GREEN ARROW SALVATION

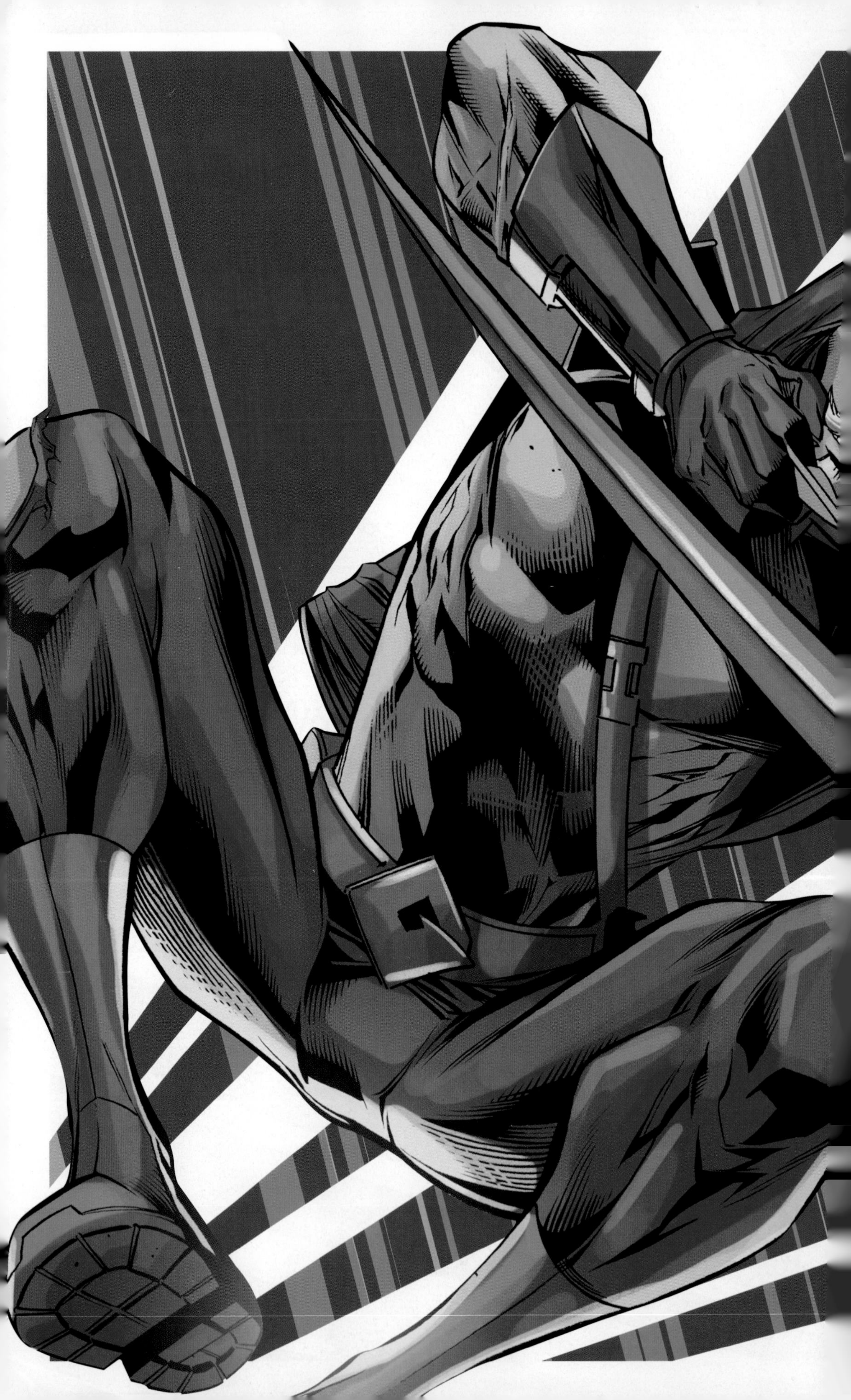

GREEN ARROW

SALVATION

J.T. Krul James Patrick Writers Diogenes Neves
Vicente Cifuentes Oclair Albert Agustin Padilla Artists
Ulises Arreola Michael Atiyeh Colorists Rob Leigh Letterer
Rodolfo Migliari Collection Cover Artist

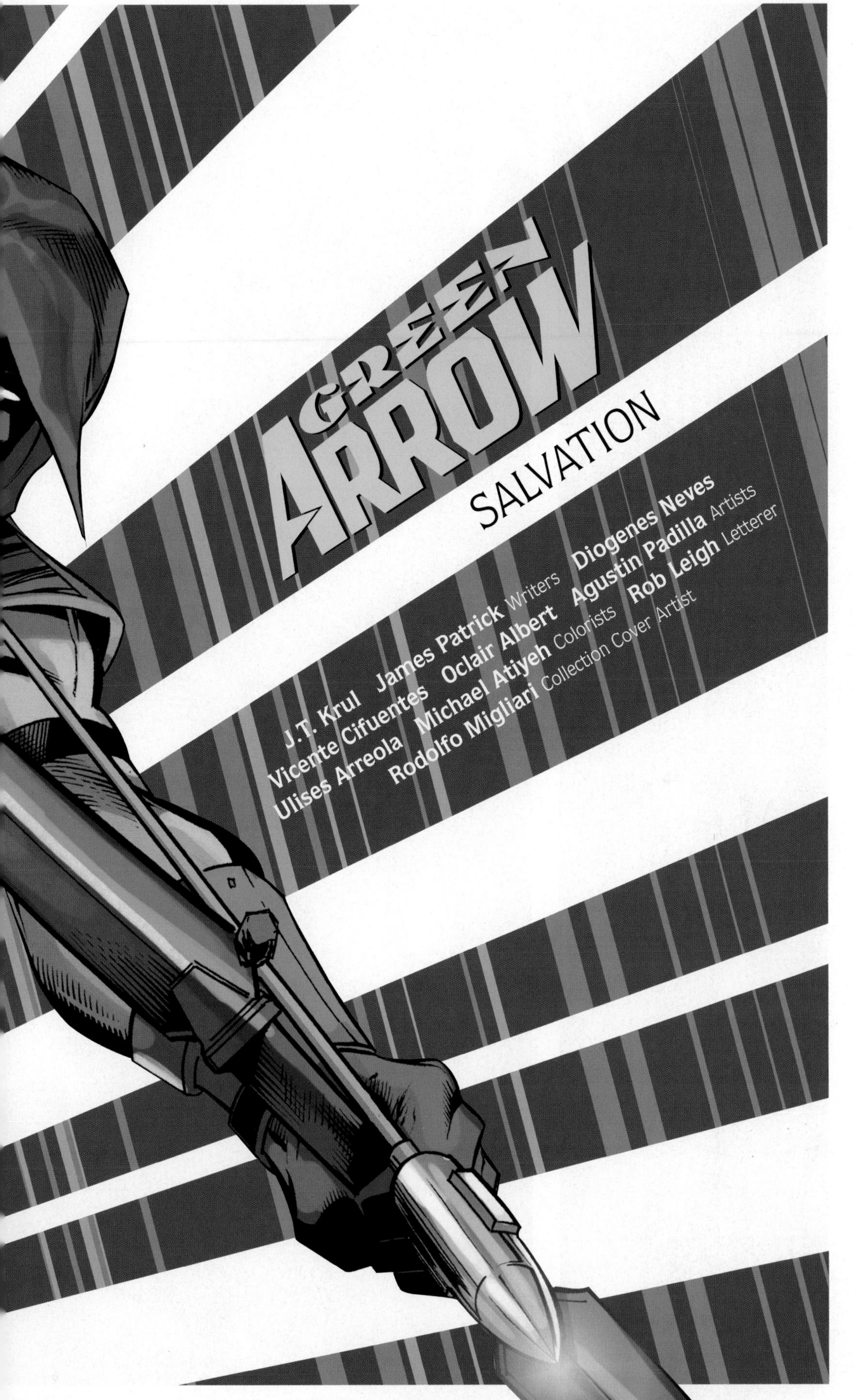

Bobbie Chase Adam Schlagman Rex Ogle Rachel Gluckstern Editors – Original Series
Katie Kubert Rickey Purdin Assistant Editors – Original Series
Peter Hamboussi Editor
Robbin Brosterman Design Director – Books

Bob Harras VP – Editor-in-Chief

Diane Nelson President
Dan DiDio and Jim Lee Co-Publishers
Geoff Johns Chief Creative Officer
John Rood Executive VP – Sales, Marketing and Business Development
Amy Genkins Senior VP – Business and Legal Affairs
Nairi Gardiner Senior VP – Finance
Jeff Boison VP – Publishing Operations
Mark Chiarello VP – Art Direction and Design
John Cunningham VP – Marketing
Terri Cunningham VP – Talent Relations and Services
Alison Gill Senior VP – Manufacturing and Operations
Hank Kanalz Senior VP – Digital
Jay Kogan VP – Business and Legal Affairs, Publishing
Jack Mahan VP – Business Affairs, Talent
Nick Napolitano VP – Manufacturing Administration
Sue Pohja VP – Book Sales
Courtney Simmons Senior VP – Publicity
Bob Wayne Senior VP – Sales

Six months ago, the central portion of Star City remained a barren wasteland following the villain Prometheus' devastating attack. With the city facing rampant crime, poverty, and corruption, it seemed that the land would be forever uninhabitable. However, with the power of the White Lantern guiding him, Deadman produced a lush, verdant forest in the city overnight. A forest as mysterious as it is beautiful.

And it is these woods that the Green Arrow now investigates and patrols. Whether it be against the Martian Manhunter or greedy corporations, Ollie has protected the land from all who would harm it.

And it seems that the forest may be returning the favor. For, even when the mysterious Isabel Rochev, a.k.a. The Queen, seized Queen Industries from Ollie and sent her Royal Guard assassins after him, from within the forest came the seemingly ancient-day Sir Galahad, ready to assist the Green Arrow in his quest....

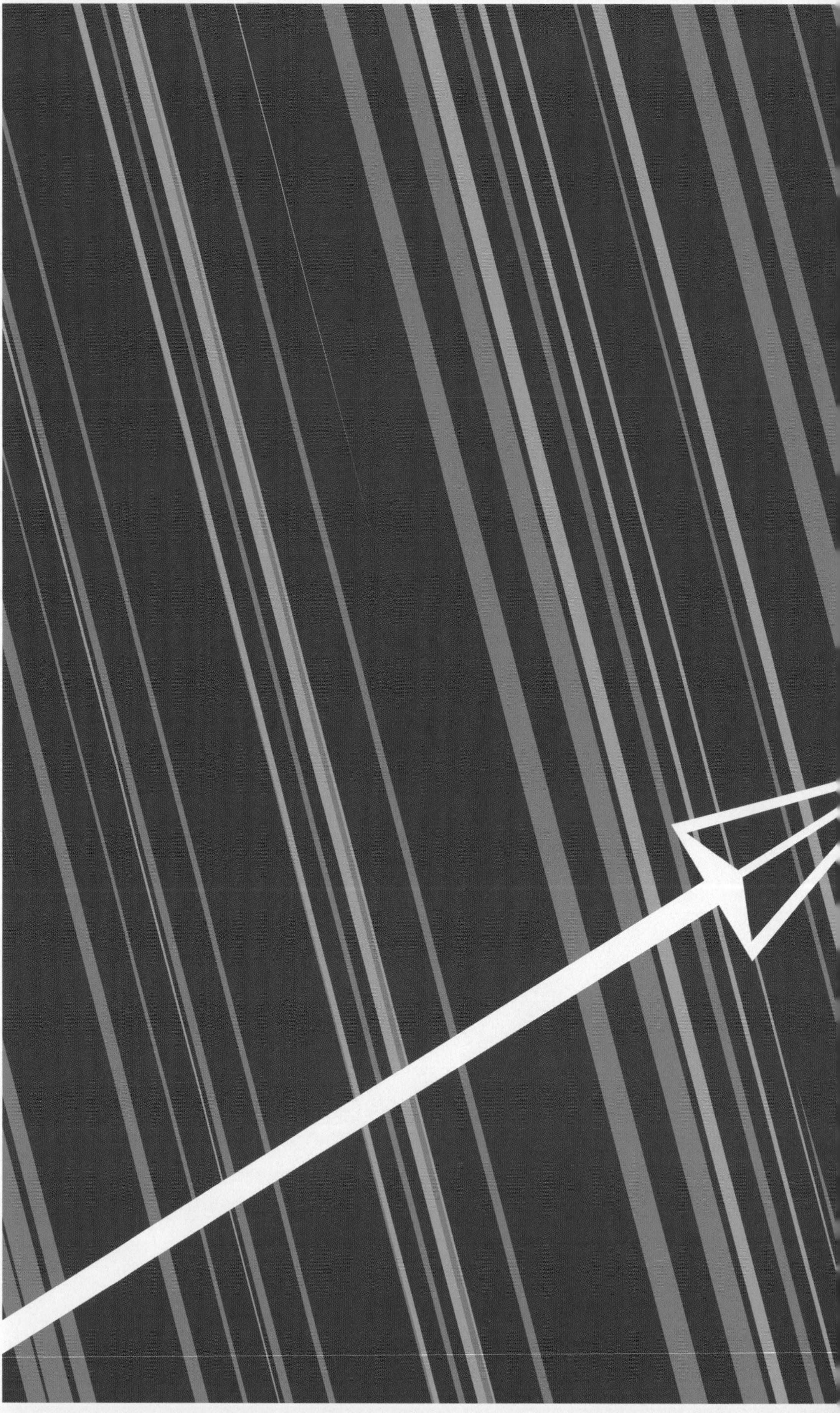

Cover by Mauro Cascioli

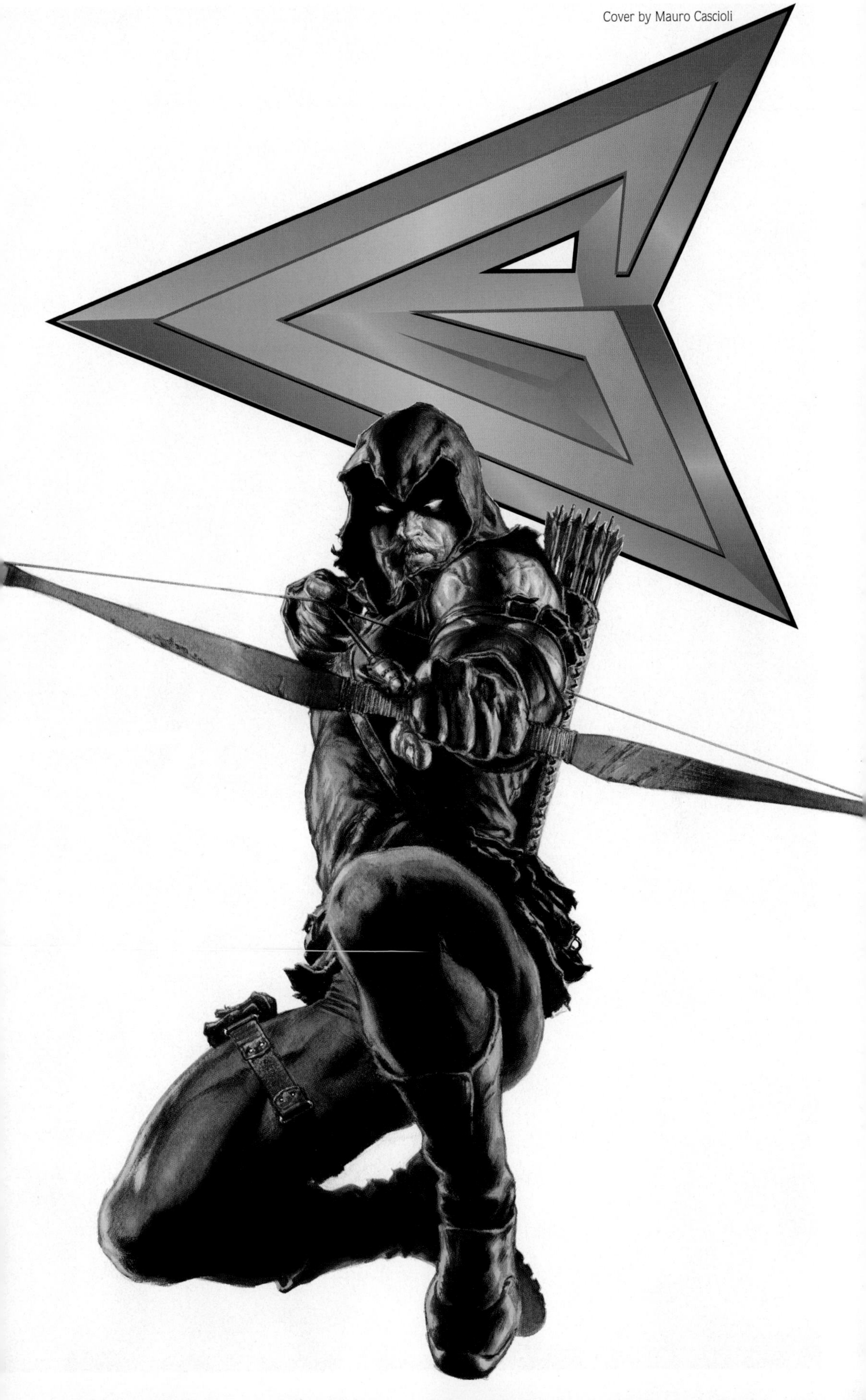

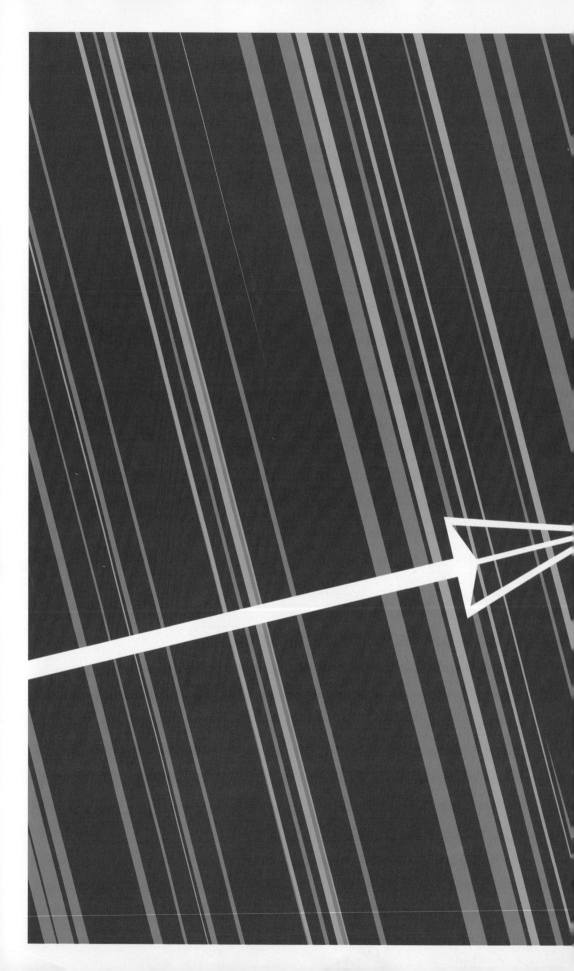

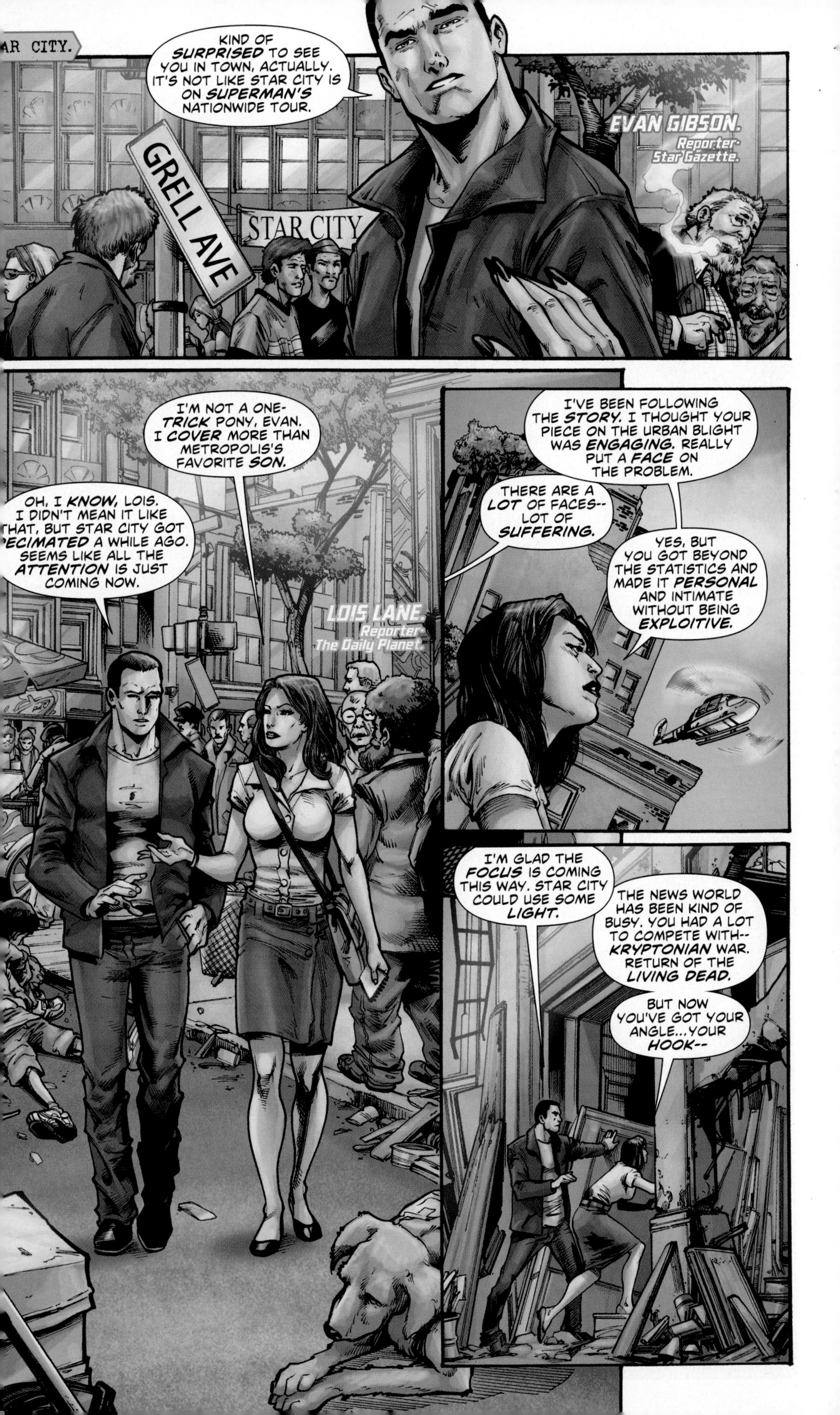
AR CITY.
KIND OF SURPRISED TO SEE YOU IN TOWN, ACTUALLY. IT'S NOT LIKE STAR CITY IS ON SUPERMAN'S NATIONWIDE TOUR.
EVAN GIBSON. Reporter- Star Gazette.
GRELL AVE
STAR CITY
I'M NOT A ONE-TRICK PONY, EVAN. I COVER MORE THAN METROPOLIS'S FAVORITE SON.
OH, I KNOW, LOIS. I DIDN'T MEAN IT LIKE THAT, BUT STAR CITY GOT ECIMATED A WHILE AGO. SEEMS LIKE ALL THE ATTENTION IS JUST COMING NOW.
LOIS LANE. Reporter- The Daily Planet.
I'VE BEEN FOLLOWING THE STORY. I THOUGHT YOUR PIECE ON THE URBAN BLIGHT WAS ENGAGING. REALLY PUT A FACE ON THE PROBLEM.
THERE ARE A LOT OF FACES-- LOT OF SUFFERING.
YES, BUT YOU GOT BEYOND THE STATISTICS AND MADE IT PERSONAL AND INTIMATE WITHOUT BEING EXPLOITIVE.
I'M GLAD THE FOCUS IS COMING THIS WAY. STAR CITY COULD USE SOME LIGHT.
THE NEWS WORLD HAS BEEN KIND OF BUSY. YOU HAD A LOT TO COMPETE WITH-- KRYPTONIAN WAR. RETURN OF THE LIVING DEAD.
BUT NOW YOU'VE GOT YOUR ANGLE...YOUR HOOK--

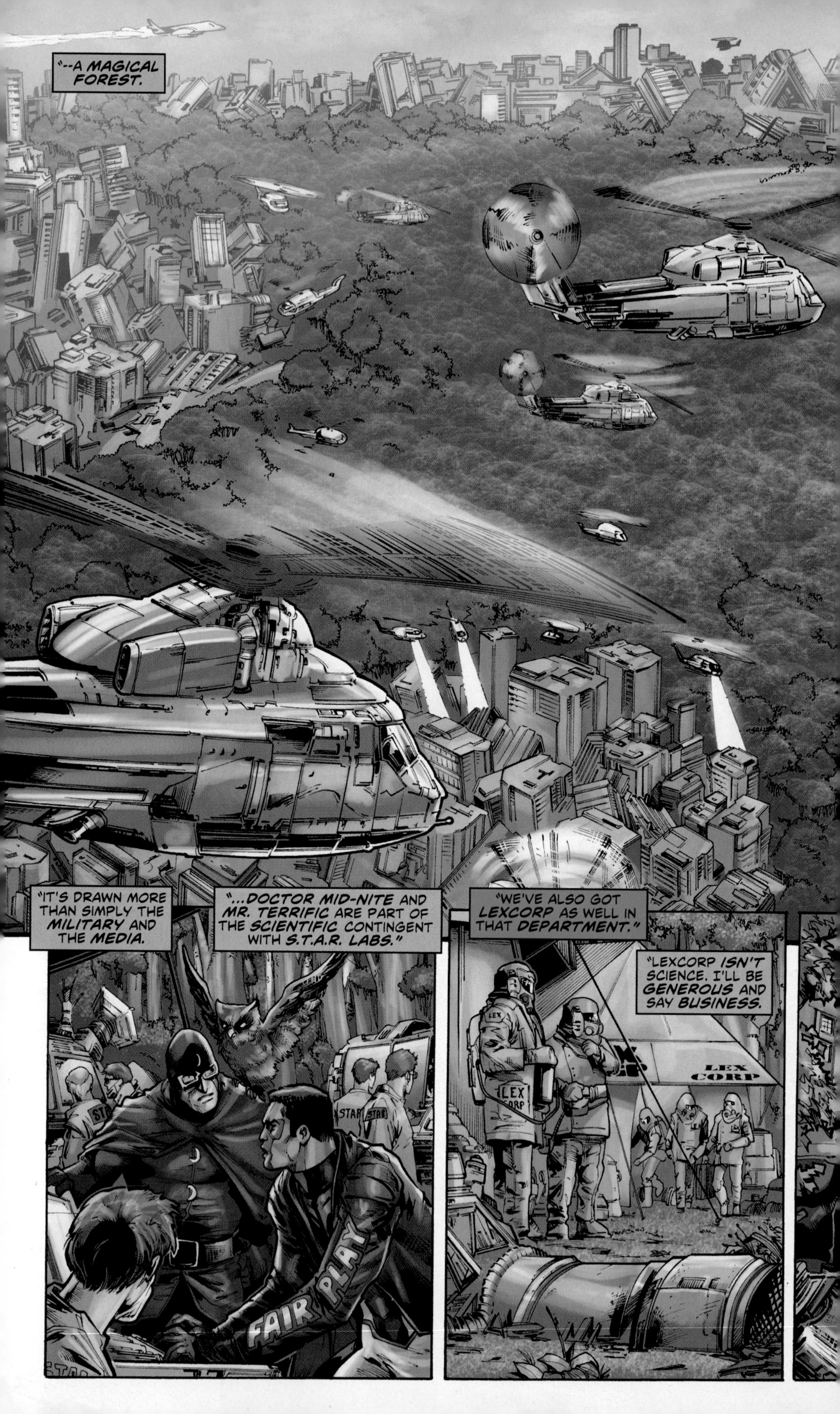
"--A MAGICAL FOREST.
"IT'S DRAWN MORE THAN SIMPLY THE MILITARY AND THE MEDIA.
"...DOCTOR MID-NITE AND MR. TERRIFIC ARE PART OF THE SCIENTIFIC CONTINGENT WITH S.T.A.R. LABS."
"WE'VE ALSO GOT LEXCORP AS WELL IN THAT DEPARTMENT."
"LEXCORP ISN'T SCIENCE. I'LL BE GENEROUS AND SAY BUSINESS.
LEX CORP
FAIR PLAY

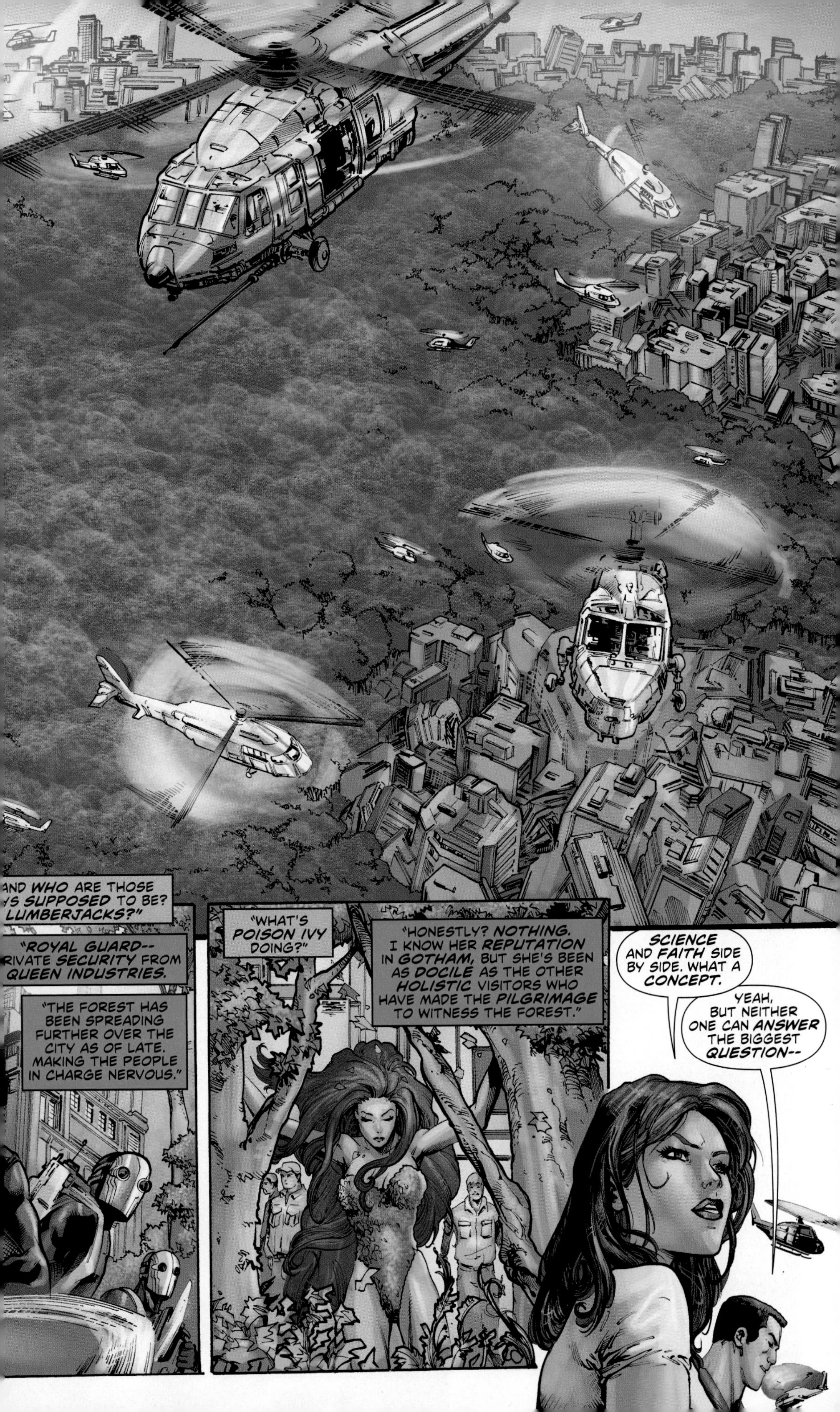

AND WHO ARE THOSE
YS SUPPOSED TO BE?
LUMBERJACKS?"
"ROYAL GUARD--
RIVATE SECURITY FROM
QUEEN INDUSTRIES.
"THE FOREST HAS BEEN SPREADING FURTHER OVER THE CITY AS OF LATE. MAKING THE PEOPLE IN CHARGE NERVOUS."
"WHAT'S POISON IVY DOING?"
"HONESTLY? NOTHING. I KNOW HER REPUTATION IN GOTHAM, BUT SHE'S BEEN AS DOCILE AS THE OTHER HOLISTIC VISITORS WHO HAVE MADE THE PILGRIMAGE TO WITNESS THE FOREST."
SCIENCE AND FAITH SIDE BY SIDE. WHAT A CONCEPT.
YEAH, BUT NEITHER ONE CAN ANSWER THE BIGGEST QUESTION--

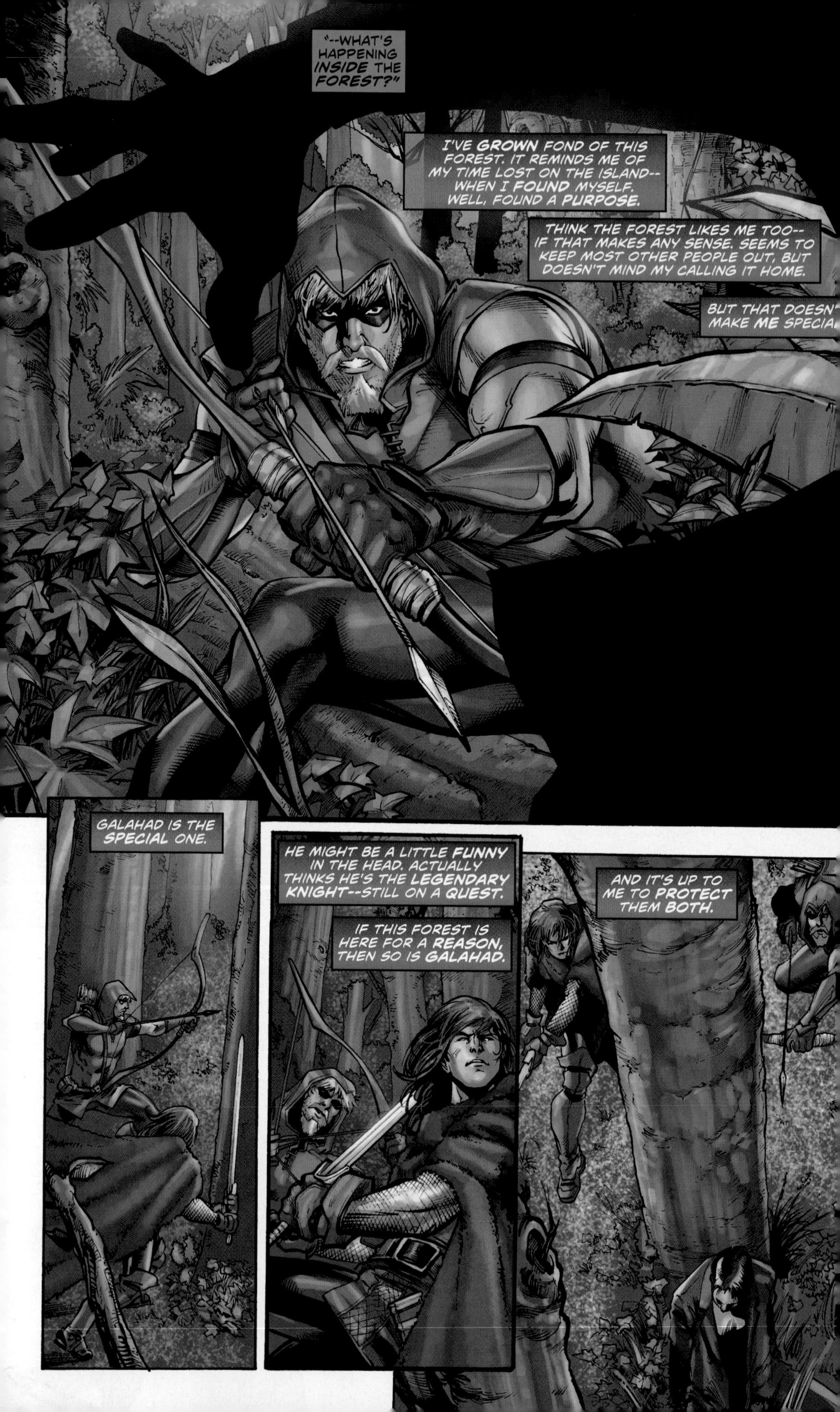
"--WHAT'S HAPPENING INSIDE THE FOREST?"
I'VE GROWN FOND OF THIS FOREST. IT REMINDS ME OF MY TIME LOST ON THE ISLAND--WHEN I FOUND MYSELF. WELL, FOUND A PURPOSE.
THINK THE FOREST LIKES ME TOO--IF THAT MAKES ANY SENSE. SEEMS TO KEEP MOST OTHER PEOPLE OUT, BUT DOESN'T MIND MY CALLING IT HOME.
BUT THAT DOESN' MAKE ME SPECIA
GALAHAD IS THE SPECIAL ONE.
HE MIGHT BE A LITTLE FUNNY IN THE HEAD. ACTUALLY THINKS HE'S THE LEGENDARY KNIGHT--STILL ON A QUEST.
IF THIS FOREST IS HERE FOR A REASON, THEN SO IS GALAHAD.
AND IT'S UP TO ME TO PROTECT THEM BOTH.

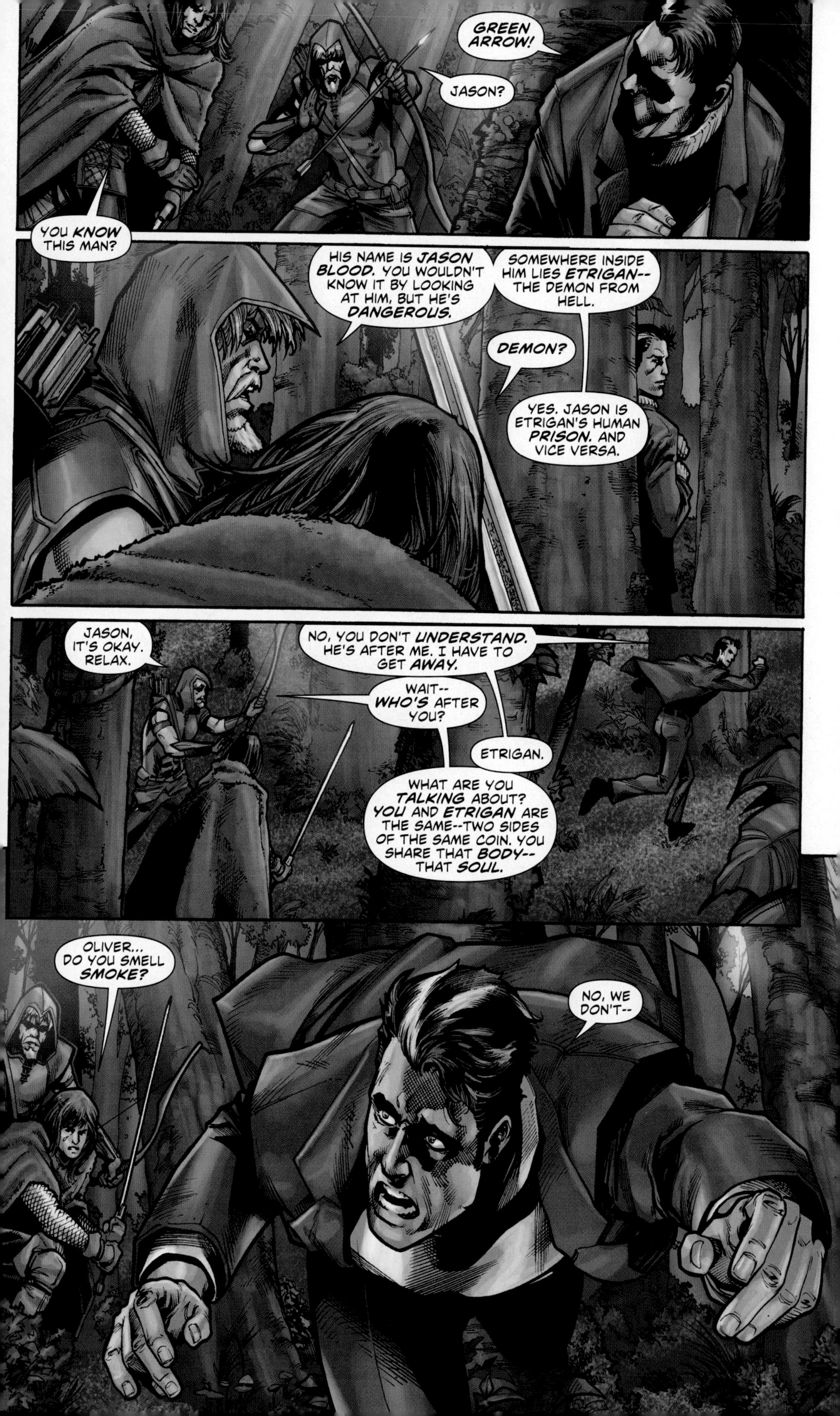
GREEN ARROW!
JASON?
YOU KNOW THIS MAN?
HIS NAME IS JASON BLOOD. YOU WOULDN'T KNOW IT BY LOOKING AT HIM, BUT HE'S DANGEROUS.
SOMEWHERE INSIDE HIM LIES ETRIGAN-- THE DEMON FROM HELL.
DEMON?
YES. JASON IS ETRIGAN'S HUMAN PRISON. AND VICE VERSA.
JASON, IT'S OKAY. RELAX.
NO, YOU DON'T UNDERSTAND. HE'S AFTER ME. I HAVE TO GET AWAY.
WAIT-- WHO'S AFTER YOU?
ETRIGAN.
WHAT ARE YOU TALKING ABOUT? YOU AND ETRIGAN ARE THE SAME--TWO SIDES OF THE SAME COIN. YOU SHARE THAT BODY-- THAT SOUL.
OLIVER... DO YOU SMELL SMOKE?
NO, WE DON'T--

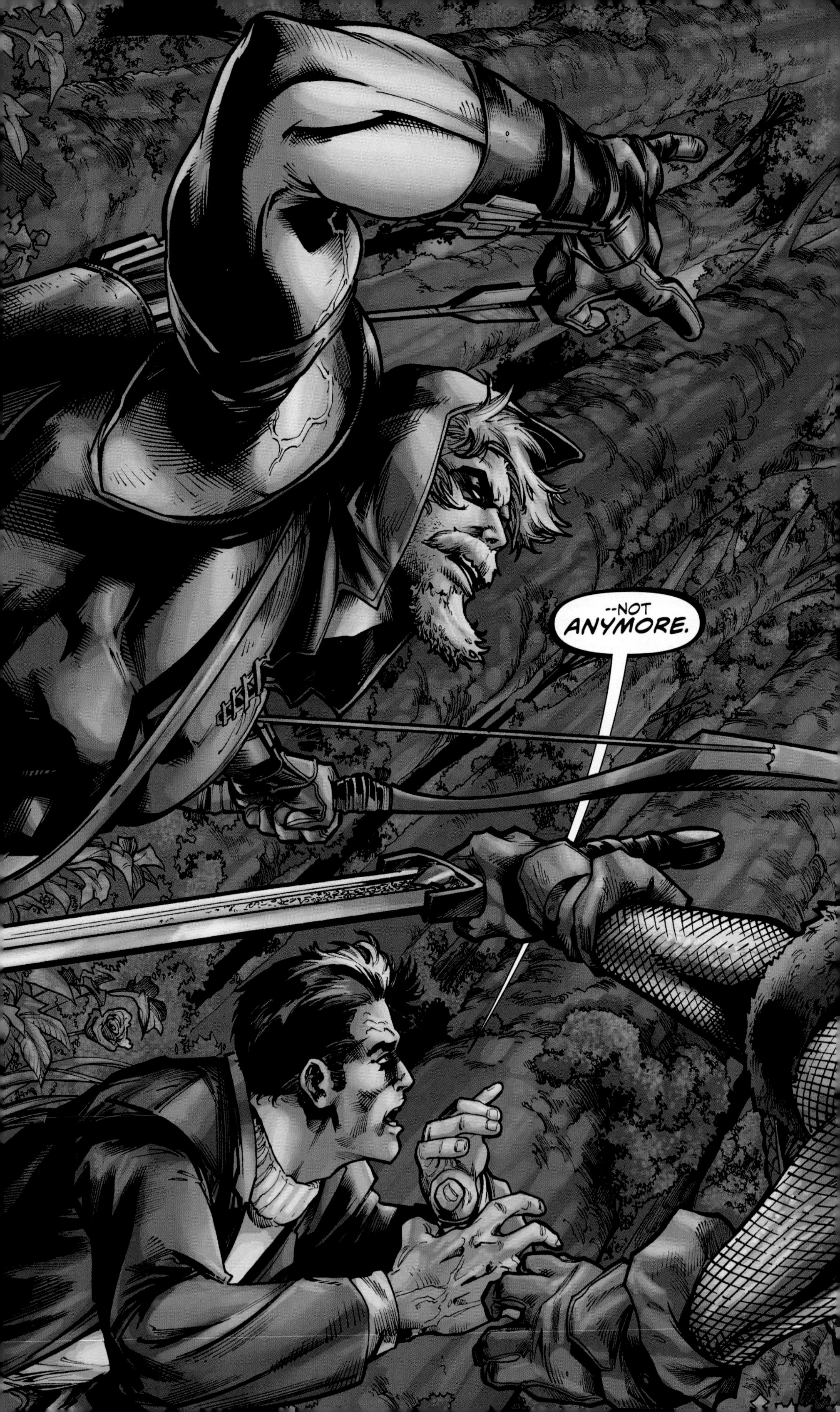
--NOT ANYMORE.

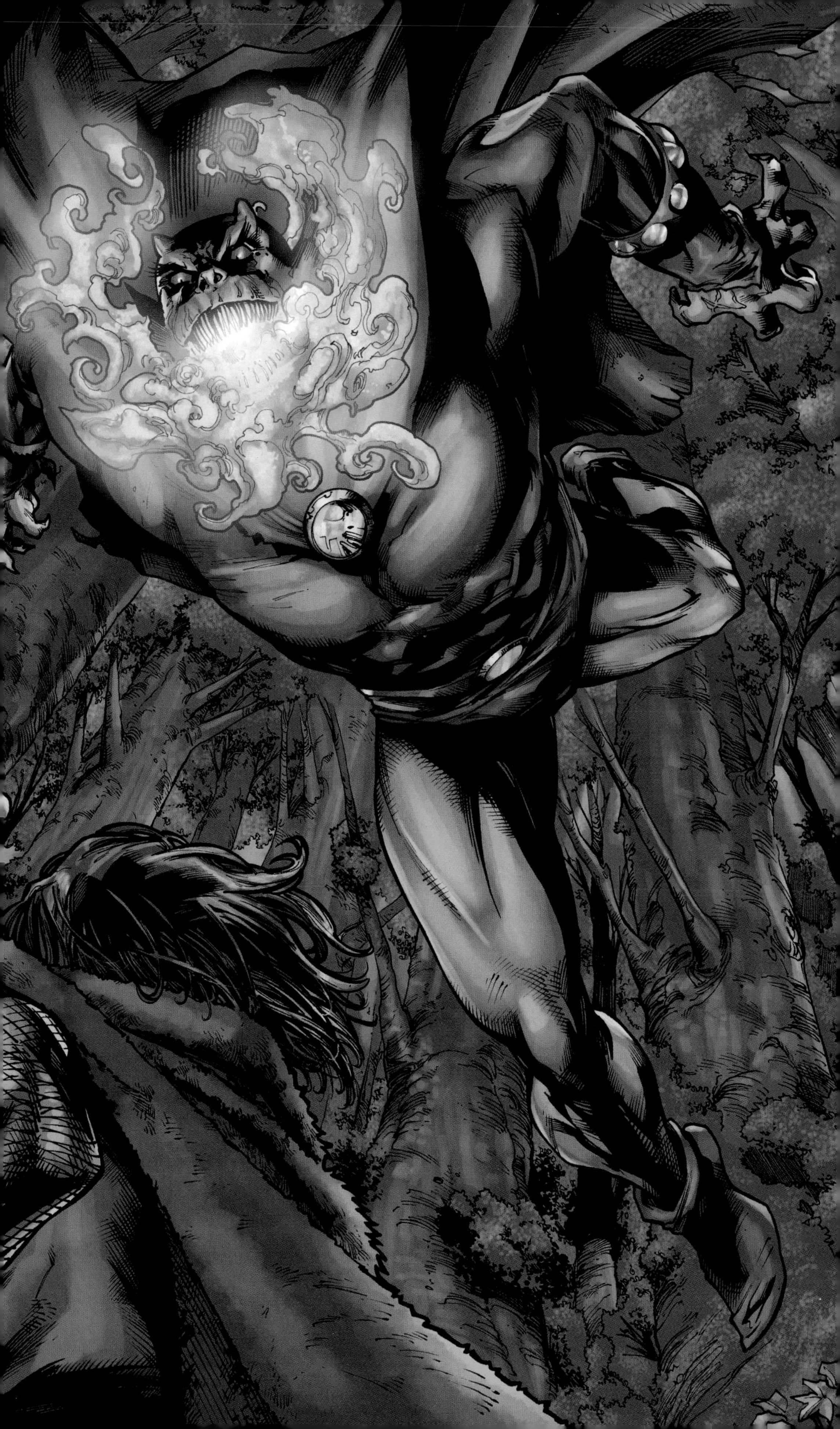

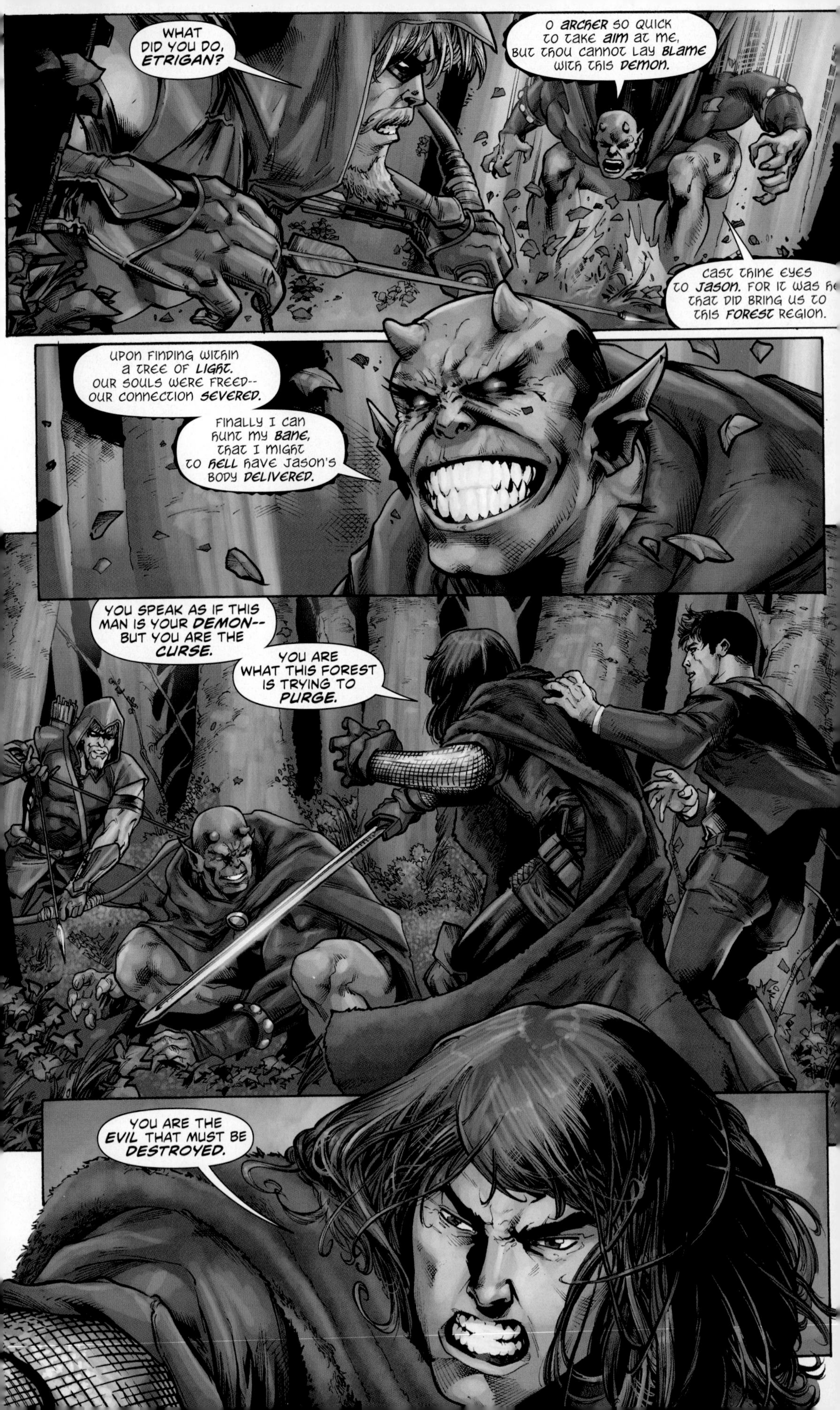
WHAT DID YOU DO, ETRIGAN?
O ARCHER SO QUICK TO TAKE AIM AT ME, BUT THOU CANNOT LAY BLAME WITH THIS DEMON.
CAST THINE EYES TO JASON. FOR IT WAS HE THAT DID BRING US TO THIS FOREST REGION.
UPON FINDING WITHIN A TREE OF LIGHT. OUR SOULS WERE FREED-- OUR CONNECTION SEVERED.
FINALLY I CAN HUNT MY BANE, THAT I MIGHT TO HELL HAVE JASON'S BODY DELIVERED.
YOU SPEAK AS IF THIS MAN IS YOUR DEMON-- BUT YOU ARE THE CURSE.
YOU ARE WHAT THIS FOREST IS TRYING TO PURGE.
YOU ARE THE EVIL THAT MUST BE DESTROYED.

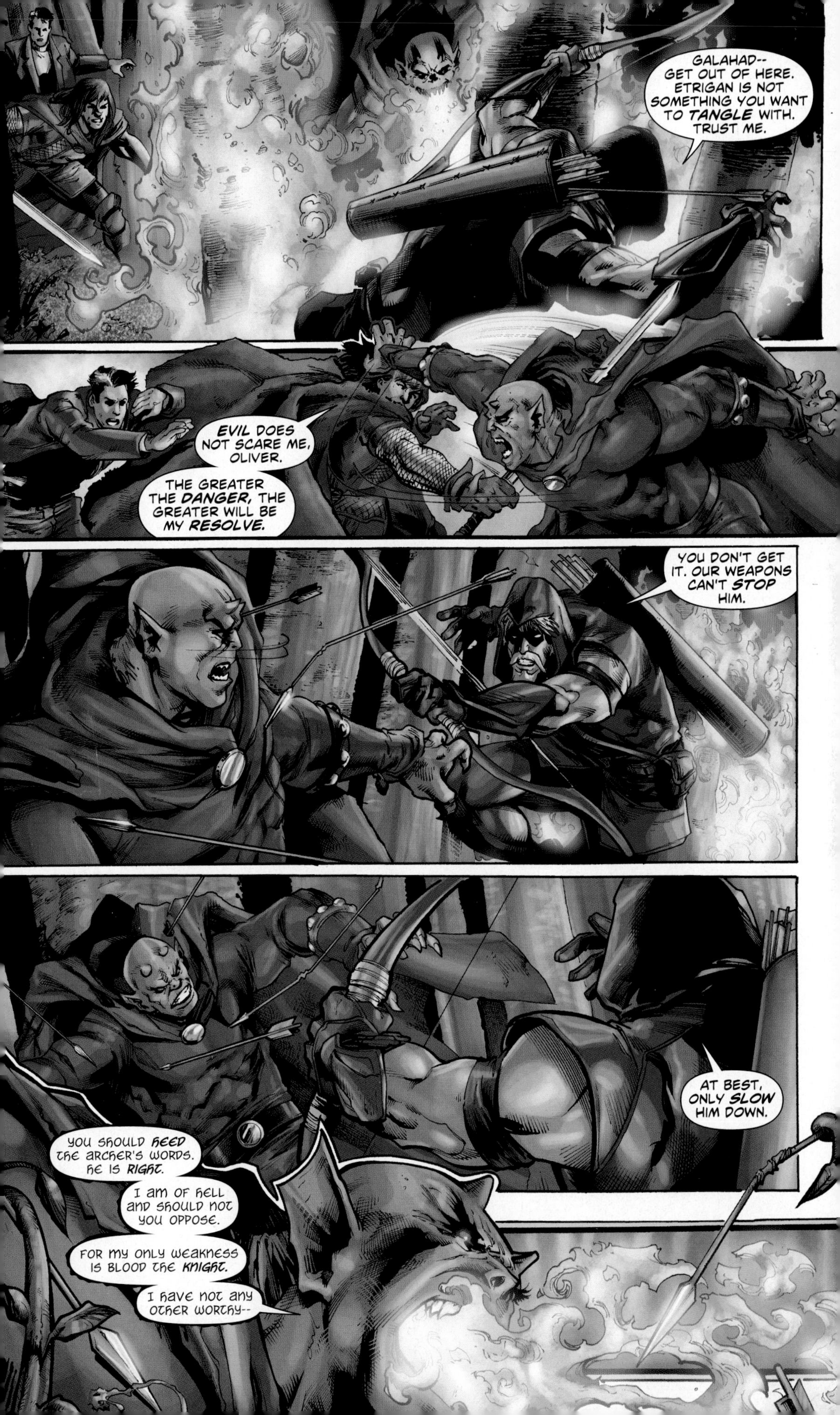
GALAHAD-- GET OUT OF HERE. ETRIGAN IS NOT SOMETHING YOU WANT TO TANGLE WITH. TRUST ME.
EVIL DOES NOT SCARE ME, OLIVER.
THE GREATER THE DANGER, THE GREATER WILL BE MY RESOLVE.
YOU DON'T GET IT. OUR WEAPONS CAN'T STOP HIM.
AT BEST, ONLY SLOW HIM DOWN.
YOU SHOULD HEED THE ARCHER'S WORDS. HE IS RIGHT.
I AM OF HELL AND SHOULD NOT YOU OPPOSE.
FOR MY ONLY WEAKNESS IS BLOOD THE KNIGHT.
I HAVE NOT ANY OTHER WORTHY--

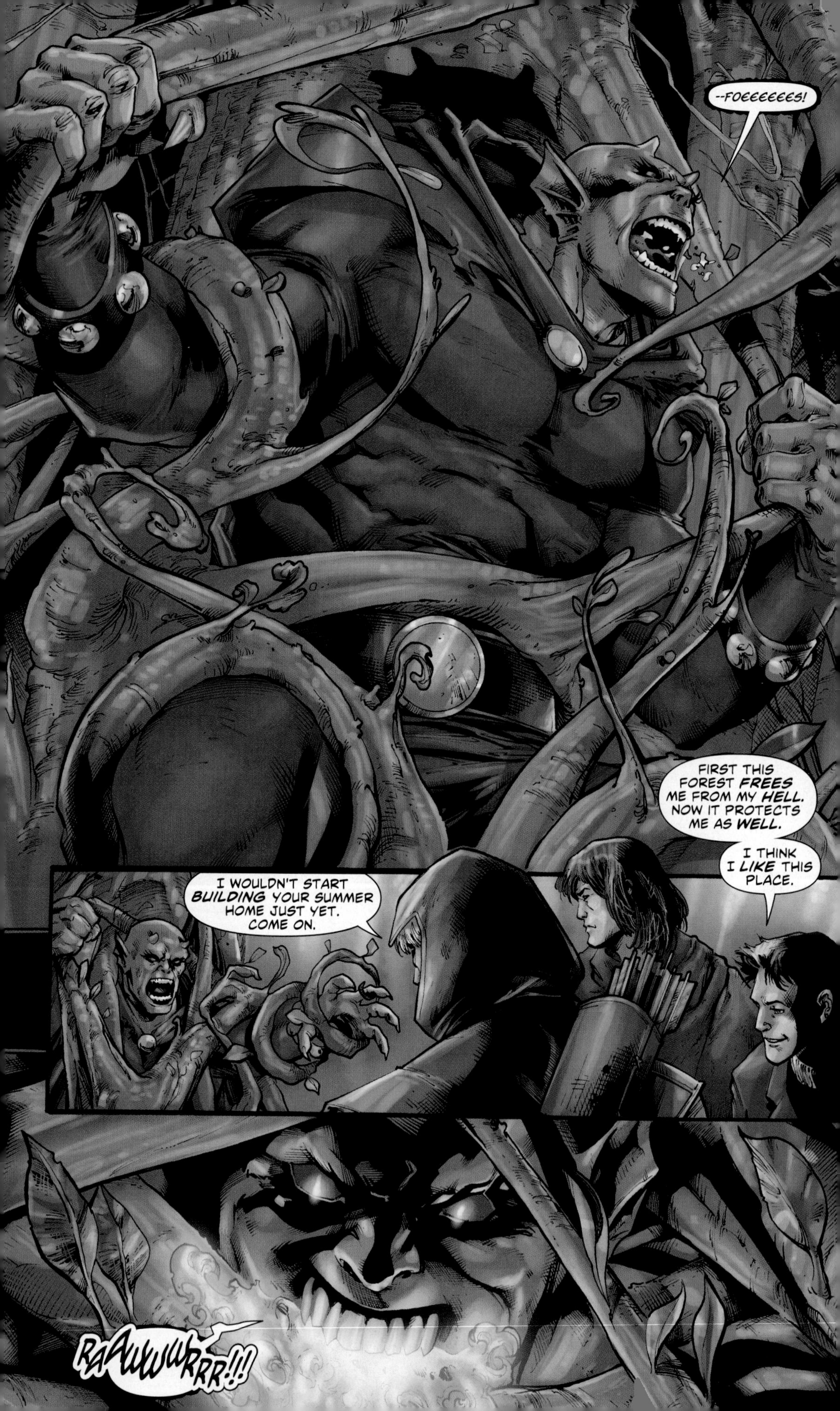
--FOEEEEEES!
FIRST THIS FOREST FREES ME FROM MY HELL. NOW IT PROTECTS ME AS WELL.
I THINK I LIKE THIS PLACE.
I WOULDN'T START BUILDING YOUR SUMMER HOME JUST YET. COME ON.
RAAWWWRRR!!!

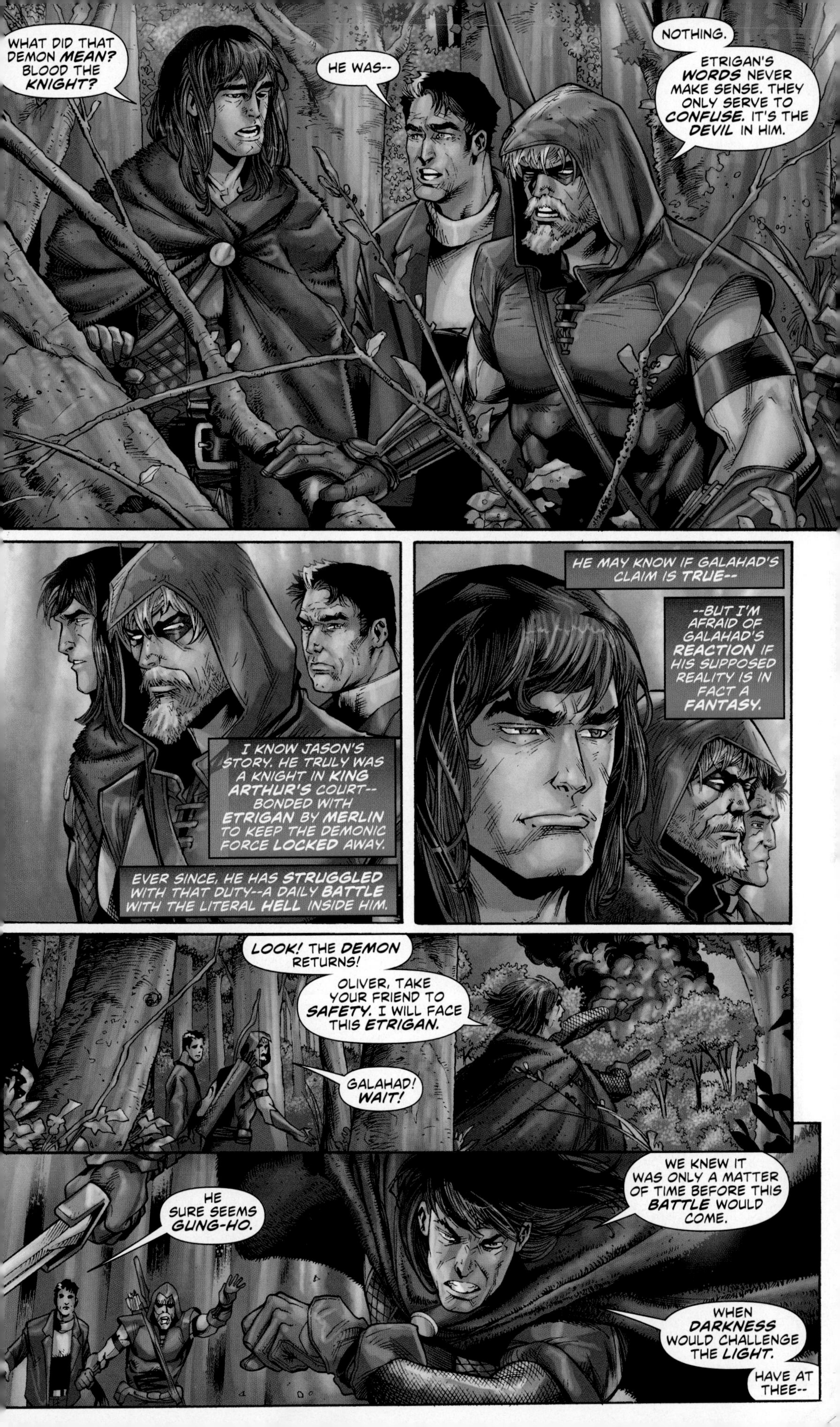
WHAT DID THAT DEMON MEAN? BLOOD THE KNIGHT?
HE WAS--
NOTHING.
ETRIGAN'S WORDS NEVER MAKE SENSE. THEY ONLY SERVE TO CONFUSE. IT'S THE DEVIL IN HIM.
I KNOW JASON'S STORY. HE TRULY WAS A KNIGHT IN KING ARTHUR'S COURT-- BONDED WITH ETRIGAN BY MERLIN TO KEEP THE DEMONIC FORCE LOCKED AWAY.
EVER SINCE, HE HAS STRUGGLED WITH THAT DUTY--A DAILY BATTLE WITH THE LITERAL HELL INSIDE HIM.
HE MAY KNOW IF GALAHAD'S CLAIM IS TRUE--
--BUT I'M AFRAID OF GALAHAD'S REACTION IF HIS SUPPOSED REALITY IS IN FACT A FANTASY.
LOOK! THE DEMON RETURNS!
OLIVER, TAKE YOUR FRIEND TO SAFETY. I WILL FACE THIS ETRIGAN.
GALAHAD! WAIT!
HE SURE SEEMS GUNG-HO.
WE KNEW IT WAS ONLY A MATTER OF TIME BEFORE THIS BATTLE WOULD COME.
WHEN DARKNESS WOULD CHALLENGE THE LIGHT.
HAVE AT THEE--

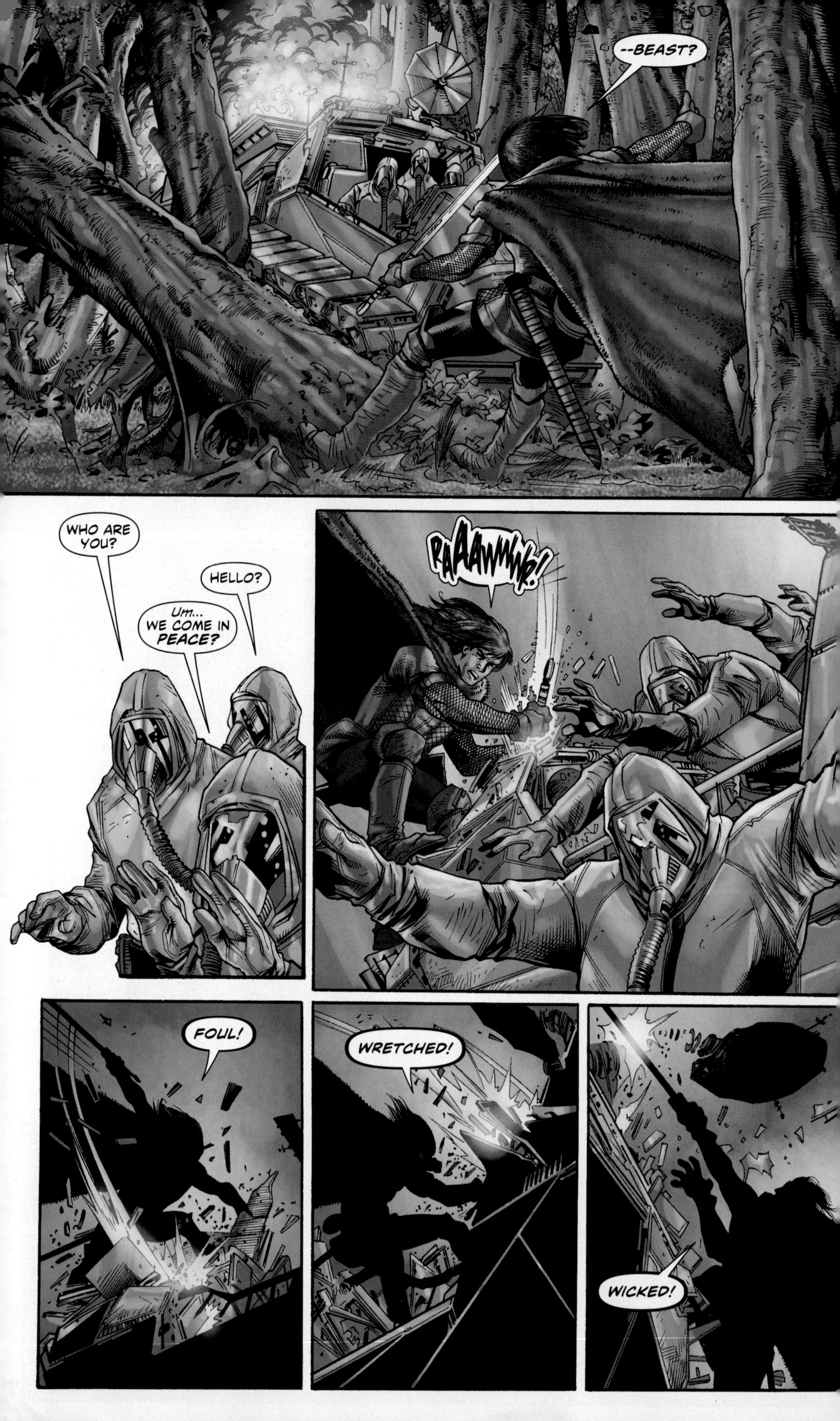
--BEAST?
WHO ARE YOU?
HELLO?
Um... WE COME IN PEACE?
RAAAWWWR!
FOUL!
WRETCHED!
WICKED!

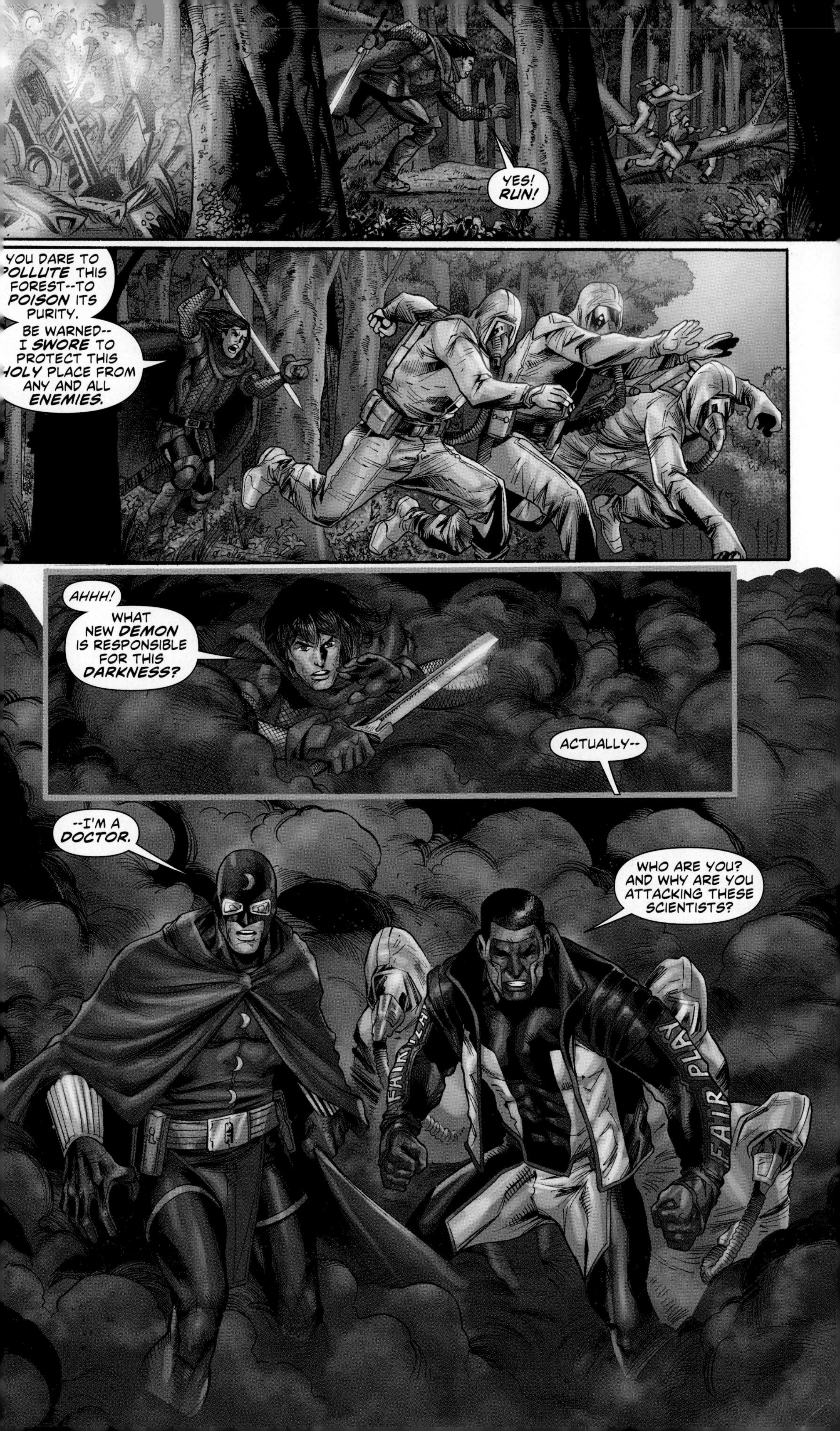
YES! RUN!
YOU DARE TO POLLUTE THIS FOREST--TO POISON ITS PURITY.
BE WARNED--I SWORE TO PROTECT THIS HOLY PLACE FROM ANY AND ALL ENEMIES.
AHHH!
WHAT NEW DEMON IS RESPONSIBLE FOR THIS DARKNESS?
ACTUALLY--
--I'M A DOCTOR.
WHO ARE YOU? AND WHY ARE YOU ATTACKING THESE SCIENTISTS?
FAIR PLAY
FAIR PLAY

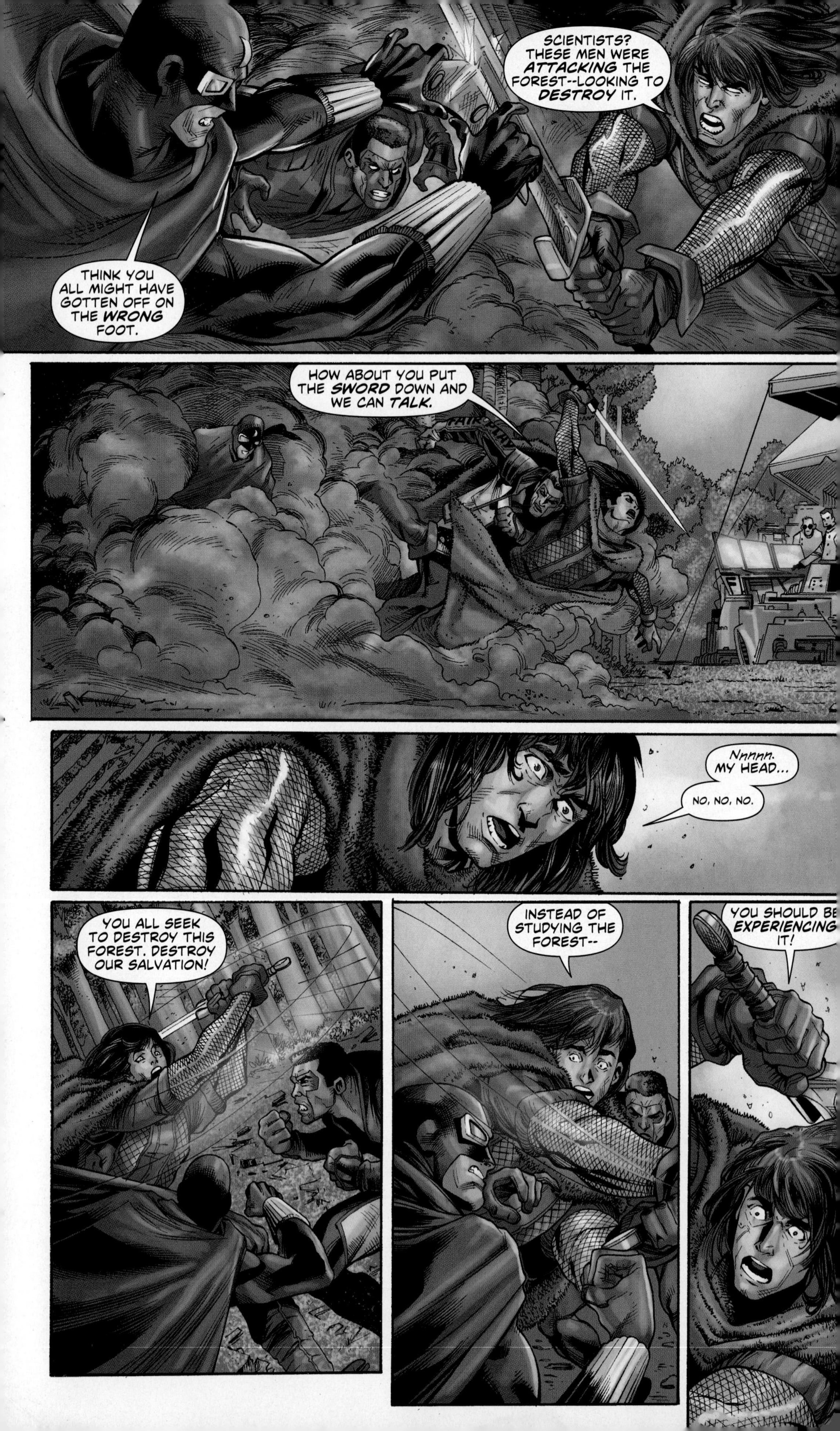
SCIENTISTS? THESE MEN WERE ATTACKING THE FOREST--LOOKING TO DESTROY IT.
THINK YOU ALL MIGHT HAVE GOTTEN OFF ON THE WRONG FOOT.
HOW ABOUT YOU PUT THE SWORD DOWN AND WE CAN TALK.
Nnnnn. MY HEAD...
NO, NO, NO.
YOU ALL SEEK TO DESTROY THIS FOREST. DESTROY OUR SALVATION!
INSTEAD OF STUDYING THE FOREST--
YOU SHOULD BE EXPERIENCING IT!

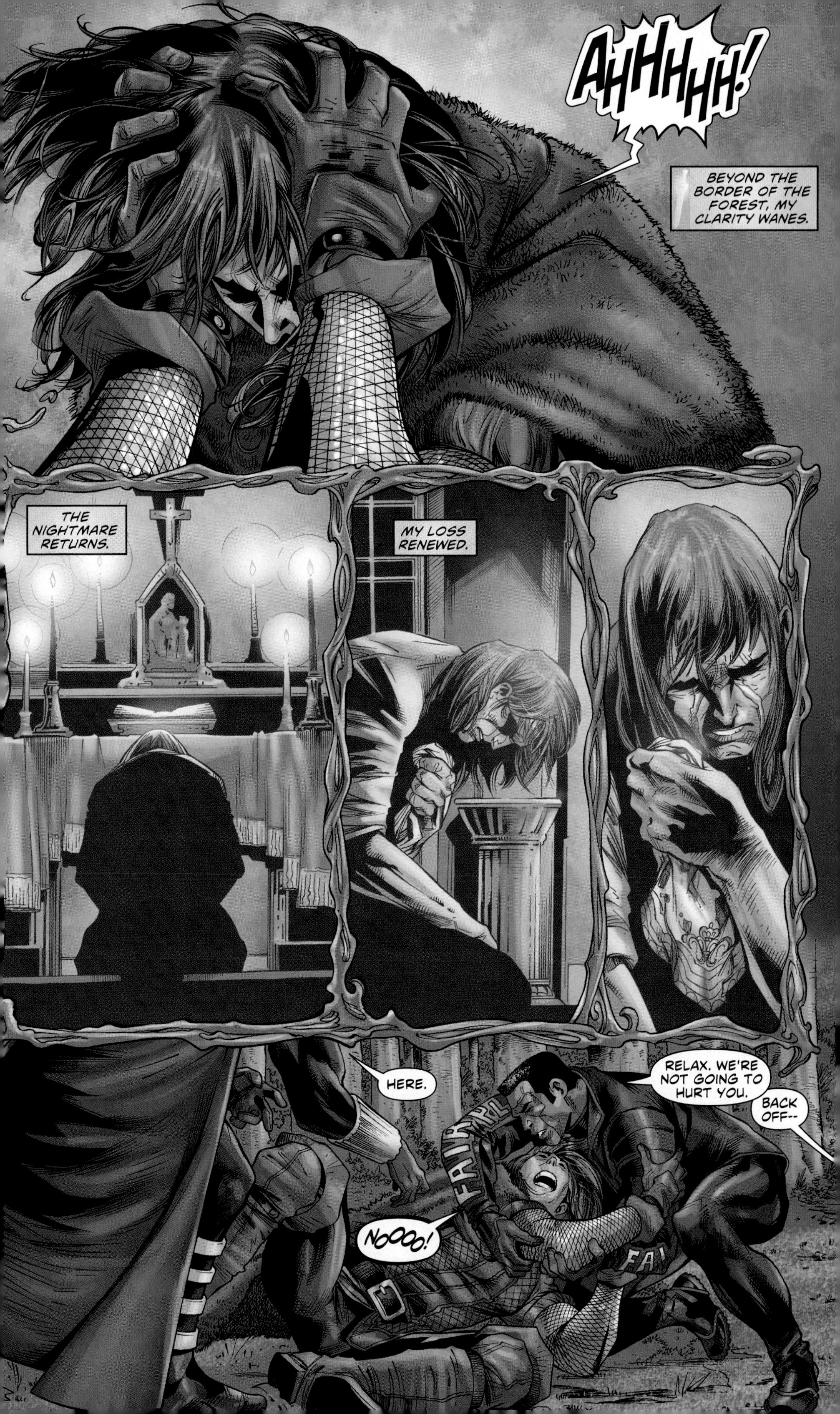
AHHHHH!
BEYOND THE BORDER OF THE FOREST, MY CLARITY WANES.
THE NIGHTMARE RETURNS.
MY LOSS RENEWED.
HERE.
RELAX. WE'RE NOT GOING TO HURT YOU.
BACK OFF--
NOOOO!

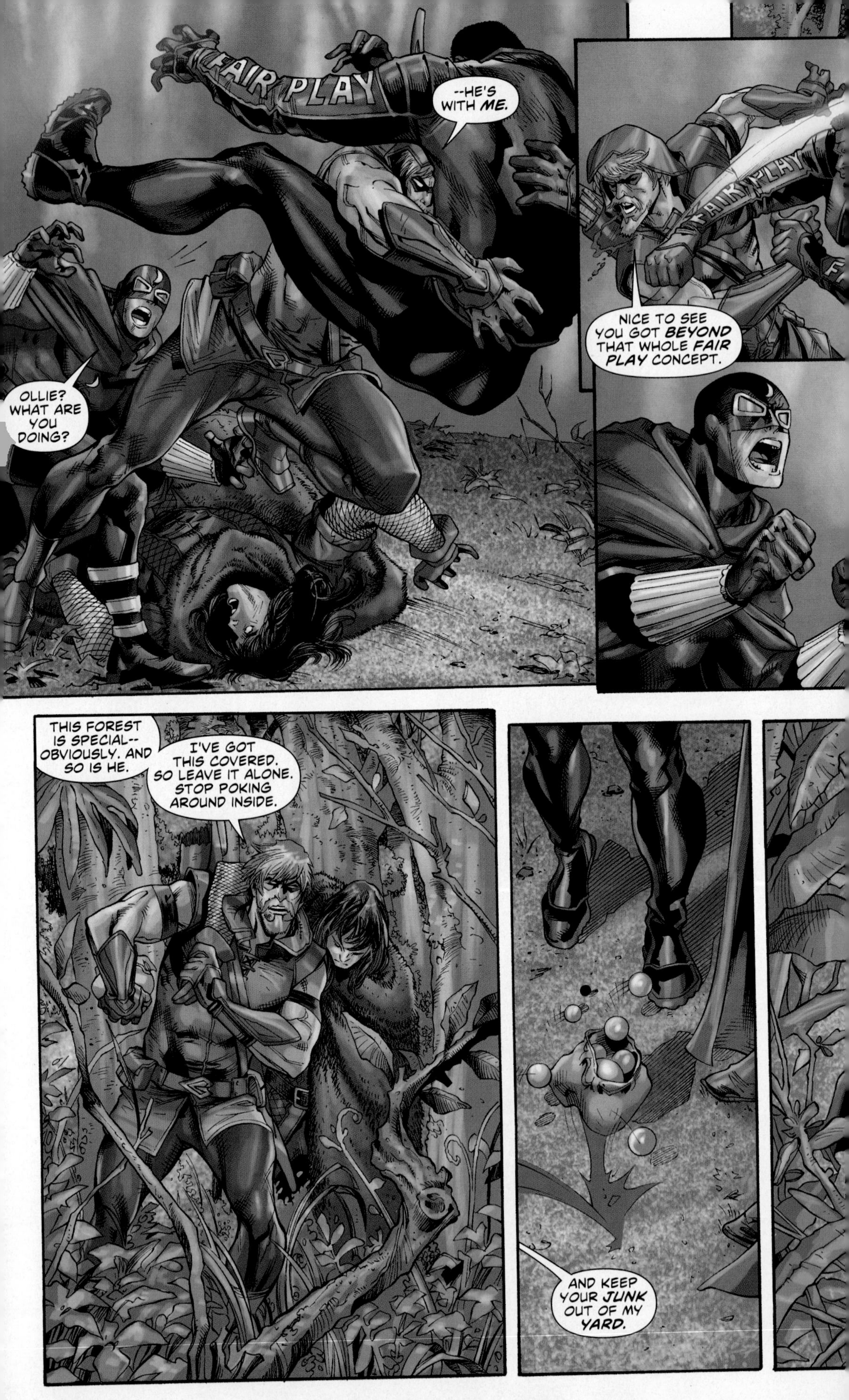
FAIR PLAY
--HE'S WITH ME.
OLLIE? WHAT ARE YOU DOING?
NICE TO SEE YOU GOT BEYOND THAT WHOLE FAIR PLAY CONCEPT.
THIS FOREST IS SPECIAL-- OBVIOUSLY. AND SO IS HE.
I'VE GOT THIS COVERED. SO LEAVE IT ALONE. STOP POKING AROUND INSIDE.
AND KEEP YOUR JUNK OUT OF MY YARD.

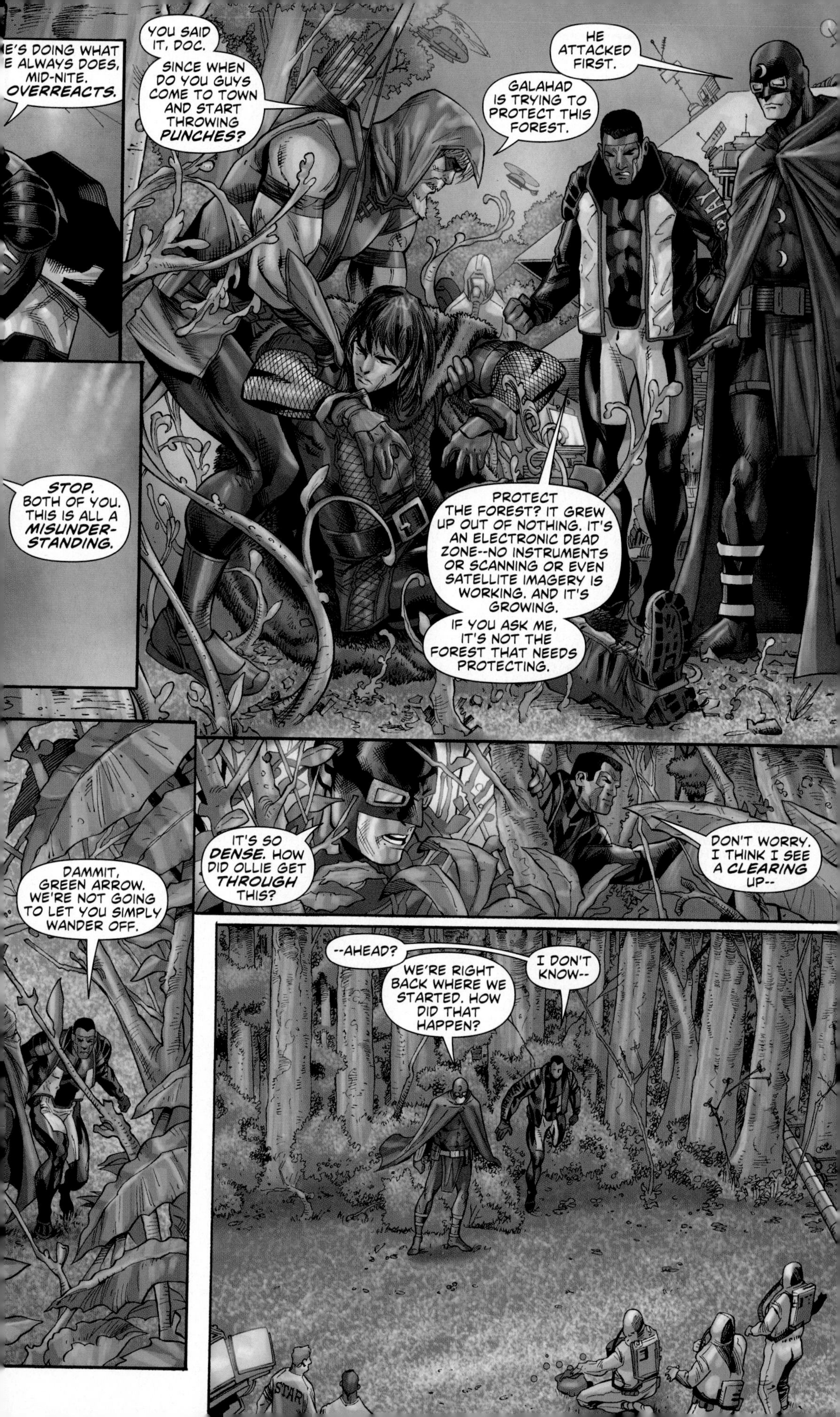
E'S DOING WHAT E ALWAYS DOES, MID-NITE. OVERREACTS.
YOU SAID IT, DOC.
SINCE WHEN DO YOU GUYS COME TO TOWN AND START THROWING PUNCHES?
HE ATTACKED FIRST.
GALAHAD IS TRYING TO PROTECT THIS FOREST.
STOP. BOTH OF YOU. THIS IS ALL A MISUNDER-STANDING.
PROTECT THE FOREST? IT GREW UP OUT OF NOTHING. IT'S AN ELECTRONIC DEAD ZONE--NO INSTRUMENTS OR SCANNING OR EVEN SATELLITE IMAGERY IS WORKING. AND IT'S GROWING.
IF YOU ASK ME, IT'S NOT THE FOREST THAT NEEDS PROTECTING.
DAMMIT, GREEN ARROW. WE'RE NOT GOING TO LET YOU SIMPLY WANDER OFF.
IT'S SO DENSE. HOW DID OLLIE GET THROUGH THIS?
DON'T WORRY. I THINK I SEE A CLEARING UP--
--AHEAD?
WE'RE RIGHT BACK WHERE WE STARTED. HOW DID THAT HAPPEN?
I DON'T KNOW--
STAR

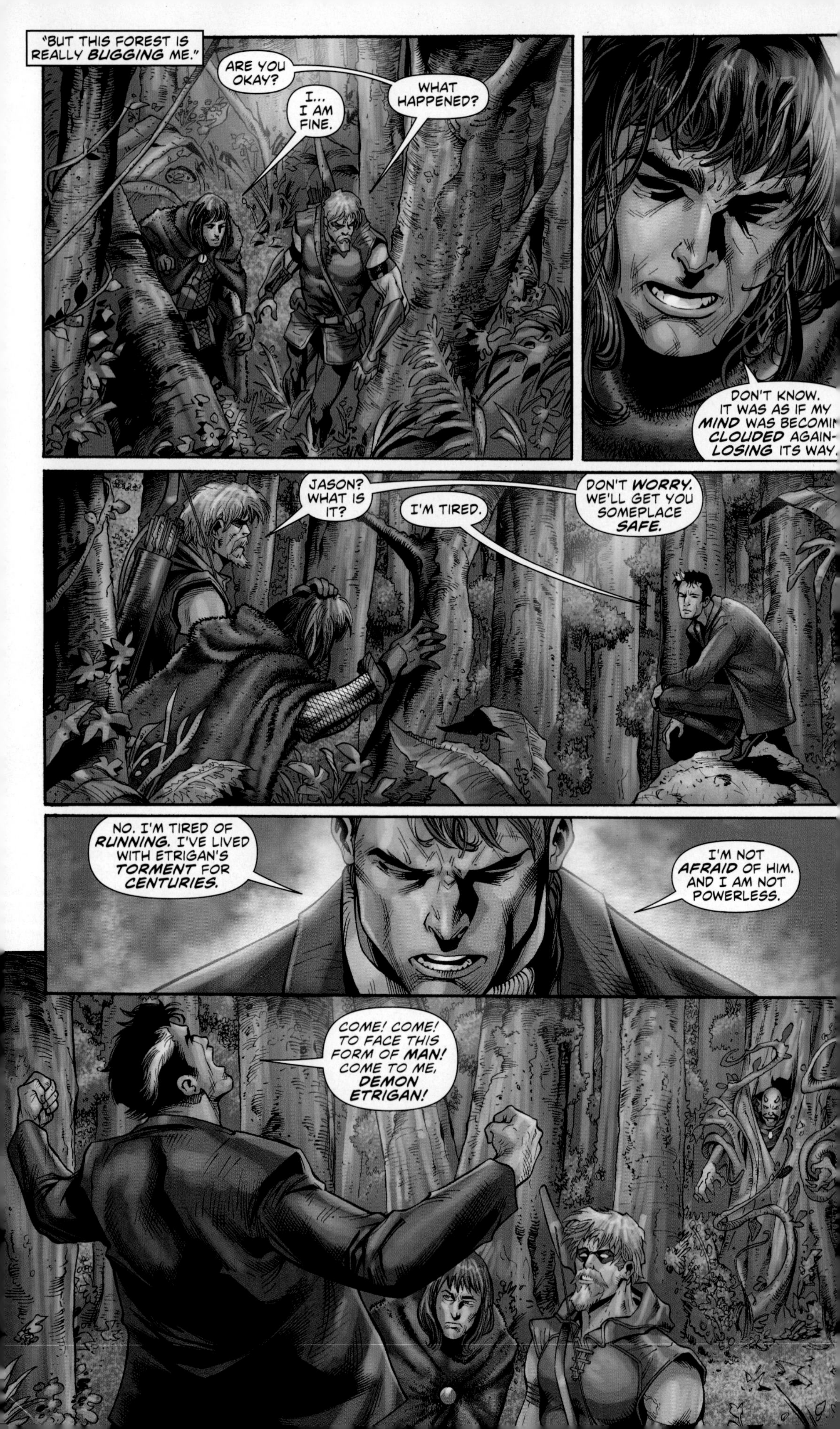
"BUT THIS FOREST IS REALLY BUGGING ME."
ARE YOU OKAY?
WHAT HAPPENED?
I... I AM FINE.
DON'T KNOW. IT WAS AS IF MY MIND WAS BECOMIN CLOUDED AGAIN-LOSING ITS WAY.
JASON? WHAT IS IT?
DON'T WORRY. WE'LL GET YOU SOMEPLACE SAFE.
I'M TIRED.
NO. I'M TIRED OF RUNNING. I'VE LIVED WITH ETRIGAN'S TORMENT FOR CENTURIES.
I'M NOT AFRAID OF HIM. AND I AM NOT POWERLESS.
COME! COME! TO FACE THIS FORM OF MAN! COME TO ME, DEMON ETRIGAN!

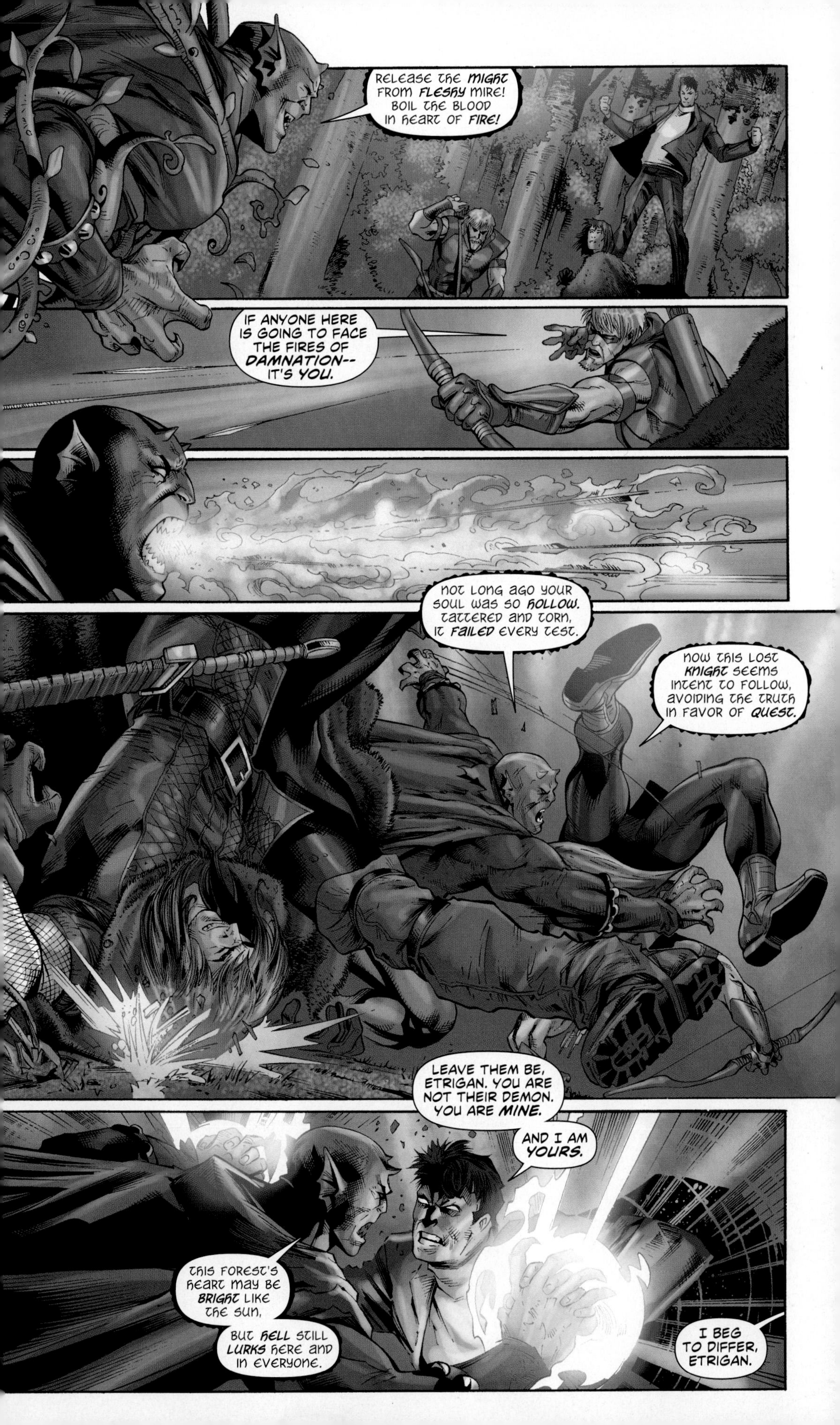

RELEASE THE MIGHT FROM FLESHY MIRE! BOIL THE BLOOD IN HEART OF FIRE!
IF ANYONE HERE IS GOING TO FACE THE FIRES OF DAMNATION-- IT'S YOU.
NOT LONG AGO YOUR SOUL WAS SO HOLLOW. TATTERED AND TORN, IT FAILED EVERY TEST.
NOW THIS LOST KNIGHT SEEMS INTENT TO FOLLOW, AVOIDING THE TRUTH IN FAVOR OF QUEST.
LEAVE THEM BE, ETRIGAN. YOU ARE NOT THEIR DEMON. YOU ARE MINE.
AND I AM YOURS.
THIS FOREST'S HEART MAY BE BRIGHT LIKE THE SUN,
BUT HELL STILL LURKS HERE AND IN EVERYONE.
I BEG TO DIFFER, ETRIGAN.

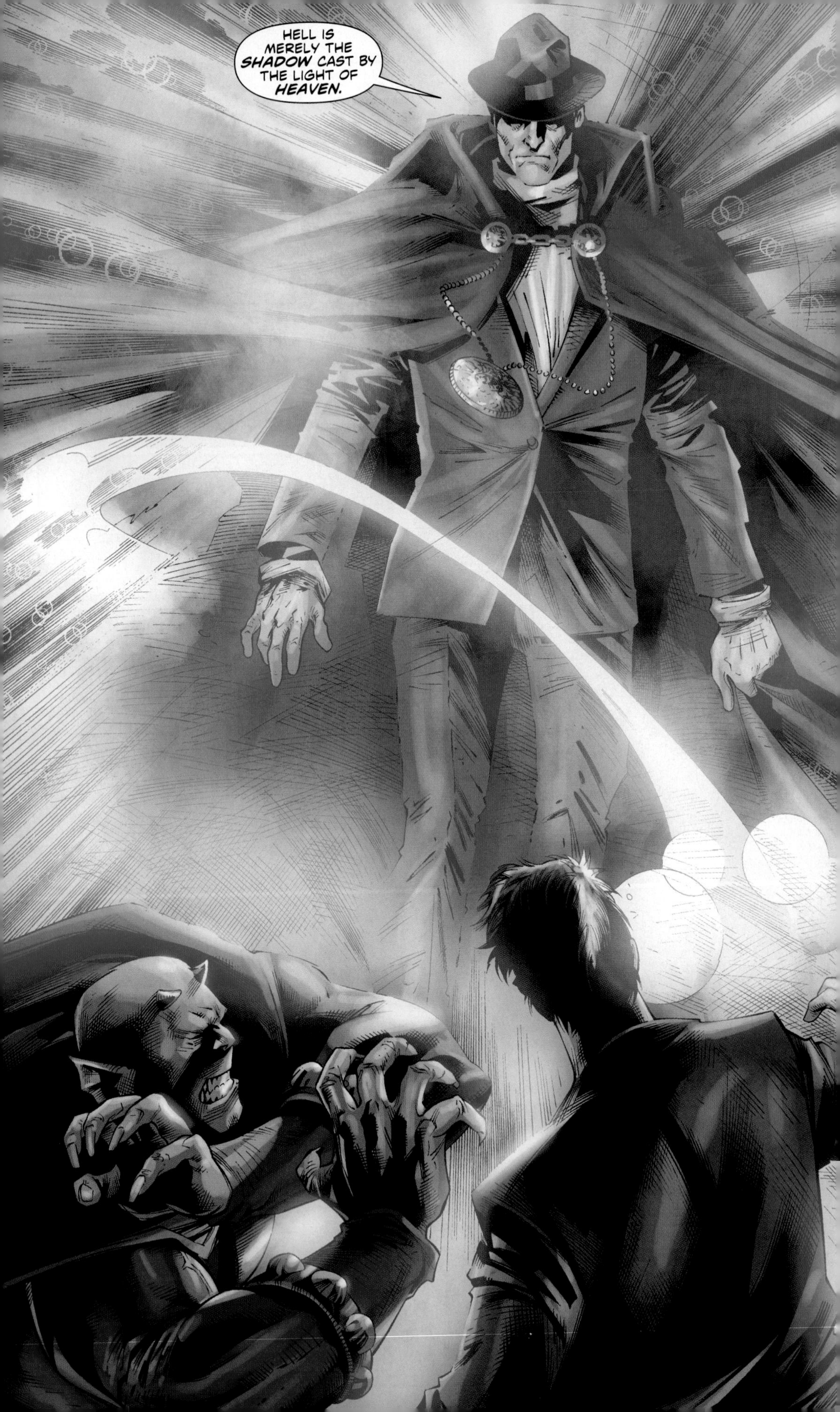
HELL IS MERELY THE *SHADOW* CAST BY THE LIGHT OF *HEAVEN.*

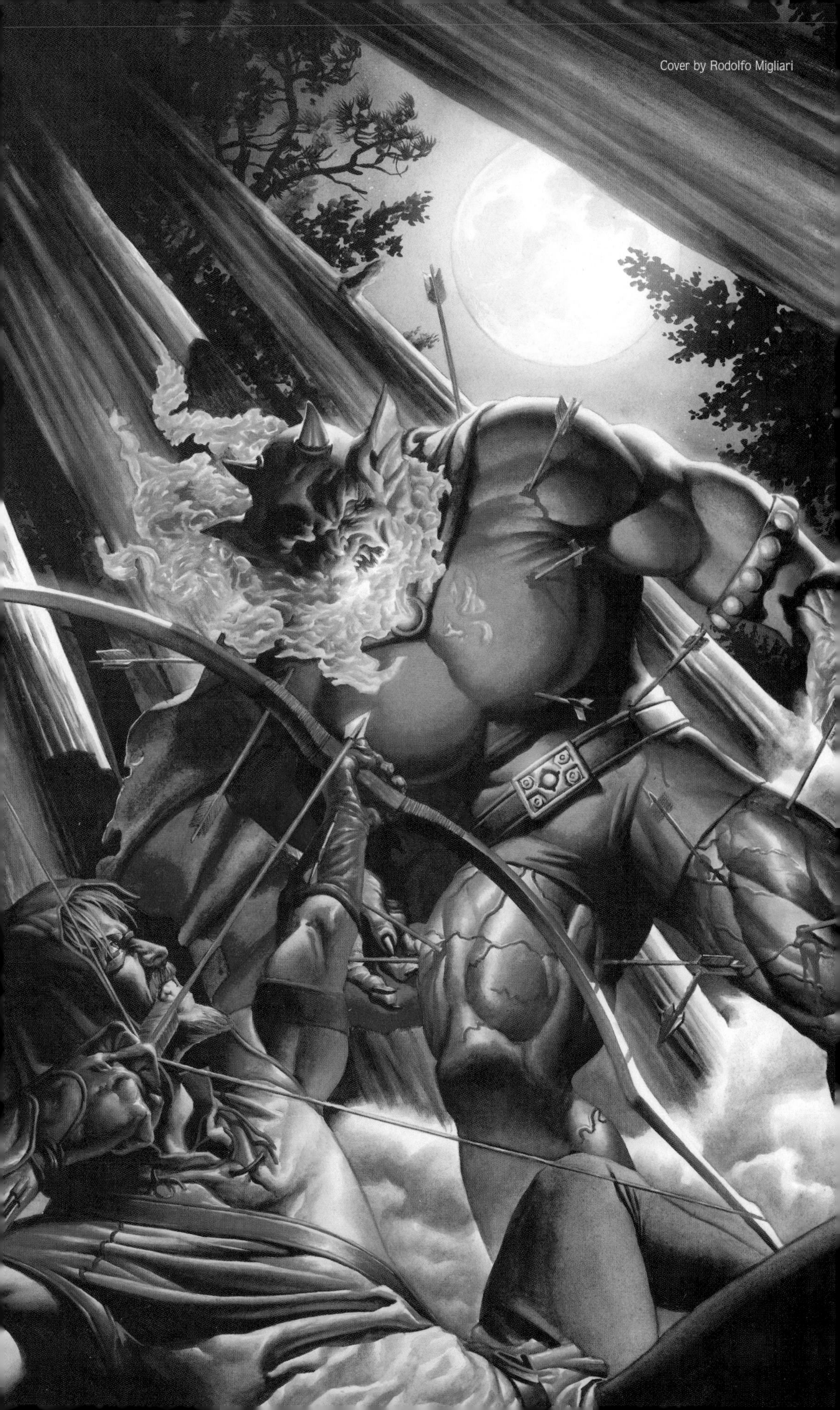

Cover by Rodolfo Migliari

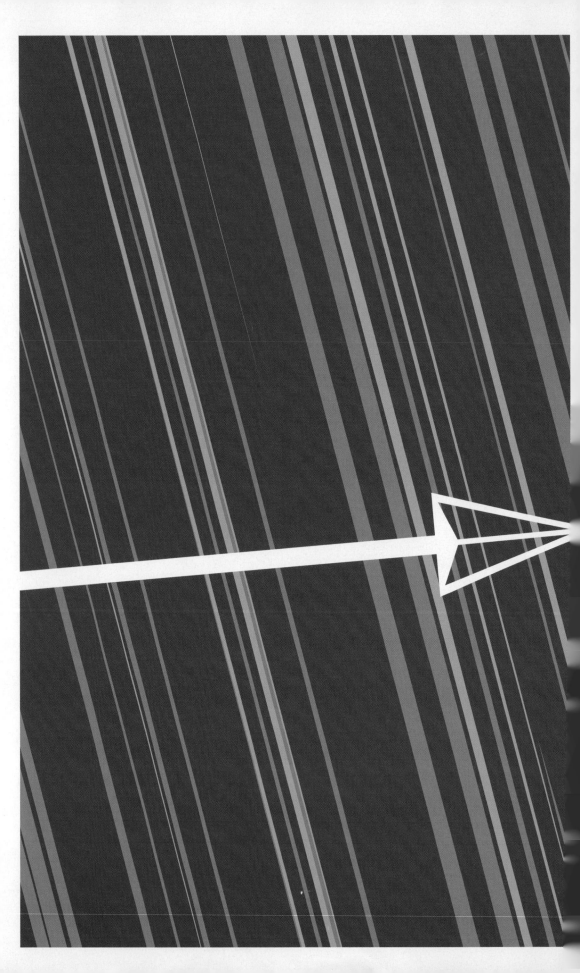

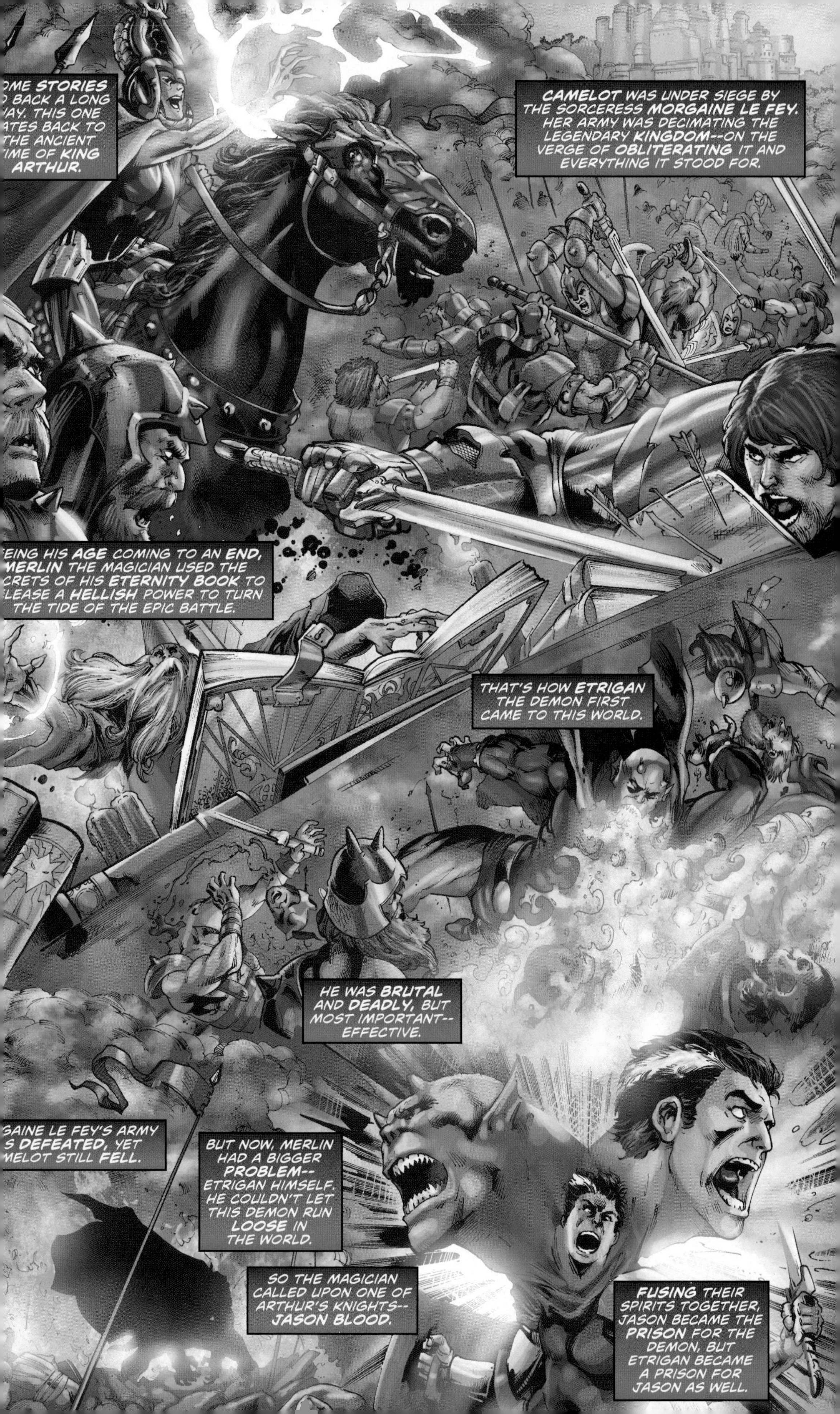
OME STORIES O BACK A LONG AY. THIS ONE ATES BACK TO THE ANCIENT TIME OF KING ARTHUR.
CAMELOT WAS UNDER SIEGE BY THE SORCERESS MORGAINE LE FEY. HER ARMY WAS DECIMATING THE LEGENDARY KINGDOM--ON THE VERGE OF OBLITERATING IT AND EVERYTHING IT STOOD FOR.
EING HIS AGE COMING TO AN END, MERLIN THE MAGICIAN USED THE CRETS OF HIS ETERNITY BOOK TO LEASE A HELLISH POWER TO TURN THE TIDE OF THE EPIC BATTLE.
THAT'S HOW ETRIGAN THE DEMON FIRST CAME TO THIS WORLD.
HE WAS BRUTAL AND DEADLY, BUT MOST IMPORTANT-- EFFECTIVE.
GAINE LE FEY'S ARMY S DEFEATED, YET MELOT STILL FELL.
BUT NOW, MERLIN HAD A BIGGER PROBLEM-- ETRIGAN HIMSELF. HE COULDN'T LET THIS DEMON RUN LOOSE IN THE WORLD.
SO THE MAGICIAN CALLED UPON ONE OF ARTHUR'S KNIGHTS-- JASON BLOOD.
FUSING THEIR SPIRITS TOGETHER, JASON BECAME THE PRISON FOR THE DEMON, BUT ETRIGAN BECAME A PRISON FOR JASON AS WELL.

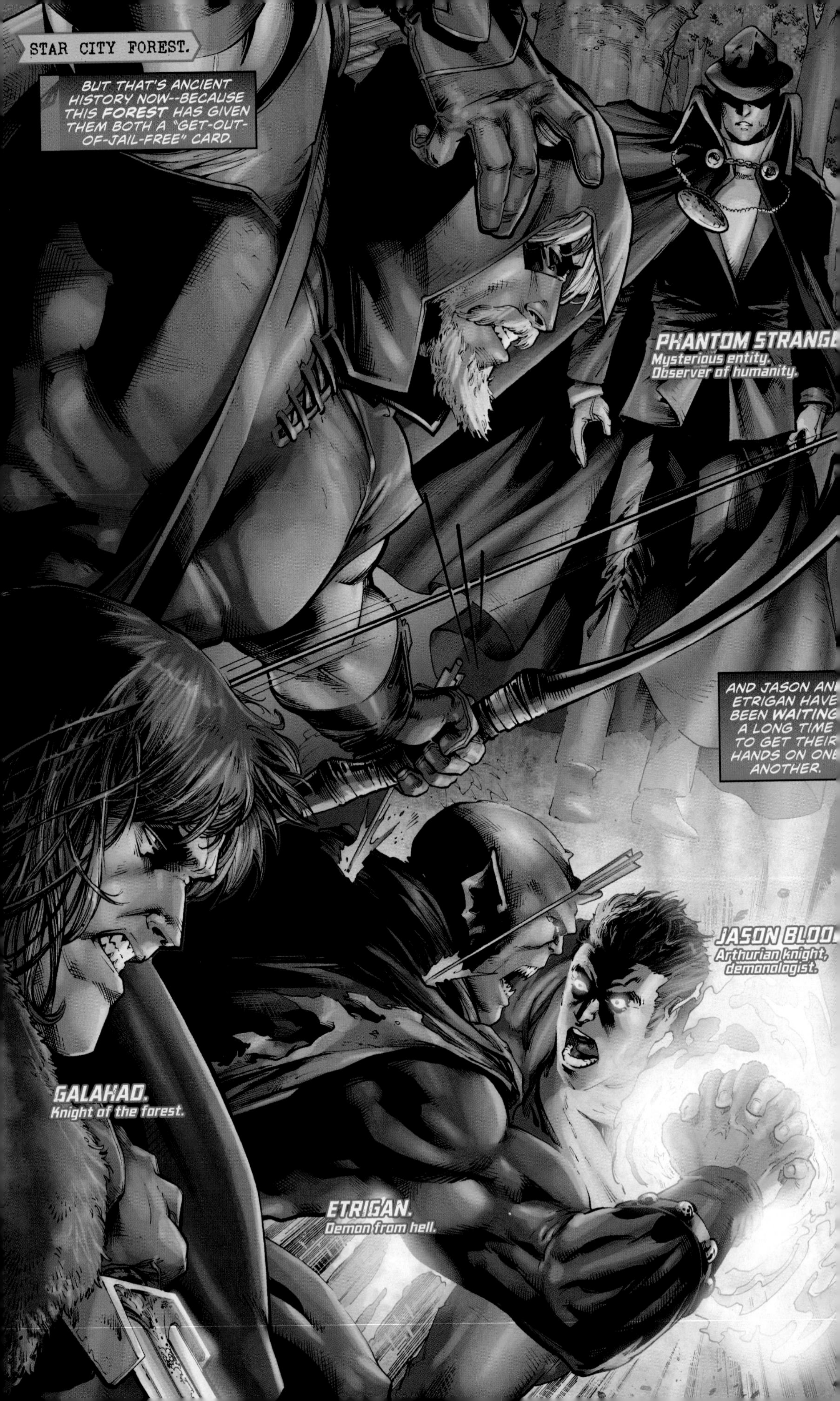
STAR CITY FOREST.
BUT THAT'S ANCIENT HISTORY NOW--BECAUSE THIS FOREST HAS GIVEN THEM BOTH A "GET-OUT-OF-JAIL-FREE" CARD.
PHANTOM STRANGE
Mysterious entity. Observer of humanity.
AND JASON AN ETRIGAN HAVE BEEN WAITING A LONG TIME TO GET THEIR HANDS ON ONE ANOTHER.
JASON BLOO.
Arthurian knight, demonologist.
GALAHAD.
Knight of the forest.
ETRIGAN.
Demon from hell.

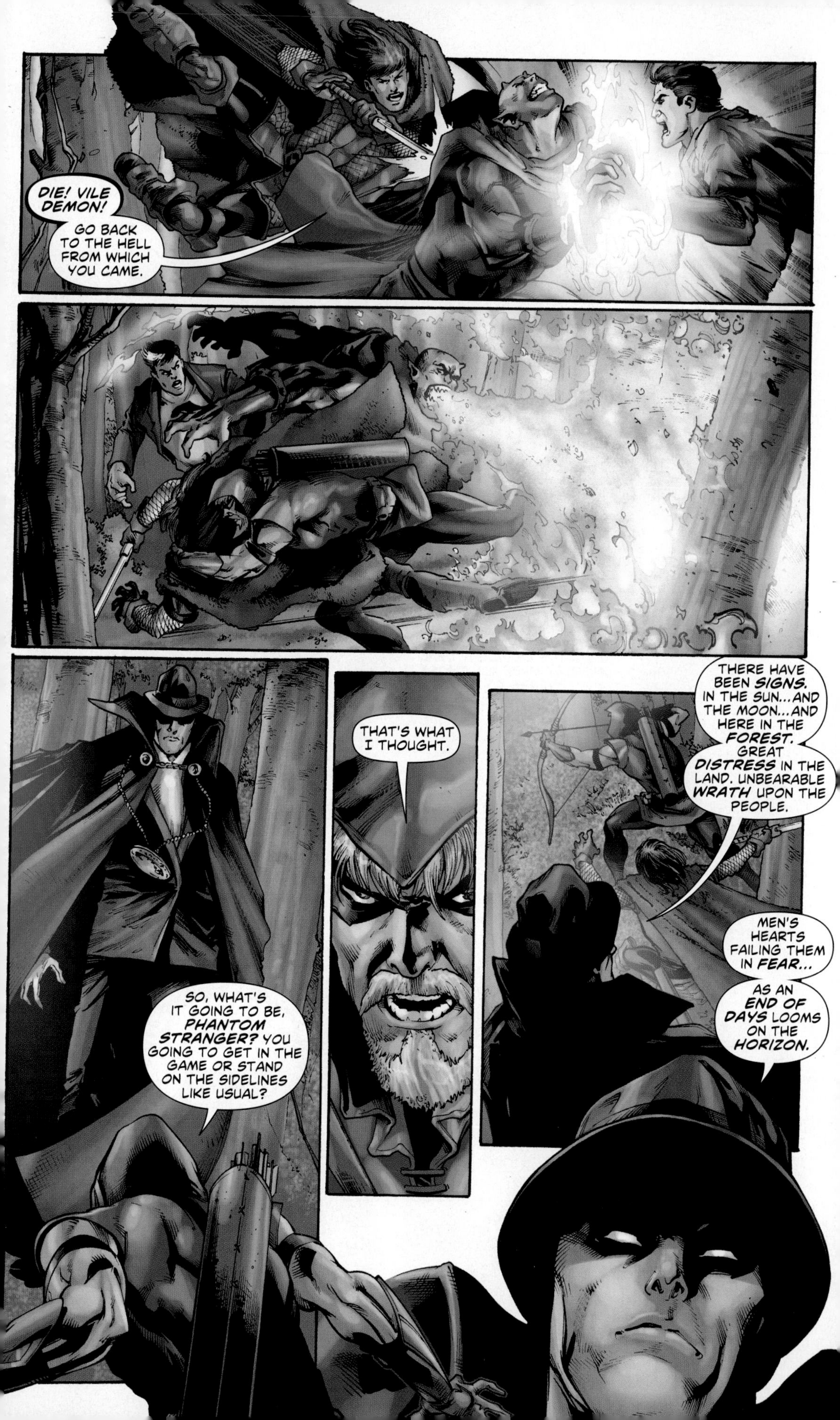
DIE! VILE DEMON!
GO BACK TO THE HELL FROM WHICH YOU CAME.
SO, WHAT'S IT GOING TO BE, PHANTOM STRANGER? YOU GOING TO GET IN THE GAME OR STAND ON THE SIDELINES LIKE USUAL?
THAT'S WHAT I THOUGHT.
THERE HAVE BEEN SIGNS. IN THE SUN...AND THE MOON...AND HERE IN THE FOREST. GREAT DISTRESS IN THE LAND. UNBEARABLE WRATH UPON THE PEOPLE.
MEN'S HEARTS FAILING THEM IN FEAR...
AS AN END OF DAYS LOOMS ON THE HORIZON.

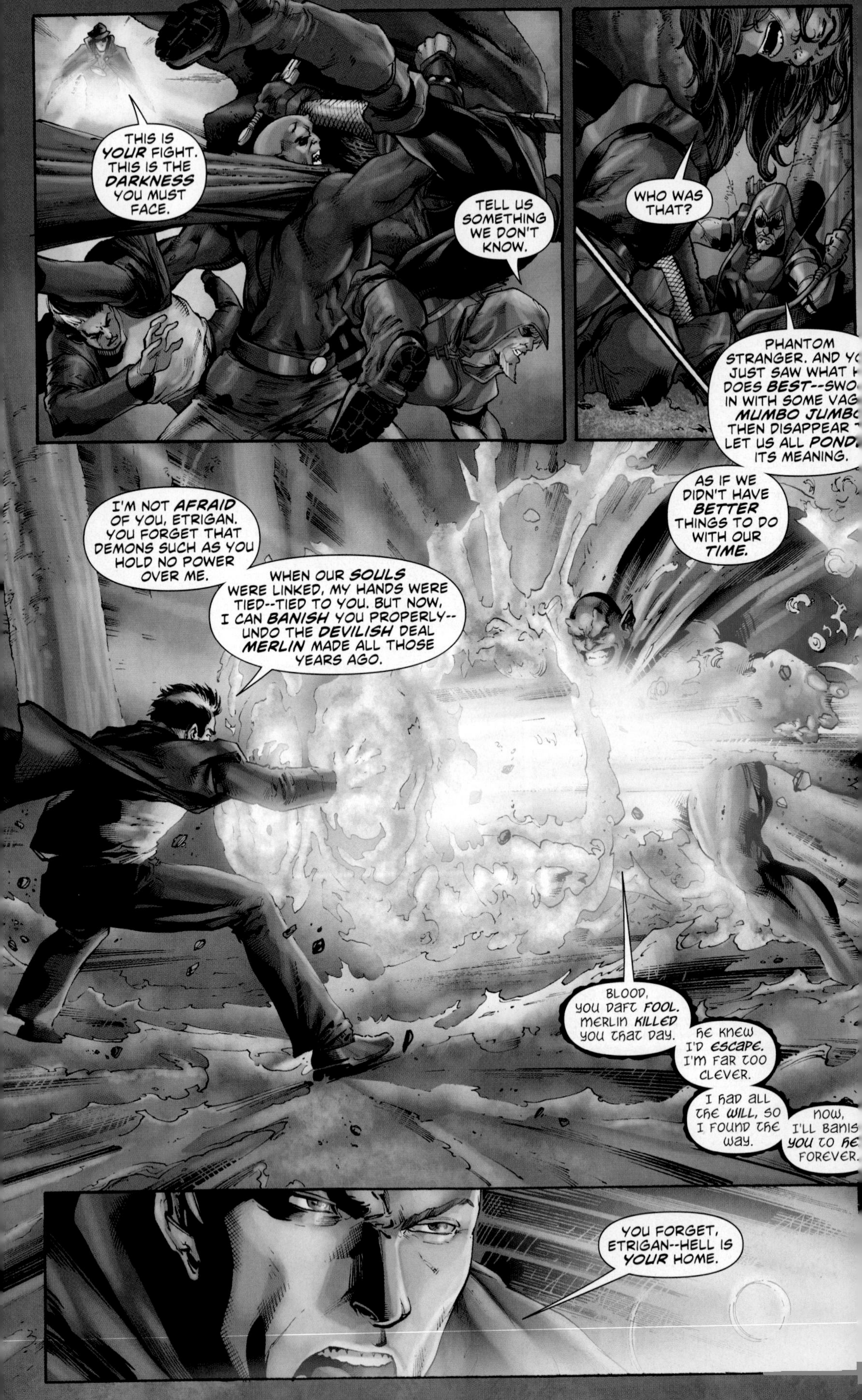

THIS IS YOUR FIGHT. THIS IS THE DARKNESS YOU MUST FACE.
TELL US SOMETHING WE DON'T KNOW.
WHO WAS THAT?
PHANTOM STRANGER. AND YO JUST SAW WHAT H DOES BEST--SWO IN WITH SOME VAG MUMBO JUMBO THEN DISAPPEAR T LET US ALL POND ITS MEANING.
AS IF WE DIDN'T HAVE BETTER THINGS TO DO WITH OUR TIME.
I'M NOT AFRAID OF YOU, ETRIGAN. YOU FORGET THAT DEMONS SUCH AS YOU HOLD NO POWER OVER ME.
WHEN OUR SOULS WERE LINKED, MY HANDS WERE TIED--TIED TO YOU. BUT NOW, I CAN BANISH YOU PROPERLY-- UNDO THE DEVILISH DEAL MERLIN MADE ALL THOSE YEARS AGO.
BLOOD, YOU DAFT FOOL. MERLIN KILLED YOU THAT DAY.
HE KNEW I'D ESCAPE. I'M FAR TOO CLEVER.
I HAD ALL THE WILL, SO I FOUND THE WAY.
NOW, I'LL BANIS YOU TO HE FOREVER.
YOU FORGET, ETRIGAN--HELL IS YOUR HOME.

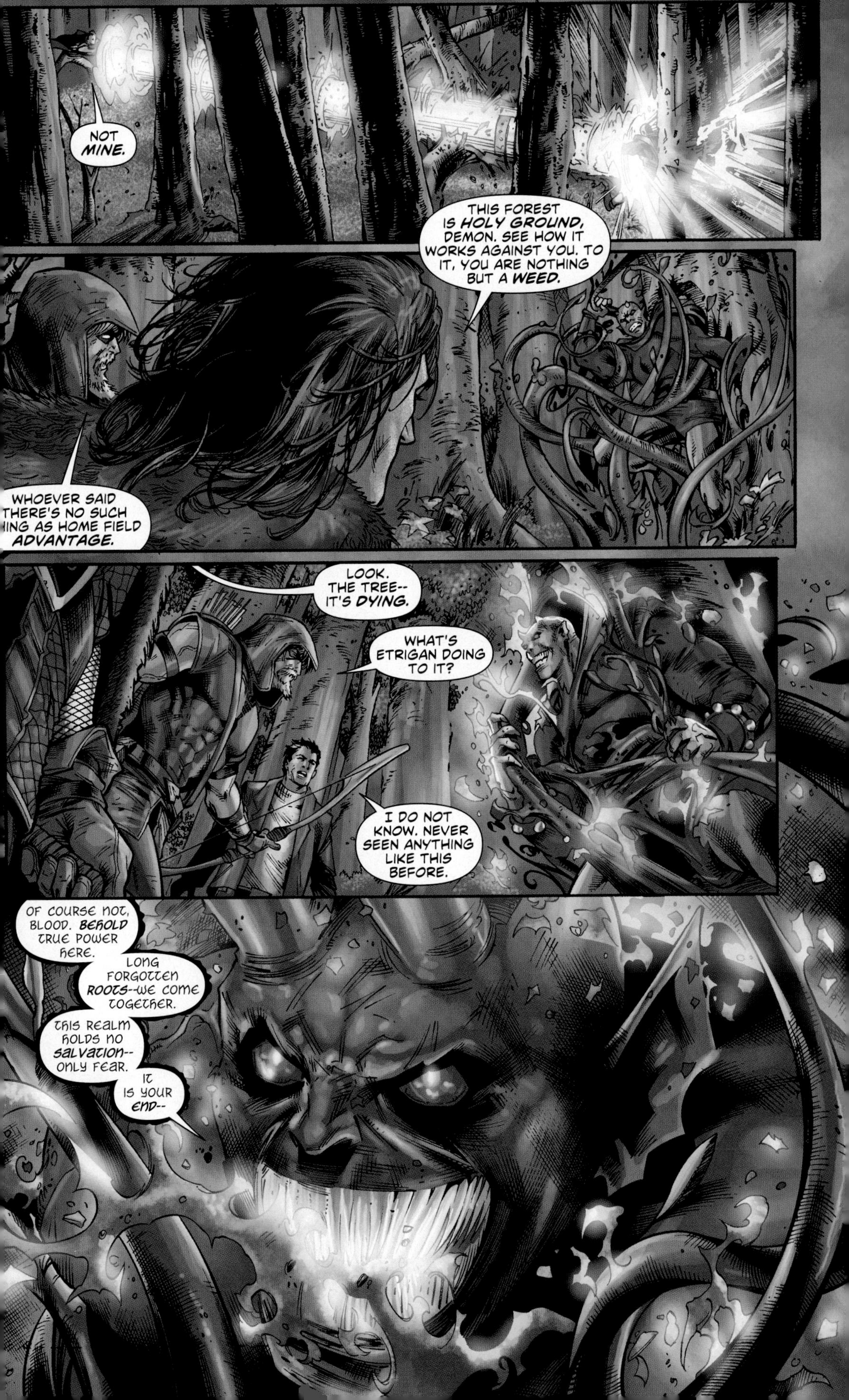

NOT MINE.
THIS FOREST IS HOLY GROUND, DEMON. SEE HOW IT WORKS AGAINST YOU. TO IT, YOU ARE NOTHING BUT A WEED.
WHOEVER SAID THERE'S NO SUCH ING AS HOME FIELD ADVANTAGE.
LOOK. THE TREE-- IT'S DYING.
WHAT'S ETRIGAN DOING TO IT?
I DO NOT KNOW. NEVER SEEN ANYTHING LIKE THIS BEFORE.
OF COURSE NOT, BLOOD. BEHOLD TRUE POWER HERE.
LONG FORGOTTEN ROOTS--WE COME TOGETHER.
THIS REALM HOLDS NO SALVATION-- ONLY FEAR.
IT IS YOUR END--

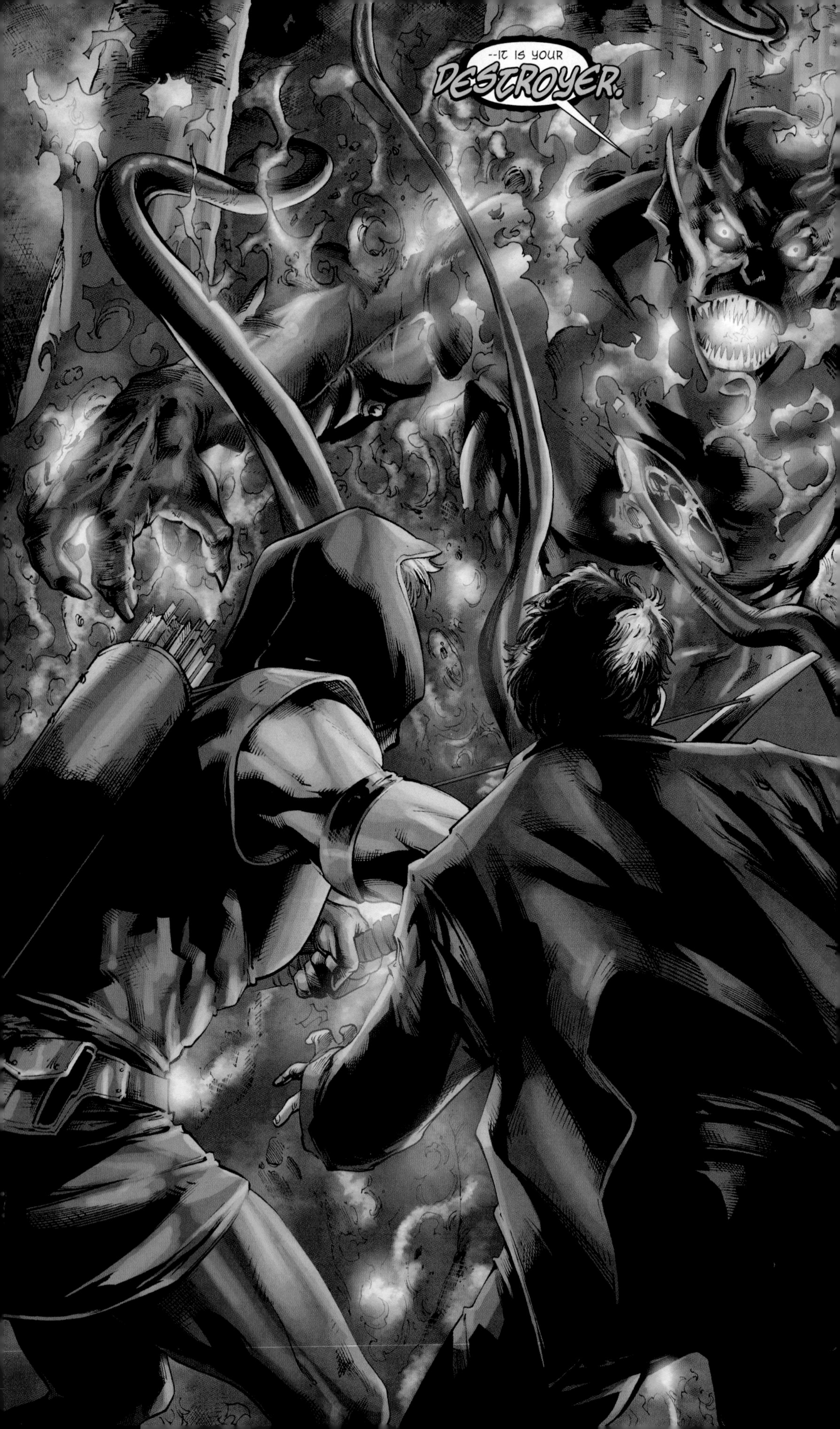
--IT IS YOUR DESTROYER.

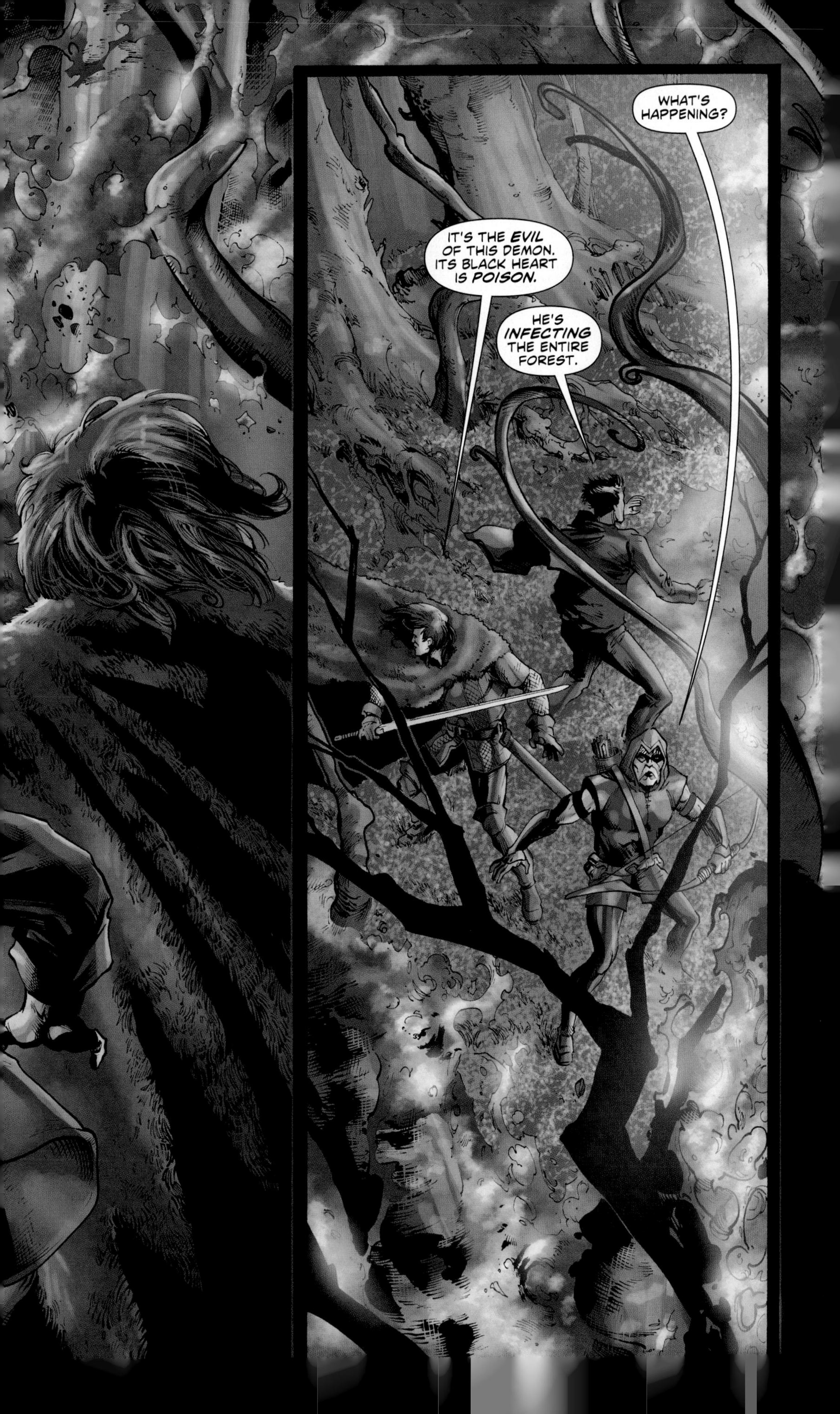
WHAT'S HAPPENING?
IT'S THE EVIL OF THIS DEMON. ITS BLACK HEART IS POISON.
HE'S INFECTING THE ENTIRE FOREST.

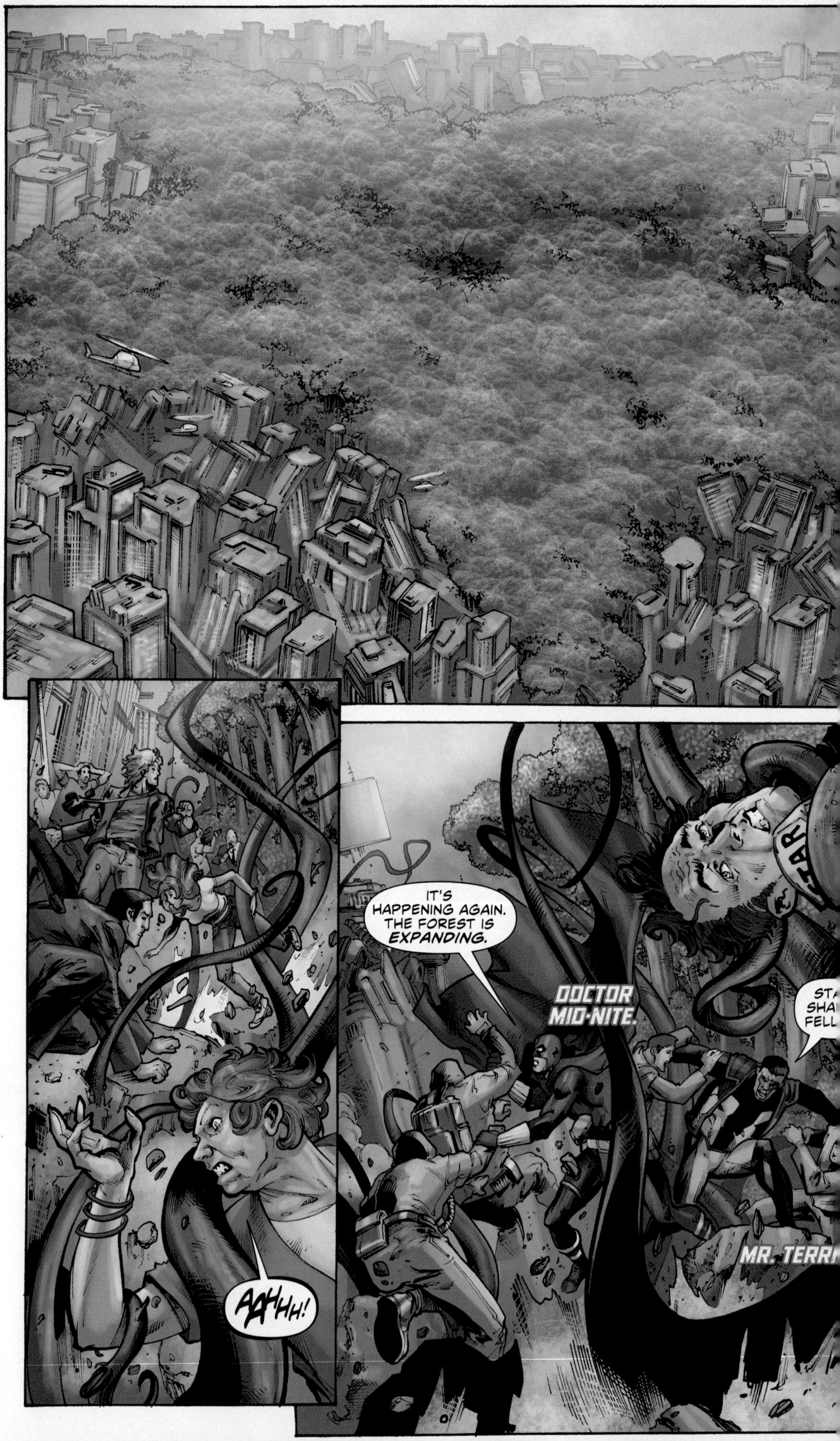
AAHHH!
IT'S HAPPENING AGAIN. THE FOREST IS EXPANDING.
DOCTOR MID-NITE.

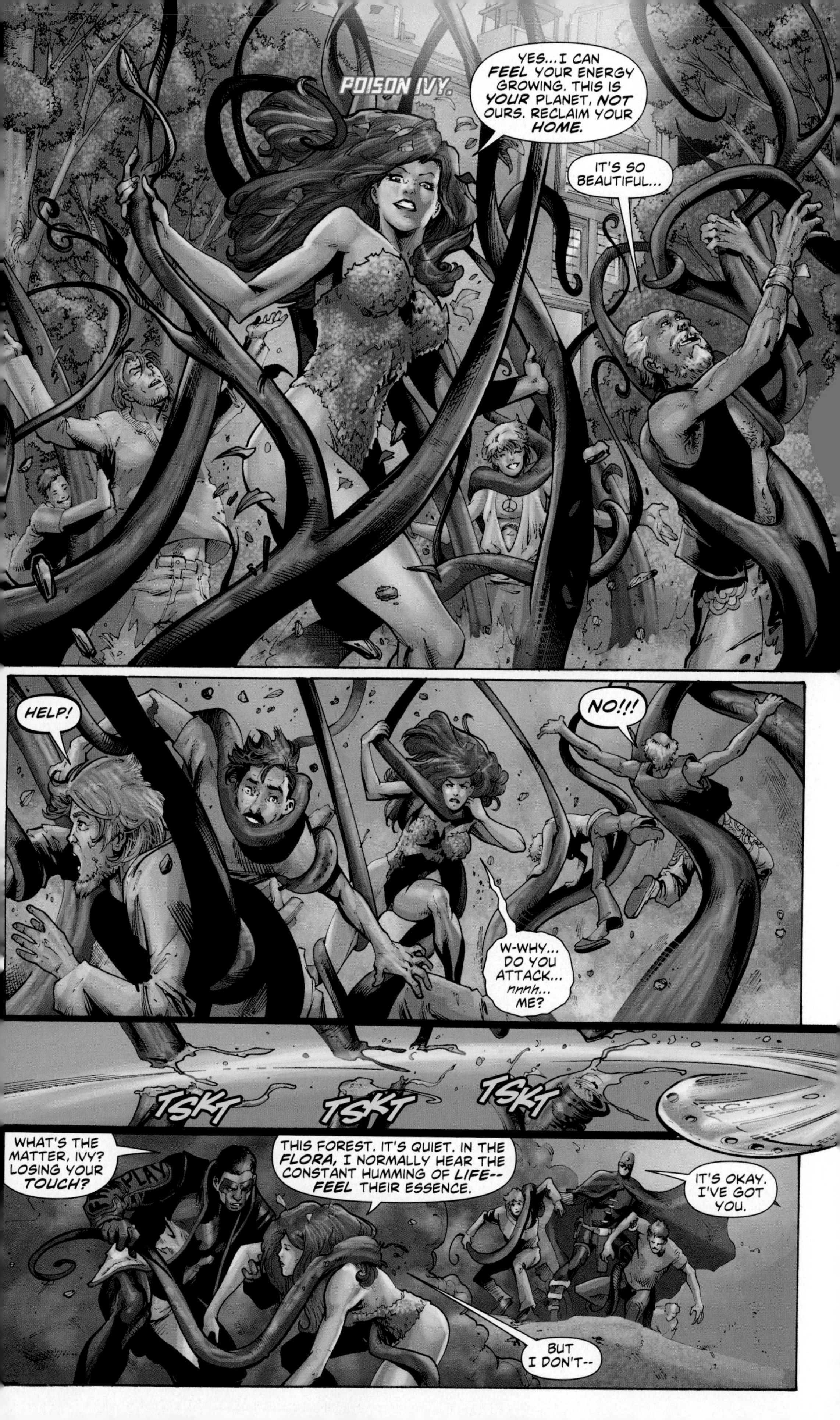
POISON IVY.
YES...I CAN FEEL YOUR ENERGY GROWING. THIS IS YOUR PLANET, NOT OURS. RECLAIM YOUR HOME.
IT'S SO BEAUTIFUL...
HELP!
NO!!!
W-WHY... DO YOU ATTACK... nnnh... ME?
TSKT
TSKT
TSKT
WHAT'S THE MATTER, IVY? LOSING YOUR TOUCH?
THIS FOREST. IT'S QUIET. IN THE FLORA, I NORMALLY HEAR THE CONSTANT HUMMING OF LIFE-- FEEL THEIR ESSENCE.
IT'S OKAY. I'VE GOT YOU.
BUT I DON'T--

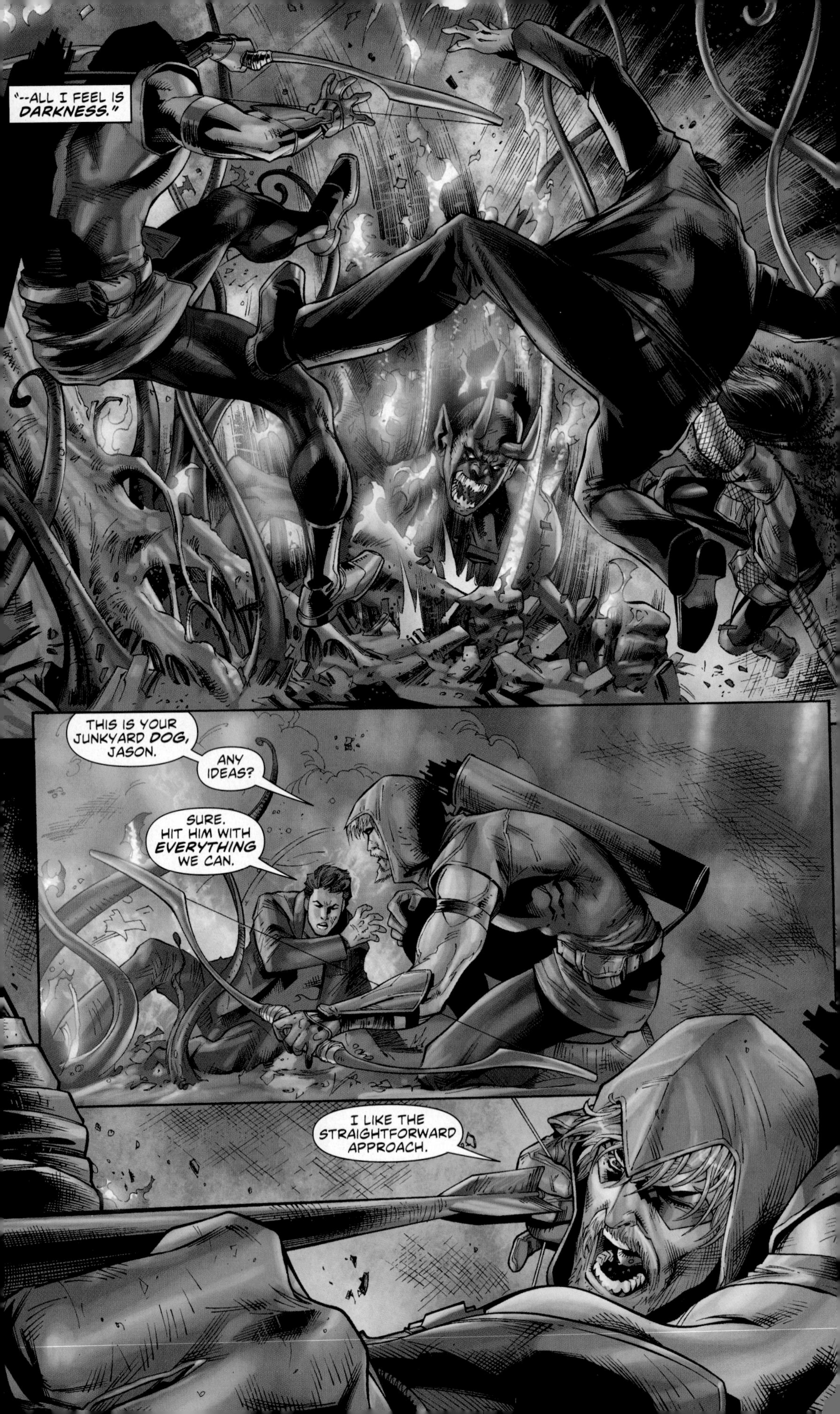
"--ALL I FEEL IS DARKNESS."
THIS IS YOUR JUNKYARD DOG, JASON.
ANY IDEAS?
SURE. HIT HIM WITH EVERYTHING WE CAN.
I LIKE THE STRAIGHTFORWARD APPROACH.

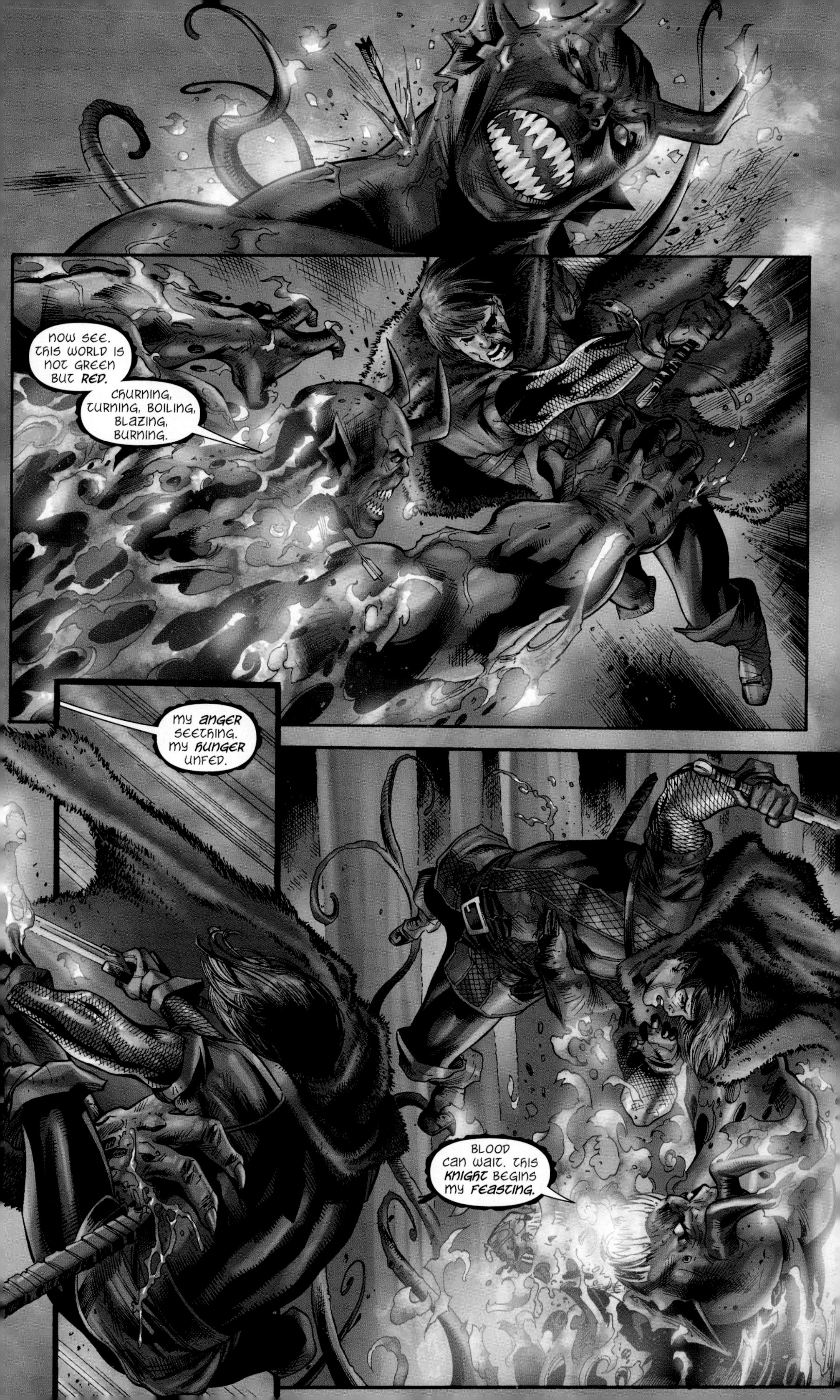
NOW SEE. THIS WORLD IS NOT GREEN BUT RED.
CHURNING, TURNING, BOILING, BLAZING, BURNING.
MY ANGER SEETHING. MY HUNGER UNFED.
BLOOD CAN WAIT. THIS KNIGHT BEGINS MY FEASTING.

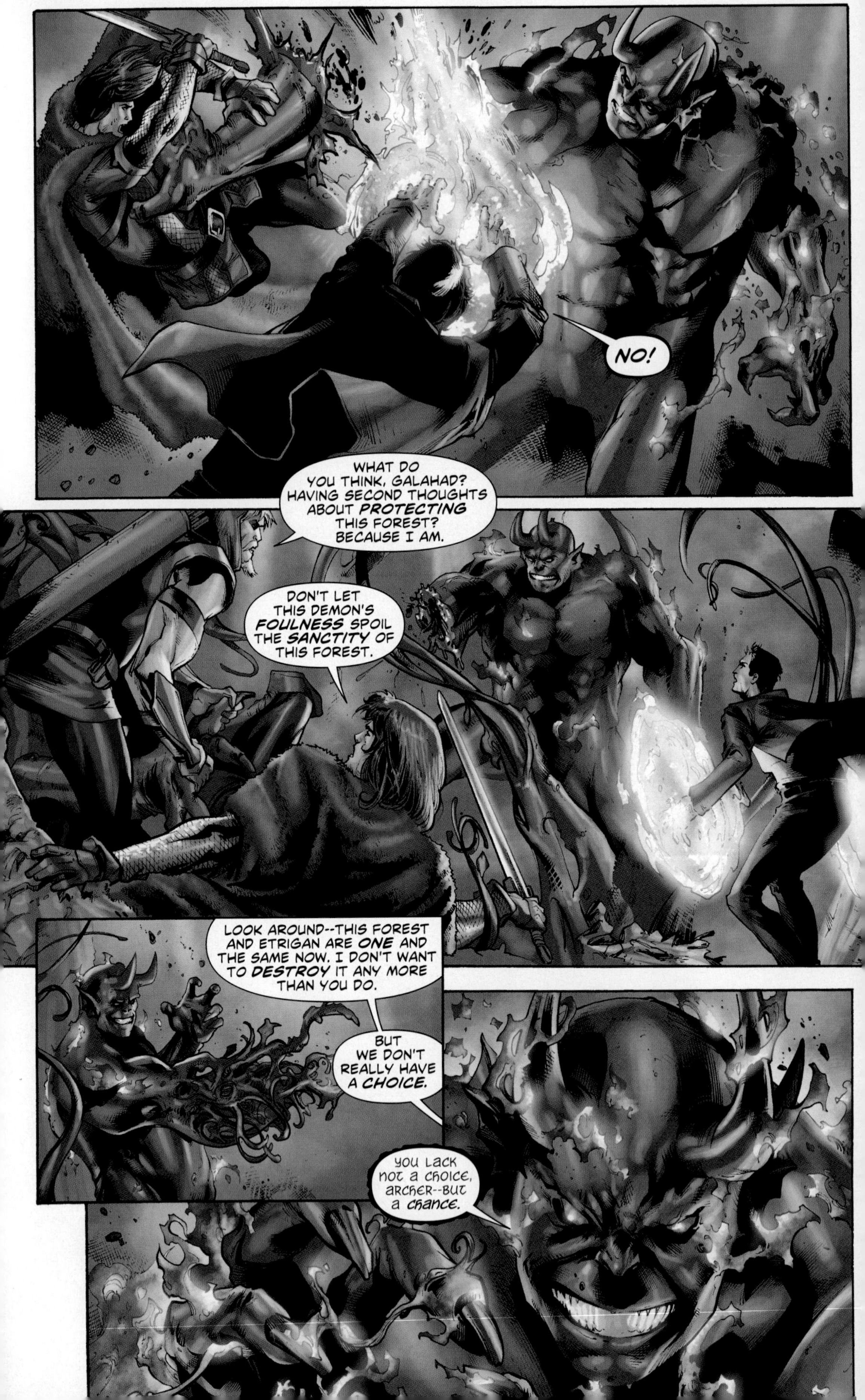
NO!
WHAT DO YOU THINK, GALAHAD? HAVING SECOND THOUGHTS ABOUT PROTECTING THIS FOREST? BECAUSE I AM.
DON'T LET THIS DEMON'S FOULNESS SPOIL THE SANCTITY OF THIS FOREST.
LOOK AROUND--THIS FOREST AND ETRIGAN ARE ONE AND THE SAME NOW. I DON'T WANT TO DESTROY IT ANY MORE THAN YOU DO.
BUT WE DON'T REALLY HAVE A CHOICE.
YOU LACK NOT A CHOICE, ARCHER--BUT A CHANCE.

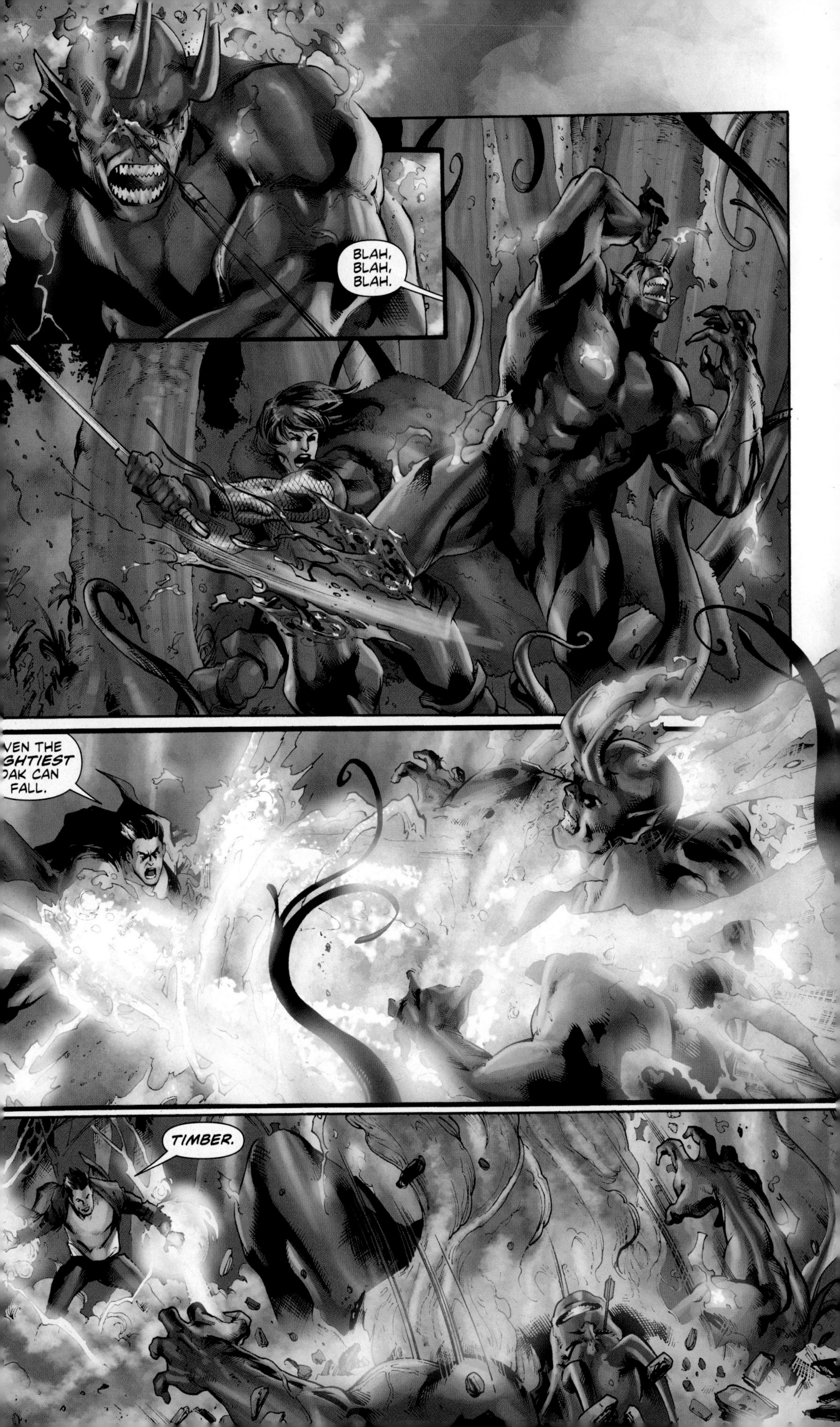
BLAH, BLAH, BLAH.
VEN THE GHTIEST OAK CAN FALL.
TIMBER.

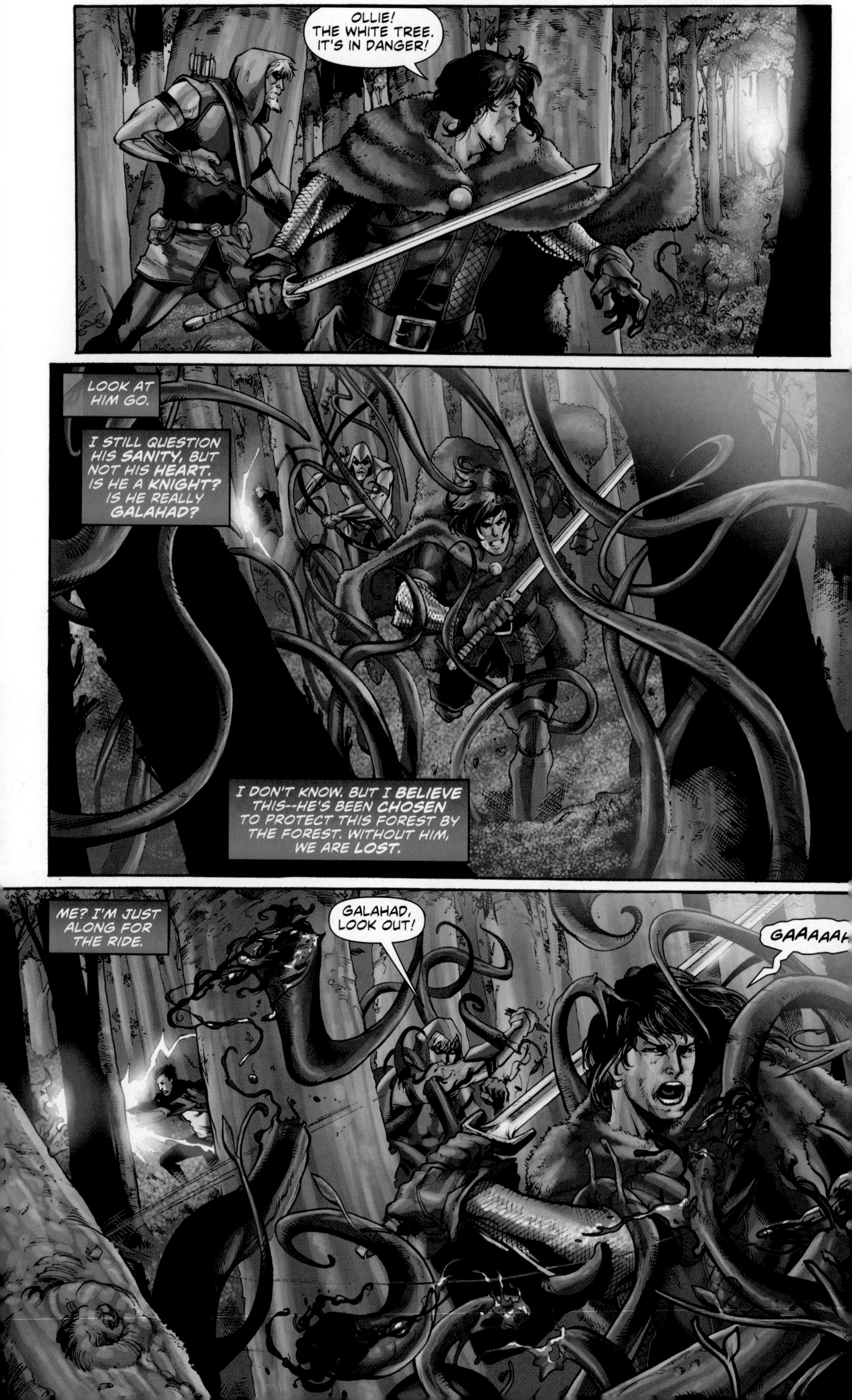
OLLIE! THE WHITE TREE. IT'S IN DANGER!
LOOK AT HIM GO.
I STILL QUESTION HIS SANITY, BUT NOT HIS HEART. IS HE A KNIGHT? IS HE REALLY GALAHAD?
I DON'T KNOW. BUT I BELIEVE THIS--HE'S BEEN CHOSEN TO PROTECT THIS FOREST BY THE FOREST. WITHOUT HIM, WE ARE LOST.
ME? I'M JUST ALONG FOR THE RIDE.
GALAHAD, LOOK OUT!
GAAAAAH

IT'S THE DEFINITION OF *OMINOUS*.

WE CANNOT LET IT *SLOW* US DOWN. THE WHITE TREE NEEDS US.

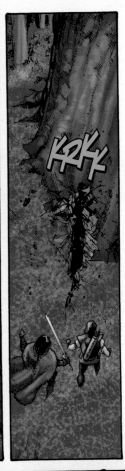

KRKK

I THINK WE NEED *IT* RIGHT ABOUT NOW.

KRKK

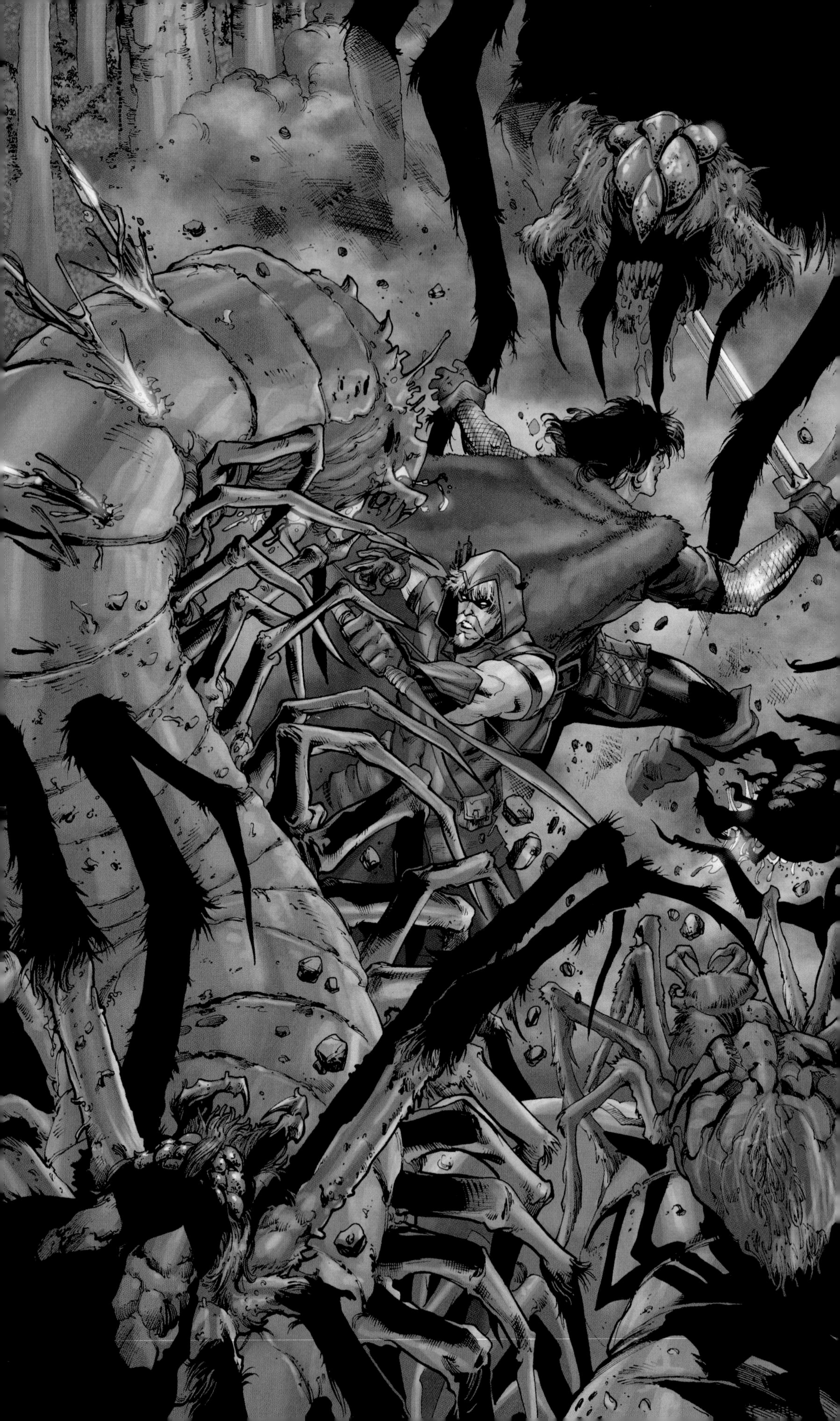

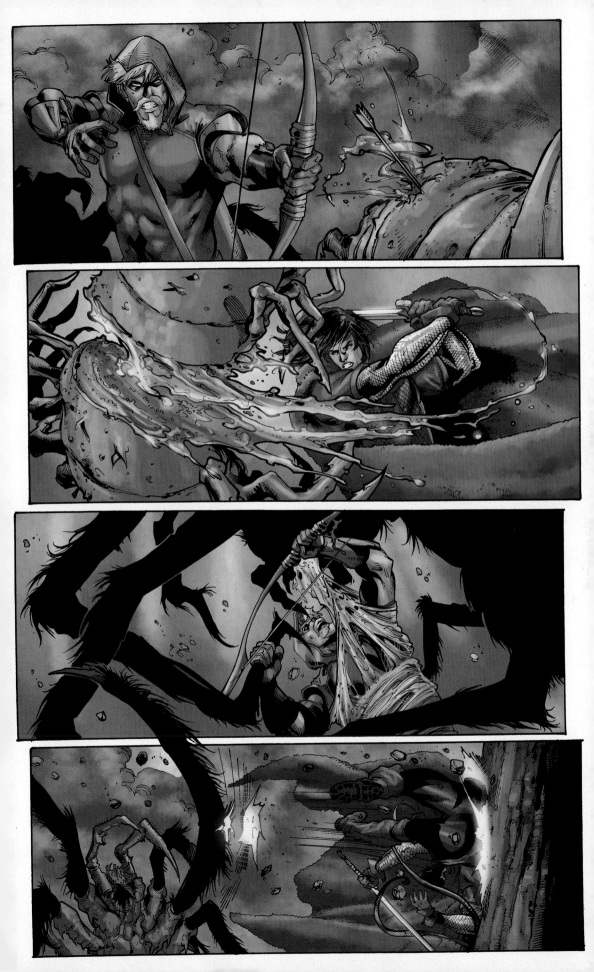

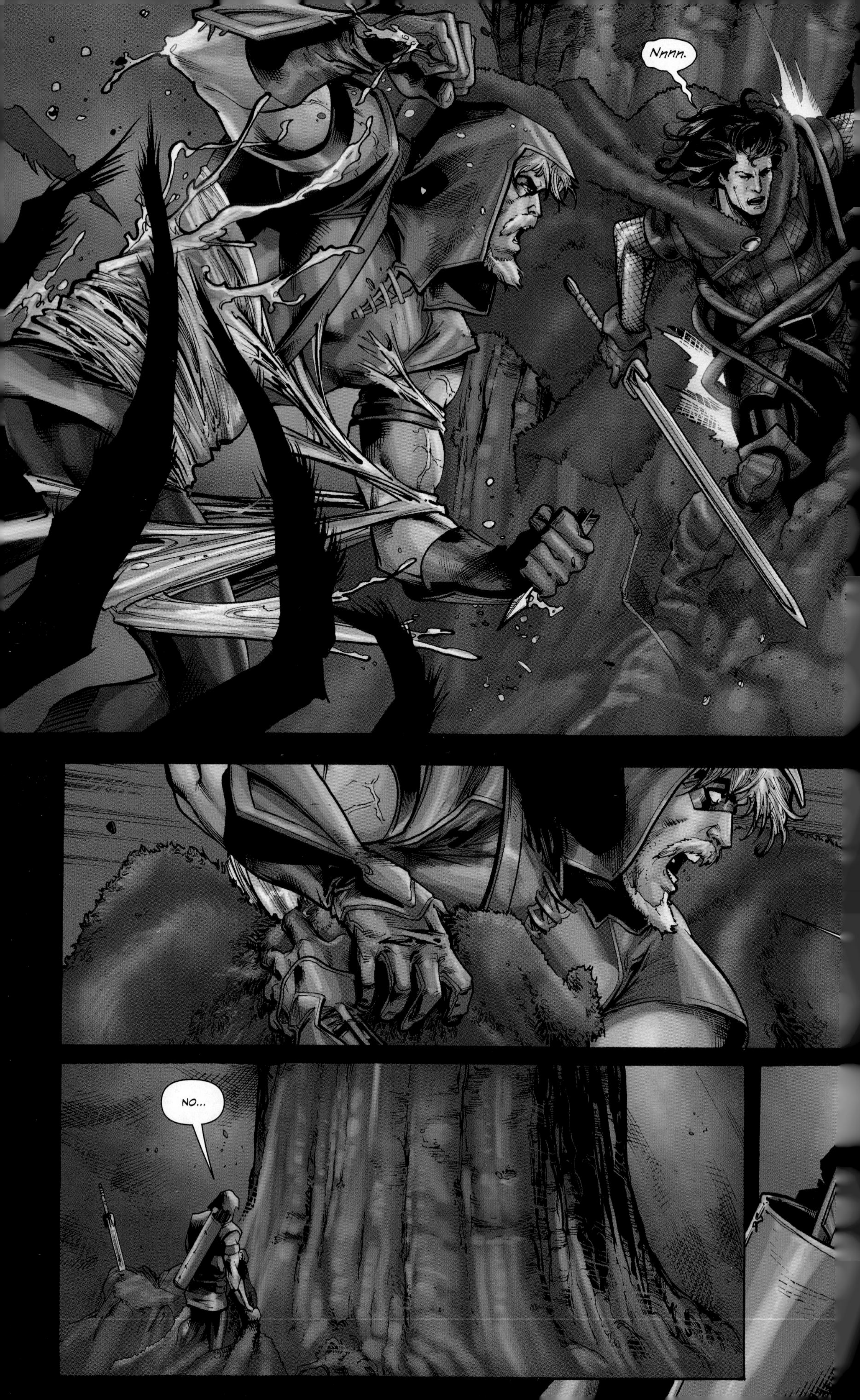
Nnnn.
NO...

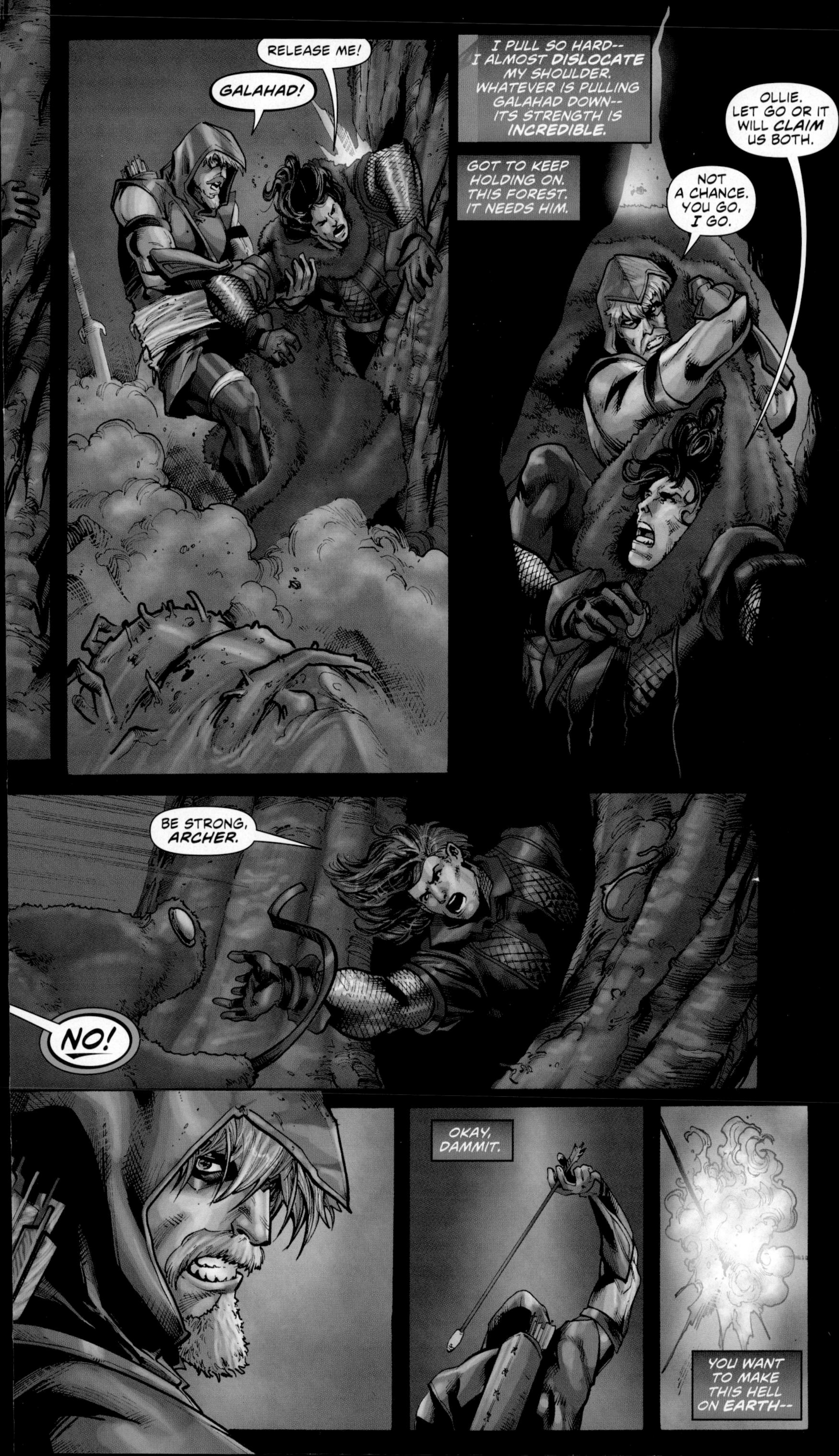
RELEASE ME!
GALAHAD!
I PULL SO HARD-- I ALMOST DISLOCATE MY SHOULDER. WHATEVER IS PULLING GALAHAD DOWN-- ITS STRENGTH IS INCREDIBLE.
GOT TO KEEP HOLDING ON. THIS FOREST. IT NEEDS HIM.
OLLIE. LET GO OR IT WILL CLAIM US BOTH.
NOT A CHANCE. YOU GO, I GO.
BE STRONG, ARCHER.
NO!
OKAY, DAMMIT.
YOU WANT TO MAKE THIS HELL ON EARTH--

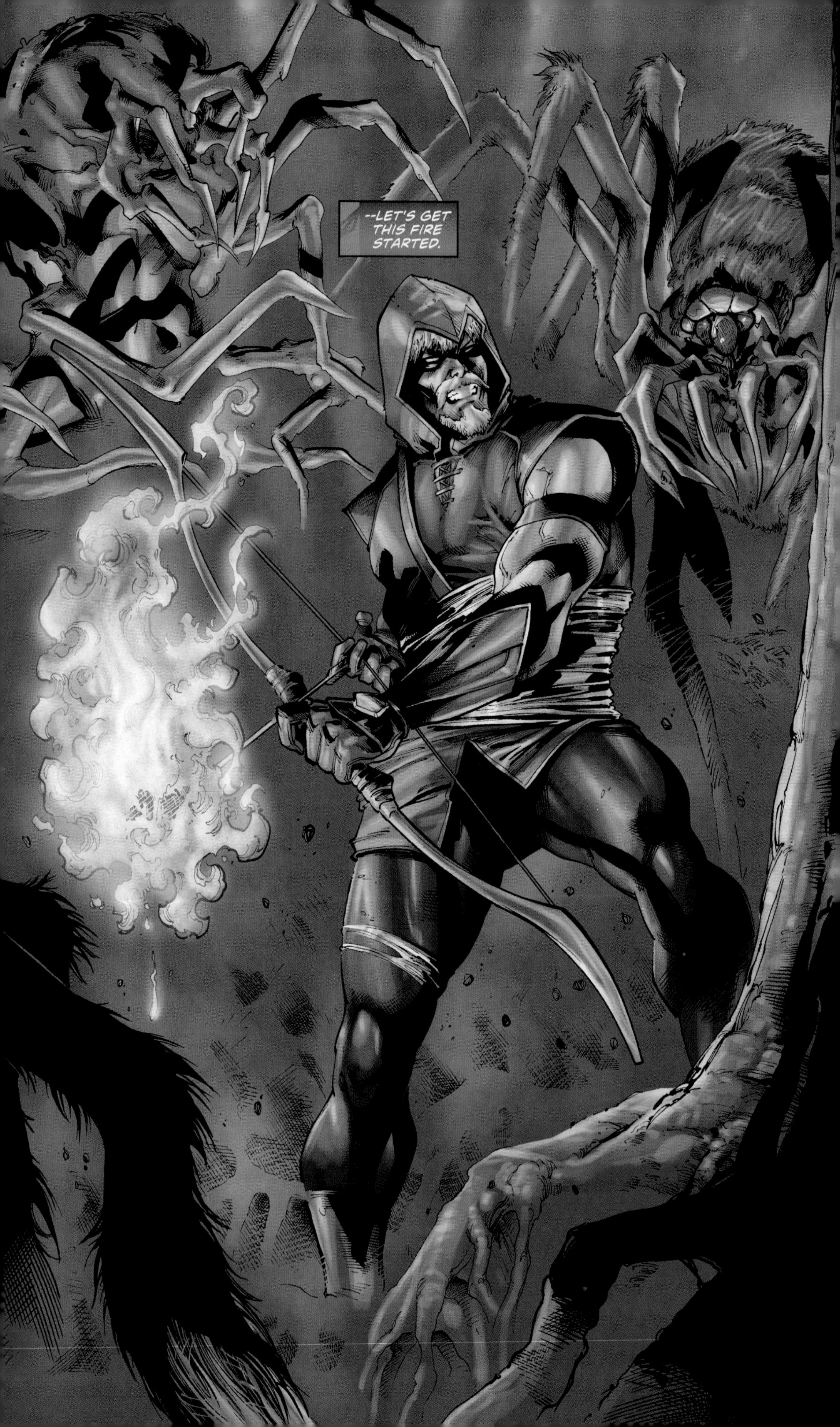
--LET'S GET THIS FIRE STARTED.

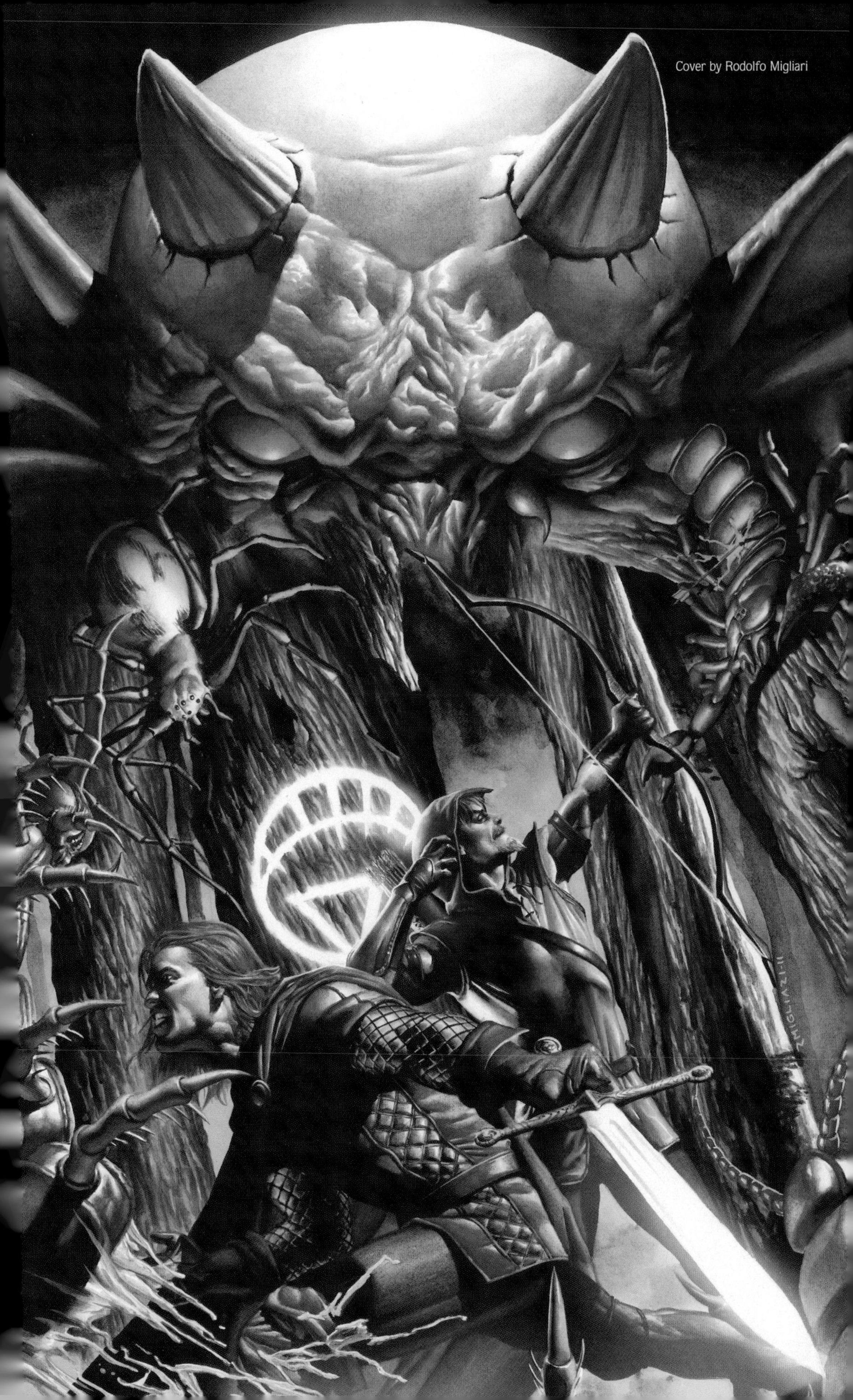

Cover by Rodolfo Migliari

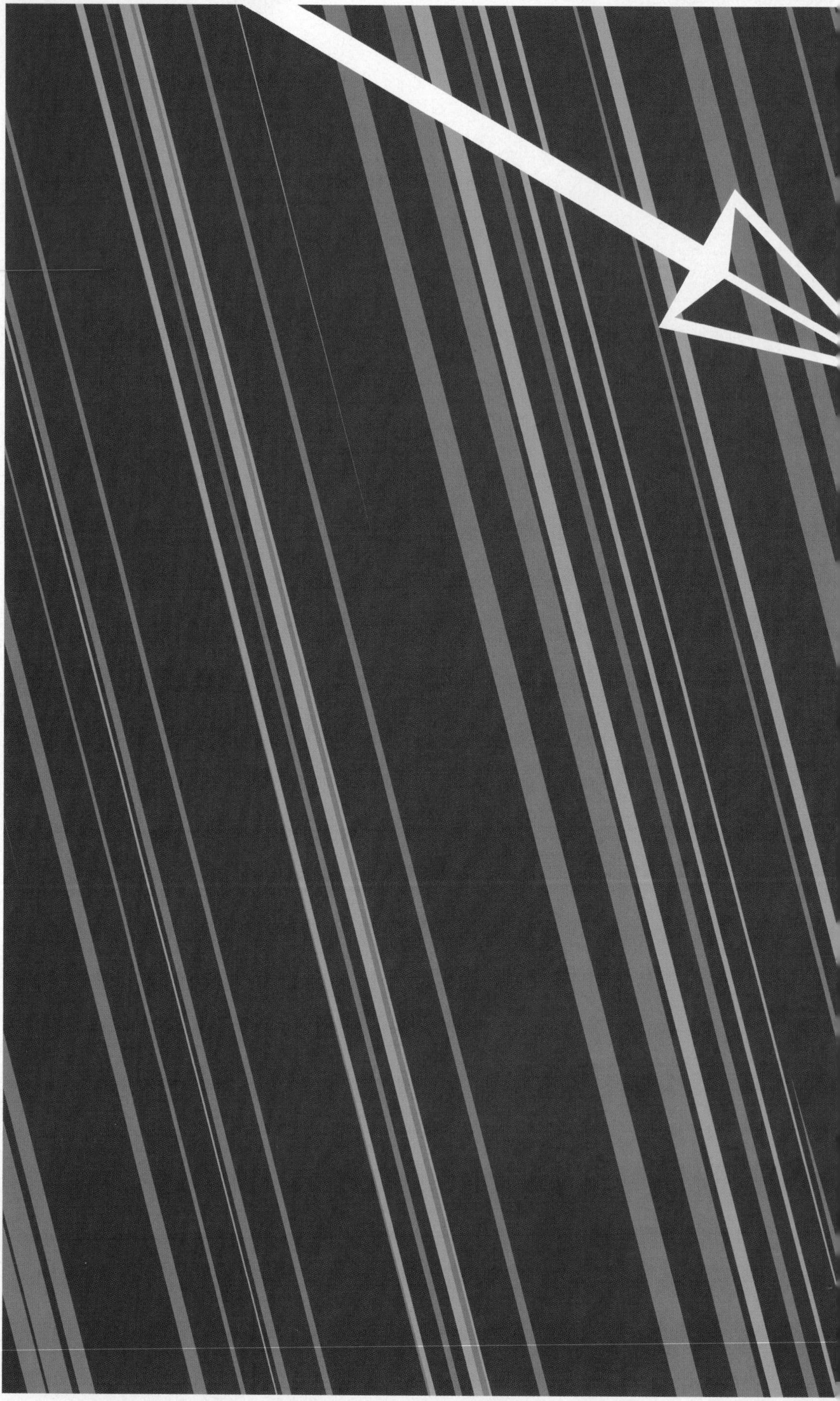

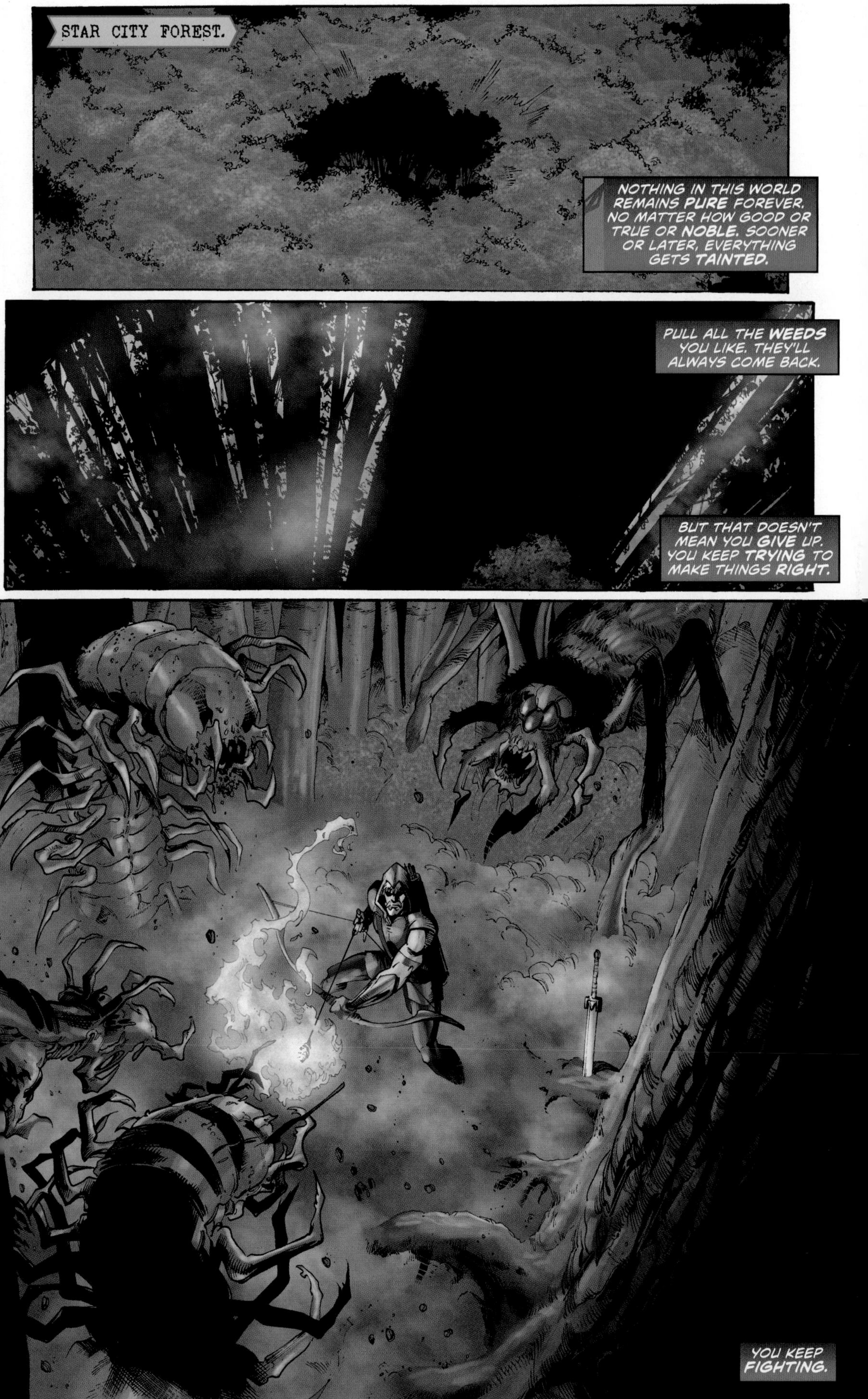
STAR CITY FOREST.
NOTHING IN THIS WORLD REMAINS PURE FOREVER. NO MATTER HOW GOOD OR TRUE OR NOBLE. SOONER OR LATER, EVERYTHING GETS TAINTED.
PULL ALL THE WEEDS YOU LIKE. THEY'LL ALWAYS COME BACK.
BUT THAT DOESN'T MEAN YOU GIVE UP. YOU KEEP TRYING TO MAKE THINGS RIGHT.
YOU KEEP FIGHTING.

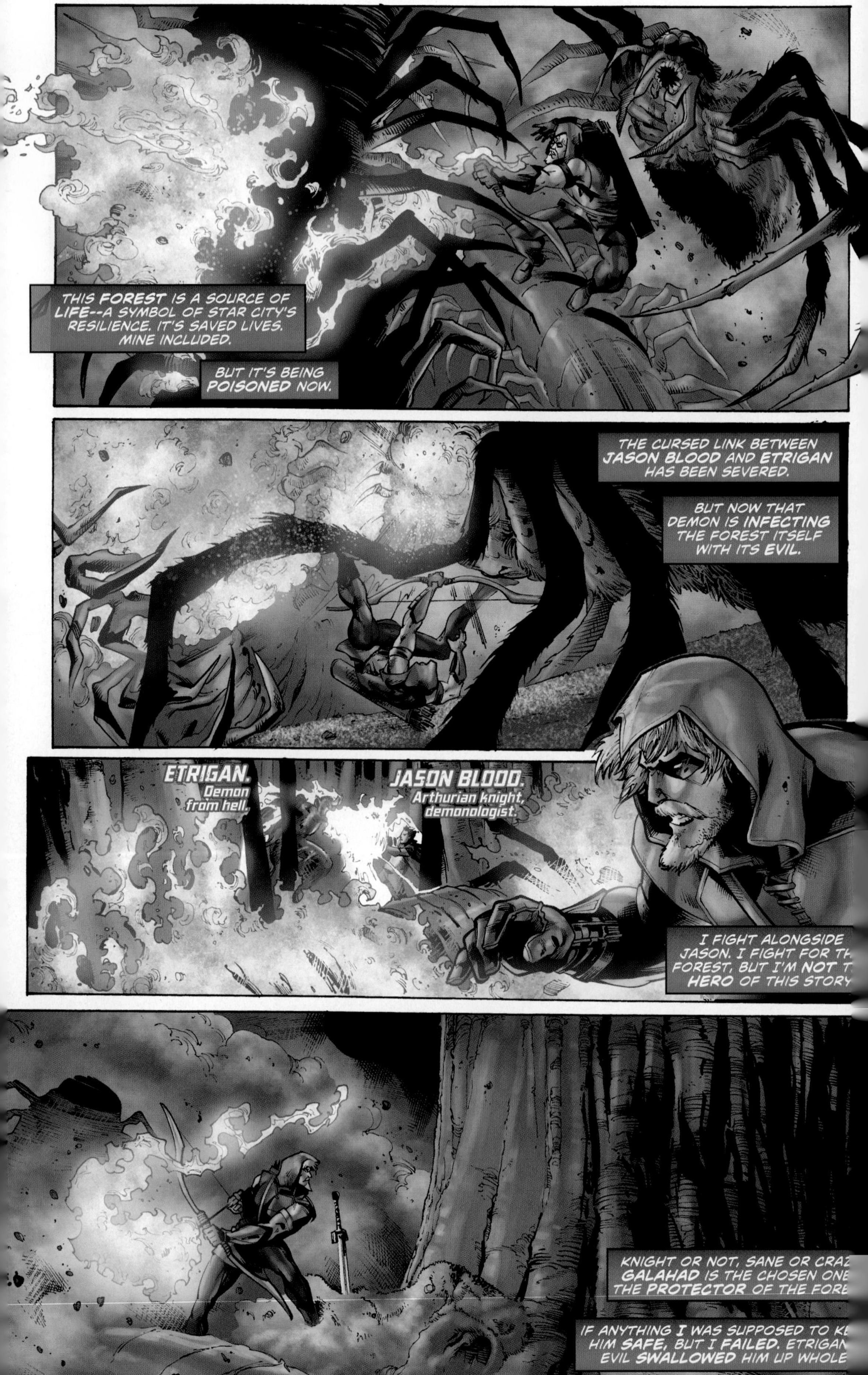
THIS FOREST IS A SOURCE OF LIFE--A SYMBOL OF STAR CITY'S RESILIENCE. IT'S SAVED LIVES. MINE INCLUDED.
BUT IT'S BEING POISONED NOW.
THE CURSED LINK BETWEEN JASON BLOOD AND ETRIGAN HAS BEEN SEVERED.
BUT NOW THAT DEMON IS INFECTING THE FOREST ITSELF WITH ITS EVIL.
ETRIGAN. Demon from hell.
JASON BLOOD. Arthurian knight, demonologist.
I FIGHT ALONGSIDE JASON. I FIGHT FOR TH FOREST, BUT I'M NOT T HERO OF THIS STORY
KNIGHT OR NOT, SANE OR CRAZ GALAHAD IS THE CHOSEN ONE THE PROTECTOR OF THE FORE
IF ANYTHING I WAS SUPPOSED TO KE HIM SAFE, BUT I FAILED. ETRIGAN EVIL SWALLOWED HIM WHOLE

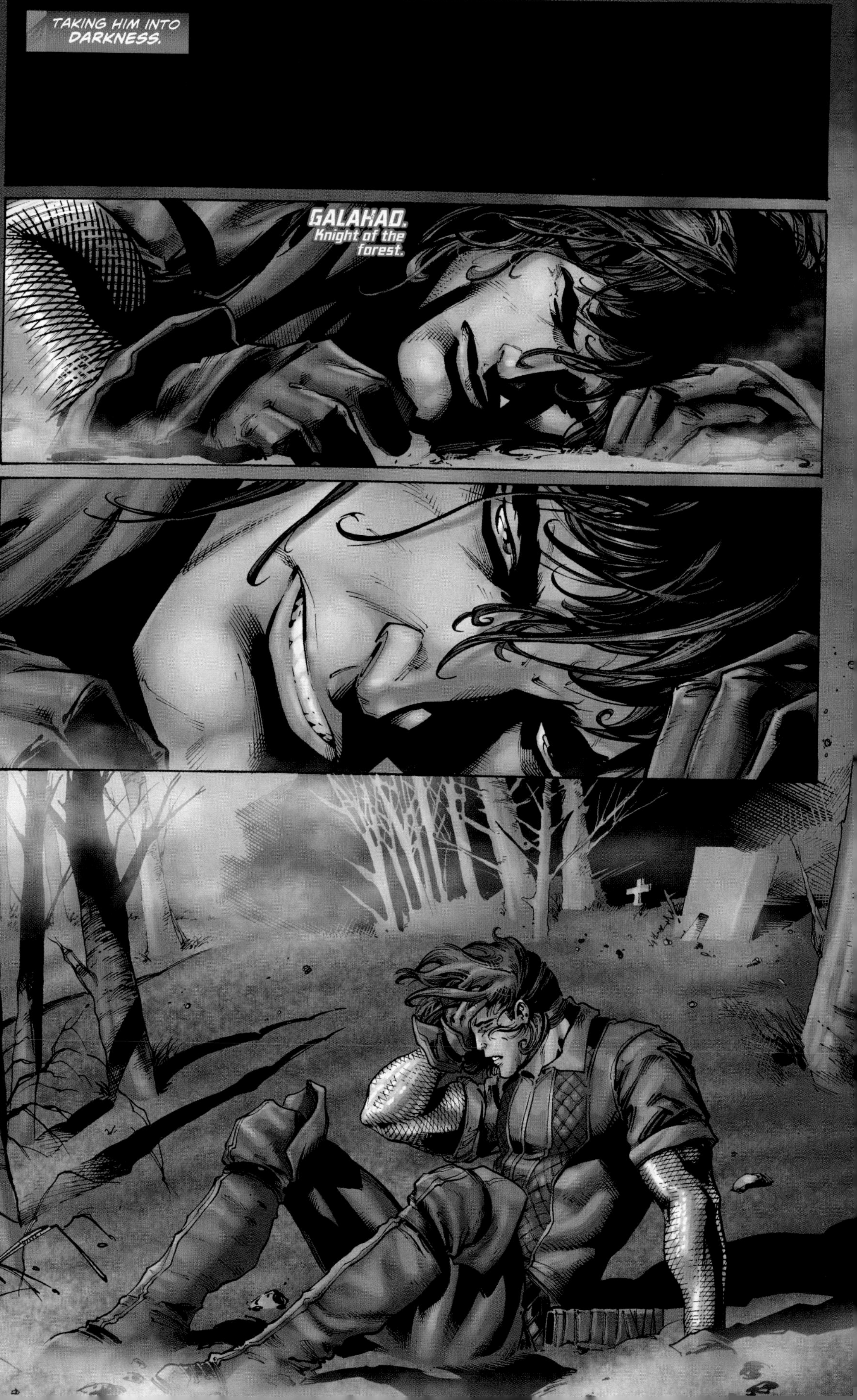
TAKING HIM INTO DARKNESS.
GALAHAD. Knight of the forest.

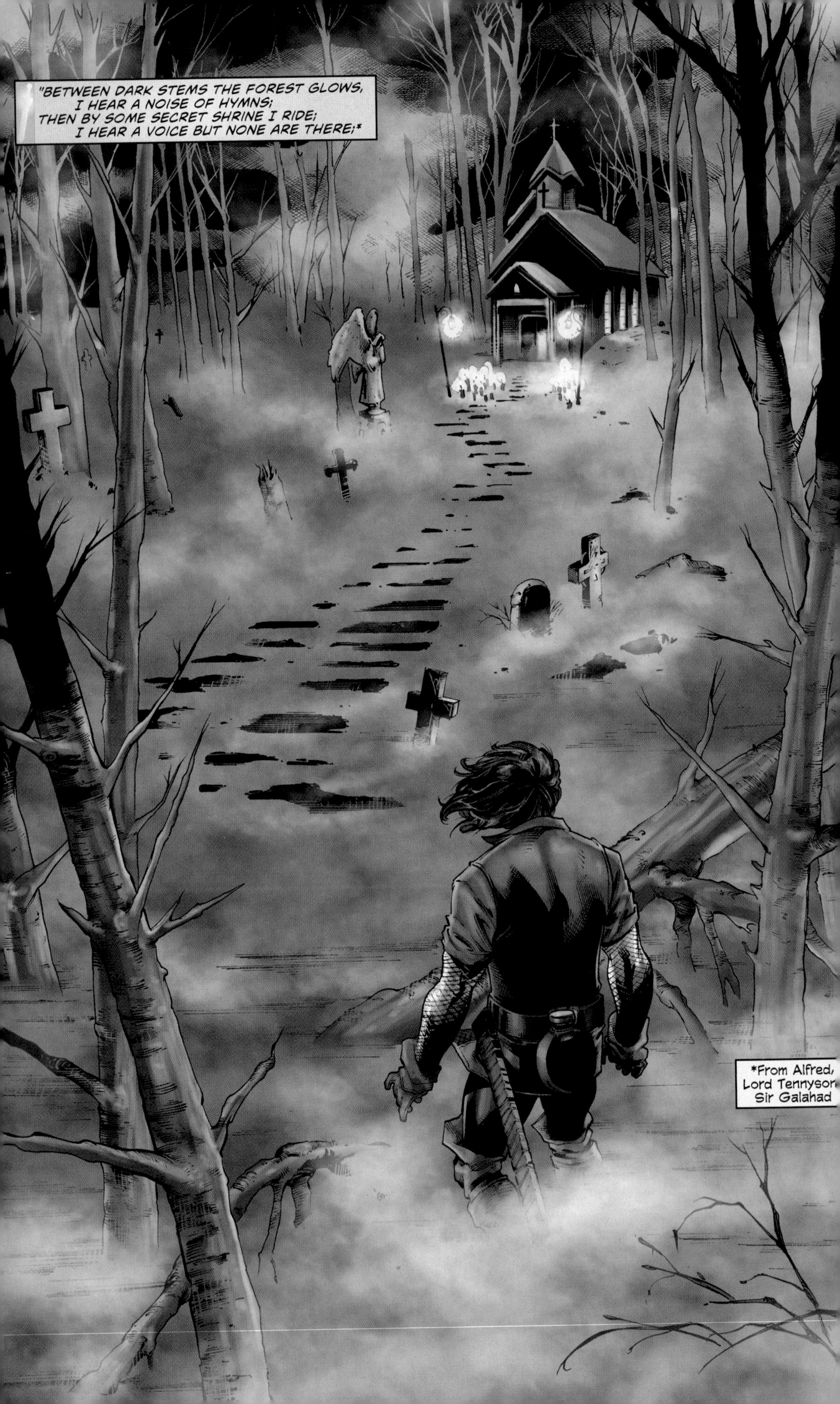
"BETWEEN DARK STEMS THE FOREST GLOWS,
I HEAR A NOISE OF HYMNS;
THEN BY SOME SECRET SHRINE I RIDE;
I HEAR A VOICE BUT NONE ARE THERE;*
*From Alfred, Lord Tennyson, Sir Galahad

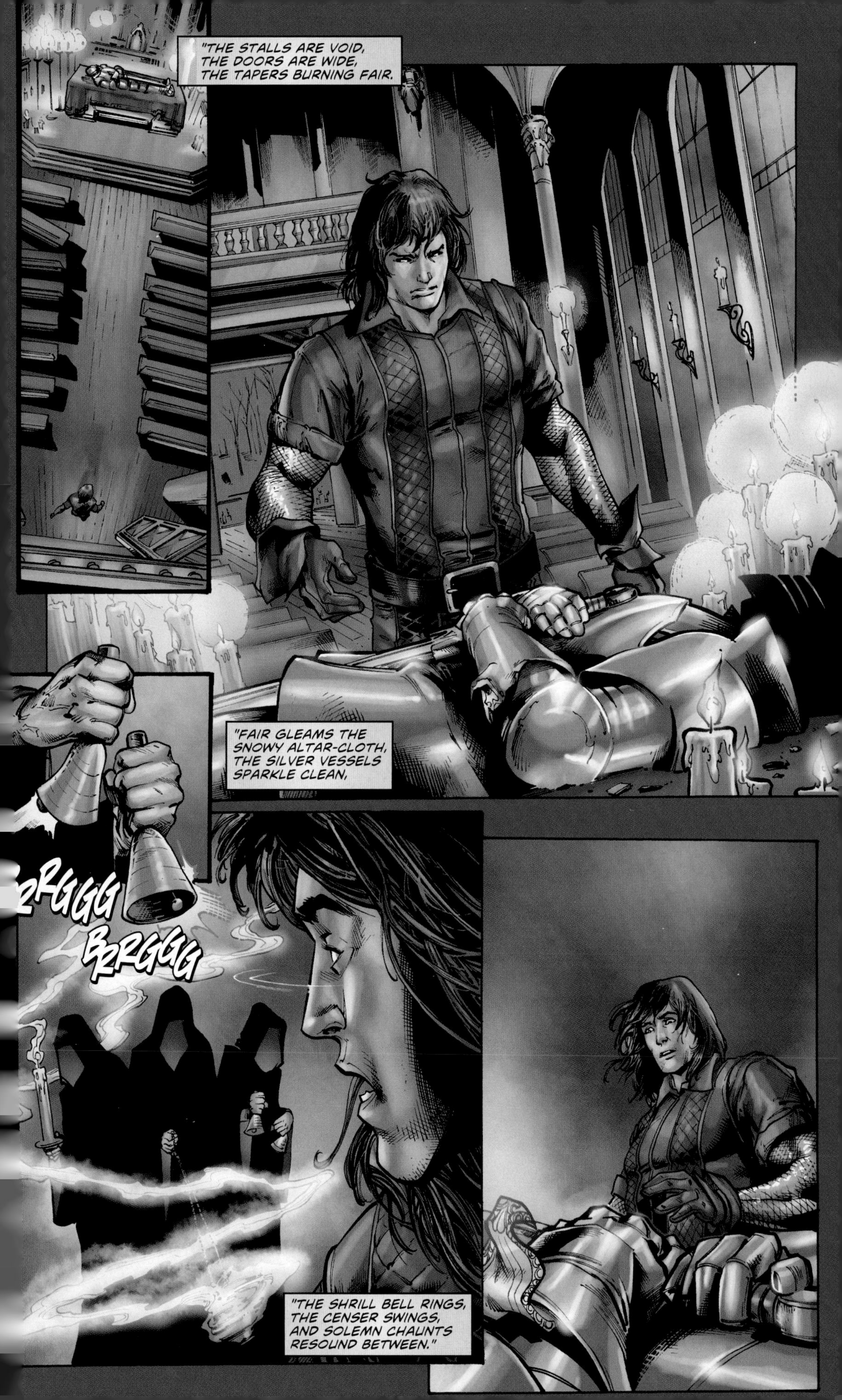
"THE STALLS ARE VOID, THE DOORS ARE WIDE, THE TAPERS BURNING FAIR.
"FAIR GLEAMS THE SNOWY ALTAR-CLOTH, THE SILVER VESSELS SPARKLE CLEAN,
BRRGGG
BRRGGG
"THE SHRILL BELL RINGS, THE CENSER SWINGS, AND SOLEMN CHAUNTS RESOUND BETWEEN."

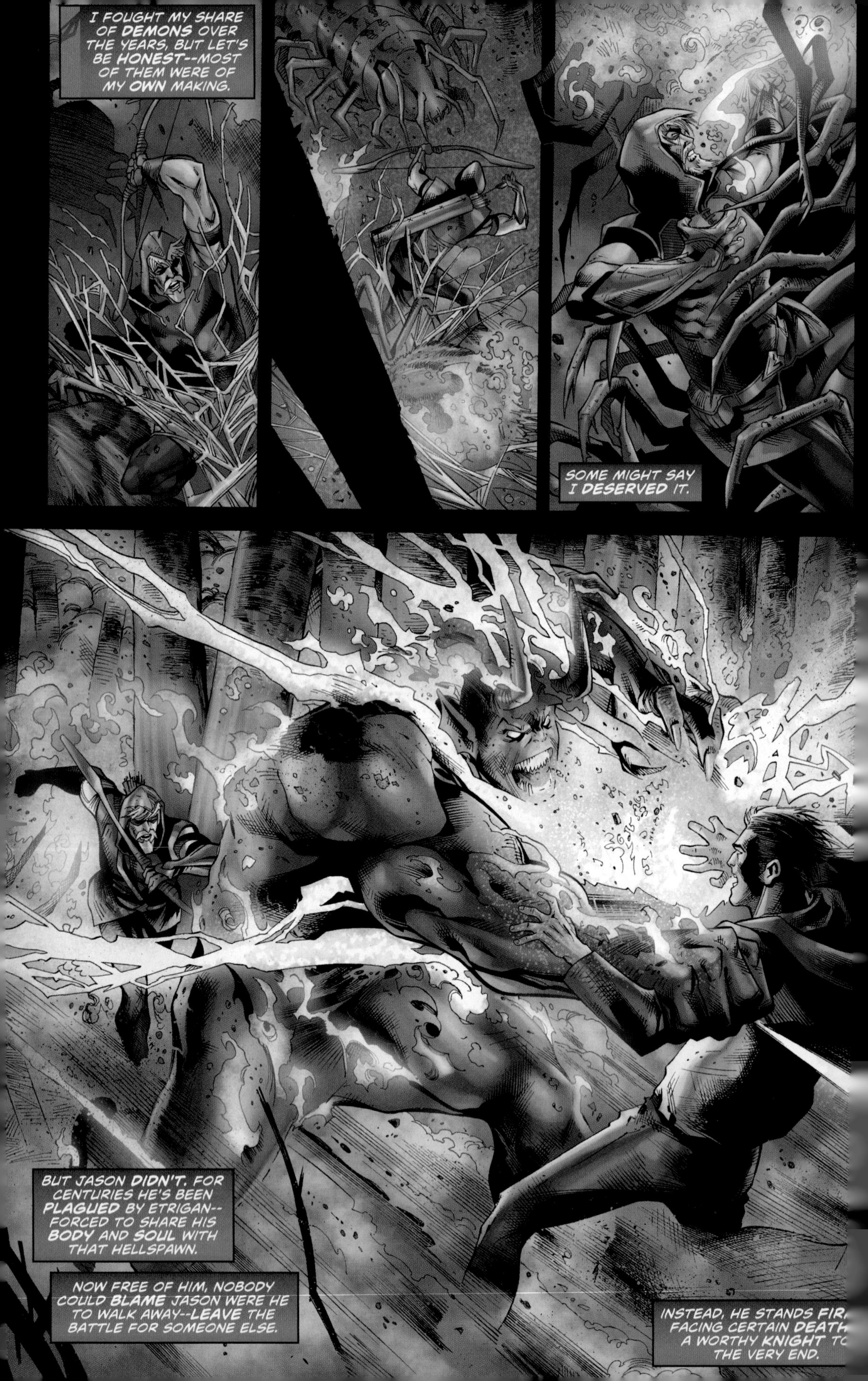
I FOUGHT MY SHARE OF DEMONS OVER THE YEARS, BUT LET'S BE HONEST--MOST OF THEM WERE OF MY OWN MAKING.
SOME MIGHT SAY I DESERVED IT.
BUT JASON DIDN'T. FOR CENTURIES HE'S BEEN PLAGUED BY ETRIGAN--FORCED TO SHARE HIS BODY AND SOUL WITH THAT HELLSPAWN.
NOW FREE OF HIM, NOBODY COULD BLAME JASON WERE HE TO WALK AWAY--LEAVE THE BATTLE FOR SOMEONE ELSE.
INSTEAD, HE STANDS FIR FACING CERTAIN DEATH A WORTHY KNIGHT TO THE VERY END.

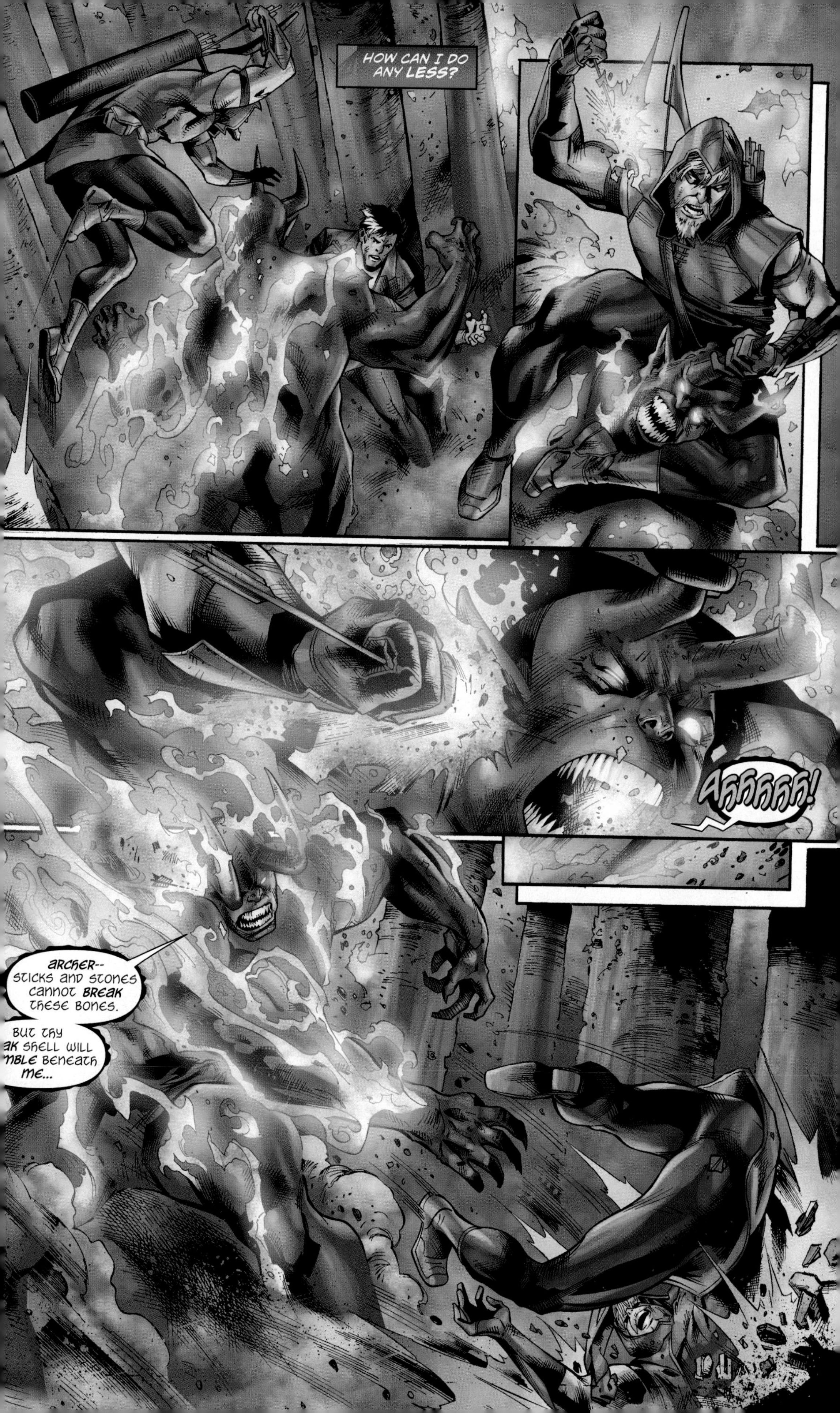

HOW CAN I DO ANY LESS?
AHHHHH!
ARCHER-- STICKS AND STONES CANNOT BREAK THESE BONES.
BUT THY
SHELL WILL
BENEATH
ME...

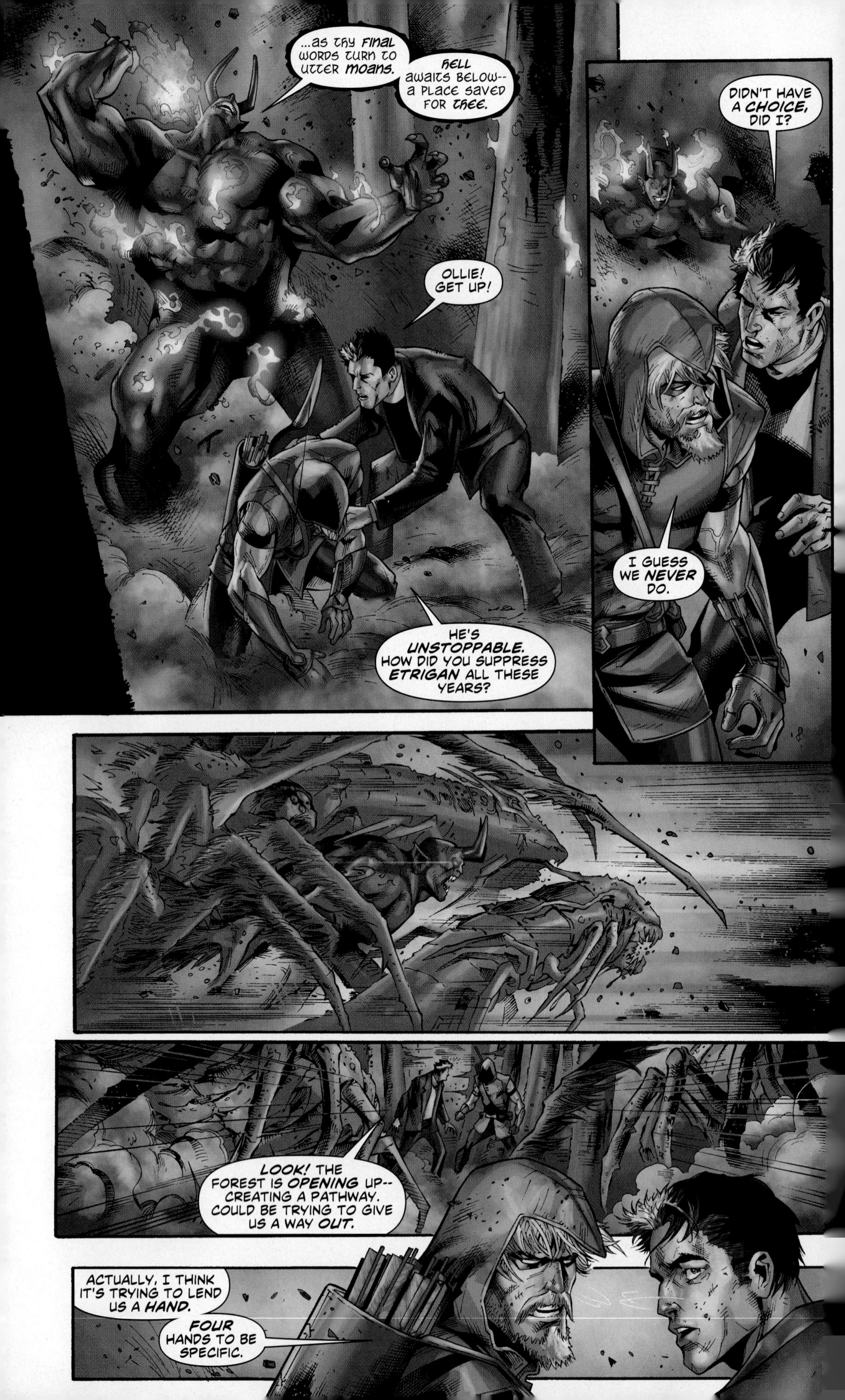
...AS THY FINAL WORDS TURN TO UTTER MOANS.
HELL AWAITS BELOW-- A PLACE SAVED FOR THEE.
OLLIE! GET UP!
HE'S UNSTOPPABLE. HOW DID YOU SUPPRESS ETRIGAN ALL THESE YEARS?
DIDN'T HAVE A CHOICE, DID I?
I GUESS WE NEVER DO.
LOOK! THE FOREST IS OPENING UP-- CREATING A PATHWAY. COULD BE TRYING TO GIVE US A WAY OUT.
ACTUALLY, I THINK IT'S TRYING TO LEND US A HAND.
FOUR HANDS TO BE SPECIFIC.

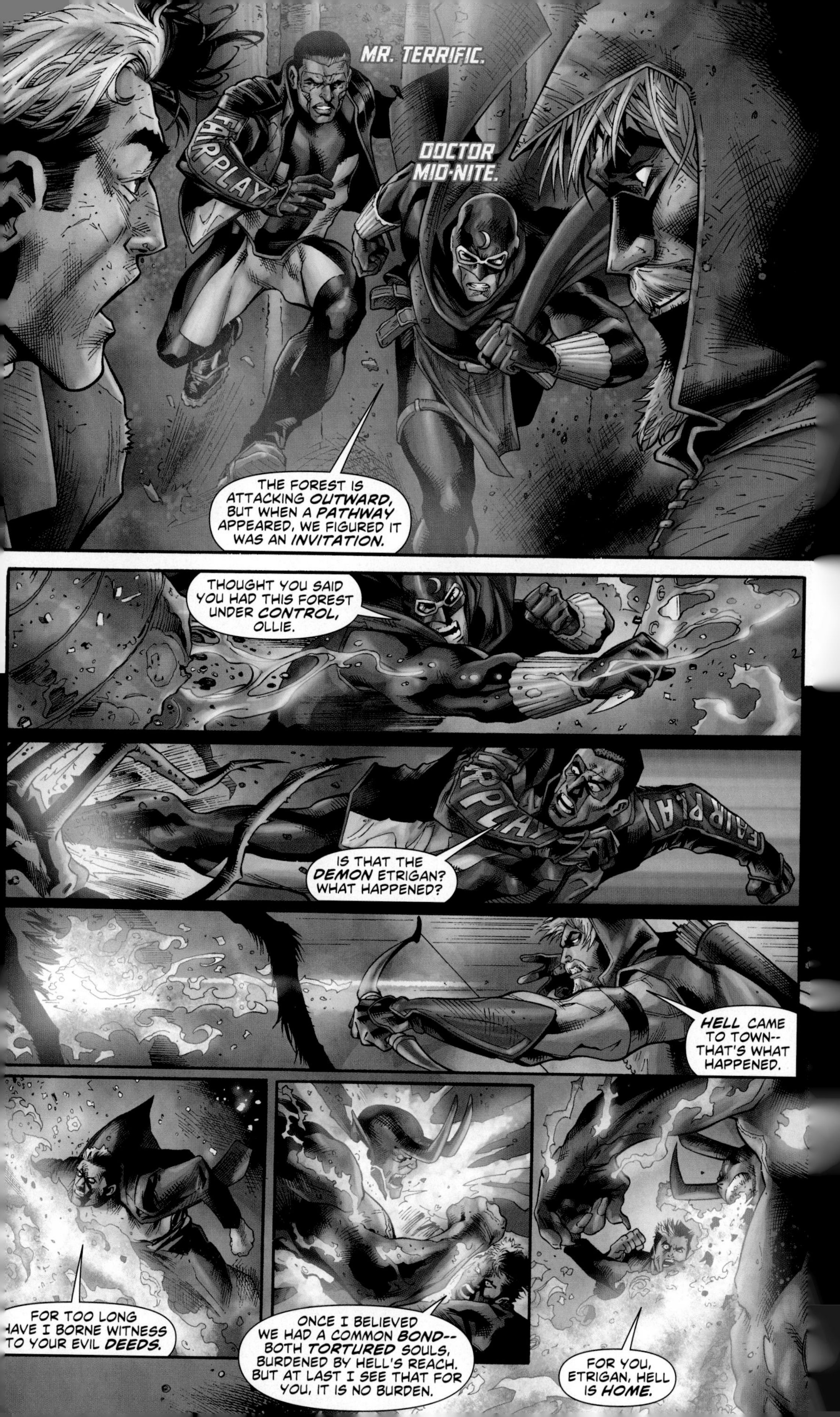
MR. TERRIFIC.
DOCTOR MID-NITE.
FAIRPLAY
THE FOREST IS ATTACKING OUTWARD, BUT WHEN A PATHWAY APPEARED, WE FIGURED IT WAS AN INVITATION.
THOUGHT YOU SAID YOU HAD THIS FOREST UNDER CONTROL, OLLIE.
IS THAT THE DEMON ETRIGAN? WHAT HAPPENED?
HELL CAME TO TOWN-- THAT'S WHAT HAPPENED.
FOR TOO LONG HAVE I BORNE WITNESS TO YOUR EVIL DEEDS.
ONCE I BELIEVED WE HAD A COMMON BOND-- BOTH TORTURED SOULS, BURDENED BY HELL'S REACH. BUT AT LAST I SEE THAT FOR YOU, IT IS NO BURDEN.
FOR YOU, ETRIGAN, HELL IS HOME.

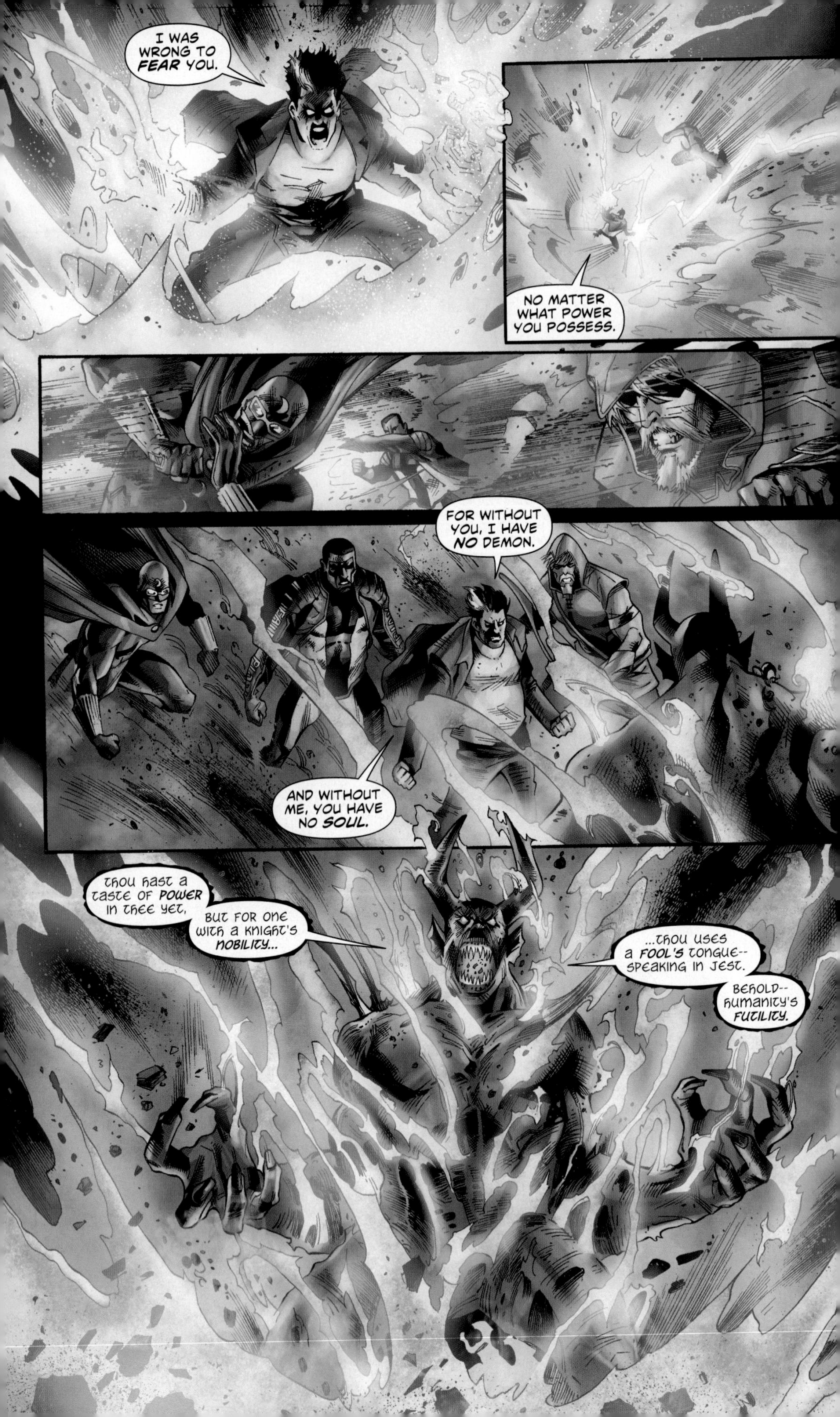
I WAS WRONG TO FEAR YOU.
NO MATTER WHAT POWER YOU POSSESS.
FOR WITHOUT YOU, I HAVE NO DEMON.
AND WITHOUT ME, YOU HAVE NO SOUL.
THOU HAST A TASTE OF POWER IN THEE YET,
BUT FOR ONE WITH A KNIGHT'S NOBILITY...
...THOU USES A FOOL'S TONGUE--SPEAKING IN JEST.
BEHOLD--HUMANITY'S FUTILITY.

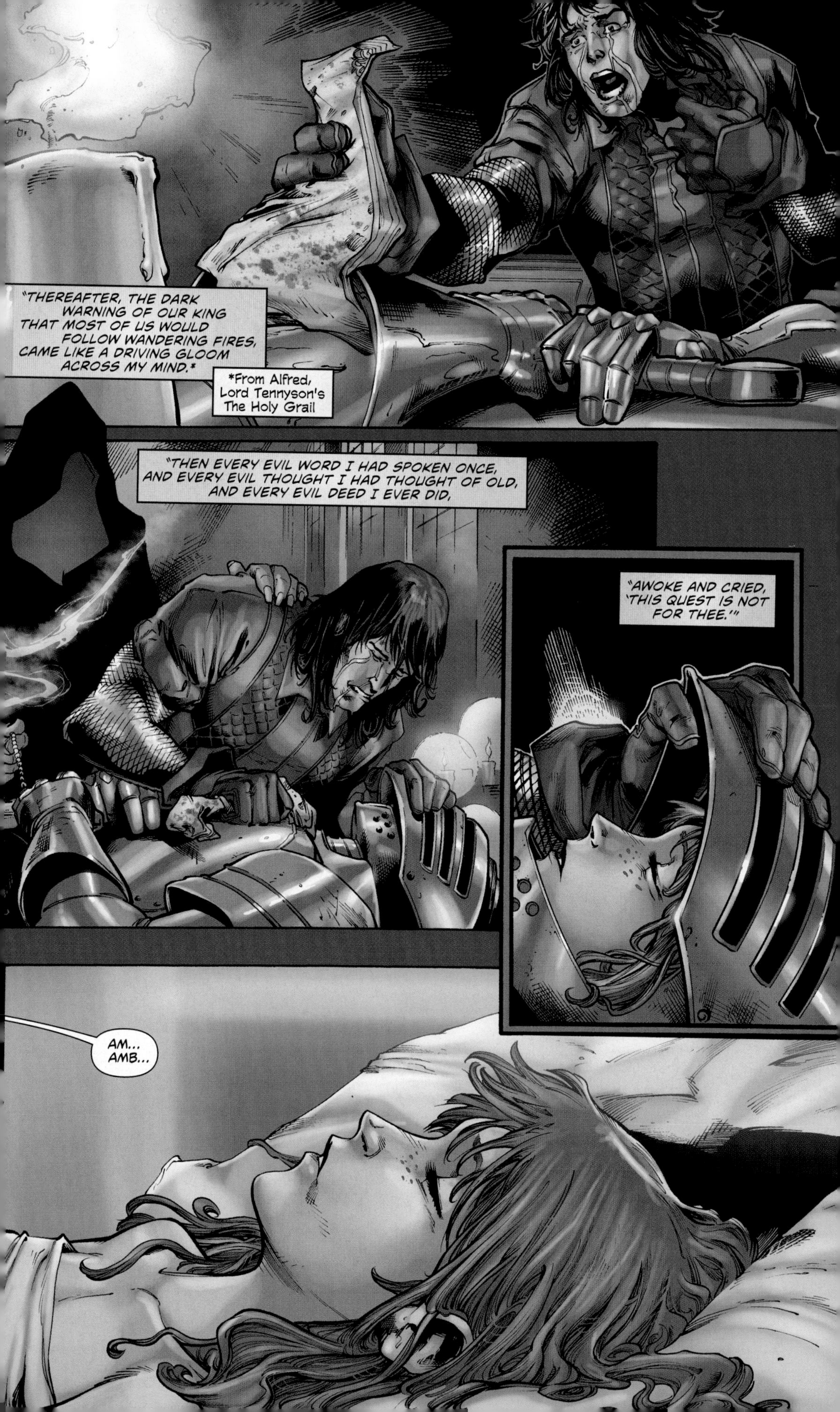
"THEREAFTER, THE DARK WARNING OF OUR KING THAT MOST OF US WOULD FOLLOW WANDERING FIRES, CAME LIKE A DRIVING GLOOM ACROSS MY MIND.*
*From Alfred, Lord Tennyson's The Holy Grail
"THEN EVERY EVIL WORD I HAD SPOKEN ONCE, AND EVERY EVIL THOUGHT I HAD THOUGHT OF OLD, AND EVERY EVIL DEED I EVER DID,
"AWOKE AND CRIED, 'THIS QUEST IS NOT FOR THEE.'"
AM... AMB...

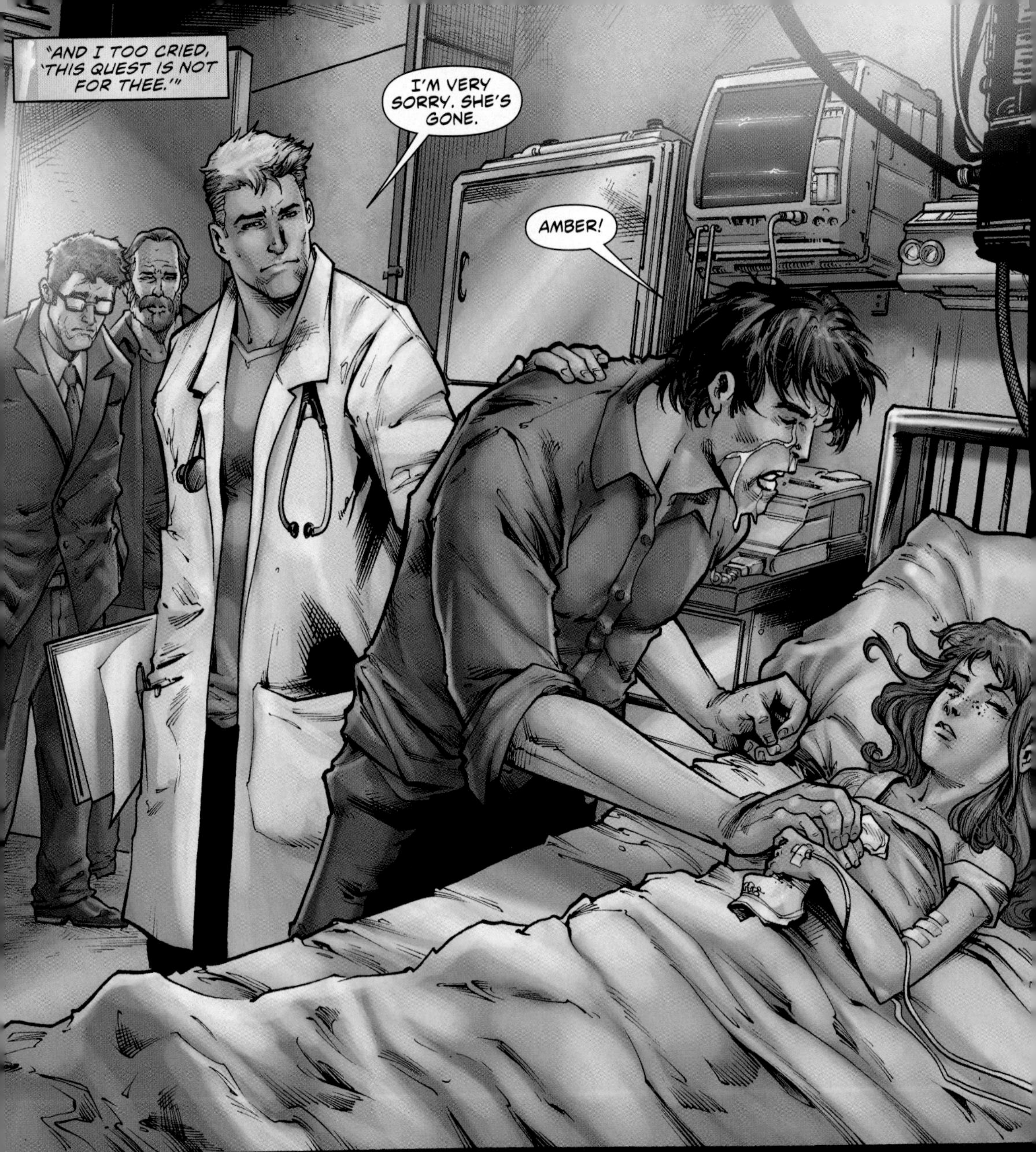
"AND I TOO CRIED, 'THIS QUEST IS NOT FOR THEE.'"
I'M VERY SORRY. SHE'S GONE.
AMBER!

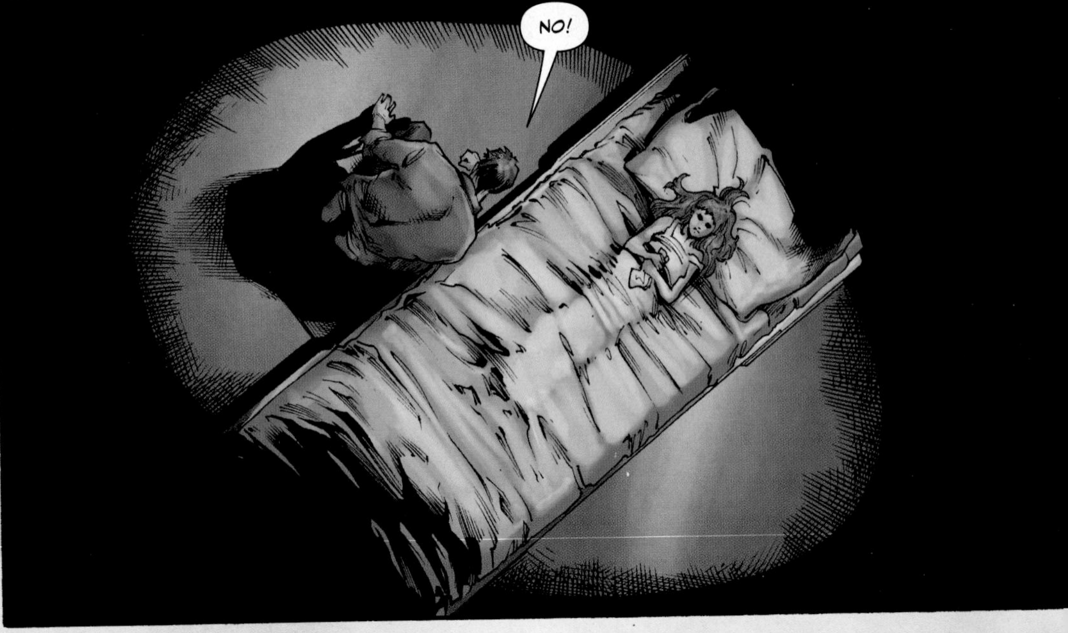
NO!

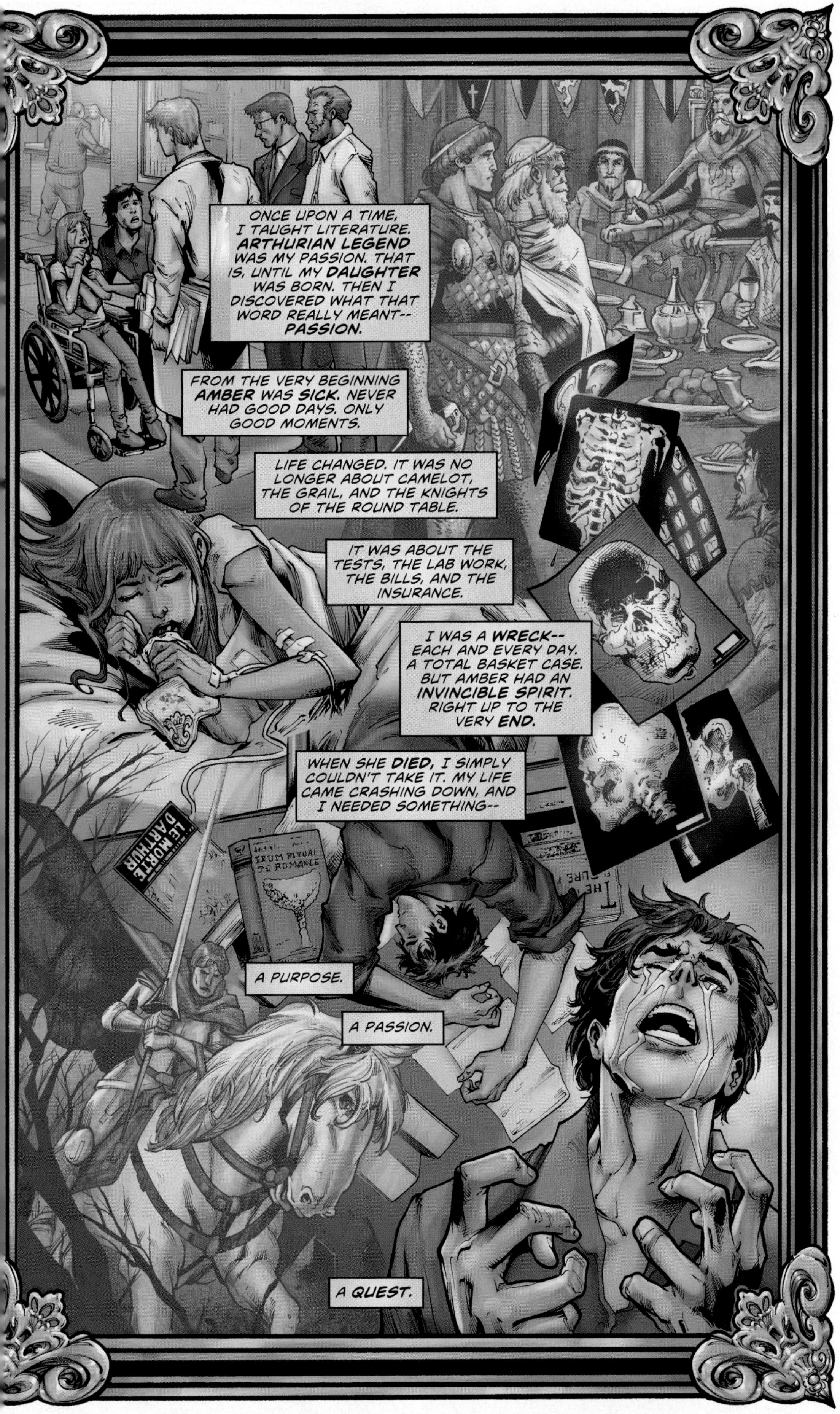
ONCE UPON A TIME, I TAUGHT LITERATURE. ARTHURIAN LEGEND WAS MY PASSION. THAT IS, UNTIL MY DAUGHTER WAS BORN. THEN I DISCOVERED WHAT THAT WORD REALLY MEANT-- PASSION.
FROM THE VERY BEGINNING AMBER WAS SICK. NEVER HAD GOOD DAYS. ONLY GOOD MOMENTS.
LIFE CHANGED. IT WAS NO LONGER ABOUT CAMELOT, THE GRAIL, AND THE KNIGHTS OF THE ROUND TABLE.
IT WAS ABOUT THE TESTS, THE LAB WORK, THE BILLS, AND THE INSURANCE.
I WAS A WRECK-- EACH AND EVERY DAY. A TOTAL BASKET CASE. BUT AMBER HAD AN INVINCIBLE SPIRIT. RIGHT UP TO THE VERY END.
WHEN SHE DIED, I SIMPLY COULDN'T TAKE IT. MY LIFE CAME CRASHING DOWN, AND I NEEDED SOMETHING--
LE MORTE DARTHUR
A PURPOSE.
A PASSION.
A QUEST.

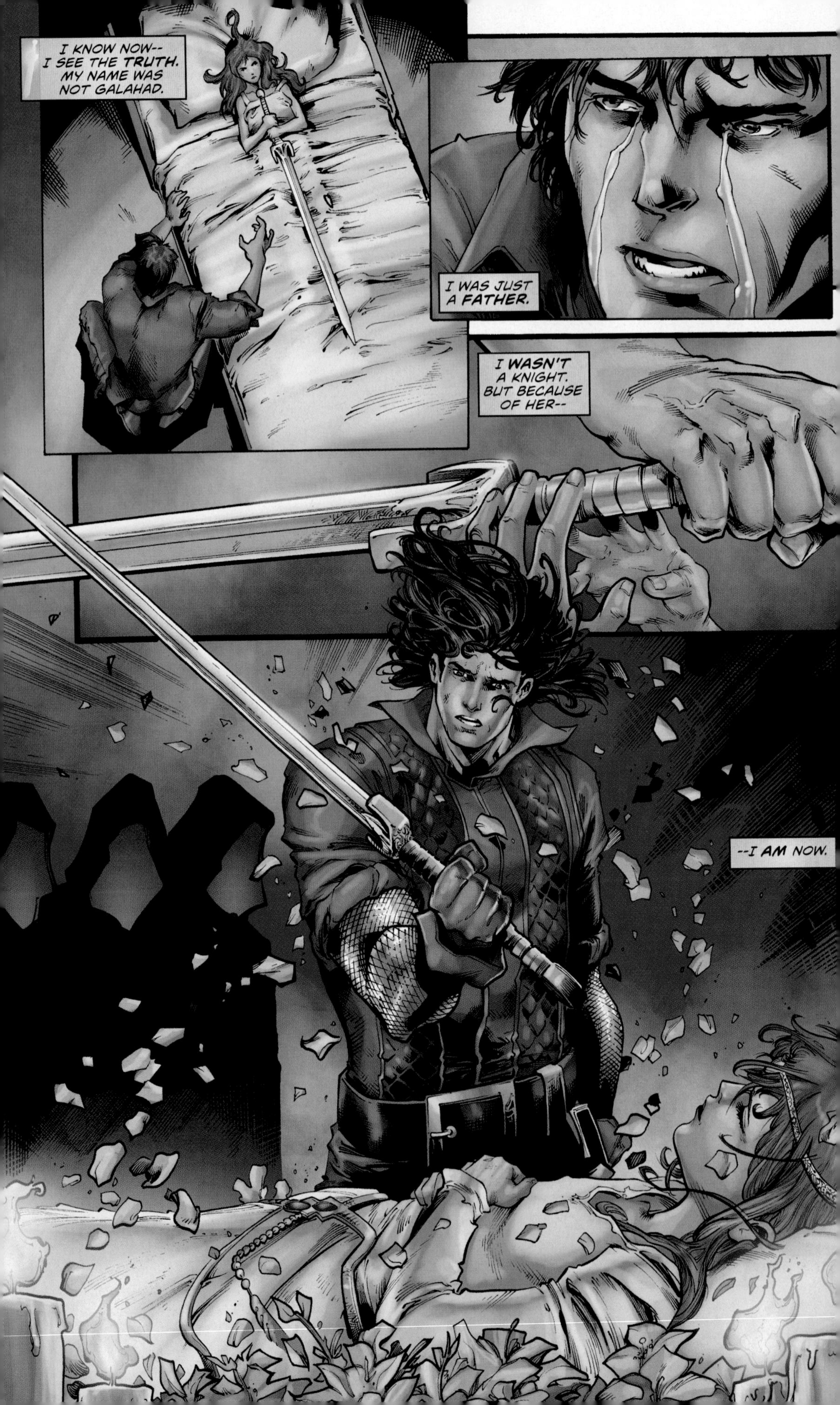
I KNOW NOW-- I SEE THE TRUTH. MY NAME WAS NOT GALAHAD.
I WAS JUST A FATHER.
I WASN'T A KNIGHT. BUT BECAUSE OF HER--
--I AM NOW.

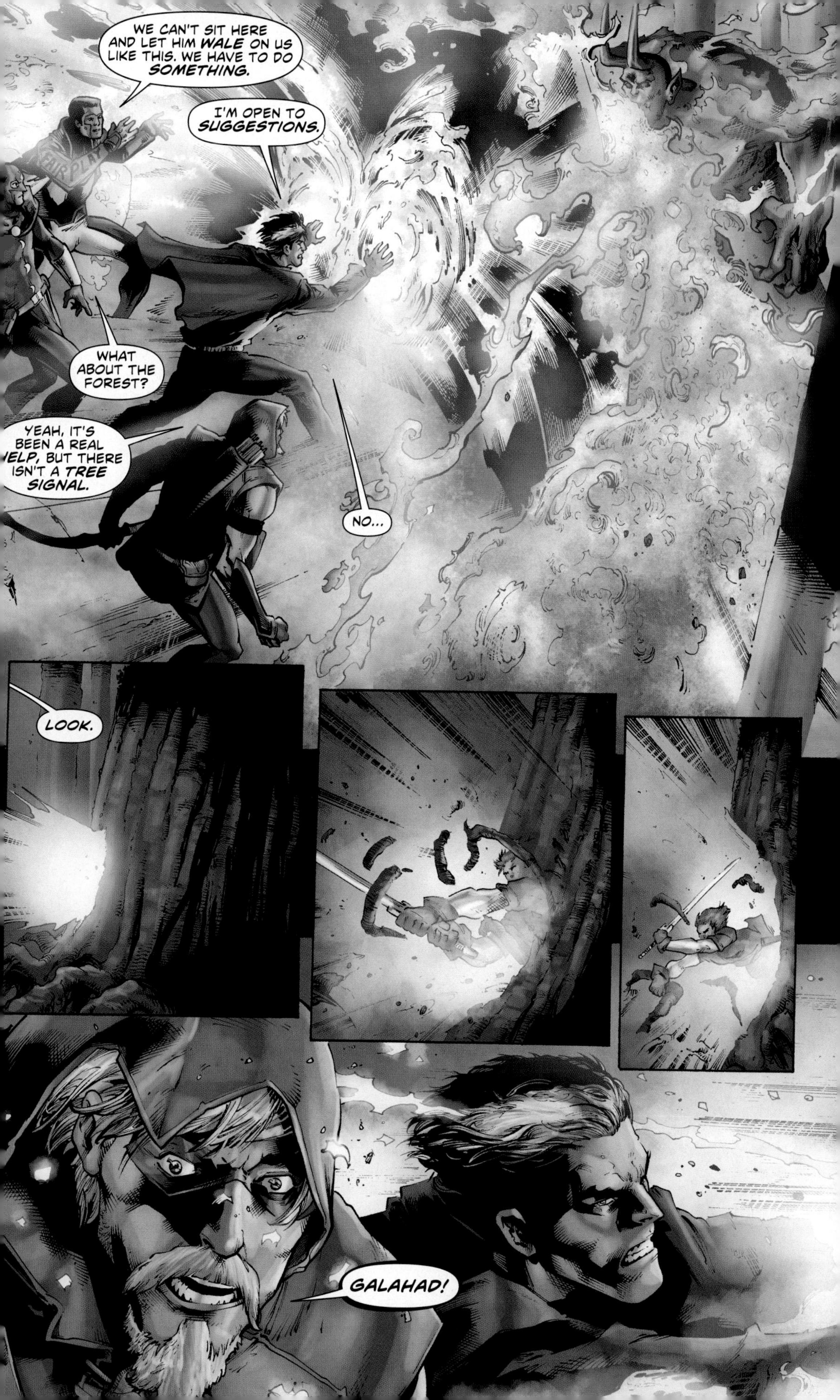
WE CAN'T SIT HERE AND LET HIM WALE ON US LIKE THIS. WE HAVE TO DO SOMETHING.
I'M OPEN TO SUGGESTIONS.
WHAT ABOUT THE FOREST?
YEAH, IT'S BEEN A REAL HELP, BUT THERE ISN'T A TREE SIGNAL.
NO...
LOOK.
GALAHAD!

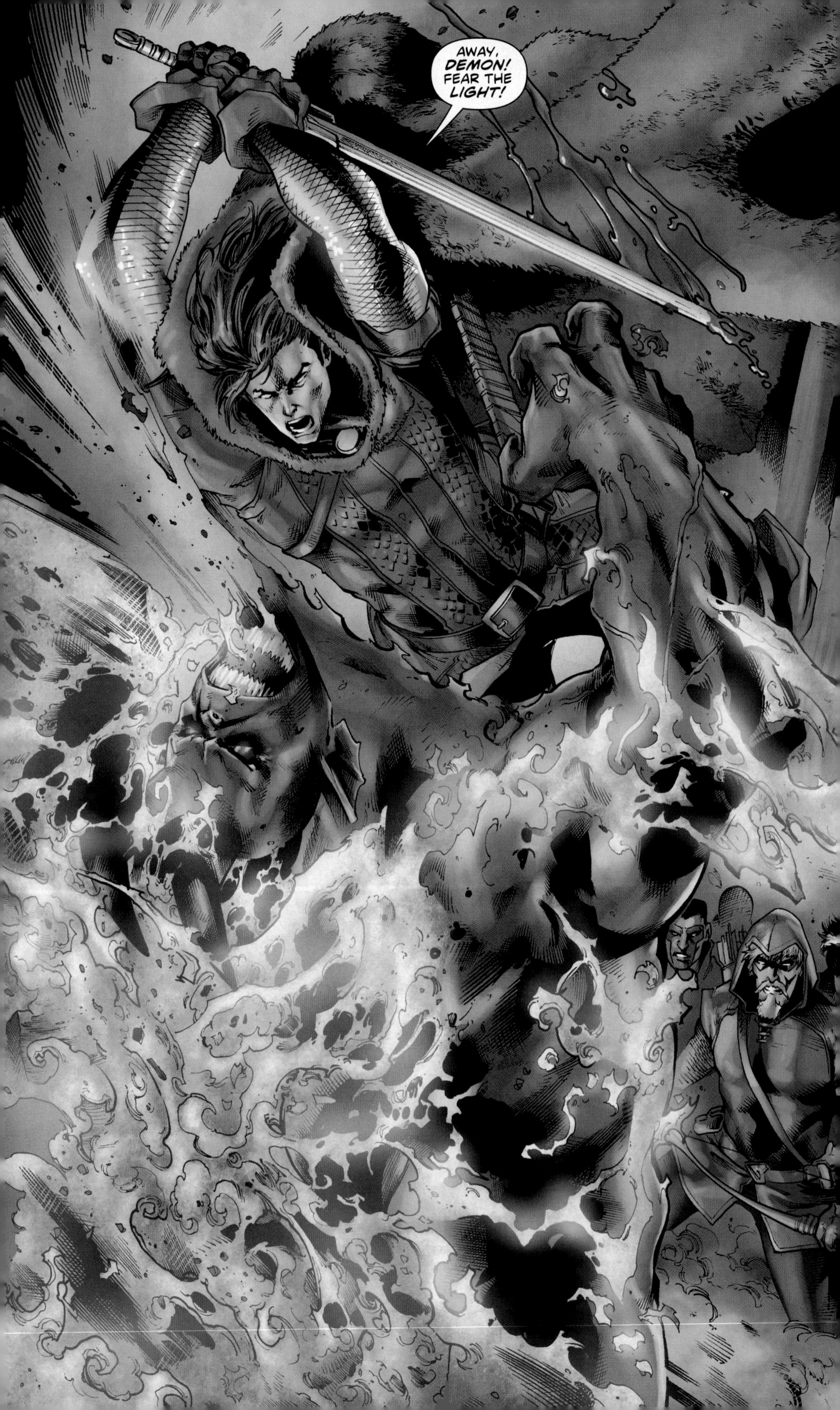
AWAY, DEMON! FEAR THE LIGHT!

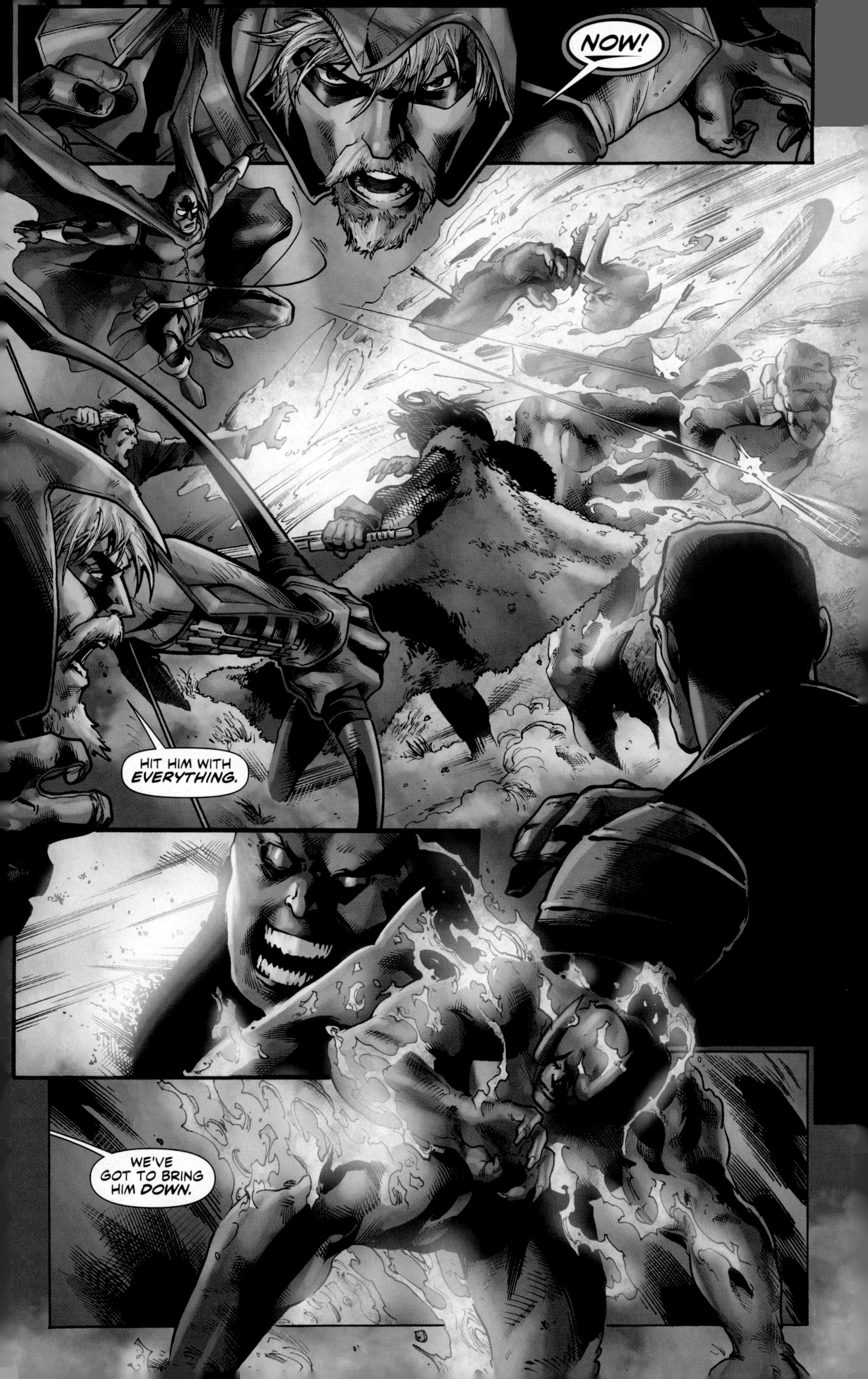
NOW!
HIT HIM WITH EVERYTHING.
WE'VE GOT TO BRING HIM DOWN.

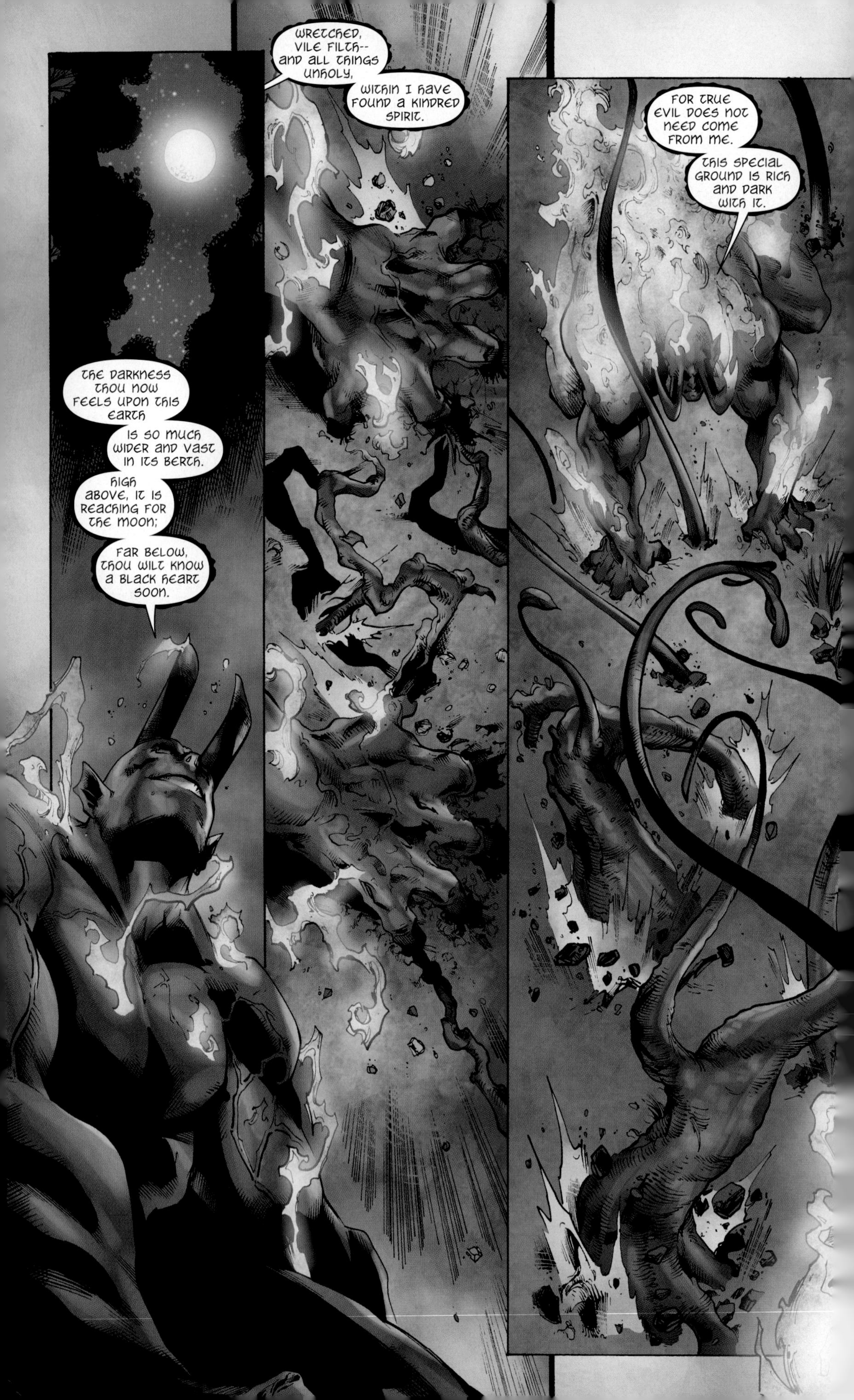

WRETCHED, VILE FILTH--AND ALL THINGS UNHOLY,
WITHIN I HAVE FOUND A KINDRED SPIRIT.
THE DARKNESS THOU NOW FEELS UPON THIS EARTH
IS SO MUCH WIDER AND VAST IN ITS BERTH.
HIGH ABOVE, IT IS REACHING FOR THE MOON;
FAR BELOW, THOU WILT KNOW A BLACK HEART SOON.
FOR TRUE EVIL DOES NOT NEED COME FROM ME.
THIS SPECIAL GROUND IS RICH AND DARK WITH IT.

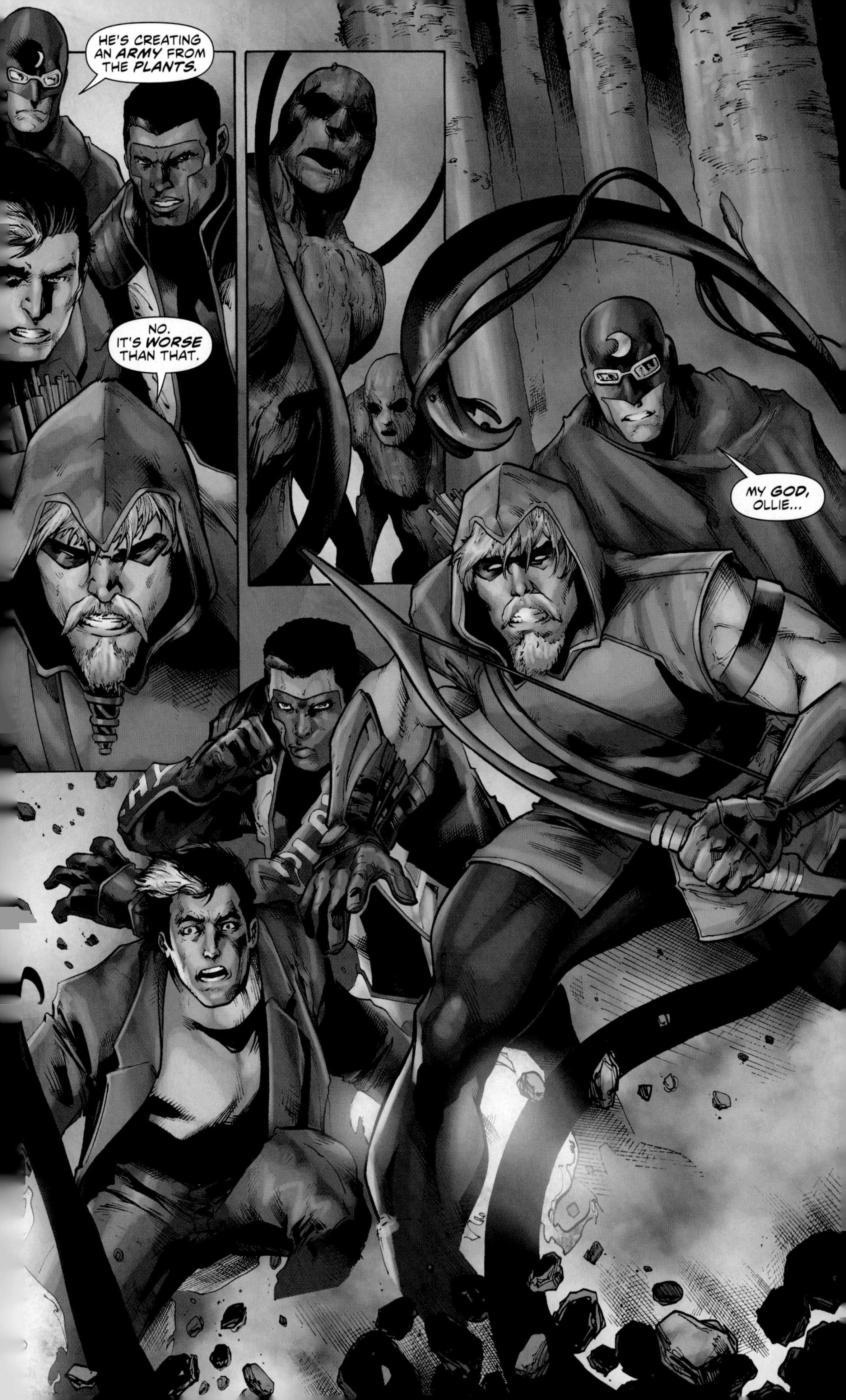
HE'S CREATING AN ARMY FROM THE PLANTS.
NO. IT'S WORSE THAN THAT.
MY GOD, OLLIE...

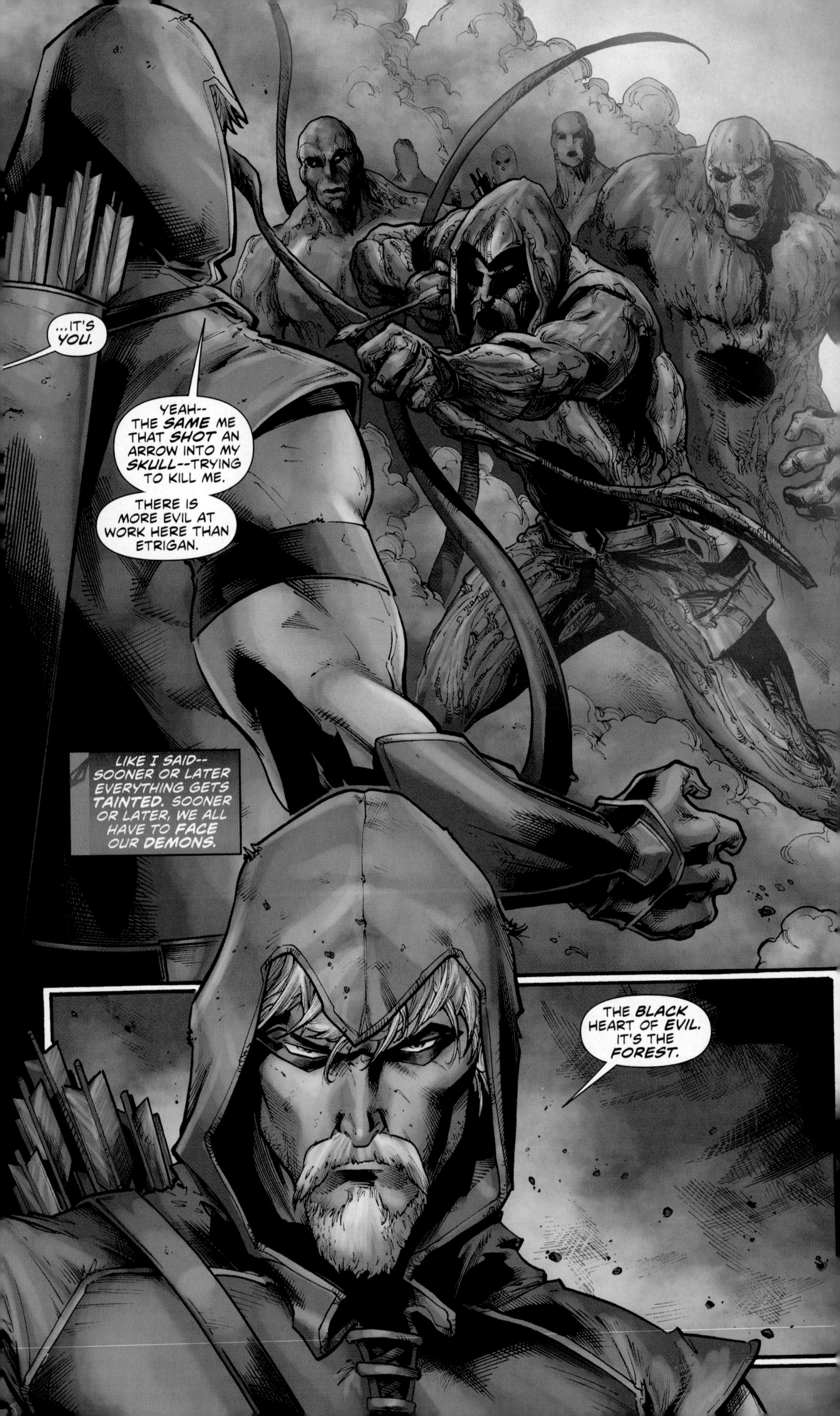

...IT'S YOU.
YEAH-- THE SAME ME THAT SHOT AN ARROW INTO MY SKULL--TRYING TO KILL ME.
THERE IS MORE EVIL AT WORK HERE THAN ETRIGAN.
LIKE I SAID-- SOONER OR LATER EVERYTHING GETS TAINTED. SOONER OR LATER, WE ALL HAVE TO FACE OUR DEMONS.
THE BLACK HEART OF EVIL. IT'S THE FOREST.

Cover by Rodolfo Migliari

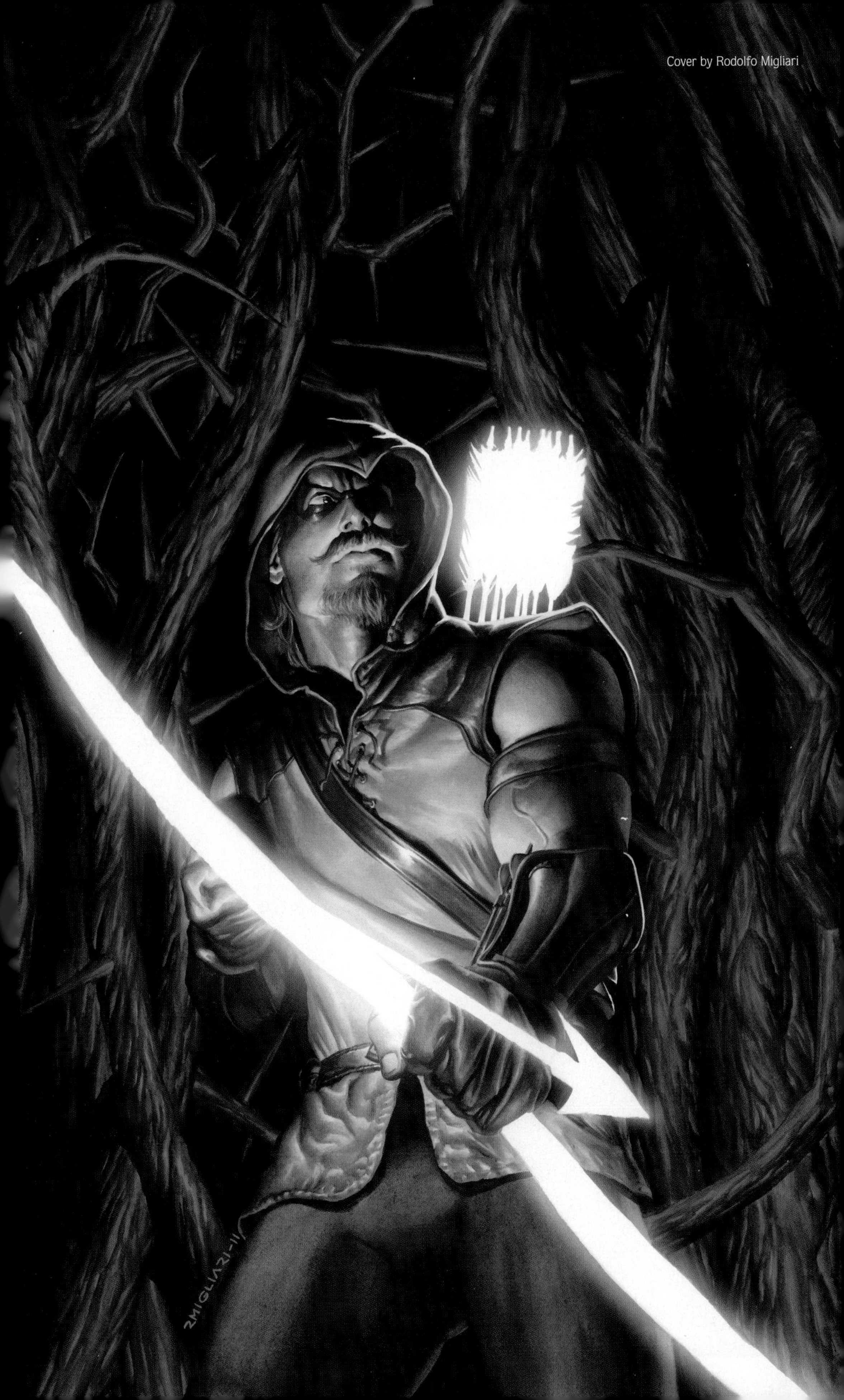

RMIGLIARI-11

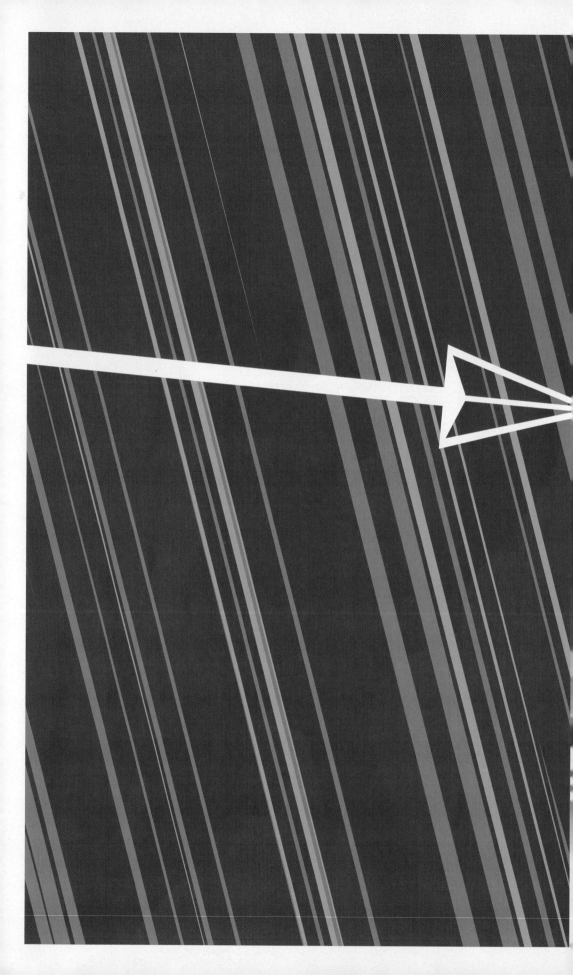

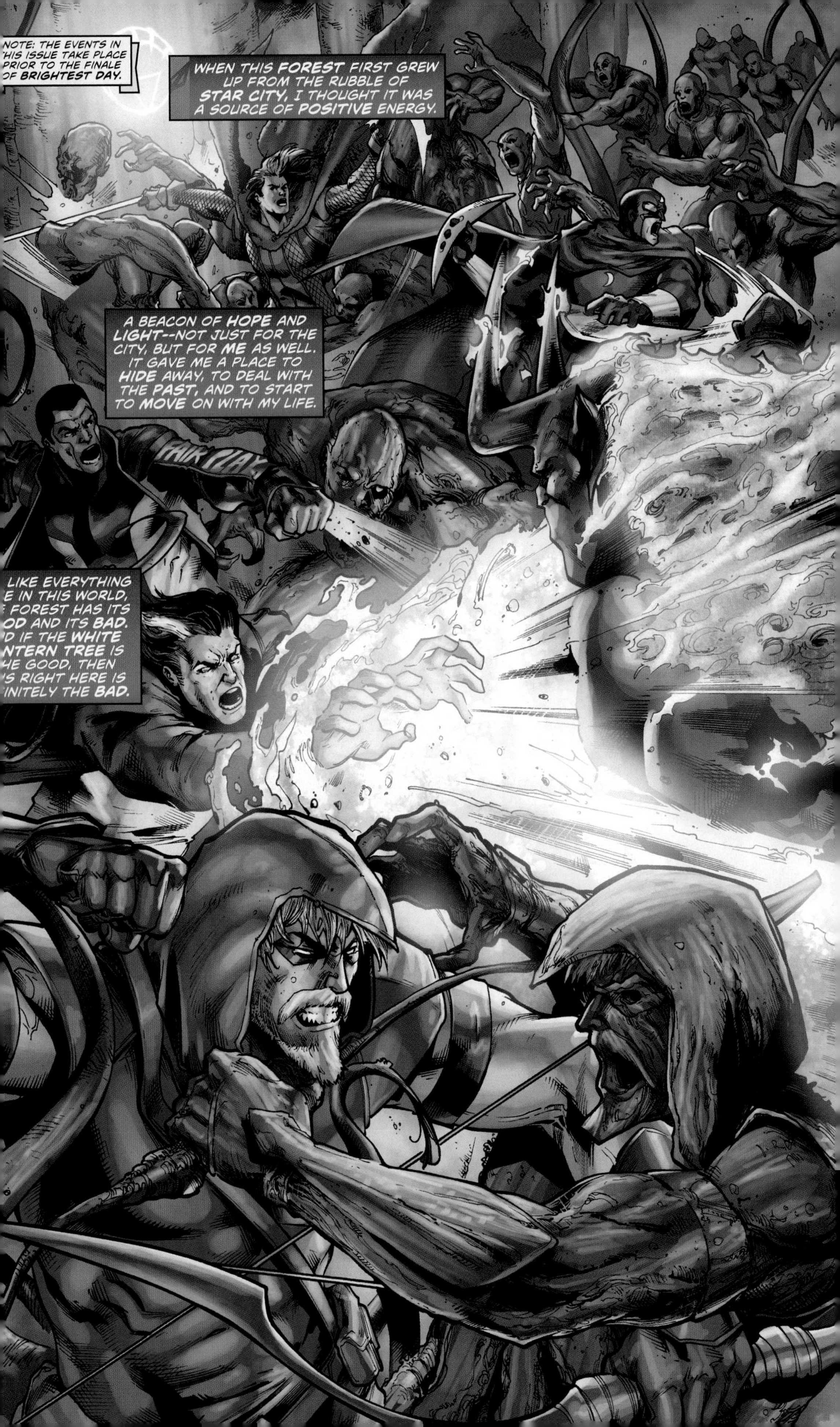
NOTE: THE EVENTS IN HIS ISSUE TAKE PLACE PRIOR TO THE FINALE OF BRIGHTEST DAY.
WHEN THIS FOREST FIRST GREW UP FROM THE RUBBLE OF STAR CITY, I THOUGHT IT WAS A SOURCE OF POSITIVE ENERGY.
A BEACON OF HOPE AND LIGHT--NOT JUST FOR THE CITY, BUT FOR ME AS WELL. IT GAVE ME A PLACE TO HIDE AWAY, TO DEAL WITH THE PAST, AND TO START TO MOVE ON WITH MY LIFE.
FAIR PLAY
LIKE EVERYTHING E IN THIS WORLD, FOREST HAS ITS OD AND ITS BAD. D IF THE WHITE NTERN TREE IS HE GOOD, THEN 'S RIGHT HERE IS INITELY THE BAD.

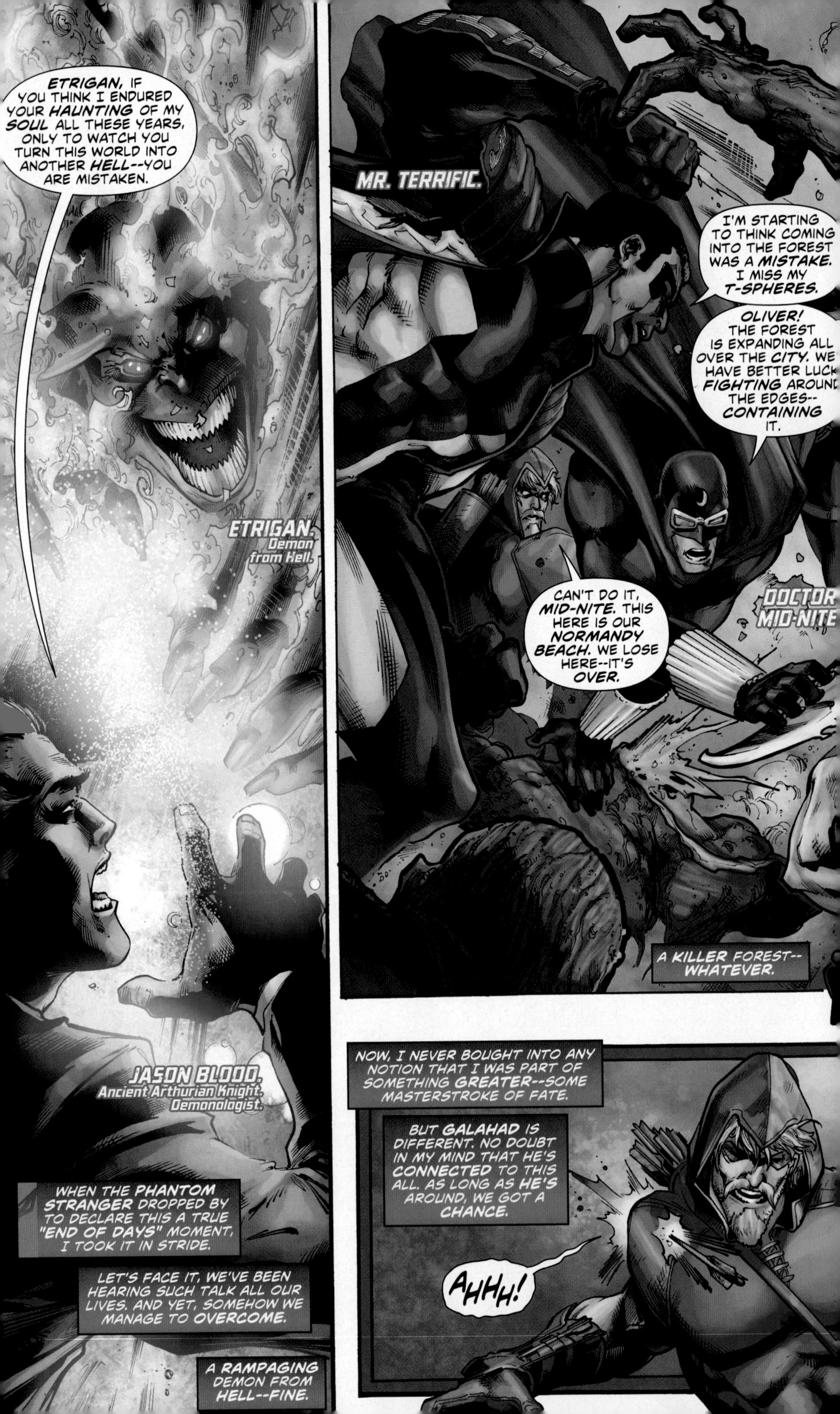
ETRIGAN, IF YOU THINK I ENDURED YOUR HAUNTING OF MY SOUL ALL THESE YEARS, ONLY TO WATCH YOU TURN THIS WORLD INTO ANOTHER HELL--YOU ARE MISTAKEN.
ETRIGAN. Demon from Hell.
JASON BLOOD. Ancient Arthurian Knight. Demonologist.
WHEN THE PHANTOM STRANGER DROPPED BY TO DECLARE THIS A TRUE "END OF DAYS" MOMENT, I TOOK IT IN STRIDE.
LET'S FACE IT, WE'VE BEEN HEARING SUCH TALK ALL OUR LIVES. AND YET, SOMEHOW WE MANAGE TO OVERCOME.
A RAMPAGING DEMON FROM HELL--FINE.
MR. TERRIFIC.
I'M STARTING TO THINK COMING INTO THE FOREST WAS A MISTAKE. I MISS MY T-SPHERES.
OLIVER! THE FOREST IS EXPANDING ALL OVER THE CITY. WE HAVE BETTER LUCK FIGHTING AROUND THE EDGES-- CONTAINING IT.
DOCTOR MID-NITE
CAN'T DO IT, MID-NITE. THIS HERE IS OUR NORMANDY BEACH. WE LOSE HERE--IT'S OVER.
A KILLER FOREST-- WHATEVER.
NOW, I NEVER BOUGHT INTO ANY NOTION THAT I WAS PART OF SOMETHING GREATER--SOME MASTERSTROKE OF FATE.
BUT GALAHAD IS DIFFERENT. NO DOUBT IN MY MIND THAT HE'S CONNECTED TO THIS ALL. AS LONG AS HE'S AROUND, WE GOT A CHANCE.
AHHH!

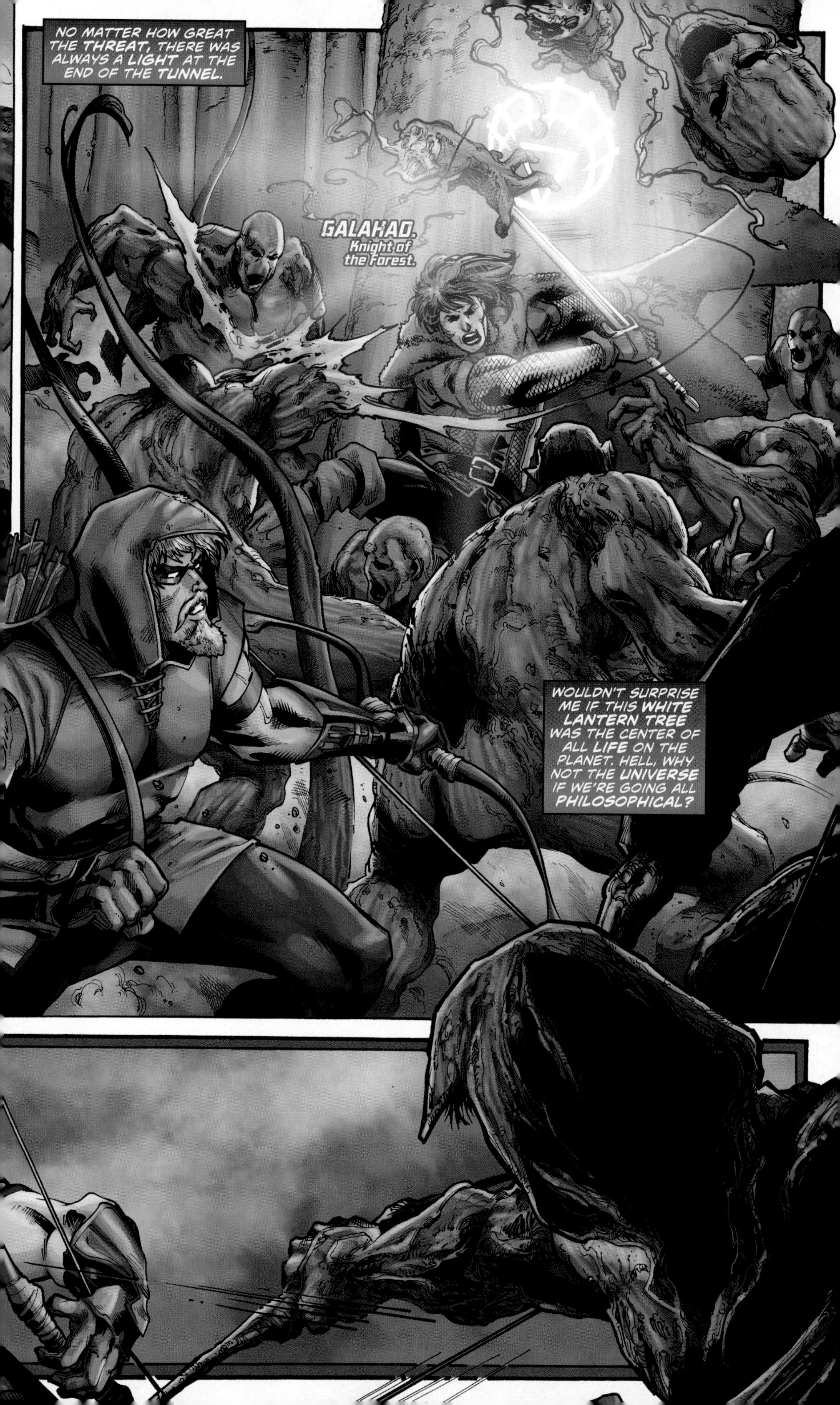
NO MATTER HOW GREAT THE THREAT, THERE WAS ALWAYS A LIGHT AT THE END OF THE TUNNEL.
GALAHAD. Knight of the Forest.
WOULDN'T SURPRISE ME IF THIS WHITE LANTERN TREE WAS THE CENTER OF ALL LIFE ON THE PLANET. HELL, WHY NOT THE UNIVERSE IF WE'RE GOING ALL PHILOSOPHICAL?

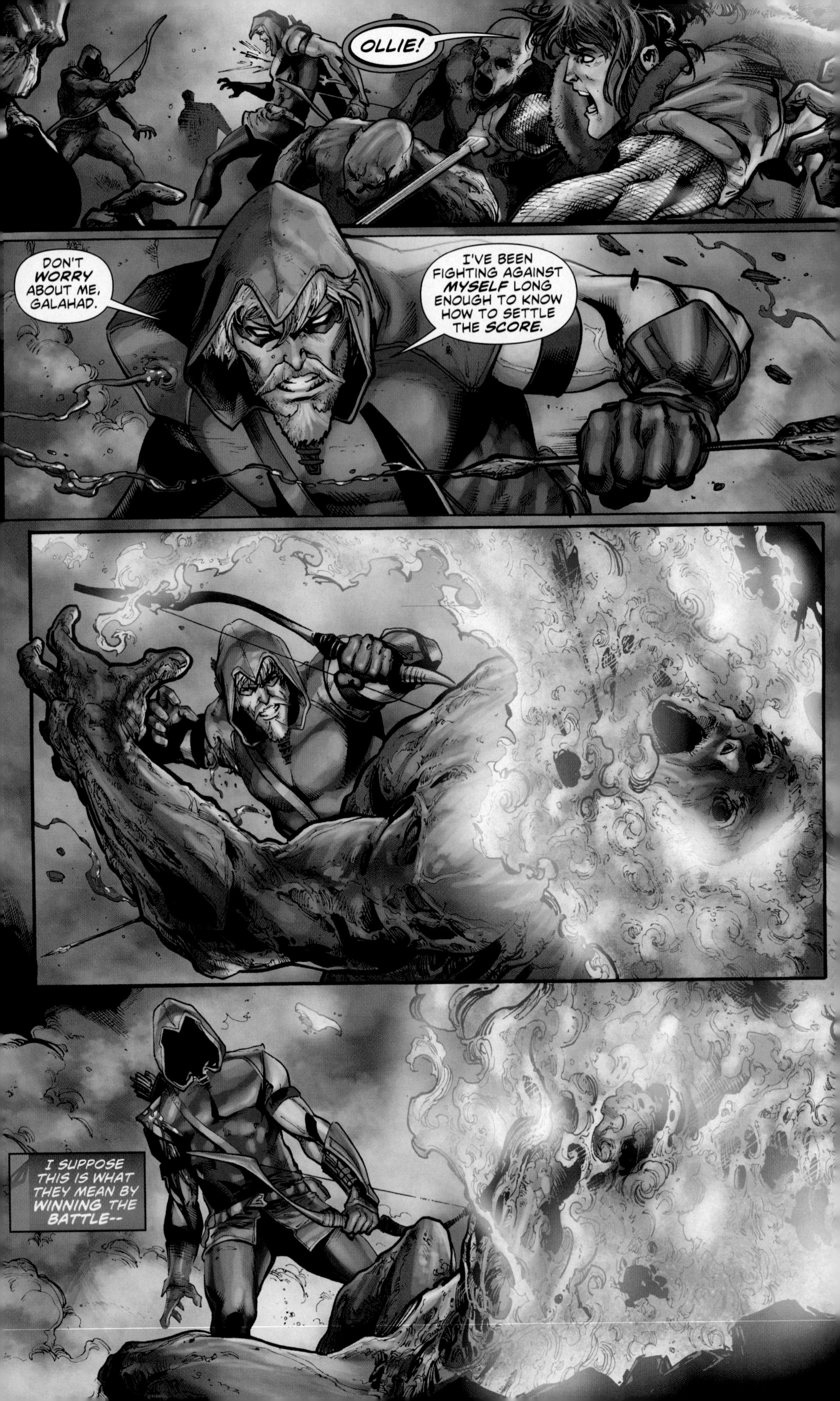
OLLIE!
DON'T WORRY ABOUT ME, GALAHAD.
I'VE BEEN FIGHTING AGAINST MYSELF LONG ENOUGH TO KNOW HOW TO SETTLE THE SCORE.
I SUPPOSE THIS IS WHAT THEY MEAN BY WINNING THE BATTLE--

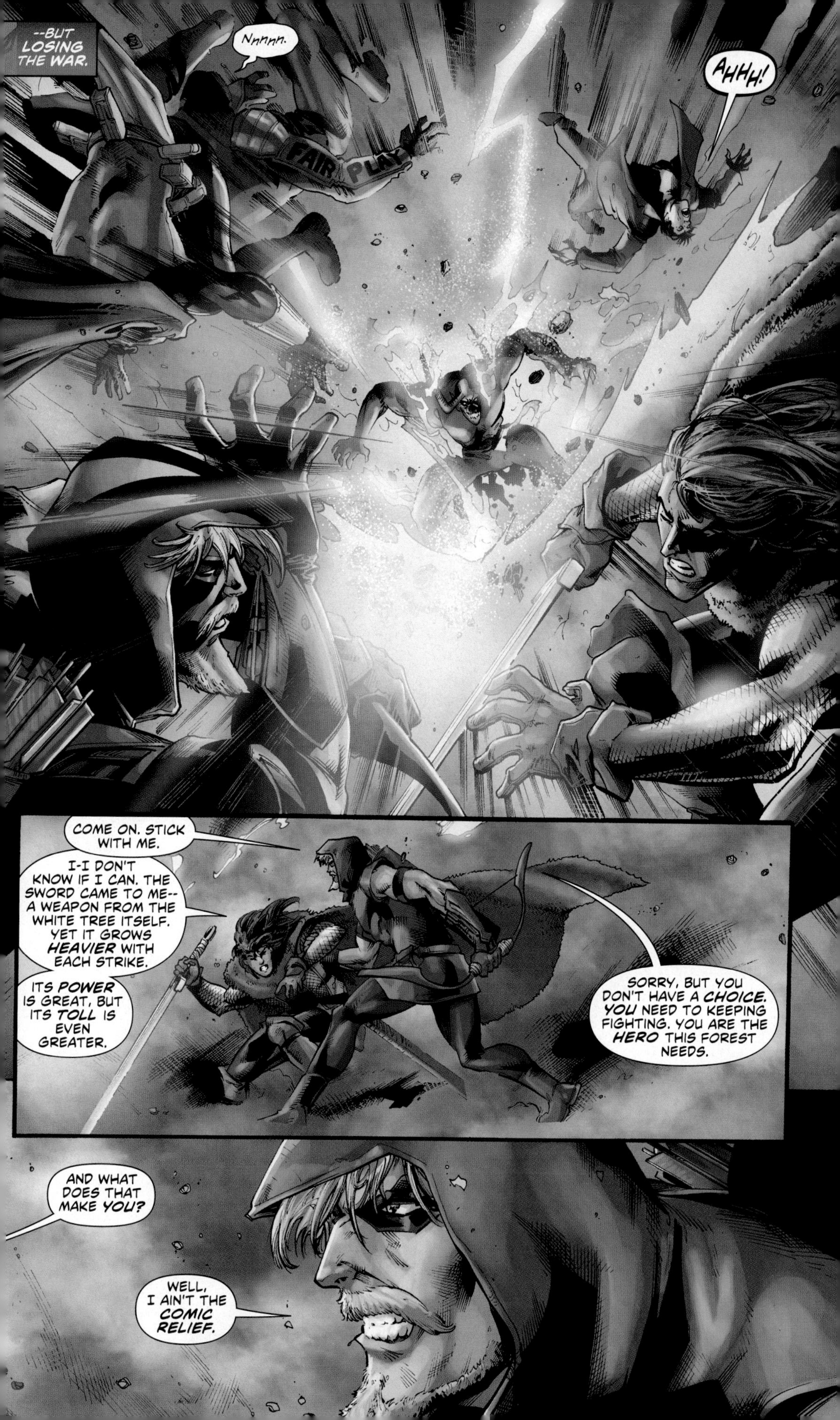
--BUT LOSING THE WAR.
Nnnnn.
AHHH!
FAIR PLAY
COME ON. STICK WITH ME.
I-I DON'T KNOW IF I CAN. THE SWORD CAME TO ME-- A WEAPON FROM THE WHITE TREE ITSELF. YET IT GROWS HEAVIER WITH EACH STRIKE.
ITS POWER IS GREAT, BUT ITS TOLL IS EVEN GREATER.
SORRY, BUT YOU DON'T HAVE A CHOICE. YOU NEED TO KEEPING FIGHTING. YOU ARE THE HERO THIS FOREST NEEDS.
AND WHAT DOES THAT MAKE YOU?
WELL, I AIN'T THE COMIC RELIEF.

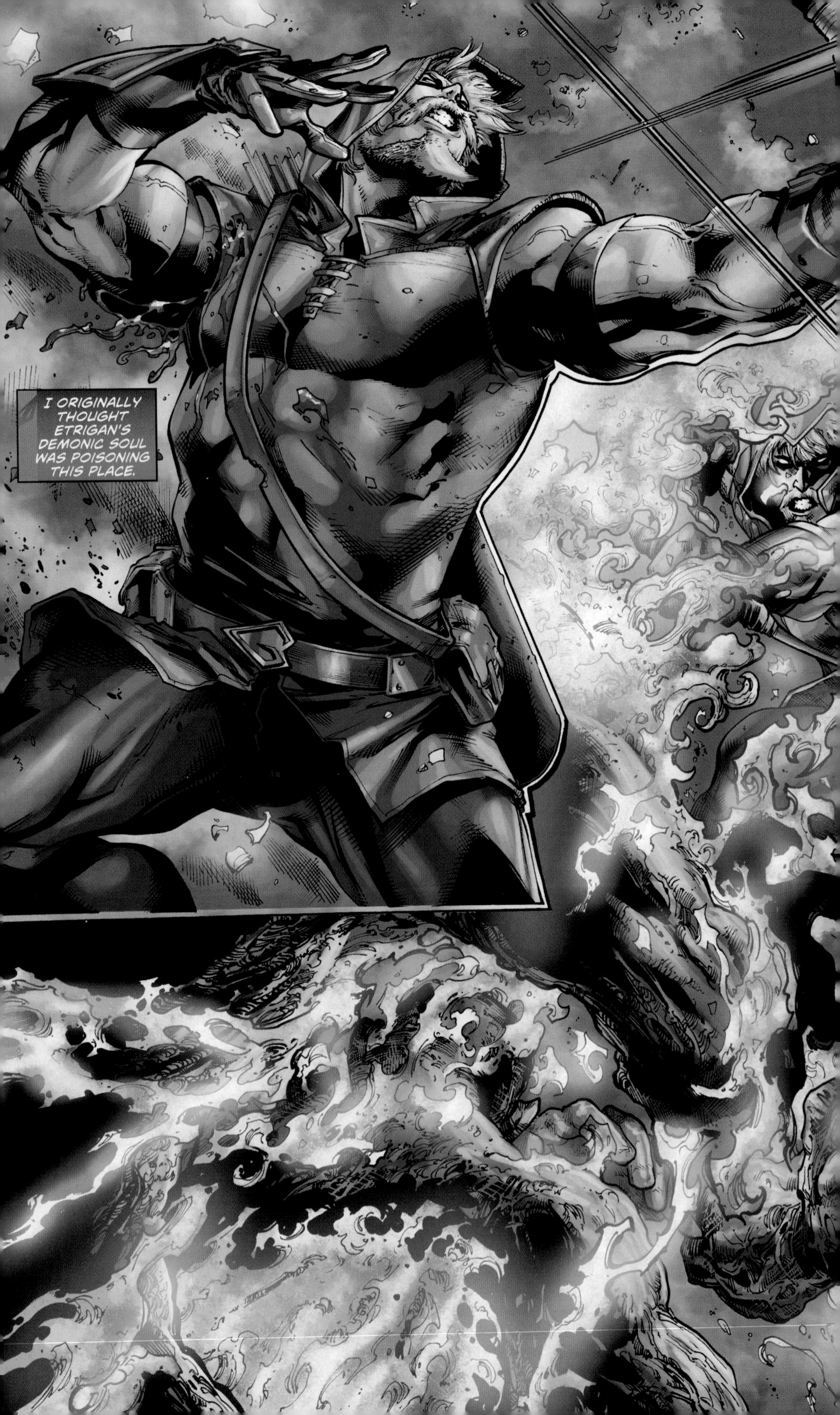
I ORIGINALLY THOUGHT ETRIGAN'S DEMONIC SOUL WAS POISONING THIS PLACE.

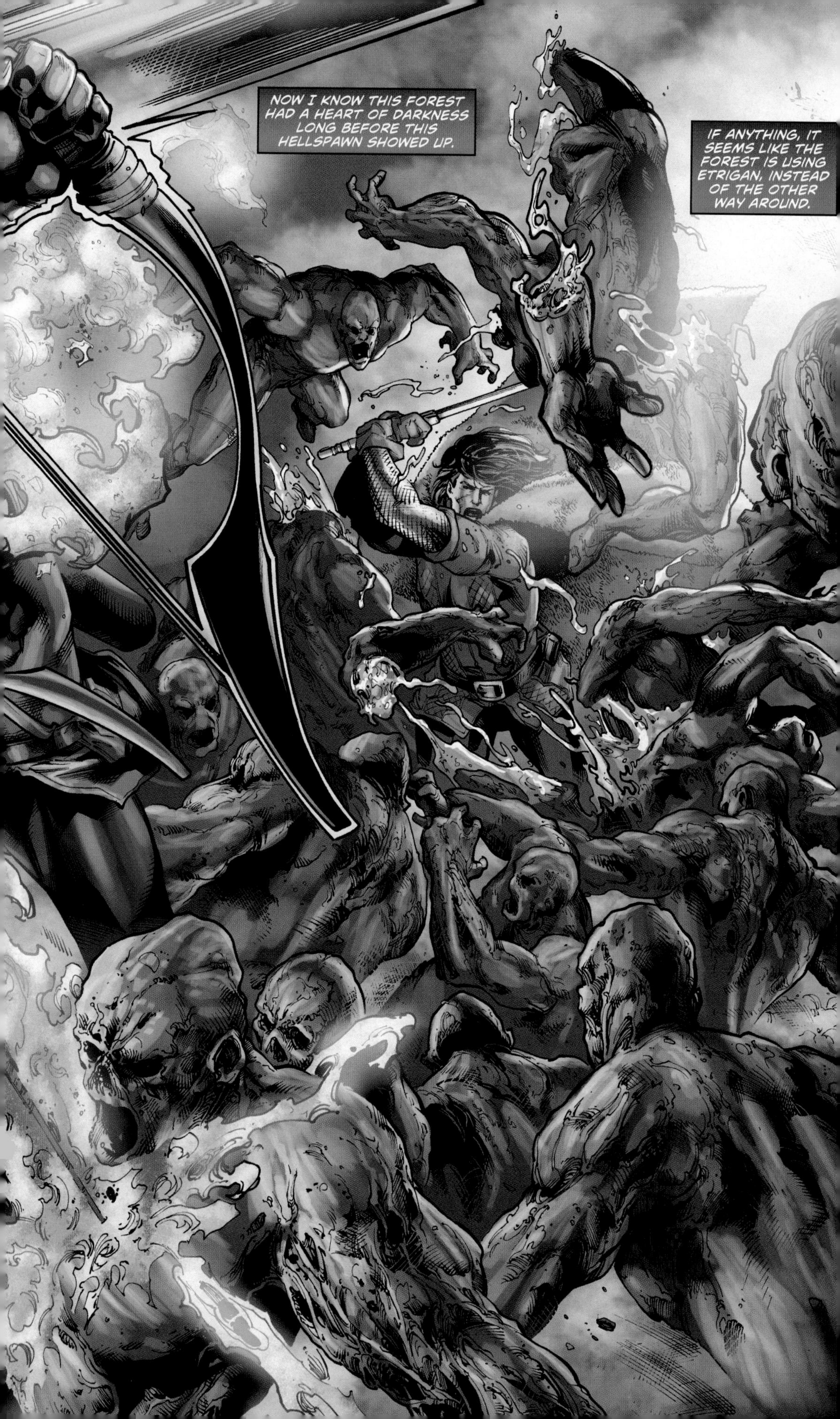
NOW I KNOW THIS FOREST HAD A HEART OF DARKNESS LONG BEFORE THIS HELLSPAWN SHOWED UP.
IF ANYTHING, IT SEEMS LIKE THE FOREST IS USING ETRIGAN, INSTEAD OF THE OTHER WAY AROUND.

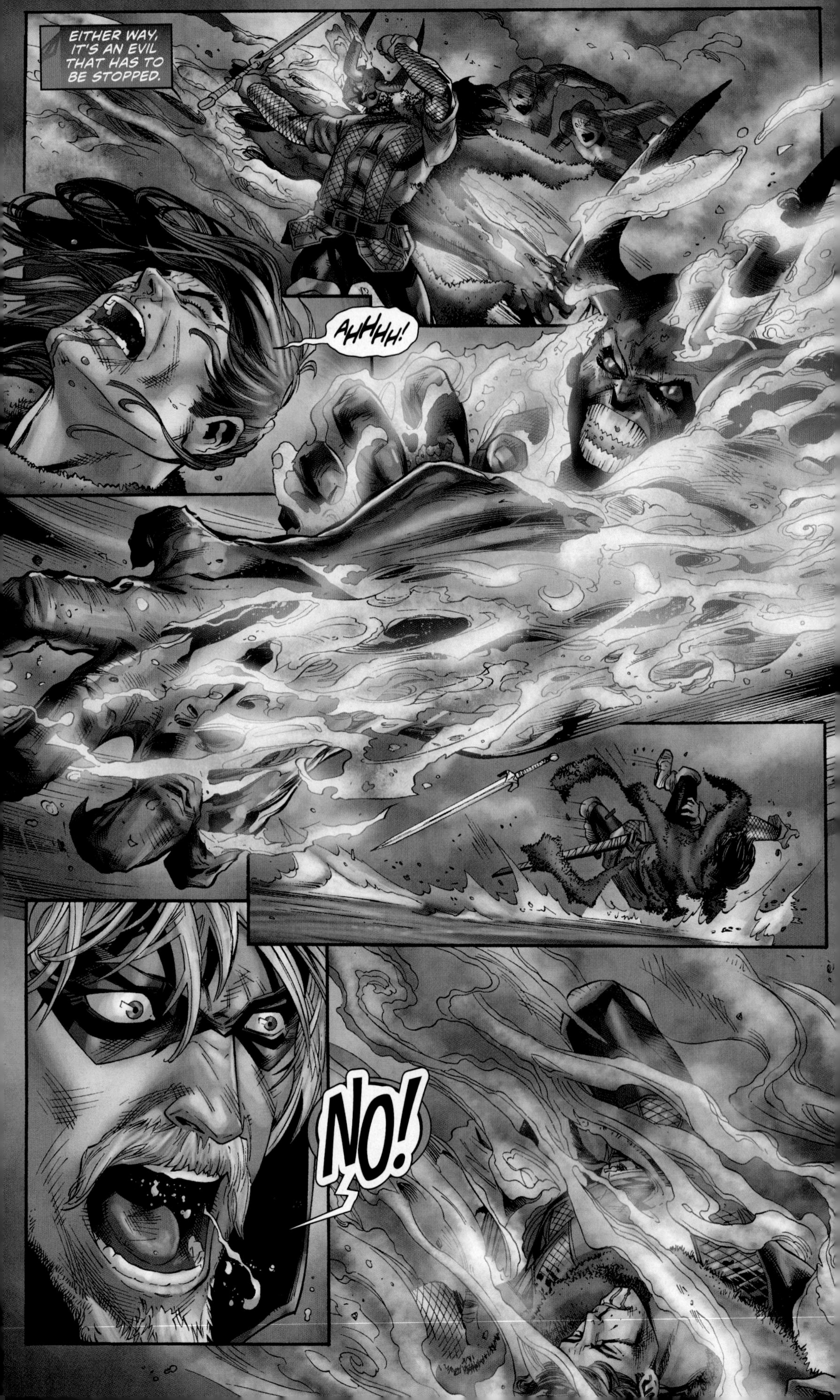
EITHER WAY, IT'S AN EVIL THAT HAS TO BE STOPPED.
AHHHH!
NO!

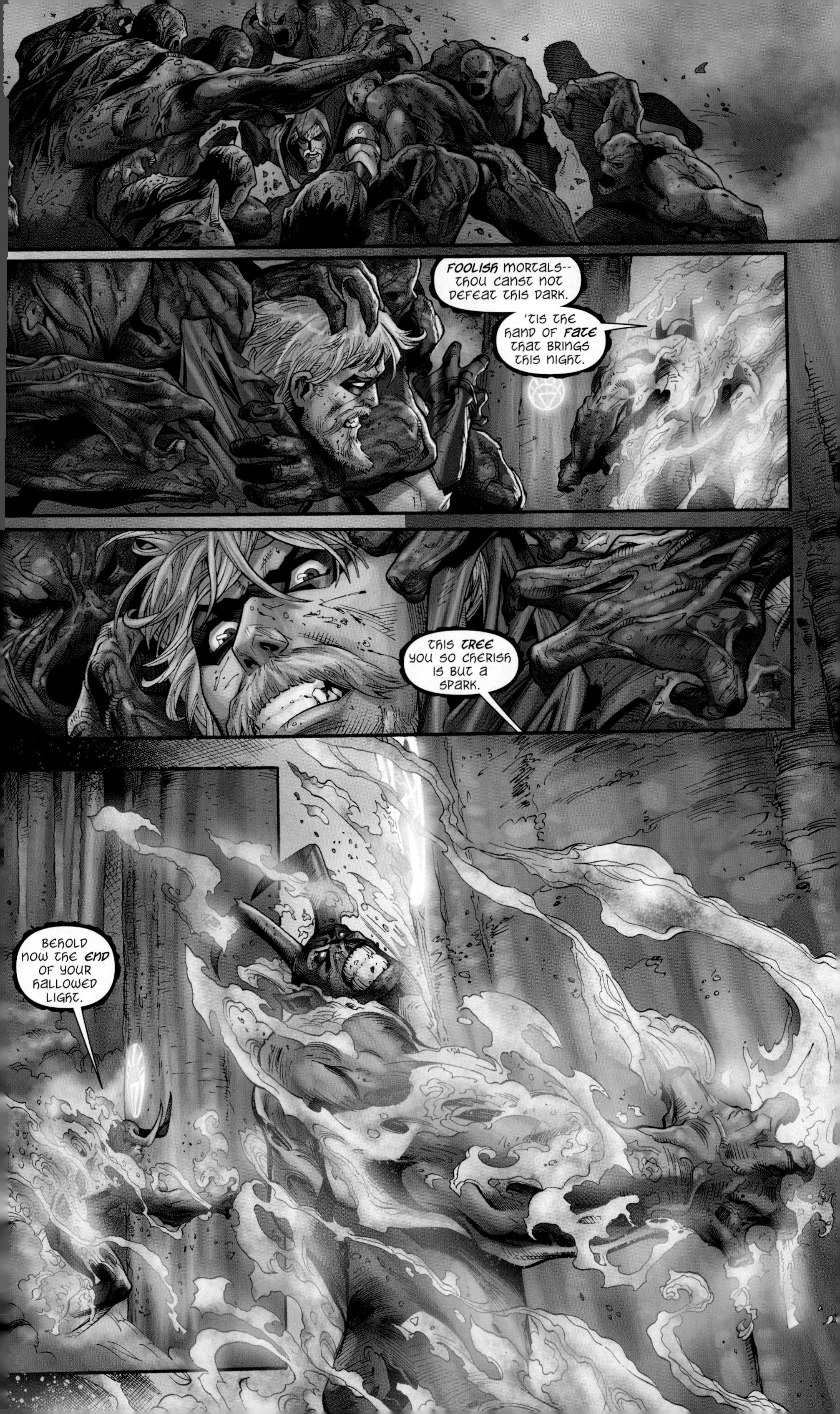
FOOLISH MORTALS--
THOU CANST NOT DEFEAT THIS DARK.
'TIS THE HAND OF FATE THAT BRINGS THIS NIGHT.
THIS TREE YOU SO CHERISH IS BUT A SPARK.
BEHOLD NOW THE END OF YOUR HALLOWED LIGHT.

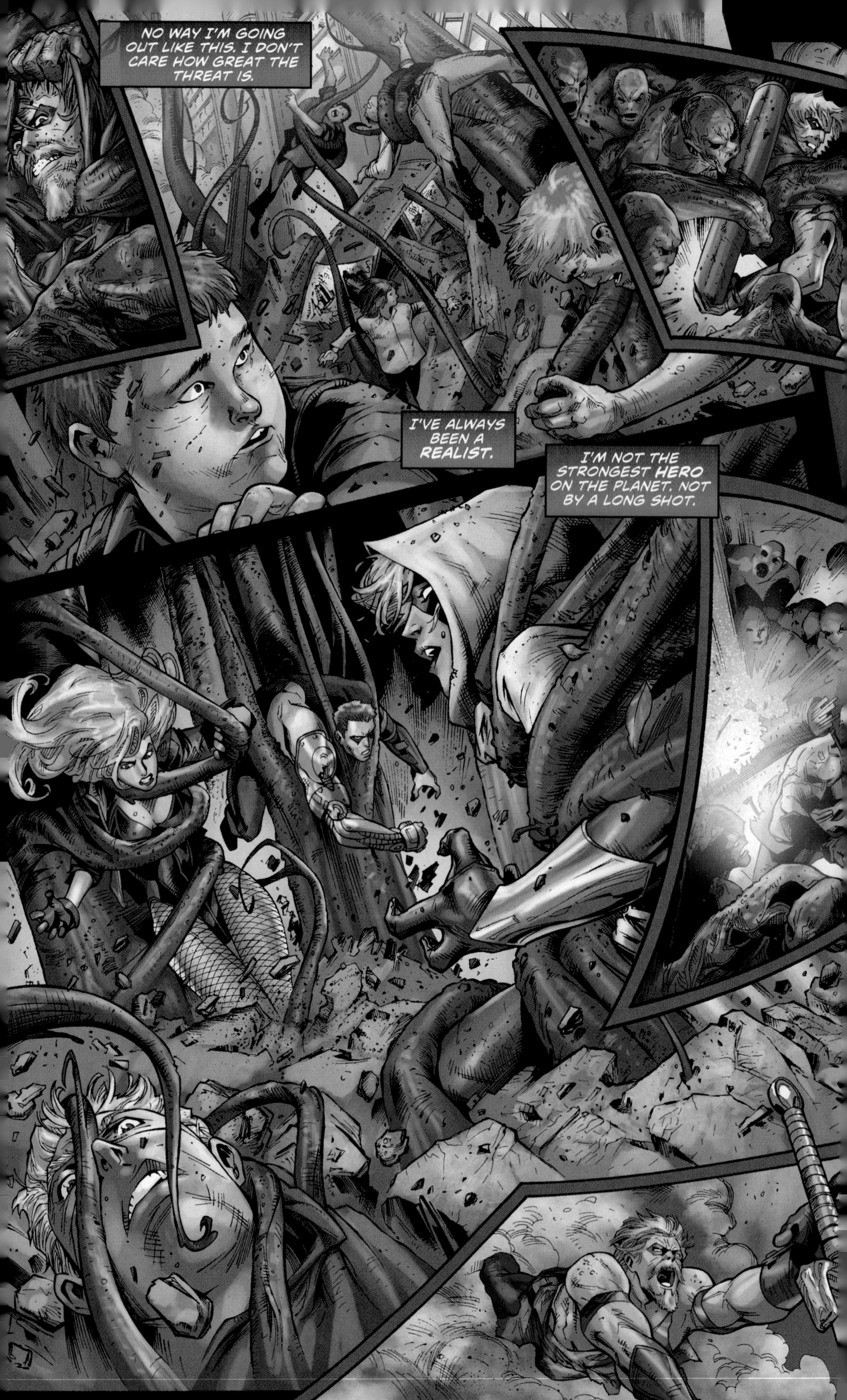
NO WAY I'M GOING OUT LIKE THIS. I DON'T CARE HOW GREAT THE THREAT IS.
I'VE ALWAYS BEEN A REALIST.
I'M NOT THE STRONGEST HERO ON THE PLANET. NOT BY A LONG SHOT.

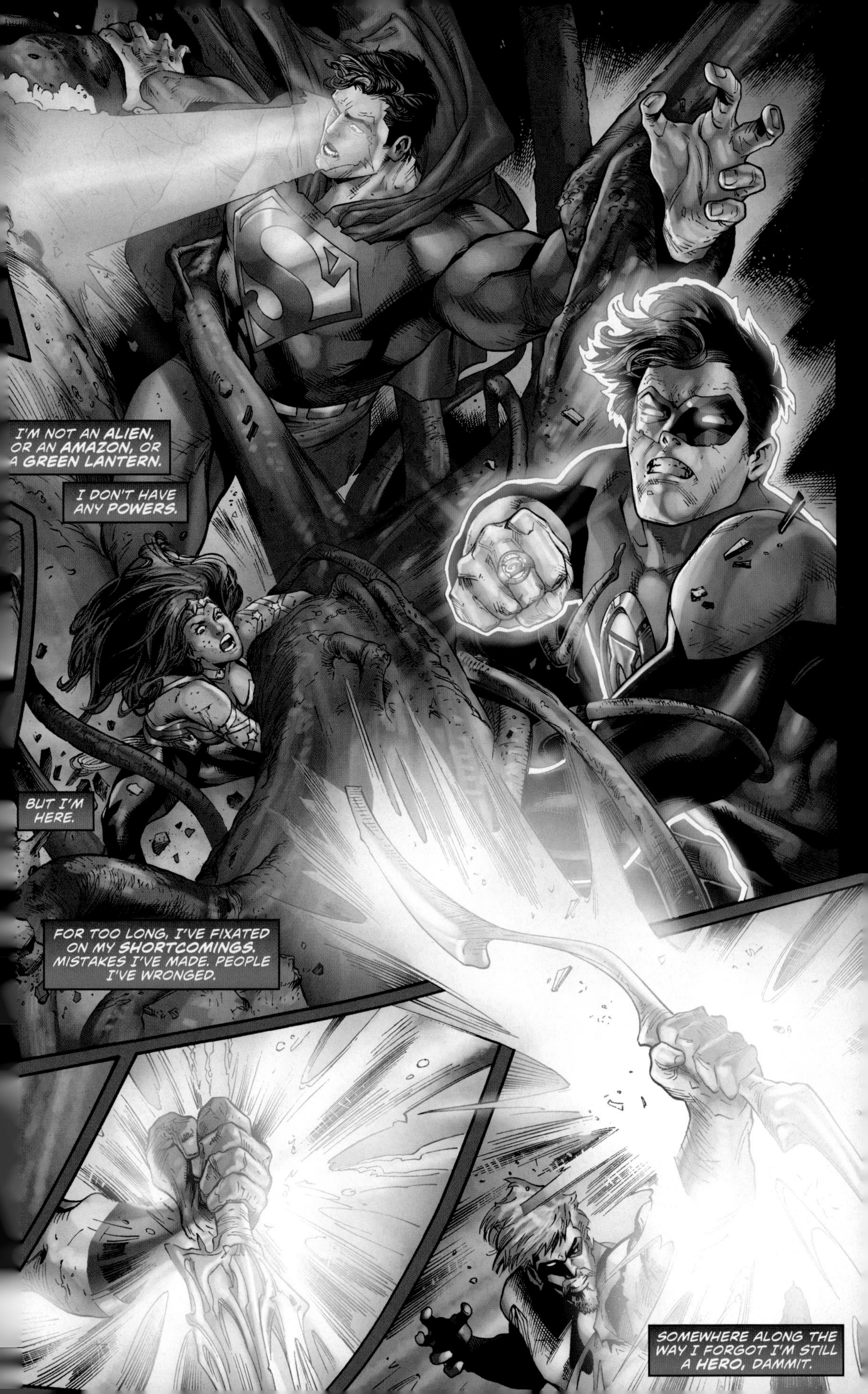
I'M NOT AN ALIEN, OR AN AMAZON, OR A GREEN LANTERN.
I DON'T HAVE ANY POWERS.
BUT I'M HERE.
FOR TOO LONG, I'VE FIXATED ON MY SHORTCOMINGS. MISTAKES I'VE MADE. PEOPLE I'VE WRONGED.
SOMEWHERE ALONG THE WAY I FORGOT I'M STILL A HERO, DAMMIT.

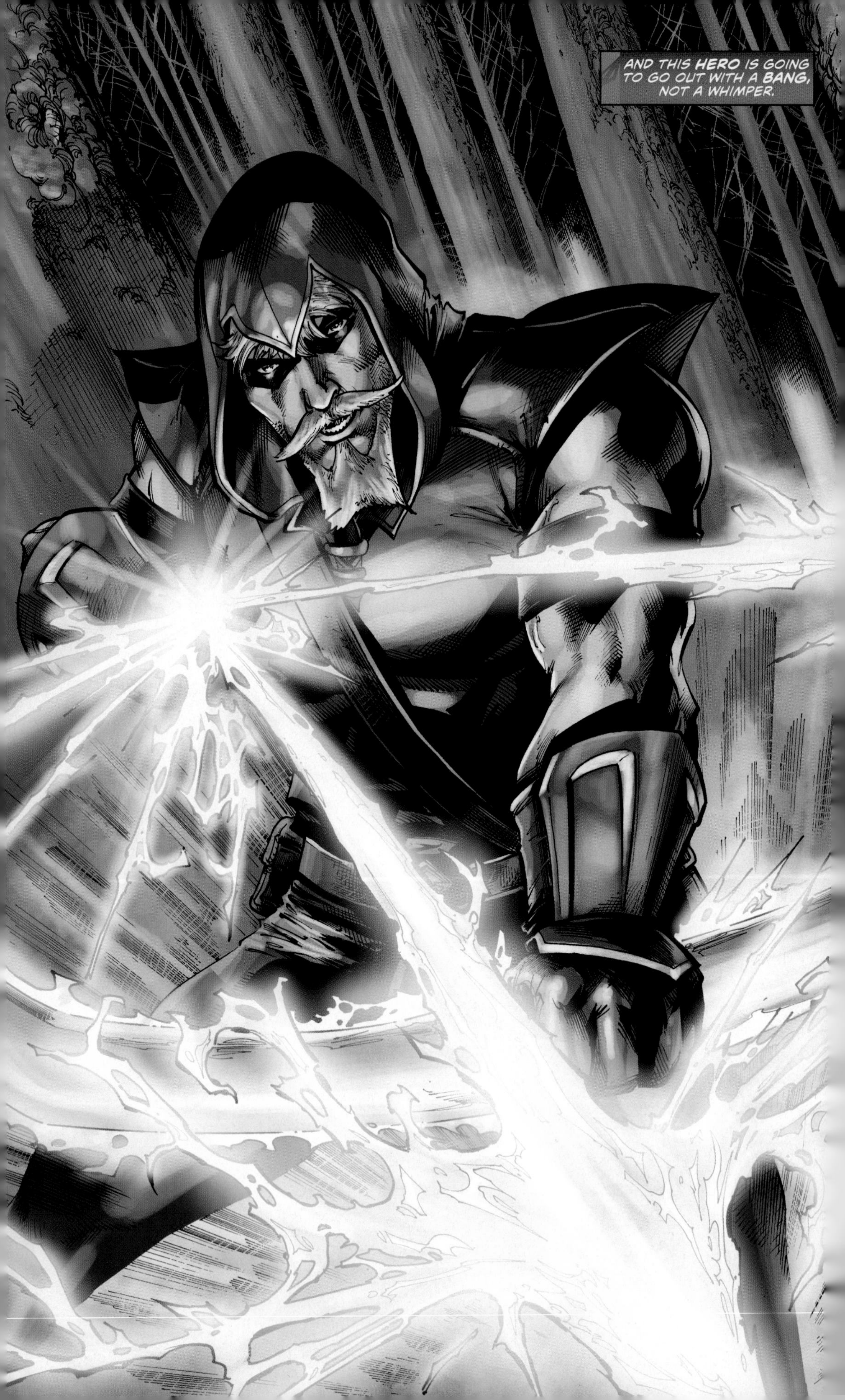
AND THIS **HERO** IS GOING TO GO OUT WITH A **BANG**, NOT A WHIMPER.

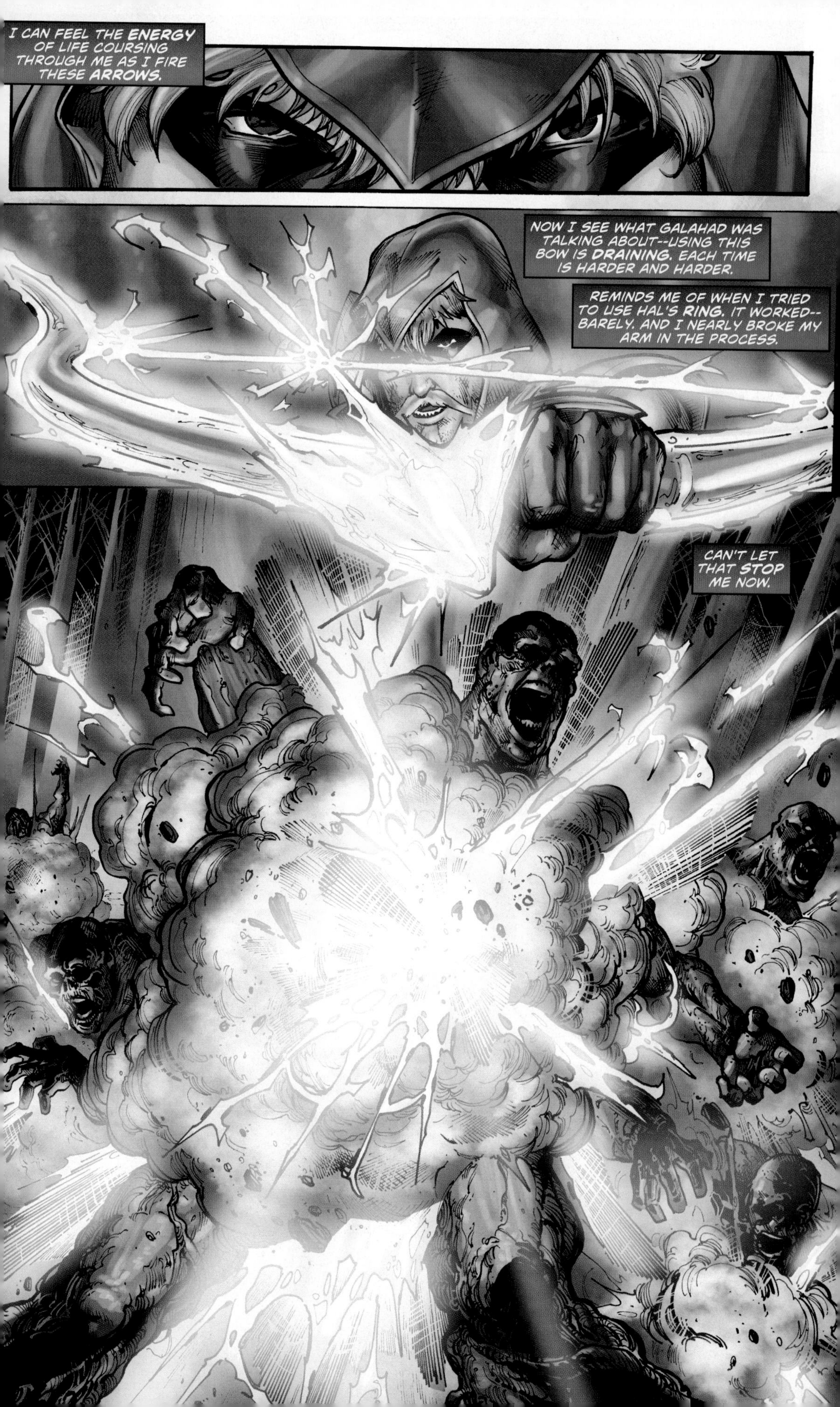
I CAN FEEL THE ENERGY OF LIFE COURSING THROUGH ME AS I FIRE THESE ARROWS.
NOW I SEE WHAT GALAHAD WAS TALKING ABOUT--USING THIS BOW IS DRAINING. EACH TIME IS HARDER AND HARDER.
REMINDS ME OF WHEN I TRIED TO USE HAL'S RING. IT WORKED--BARELY. AND I NEARLY BROKE MY ARM IN THE PROCESS.
CAN'T LET THAT STOP ME NOW.

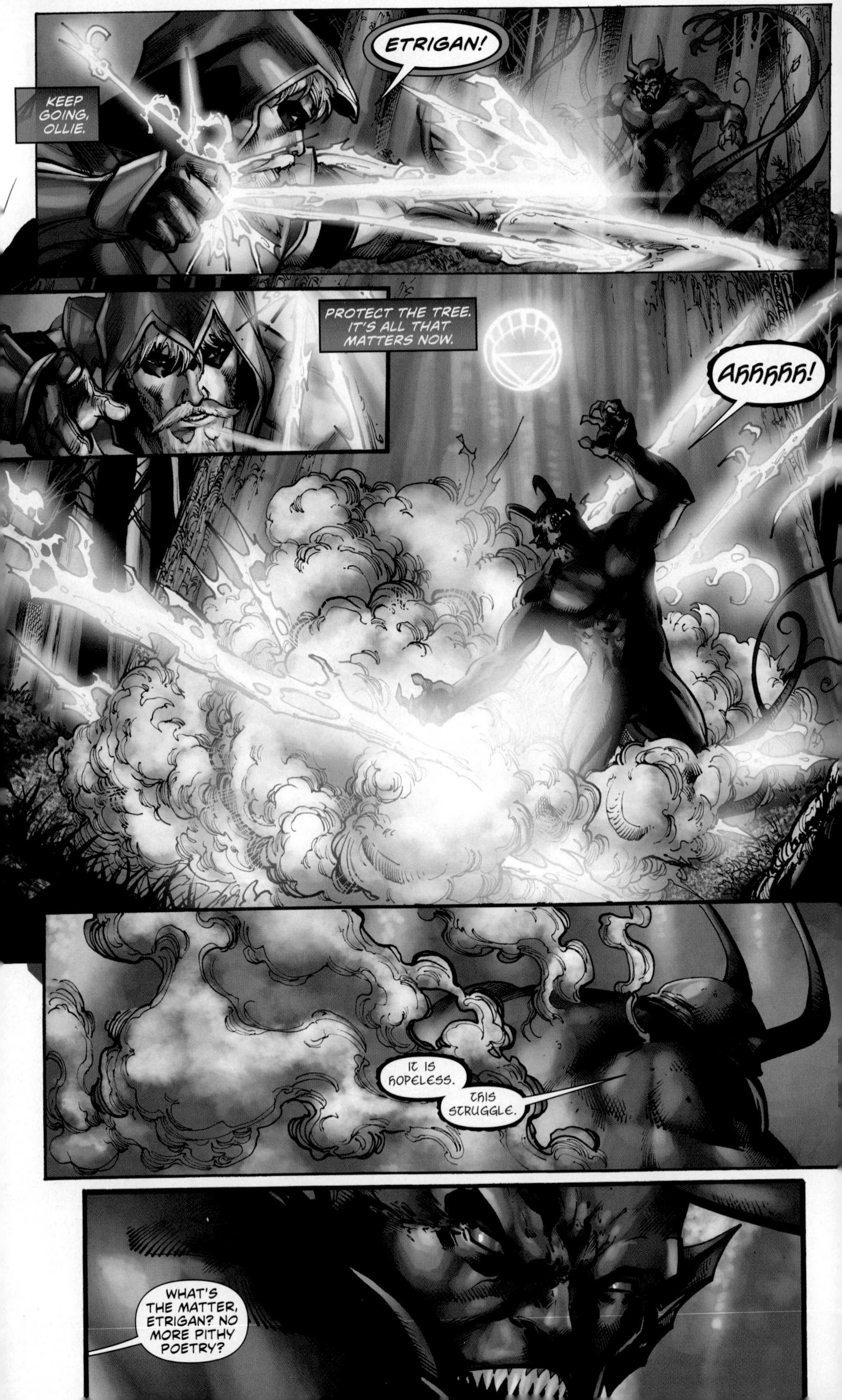
KEEP GOING, OLLIE.
ETRIGAN!
PROTECT THE TREE. IT'S ALL THAT MATTERS NOW.
AHHHHH!
IT IS HOPELESS.
THIS STRUGGLE.
WHAT'S THE MATTER, ETRIGAN? NO MORE PITHY POETRY?

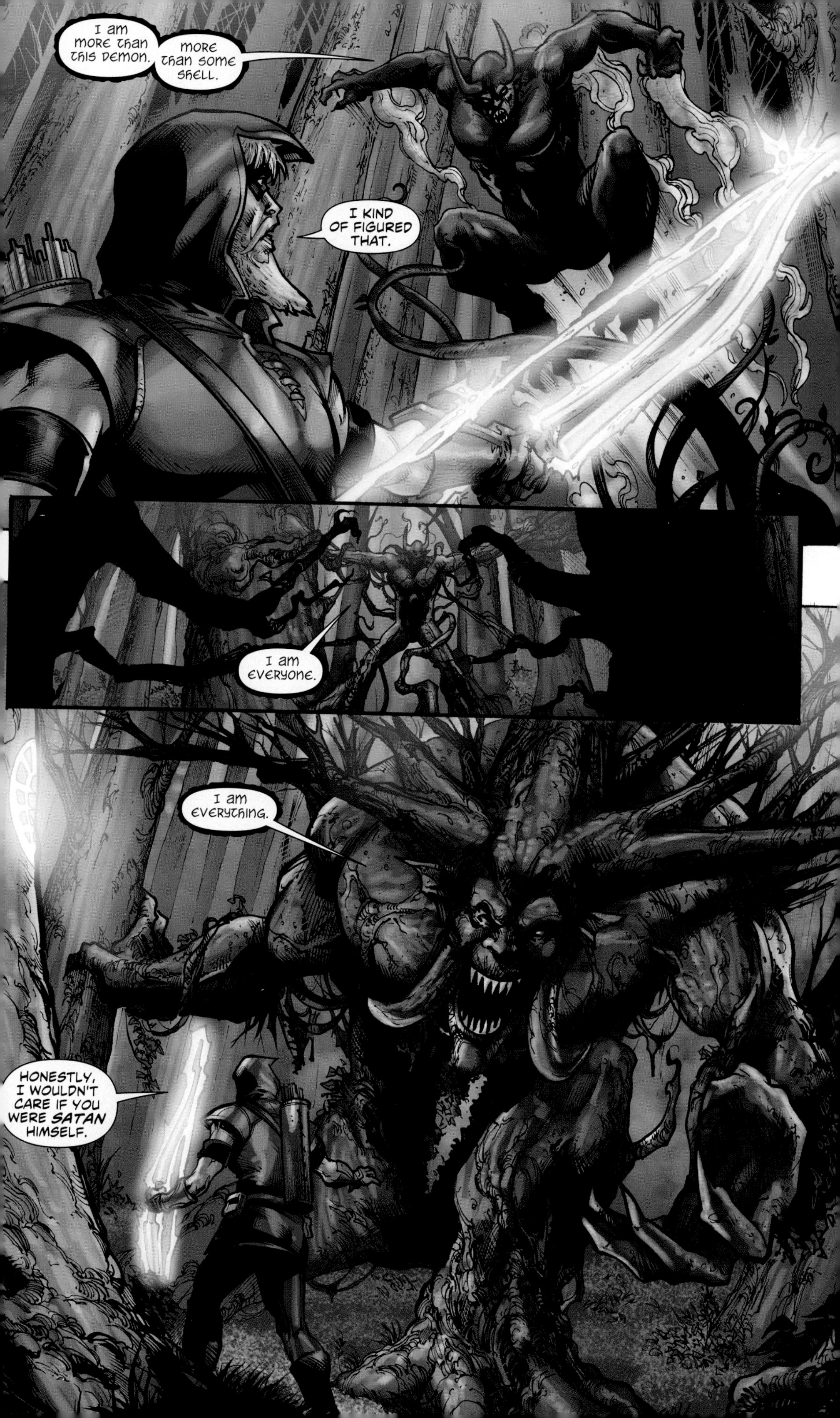

I am more than this demon.
more than some shell.
I KIND OF FIGURED THAT.
I am everyone.
I am everything.
HONESTLY, I WOULDN'T CARE IF YOU WERE *SATAN* HIMSELF.

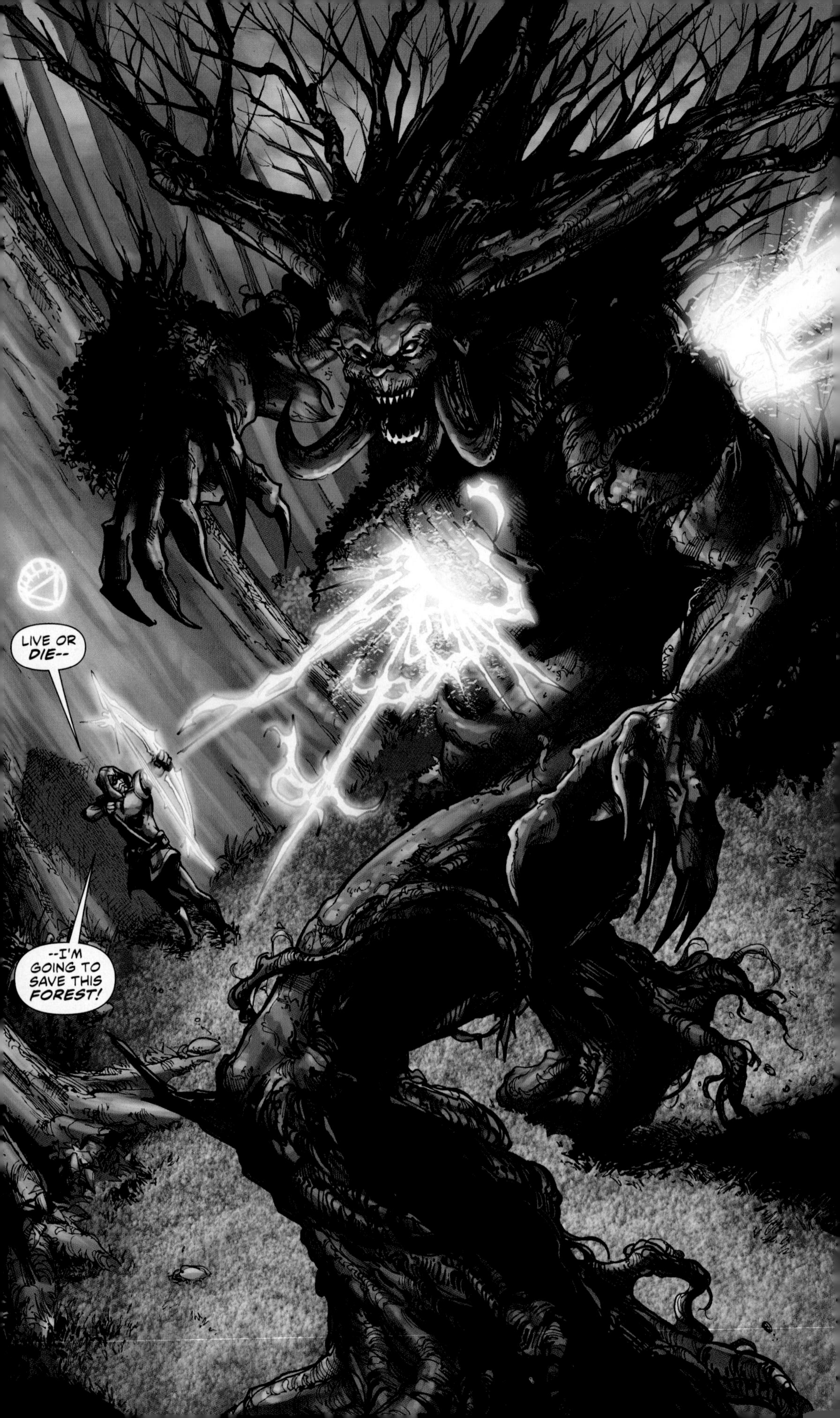
LIVE OR DIE--
--I'M GOING TO SAVE THIS FOREST!

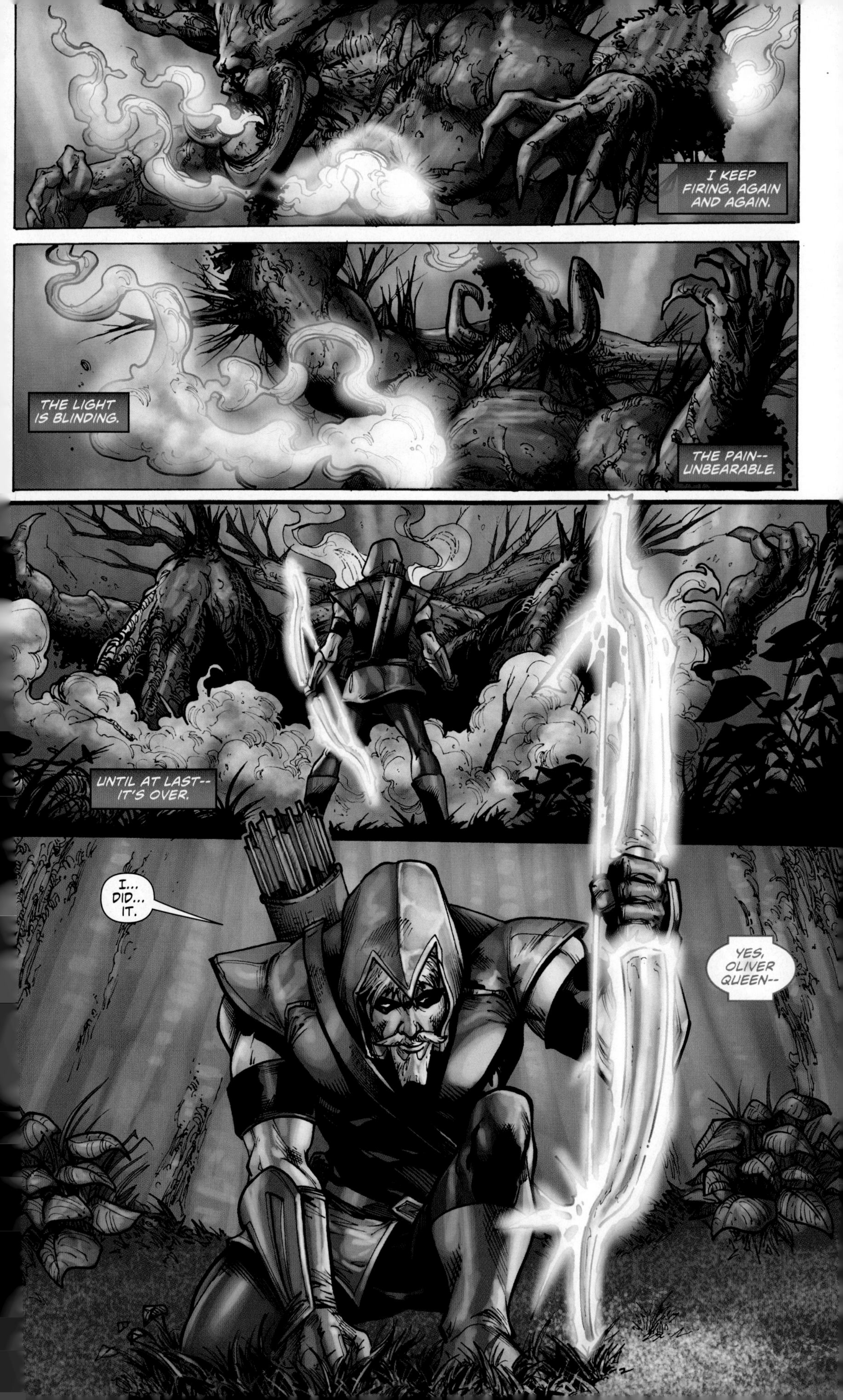
I KEEP FIRING. AGAIN AND AGAIN.
THE LIGHT IS BLINDING.
THE PAIN-- UNBEARABLE.
UNTIL AT LAST-- IT'S OVER.
I... DID... IT.
YES, OLIVER QUEEN--

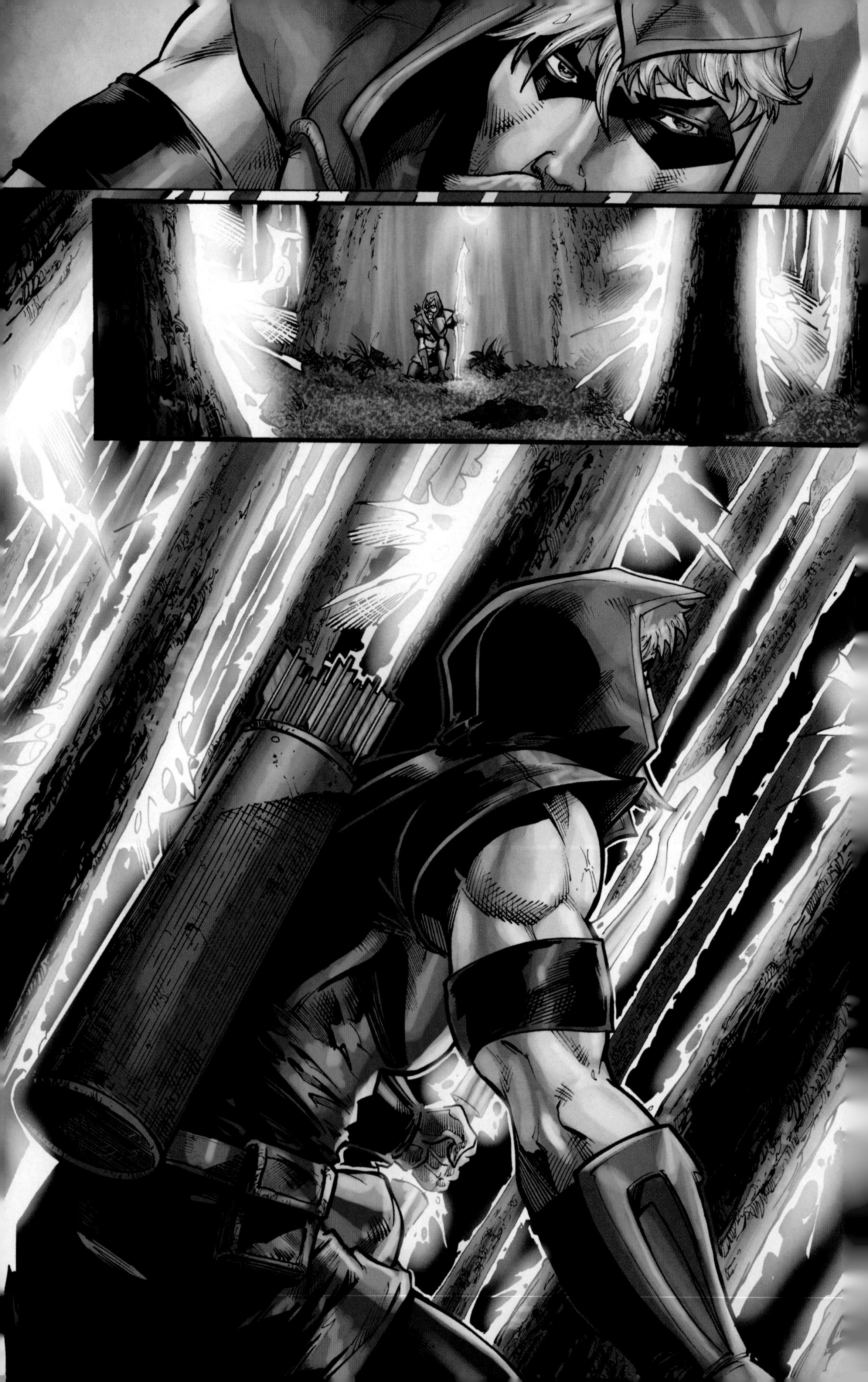

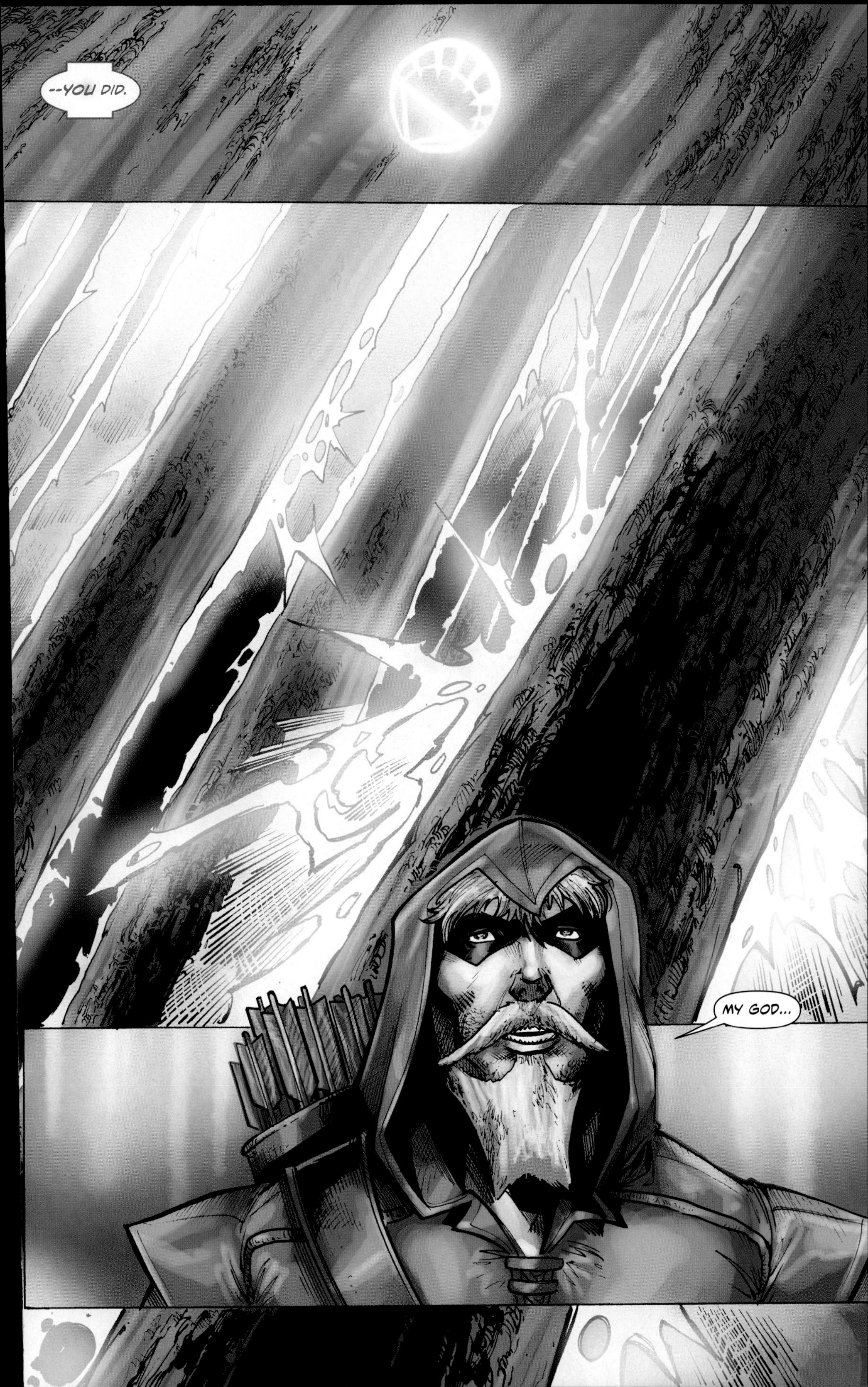
--YOU DID.
MY GOD...

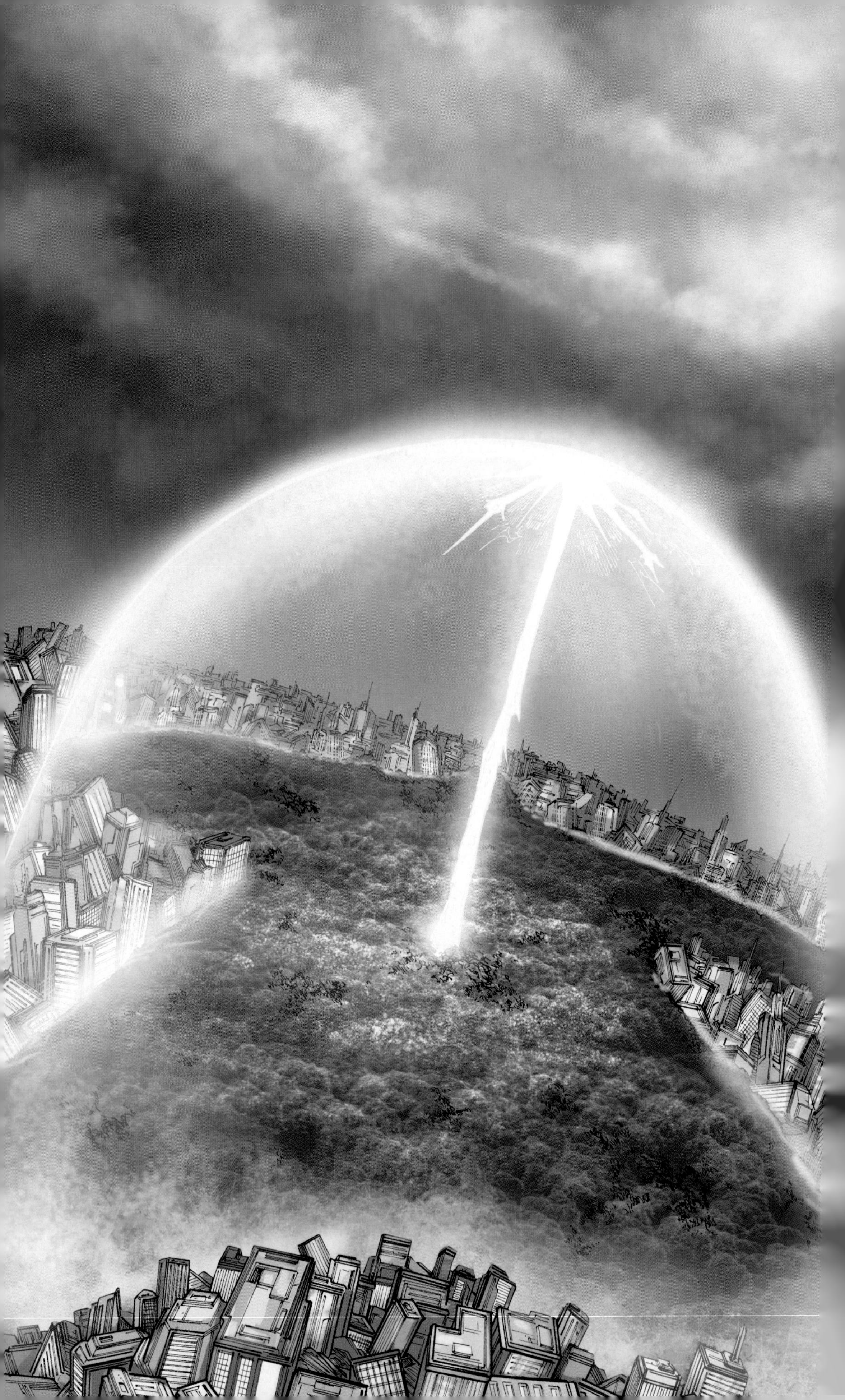

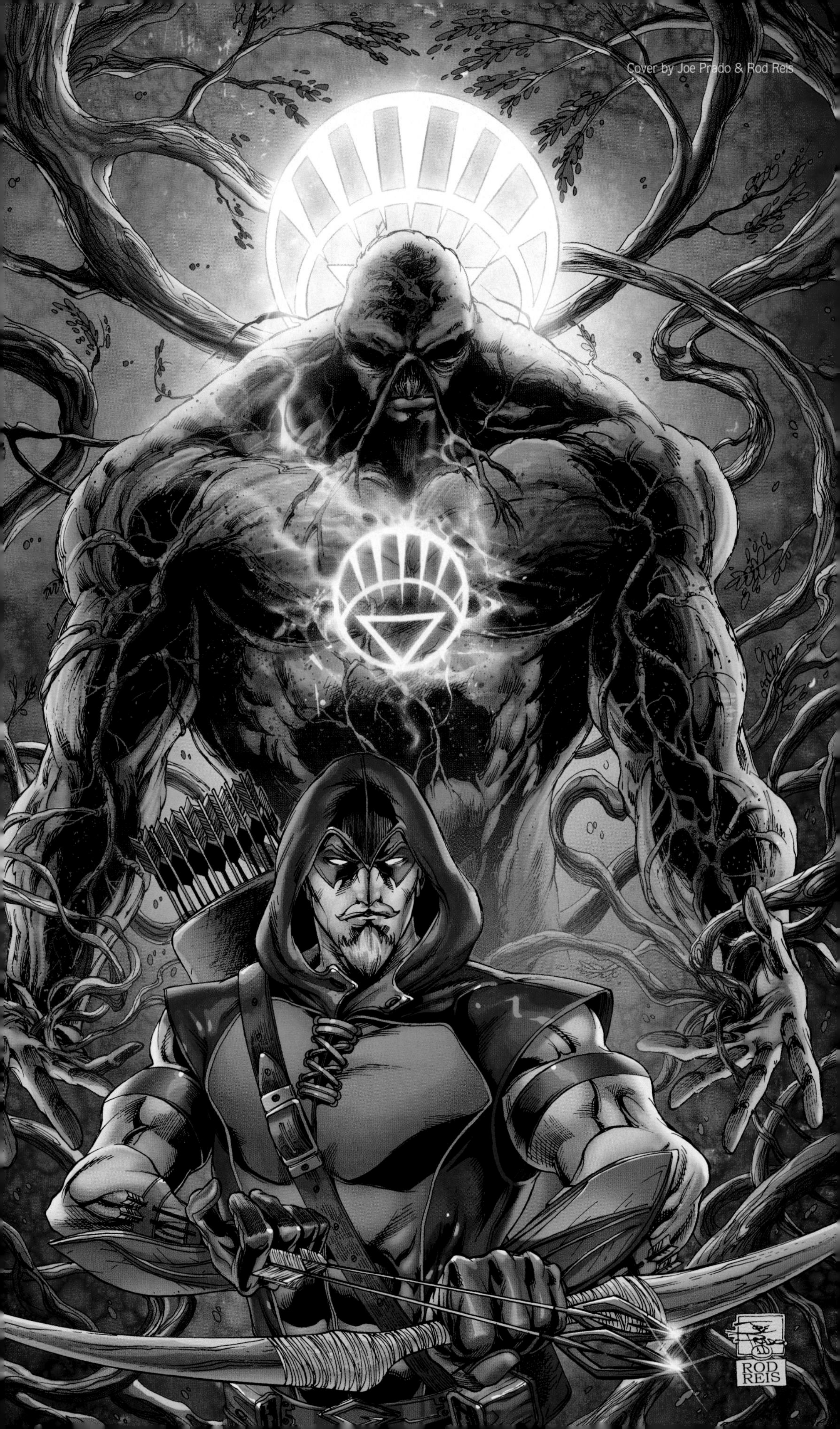
Cover by Joe Prado & Rod Reis
ROD
REIS

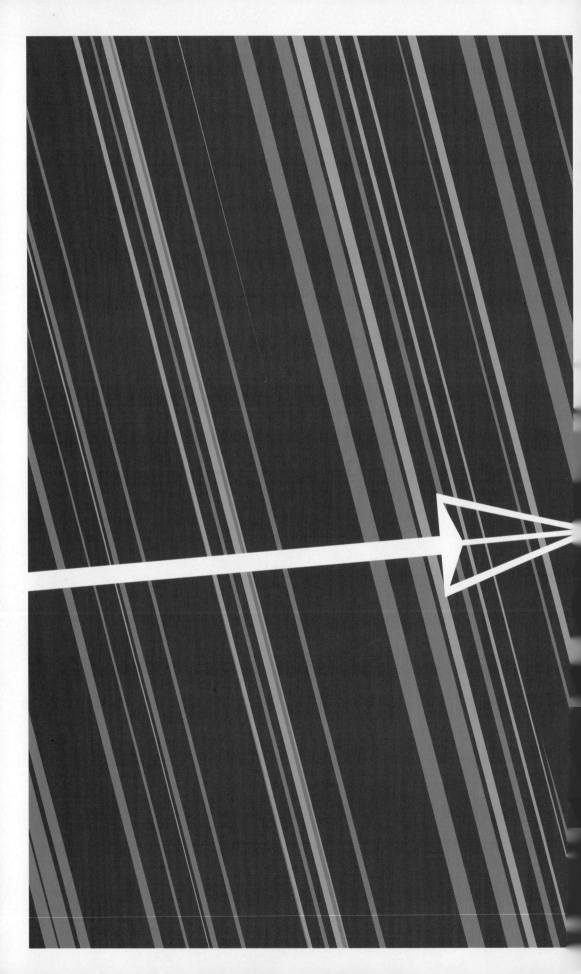

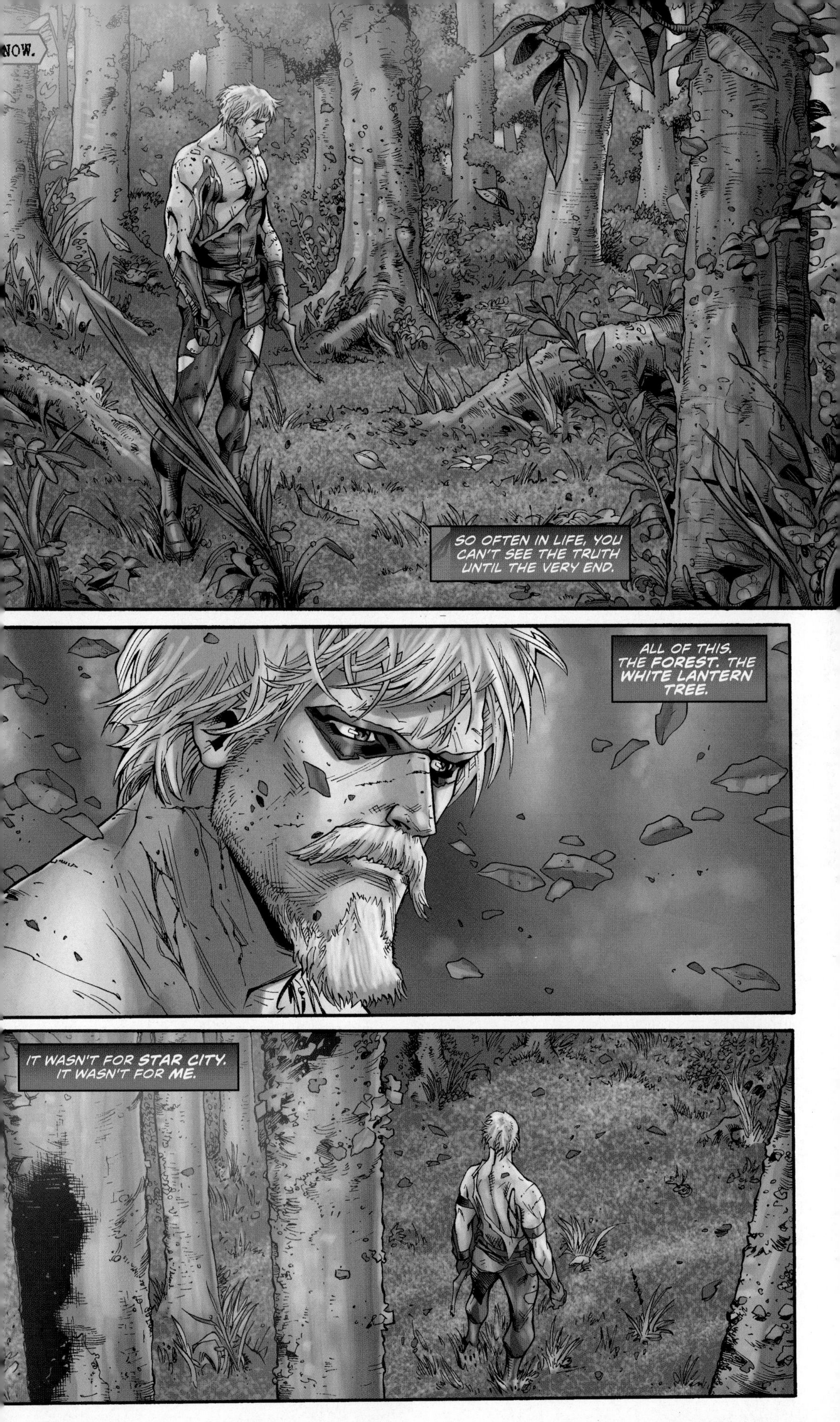
NOW.
SO OFTEN IN LIFE, YOU CAN'T SEE THE TRUTH UNTIL THE VERY END.
ALL OF THIS. THE FOREST. THE WHITE LANTERN TREE.
IT WASN'T FOR STAR CITY. IT WASN'T FOR ME.

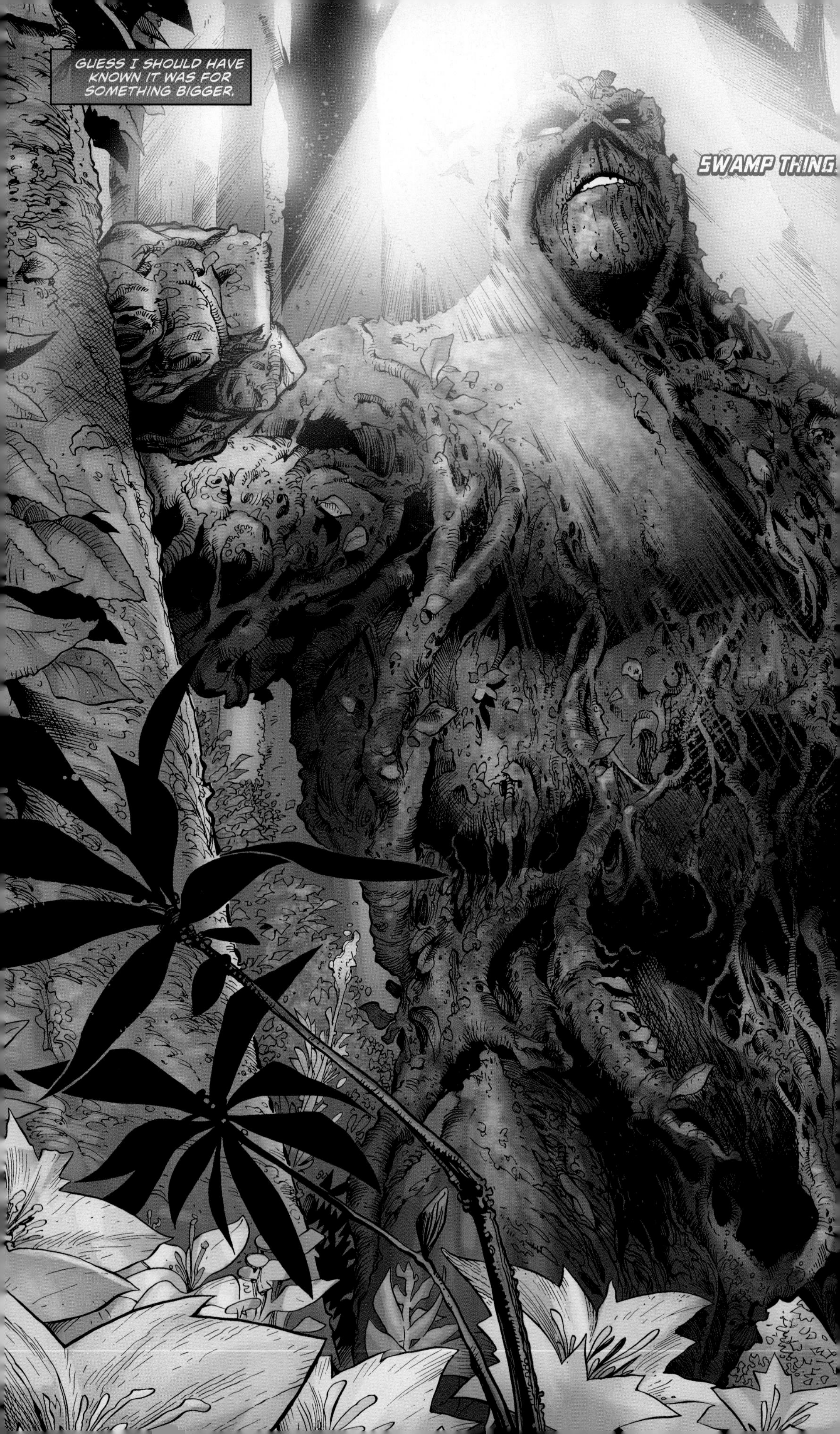
GUESS I SHOULD HAVE KNOWN IT WAS FOR SOMETHING BIGGER.
SWAMP THING.

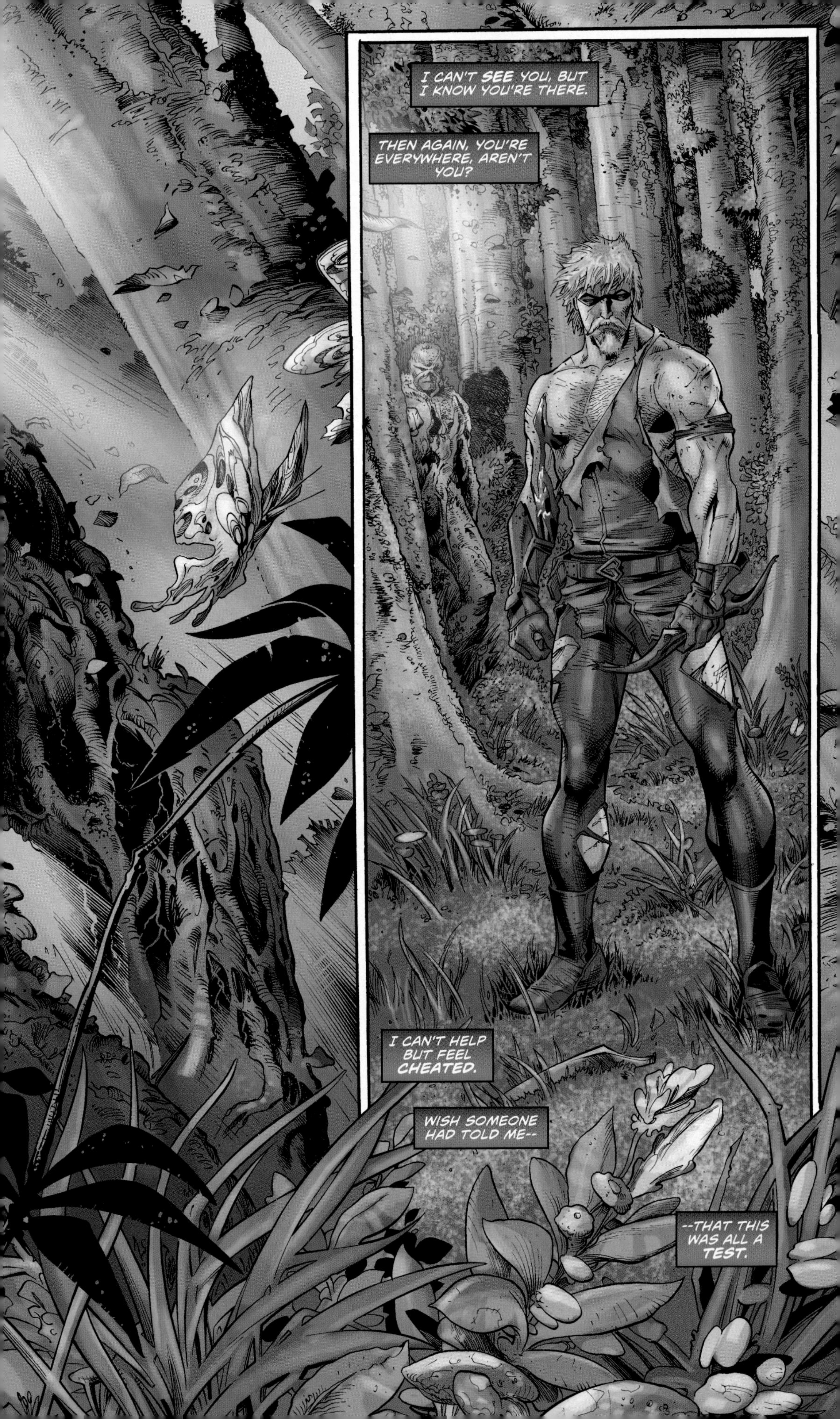
I CAN'T SEE YOU, BUT I KNOW YOU'RE THERE.
THEN AGAIN, YOU'RE EVERYWHERE, AREN'T YOU?
I CAN'T HELP BUT FEEL CHEATED.
WISH SOMEONE HAD TOLD ME--
--THAT THIS WAS ALL A TEST.

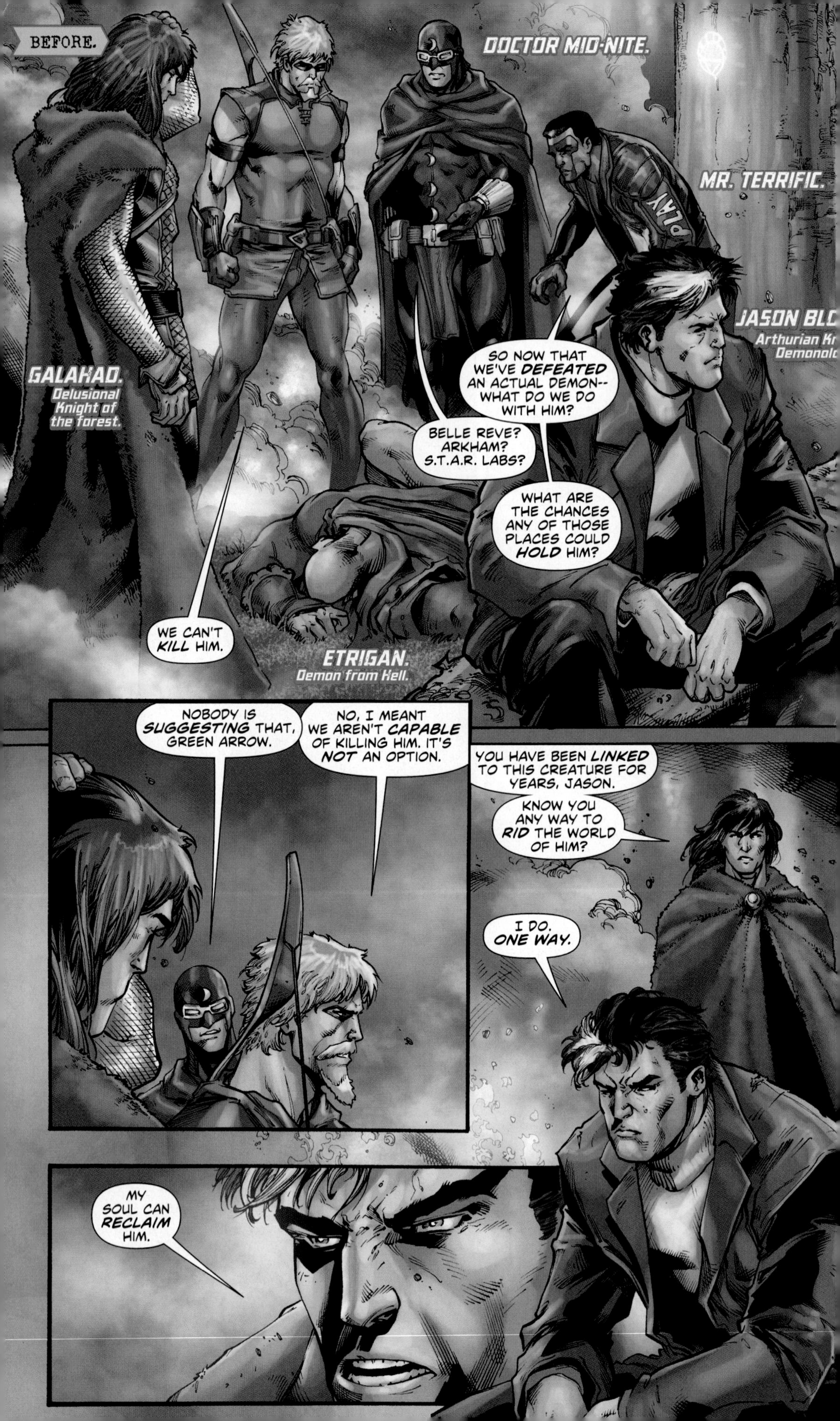
BEFORE.
DOCTOR MID-NITE.
MR. TERRIFIC.
JASON BLC
Arthurian Kr
Demonolc
GALAHAD.
Delusional Knight of the forest.
SO NOW THAT WE'VE DEFEATED AN ACTUAL DEMON-- WHAT DO WE DO WITH HIM?
BELLE REVE? ARKHAM? S.T.A.R. LABS?
WHAT ARE THE CHANCES ANY OF THOSE PLACES COULD HOLD HIM?
WE CAN'T KILL HIM.
ETRIGAN.
Demon from Hell.
NOBODY IS SUGGESTING THAT, GREEN ARROW.
NO, I MEANT WE AREN'T CAPABLE OF KILLING HIM. IT'S NOT AN OPTION.
YOU HAVE BEEN LINKED TO THIS CREATURE FOR YEARS, JASON.
KNOW YOU ANY WAY TO RID THE WORLD OF HIM?
I DO. ONE WAY.
MY SOUL CAN RECLAIM HIM.

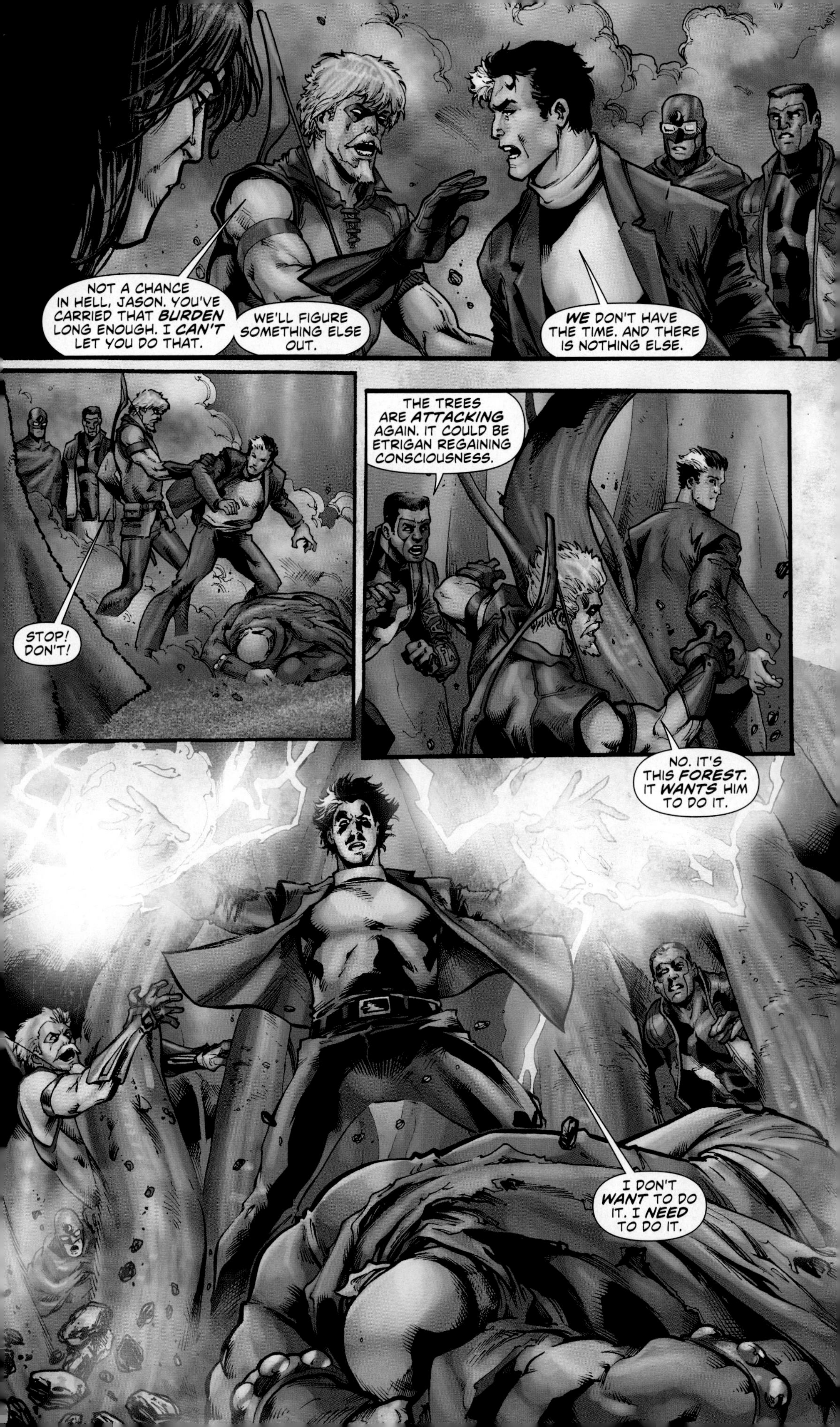
NOT A CHANCE IN HELL, JASON. YOU'VE CARRIED THAT BURDEN LONG ENOUGH. I CAN'T LET YOU DO THAT.
WE'LL FIGURE SOMETHING ELSE OUT.
WE DON'T HAVE THE TIME. AND THERE IS NOTHING ELSE.
STOP! DON'T!
THE TREES ARE ATTACKING AGAIN. IT COULD BE ETRIGAN REGAINING CONSCIOUSNESS.
NO. IT'S THIS FOREST. IT WANTS HIM TO DO IT.
I DON'T WANT TO DO IT. I NEED TO DO IT.

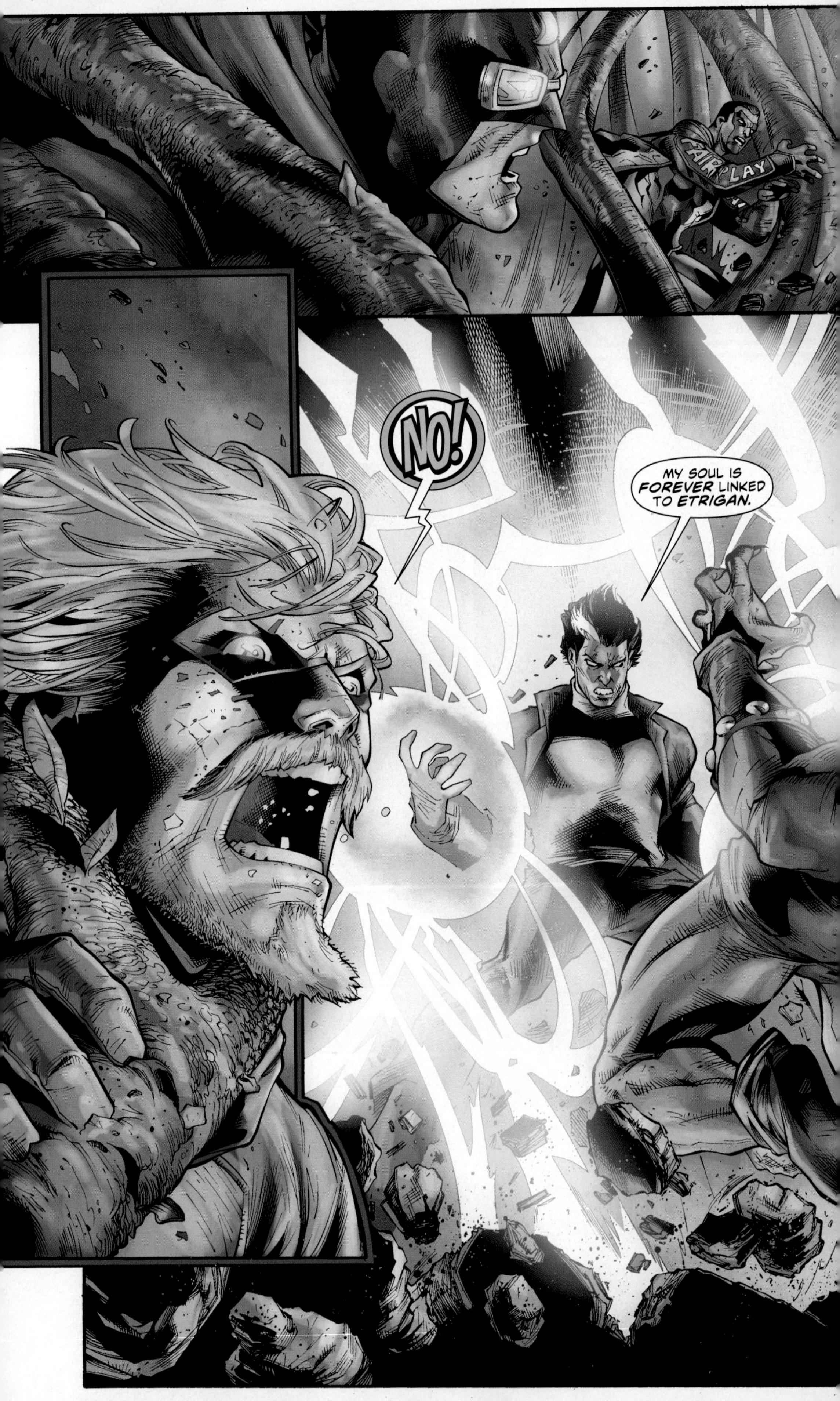
FAIRPLAY
NO!
MY SOUL IS FOREVER LINKED TO ETRIGAN.

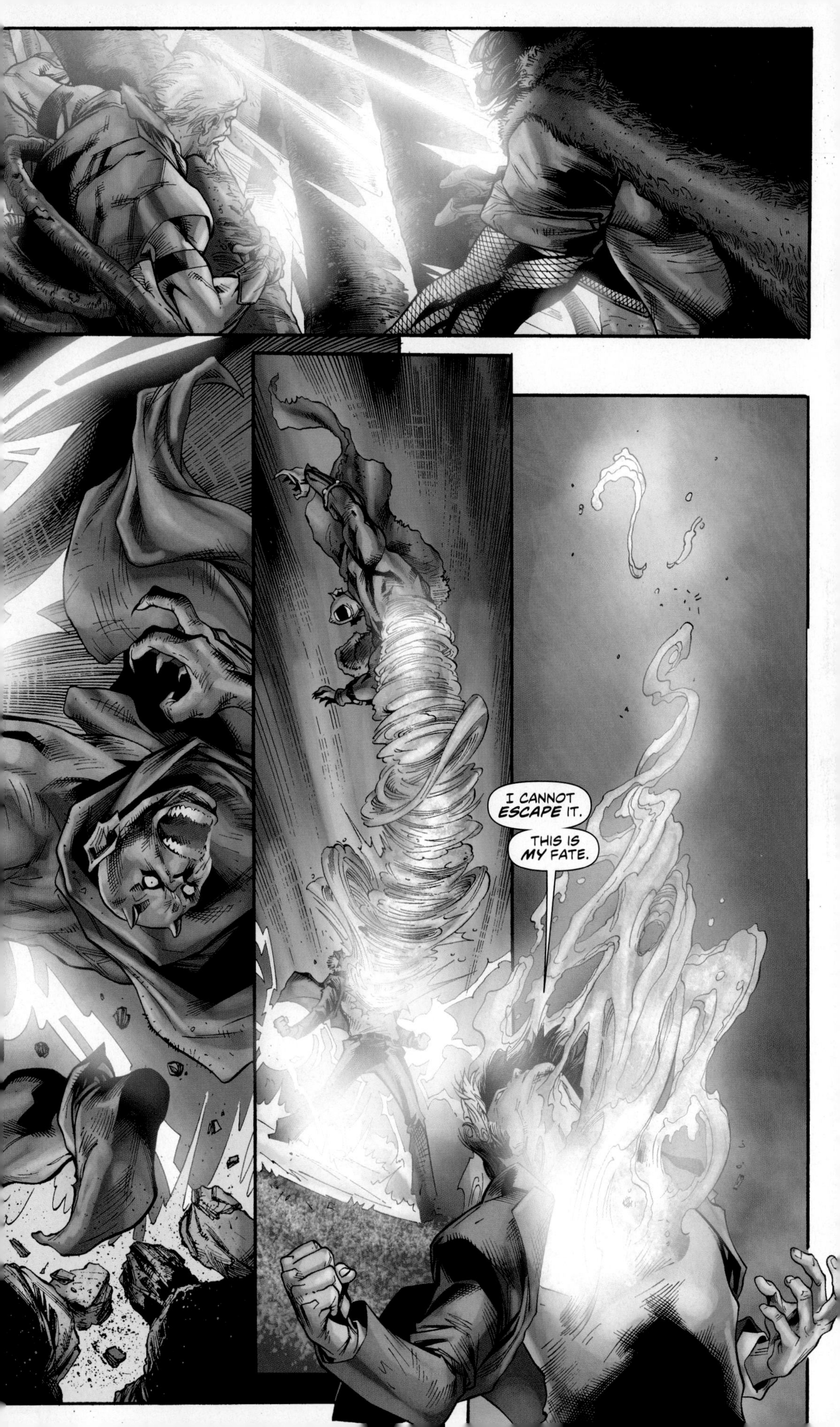
I CANNOT ESCAPE IT.
THIS IS MY FATE.

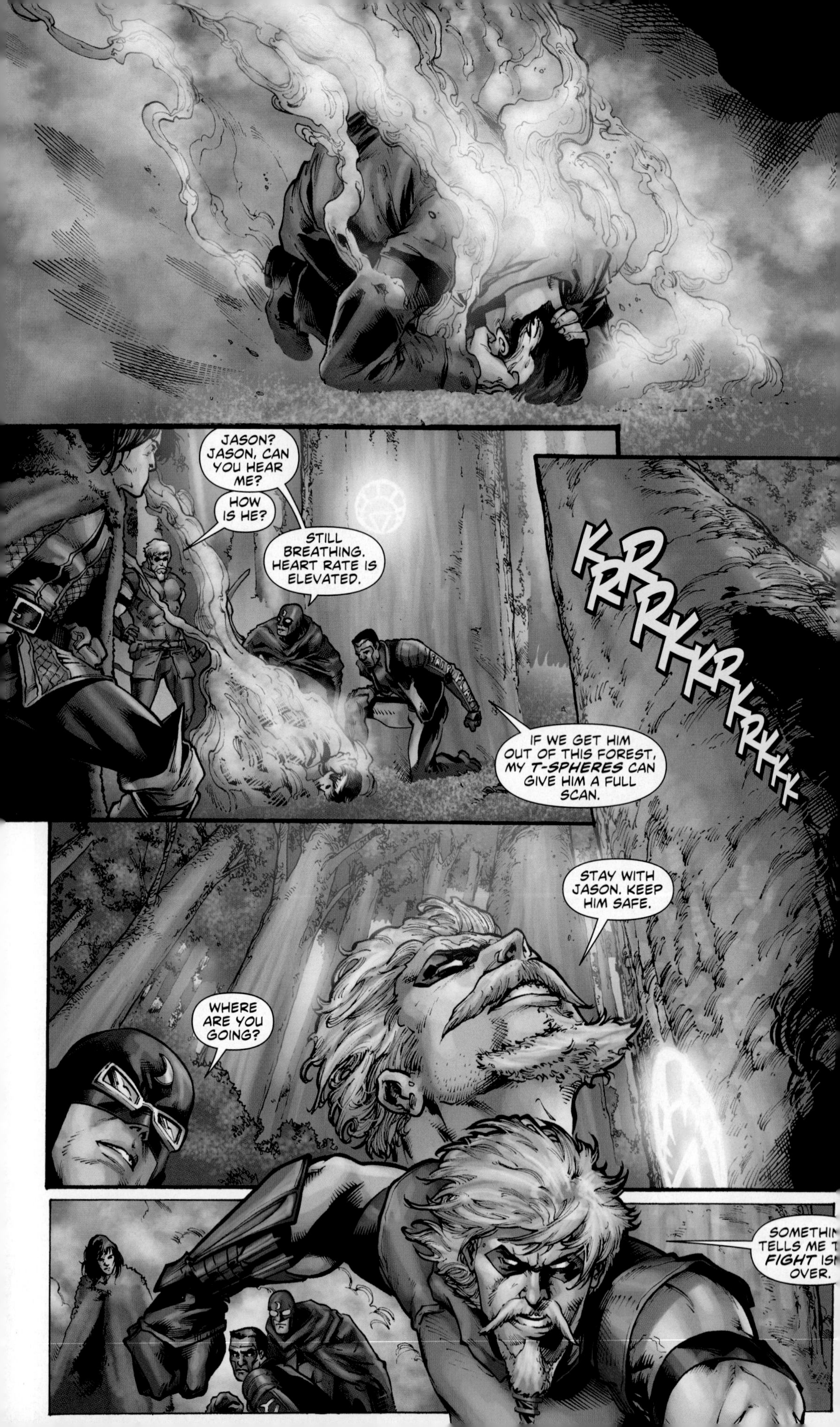

JASON? JASON, CAN YOU HEAR ME?
HOW IS HE?
STILL BREATHING. HEART RATE IS ELEVATED.
IF WE GET HIM OUT OF THIS FOREST, MY *T-SPHERES* CAN GIVE HIM A FULL SCAN.
KRRRKKRRKRKKK
STAY WITH JASON. KEEP HIM SAFE.
WHERE ARE YOU GOING?
SOMETHIN TELLS ME T *FIGHT* ISN OVER.

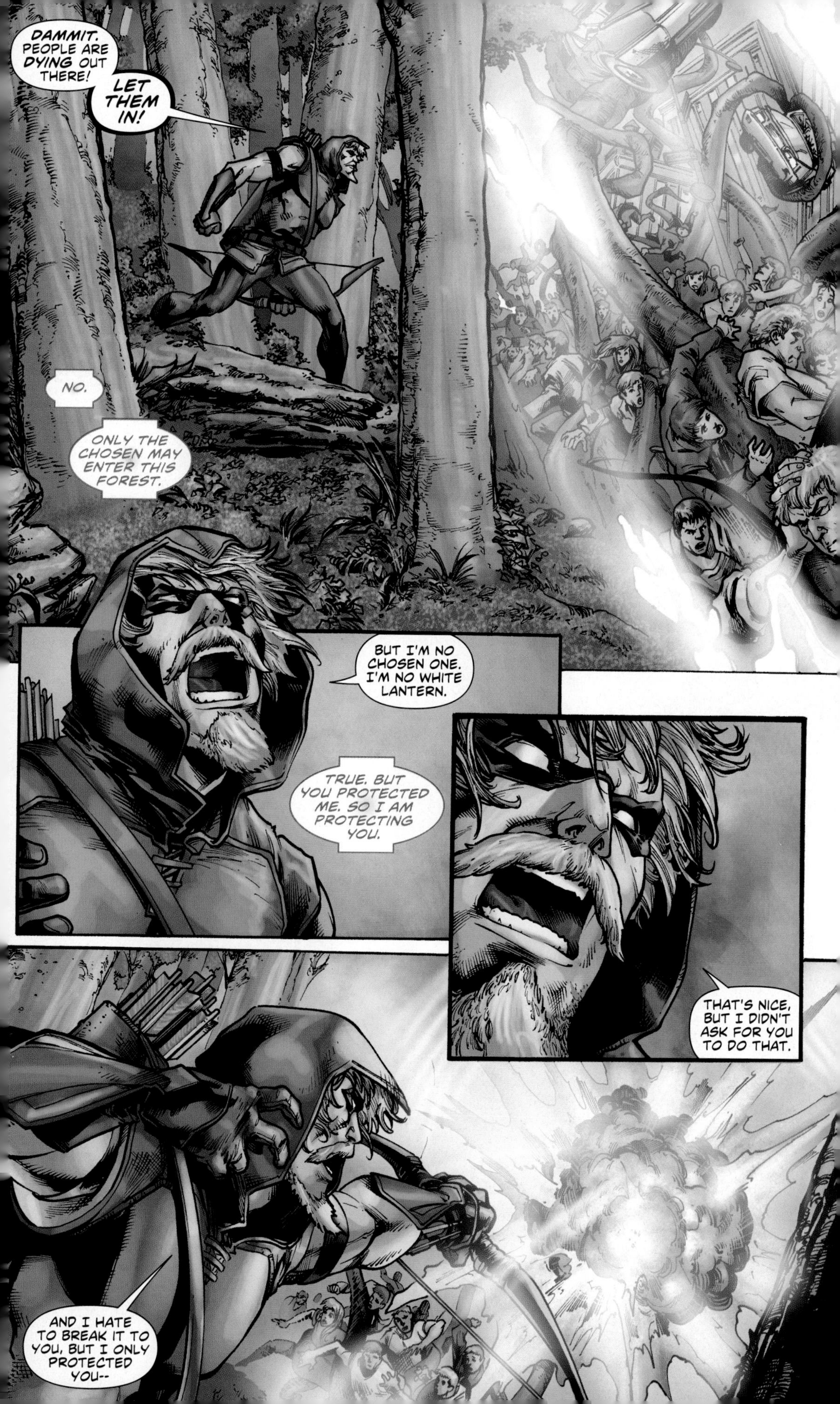
DAMMIT. PEOPLE ARE DYING OUT THERE!
LET THEM IN!
NO.
ONLY THE CHOSEN MAY ENTER THIS FOREST.
BUT I'M NO CHOSEN ONE. I'M NO WHITE LANTERN.
TRUE. BUT YOU PROTECTED ME. SO I AM PROTECTING YOU.
THAT'S NICE, BUT I DIDN'T ASK FOR YOU TO DO THAT.
AND I HATE TO BREAK IT TO YOU, BUT I ONLY PROTECTED YOU--

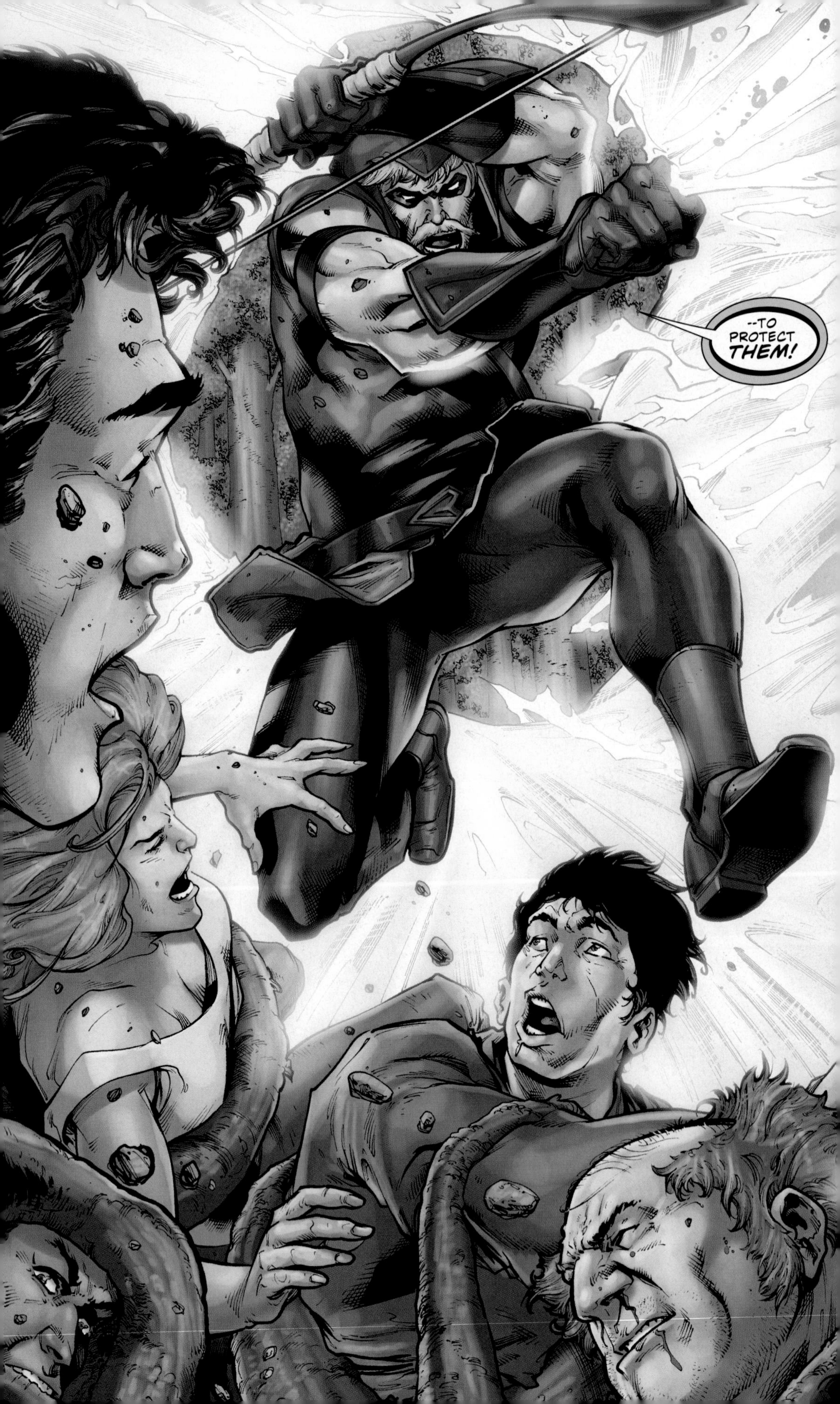
--TO PROTECT THEM!

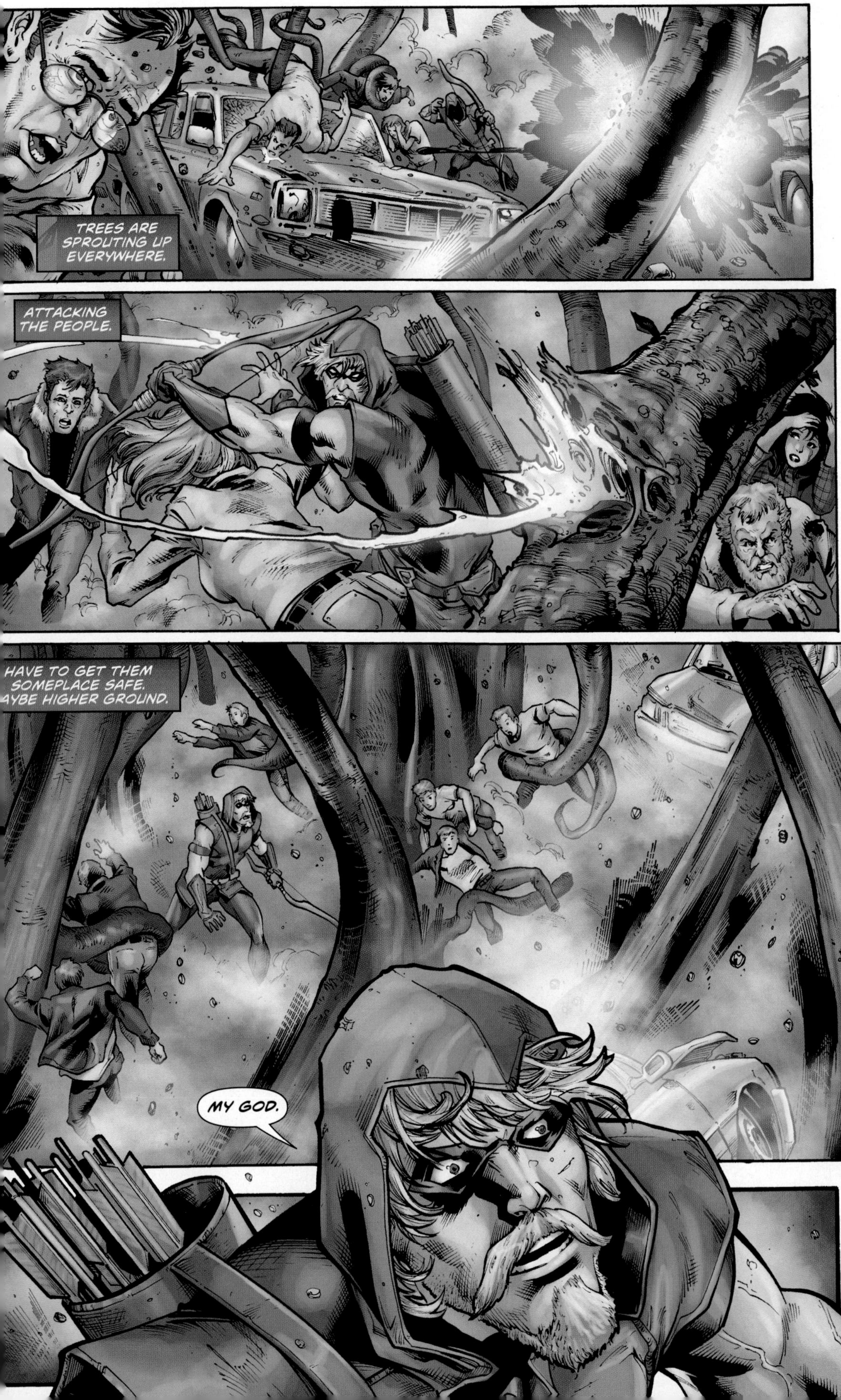
TREES ARE SPROUTING UP EVERYWHERE.
ATTACKING THE PEOPLE.
HAVE TO GET THEM SOMEPLACE SAFE. AYBE HIGHER GROUND.
MY GOD.

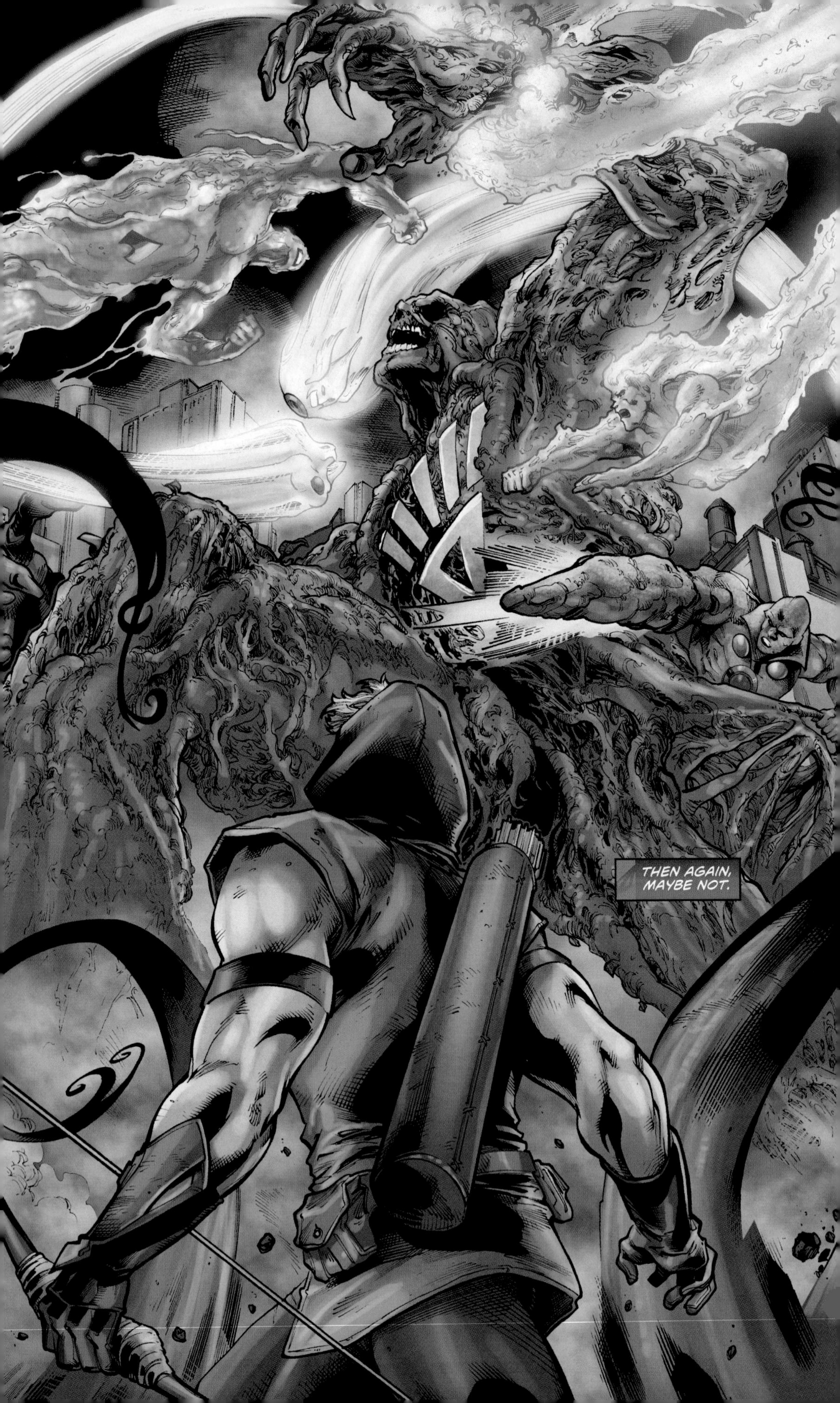
THEN AGAIN, MAYBE NOT.

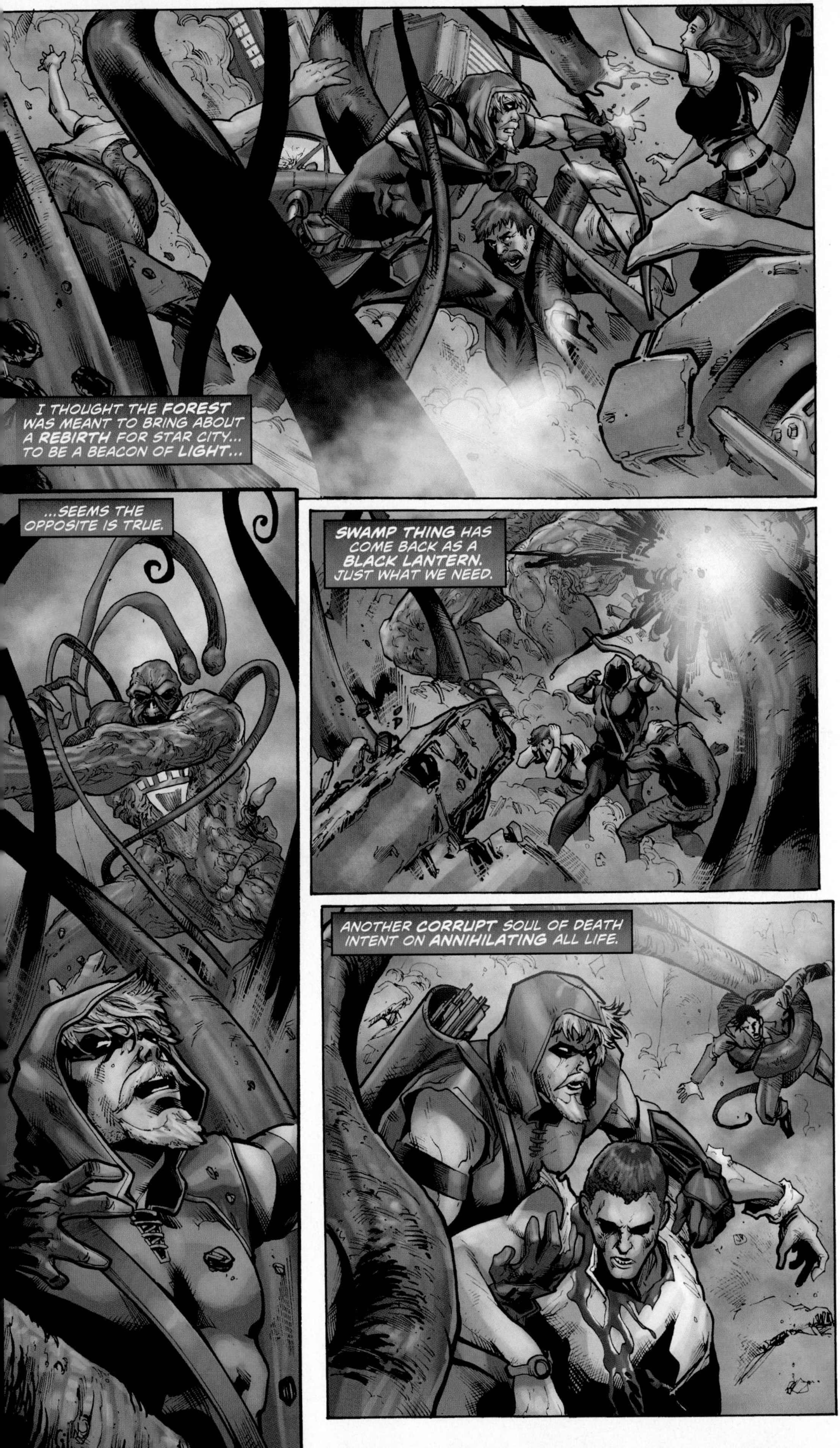
I THOUGHT THE FOREST WAS MEANT TO BRING ABOUT A REBIRTH FOR STAR CITY... TO BE A BEACON OF LIGHT...
...SEEMS THE OPPOSITE IS TRUE.
SWAMP THING HAS COME BACK AS A BLACK LANTERN. JUST WHAT WE NEED.
ANOTHER CORRUPT SOUL OF DEATH INTENT ON ANNIHILATING ALL LIFE.

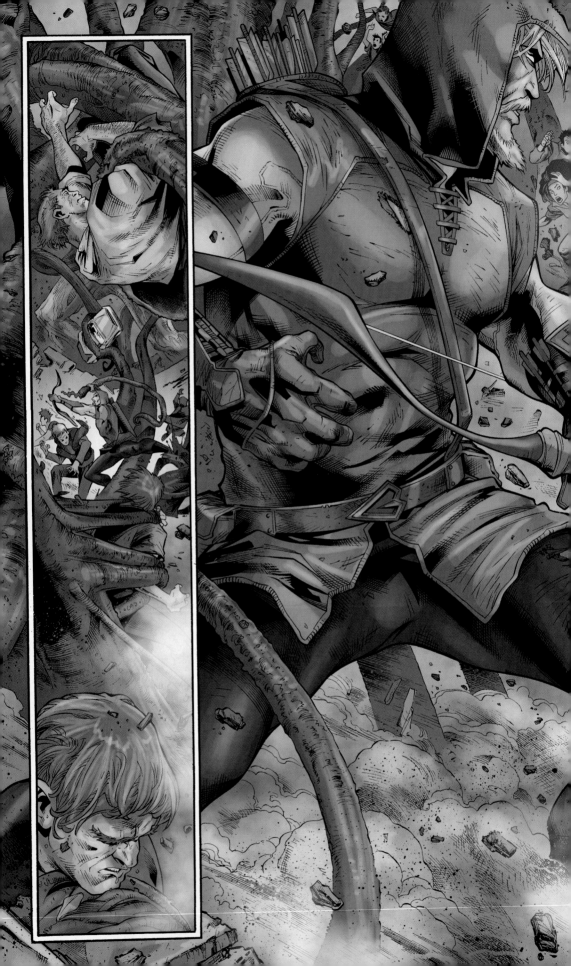

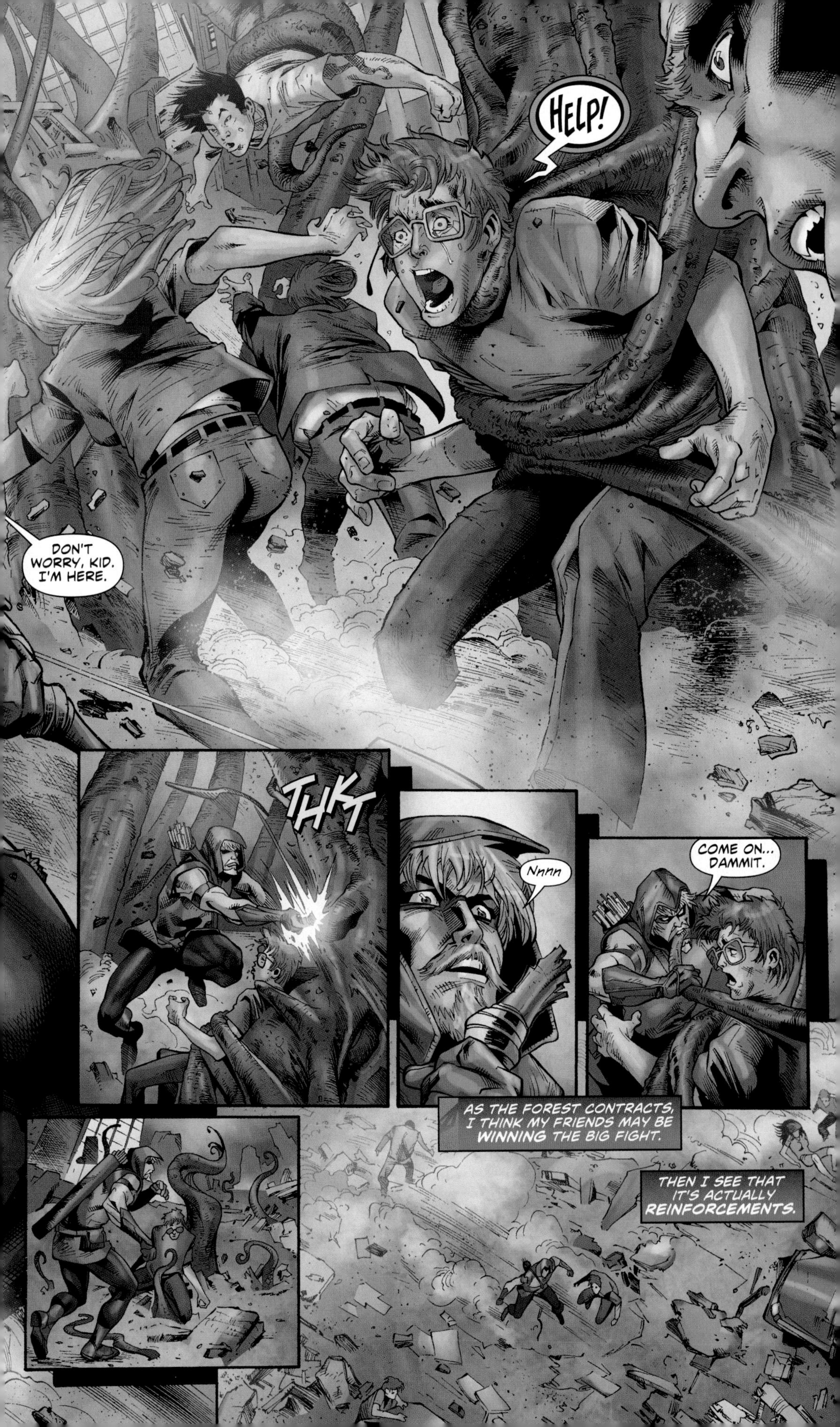
HELP!
DON'T WORRY, KID. I'M HERE.
THKT
Nnnn
COME ON... DAMMIT.
AS THE FOREST CONTRACTS, I THINK MY FRIENDS MAY BE WINNING THE BIG FIGHT.
THEN I SEE THAT IT'S ACTUALLY REINFORCEMENTS.

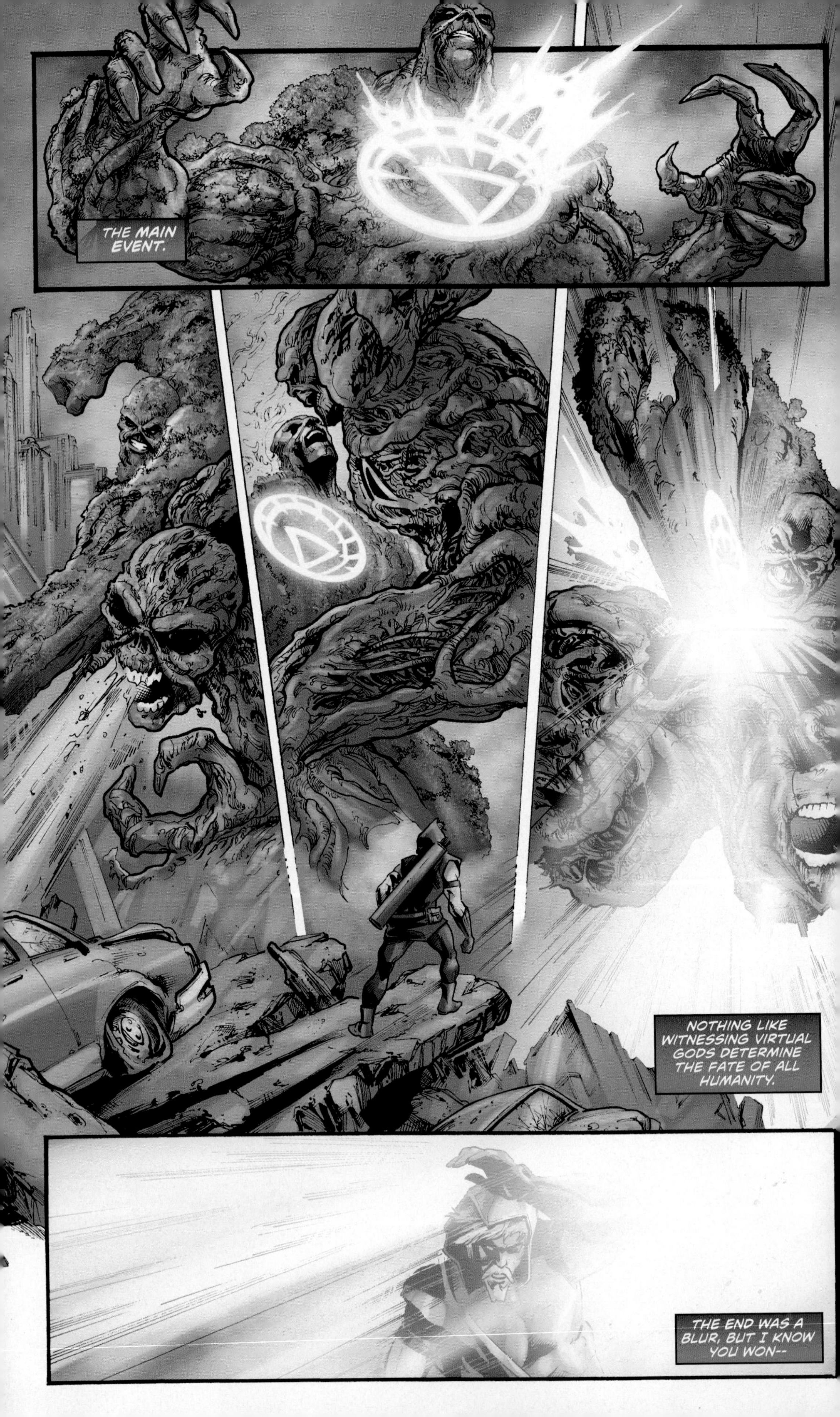
THE MAIN EVENT.
NOTHING LIKE WITNESSING VIRTUAL GODS DETERMINE THE FATE OF ALL HUMANITY.
THE END WAS A BLUR, BUT I KNOW YOU WON--

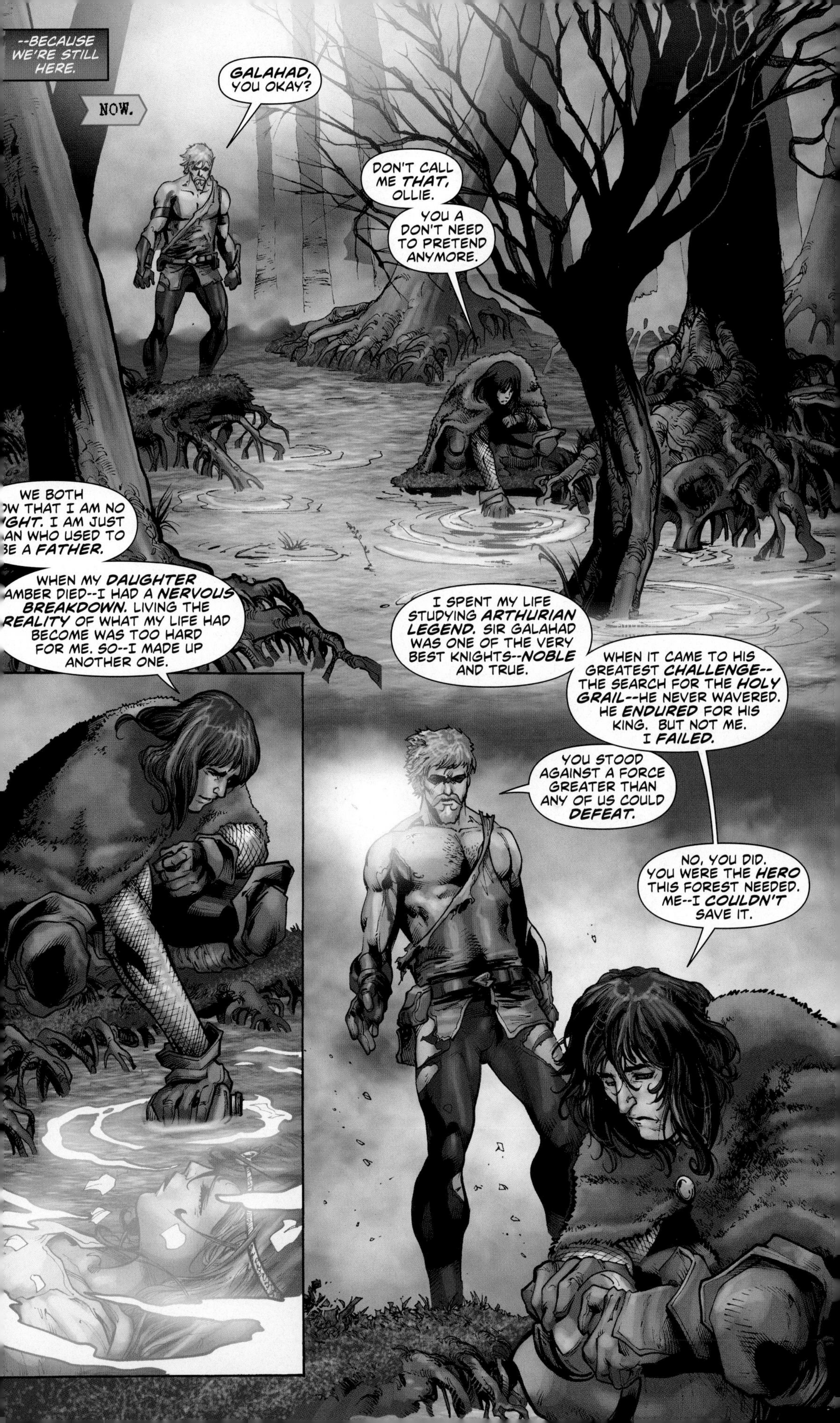

--BECAUSE WE'RE STILL HERE.
NOW.
GALAHAD, YOU OKAY?
DON'T CALL ME THAT, OLLIE.
YOU A DON'T NEED TO PRETEND ANYMORE.
WE BOTH OW THAT I AM NO IGHT. I AM JUST AN WHO USED TO E A FATHER.
WHEN MY DAUGHTER AMBER DIED--I HAD A NERVOUS BREAKDOWN. LIVING THE REALITY OF WHAT MY LIFE HAD BECOME WAS TOO HARD FOR ME. SO--I MADE UP ANOTHER ONE.
I SPENT MY LIFE STUDYING ARTHURIAN LEGEND. SIR GALAHAD WAS ONE OF THE VERY BEST KNIGHTS--NOBLE AND TRUE.
WHEN IT CAME TO HIS GREATEST CHALLENGE-- THE SEARCH FOR THE HOLY GRAIL--HE NEVER WAVERED. HE ENDURED FOR HIS KING. BUT NOT ME. I FAILED.
YOU STOOD AGAINST A FORCE GREATER THAN ANY OF US COULD DEFEAT.
NO, YOU DID. YOU WERE THE HERO THIS FOREST NEEDED. ME--I COULDN'T SAVE IT.

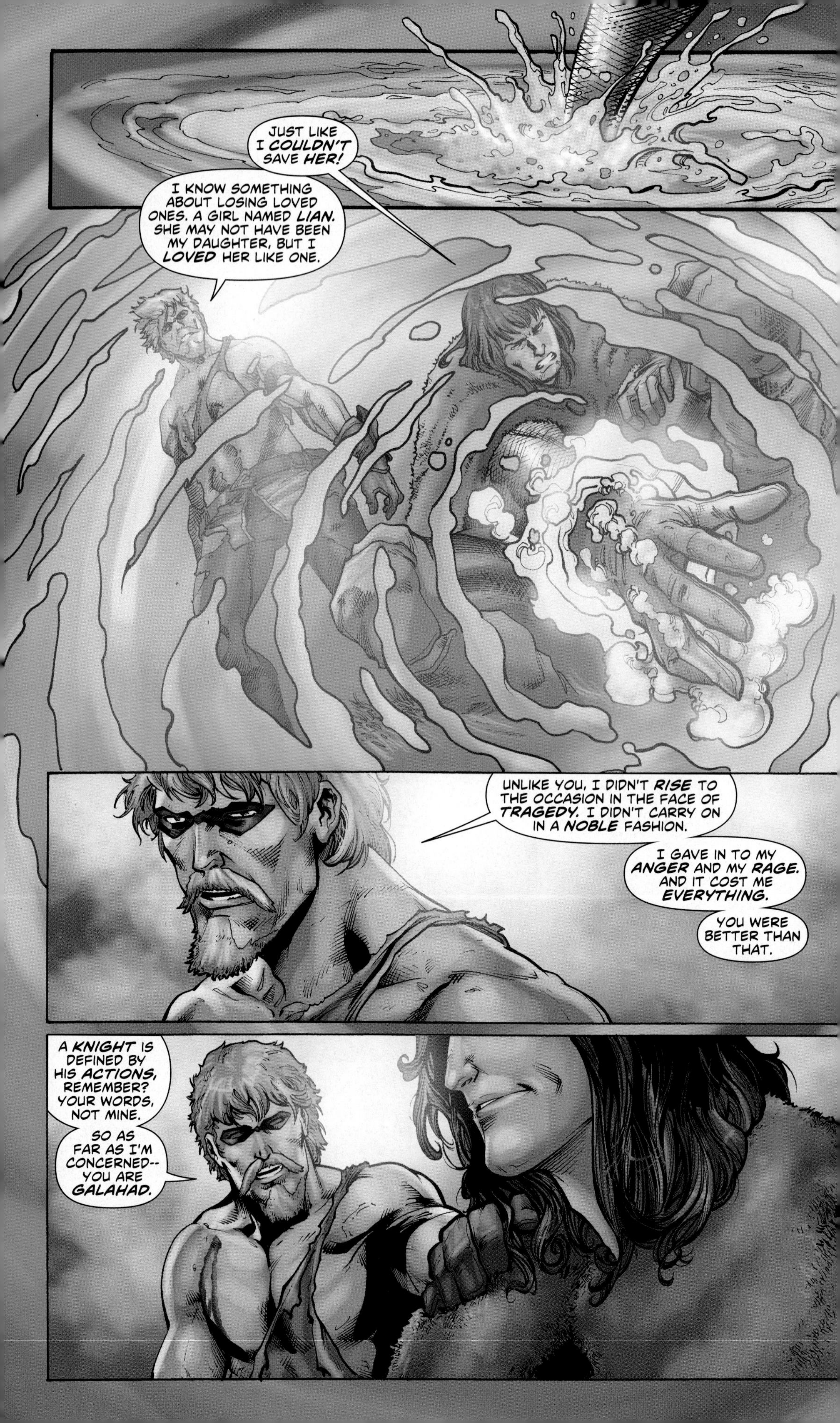
JUST LIKE I COULDN'T SAVE HER!
I KNOW SOMETHING ABOUT LOSING LOVED ONES. A GIRL NAMED LIAN. SHE MAY NOT HAVE BEEN MY DAUGHTER, BUT I LOVED HER LIKE ONE.
UNLIKE YOU, I DIDN'T RISE TO THE OCCASION IN THE FACE OF TRAGEDY. I DIDN'T CARRY ON IN A NOBLE FASHION.
I GAVE IN TO MY ANGER AND MY RAGE. AND IT COST ME EVERYTHING.
YOU WERE BETTER THAN THAT.
A KNIGHT IS DEFINED BY HIS ACTIONS, REMEMBER? YOUR WORDS, NOT MINE.
SO AS FAR AS I'M CONCERNED-- YOU ARE GALAHAD.

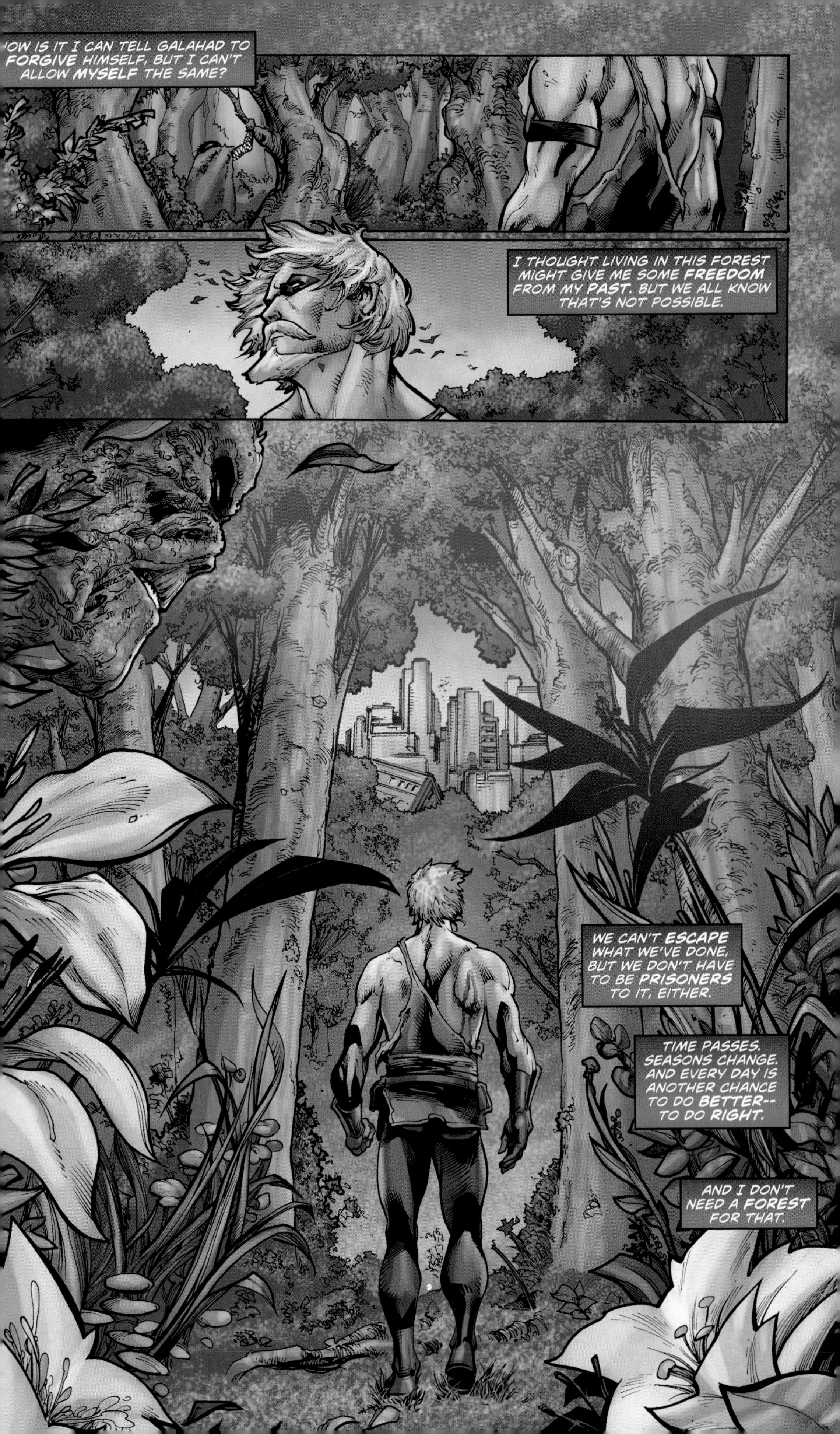
HOW IS IT I CAN TELL GALAHAD TO FORGIVE HIMSELF, BUT I CAN'T ALLOW MYSELF THE SAME?
I THOUGHT LIVING IN THIS FOREST MIGHT GIVE ME SOME FREEDOM FROM MY PAST. BUT WE ALL KNOW THAT'S NOT POSSIBLE.
WE CAN'T ESCAPE WHAT WE'VE DONE, BUT WE DON'T HAVE TO BE PRISONERS TO IT, EITHER.
TIME PASSES. SEASONS CHANGE. AND EVERY DAY IS ANOTHER CHANCE TO DO BETTER-- TO DO RIGHT.
AND I DON'T NEED A FOREST FOR THAT.

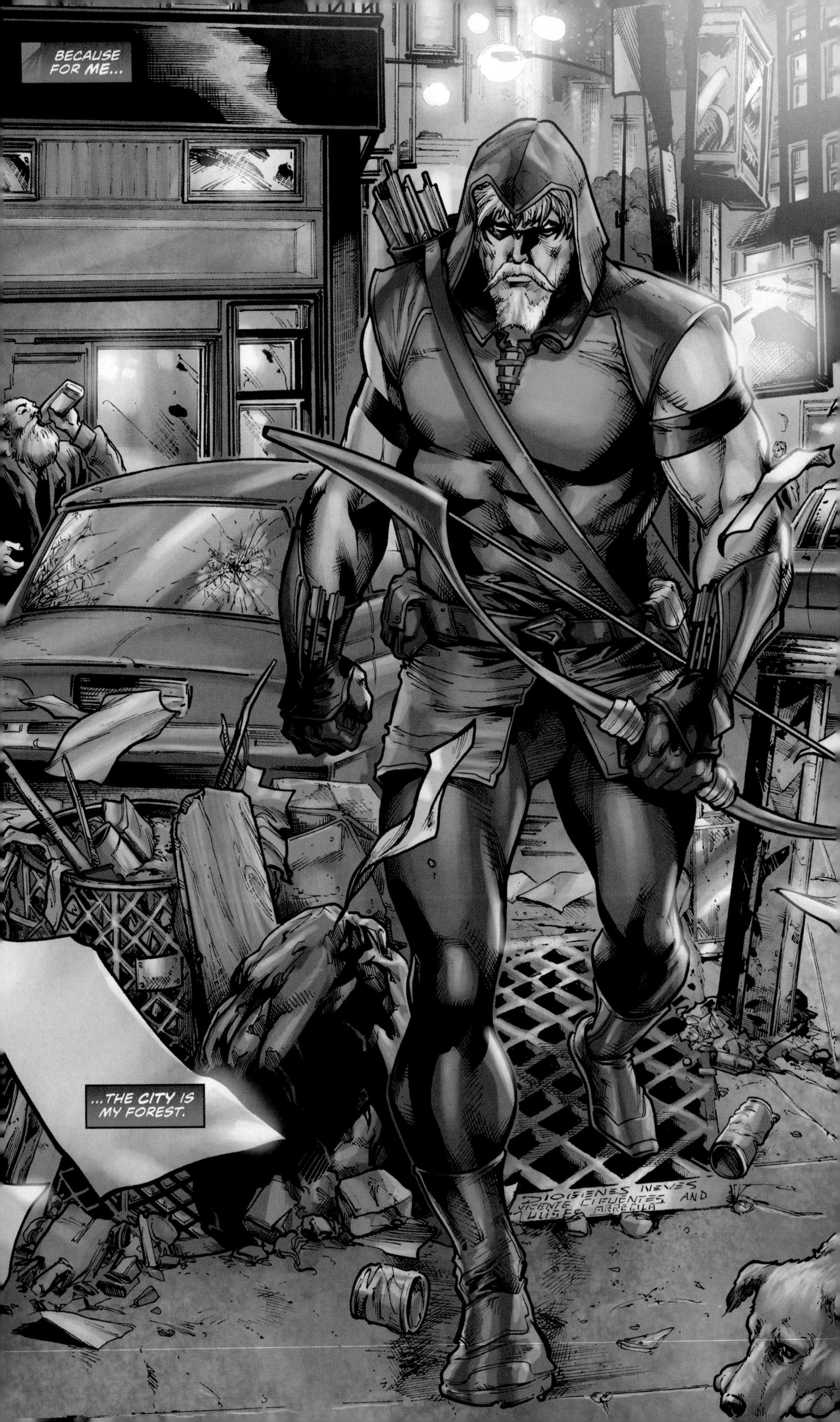
BECAUSE FOR ME...
DIOGENES NEVES
VICENTE CIFUENTES AND
ULISES ARREOLA
...THE CITY IS MY FOREST.

Cover by Josh Middleton

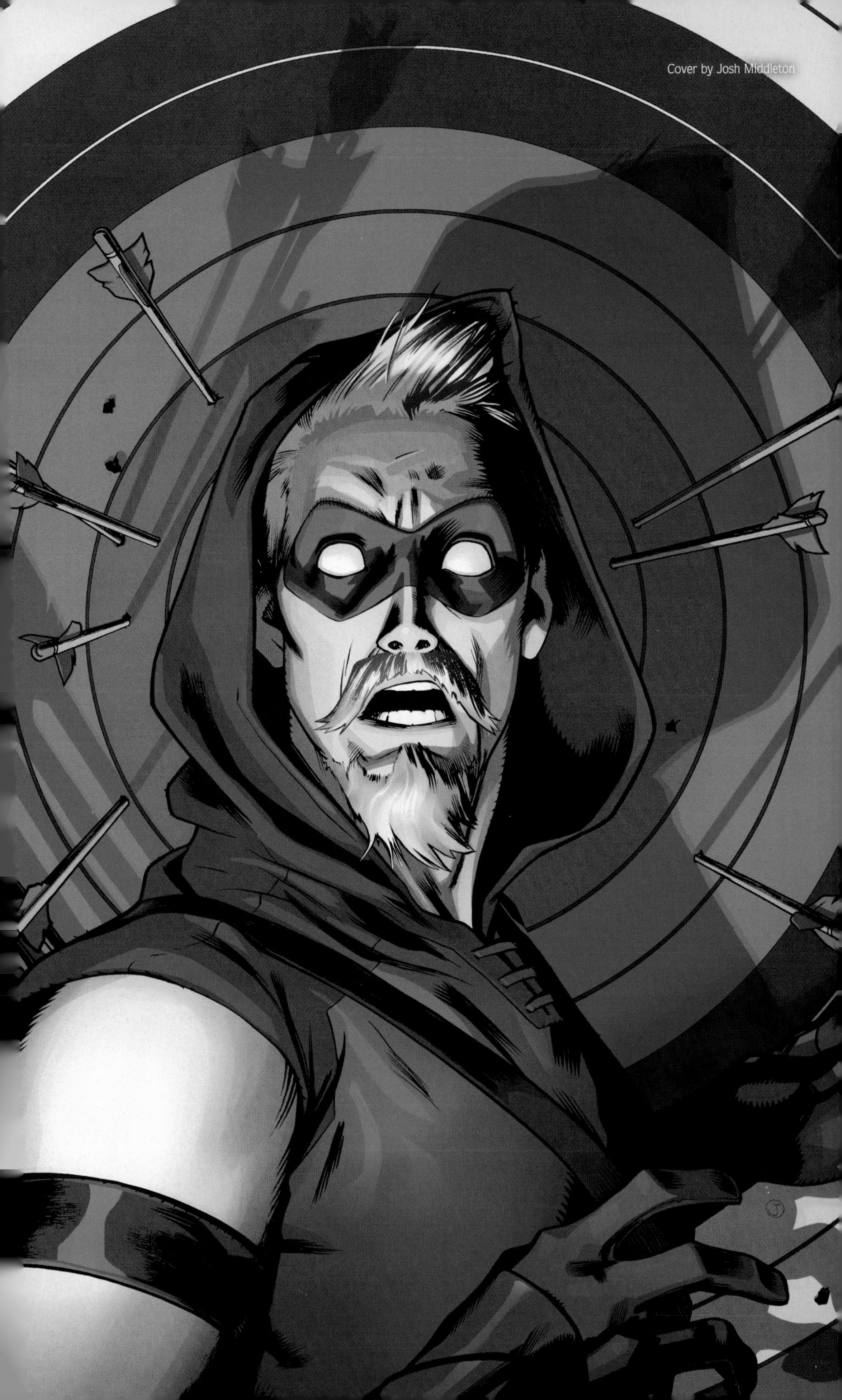

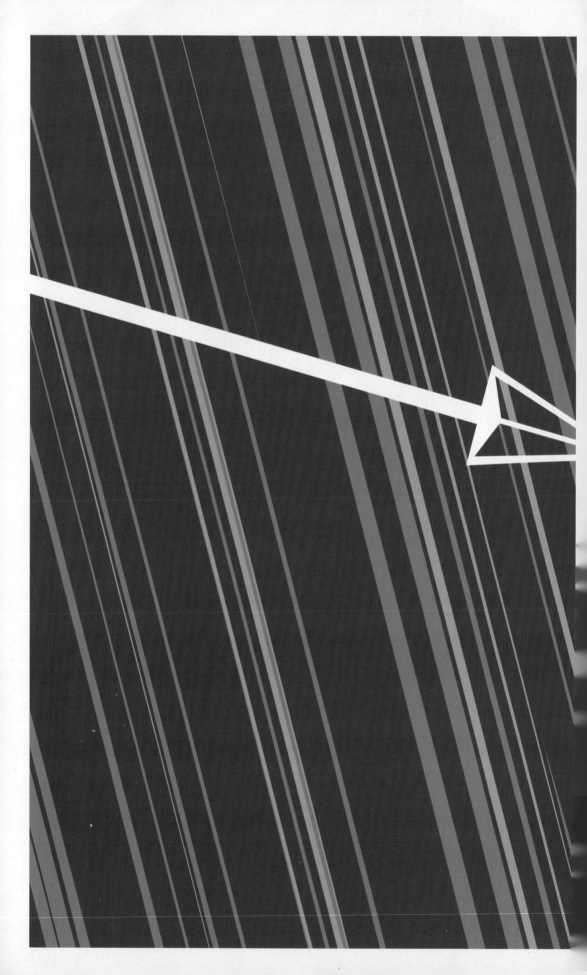

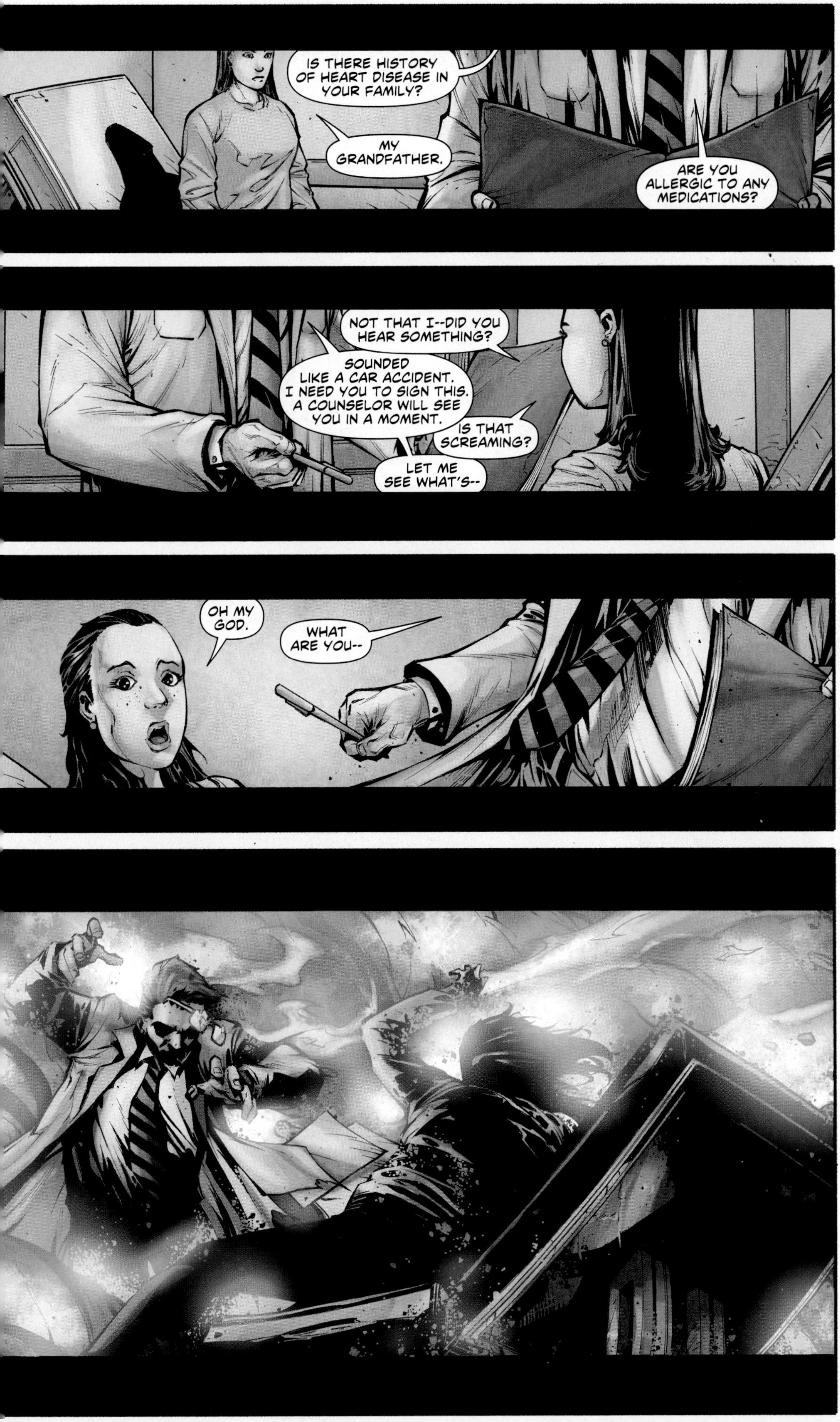
IS THERE HISTORY OF HEART DISEASE IN YOUR FAMILY?
MY GRANDFATHER.
ARE YOU ALLERGIC TO ANY MEDICATIONS?
NOT THAT I--DID YOU HEAR SOMETHING?
SOUNDED LIKE A CAR ACCIDENT. I NEED YOU TO SIGN THIS. A COUNSELOR WILL SEE YOU IN A MOMENT.
IS THAT SCREAMING?
LET ME SEE WHAT'S--
OH MY GOD.
WHAT ARE YOU--

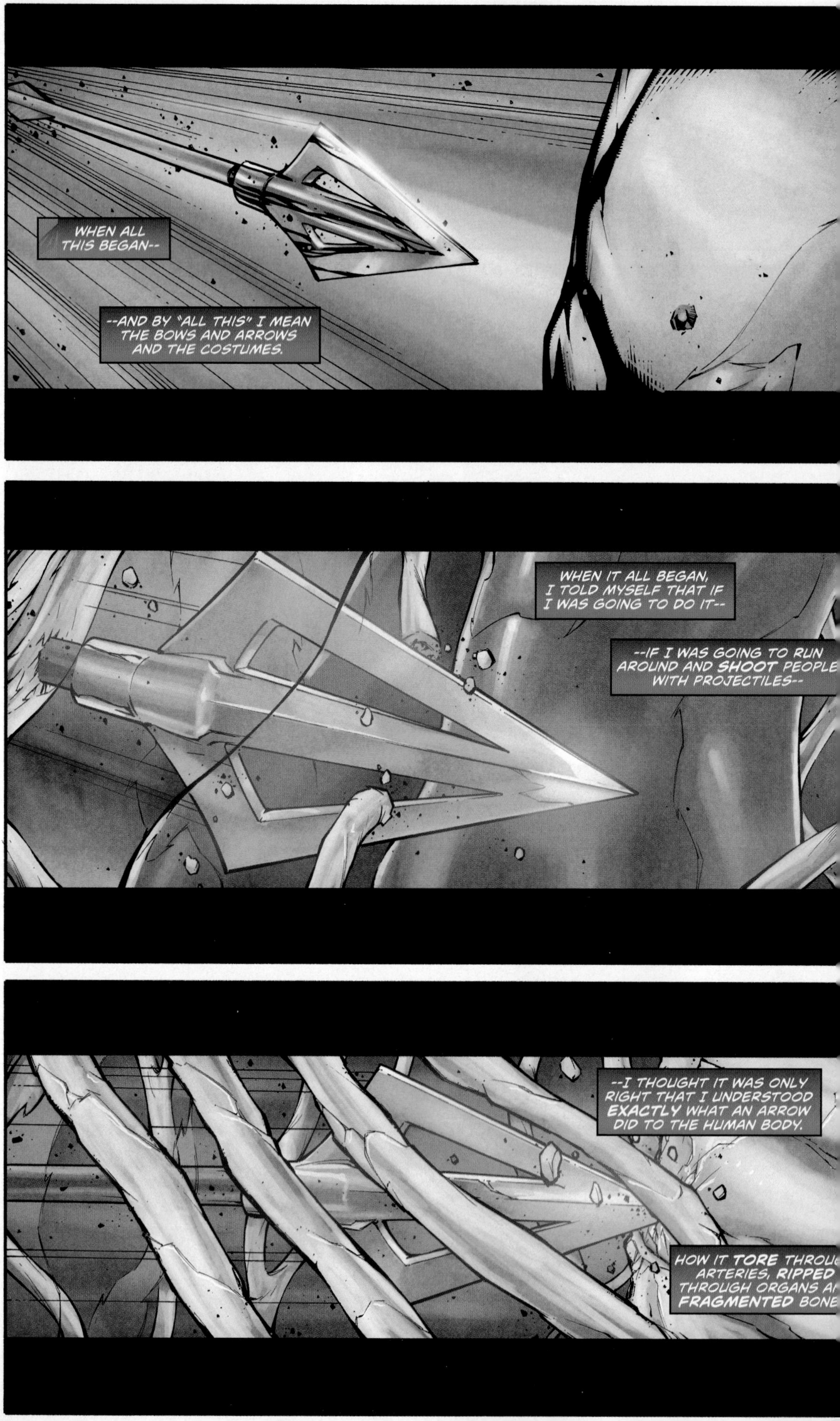
WHEN ALL THIS BEGAN--
--AND BY "ALL THIS" I MEAN THE BOWS AND ARROWS AND THE COSTUMES.
WHEN IT ALL BEGAN, I TOLD MYSELF THAT IF I WAS GOING TO DO IT--
--IF I WAS GOING TO RUN AROUND AND SHOOT PEOPLE WITH PROJECTILES--
--I THOUGHT IT WAS ONLY RIGHT THAT I UNDERSTOOD EXACTLY WHAT AN ARROW DID TO THE HUMAN BODY.
HOW IT TORE THROU ARTERIES, RIPPED THROUGH ORGANS A FRAGMENTED BONE

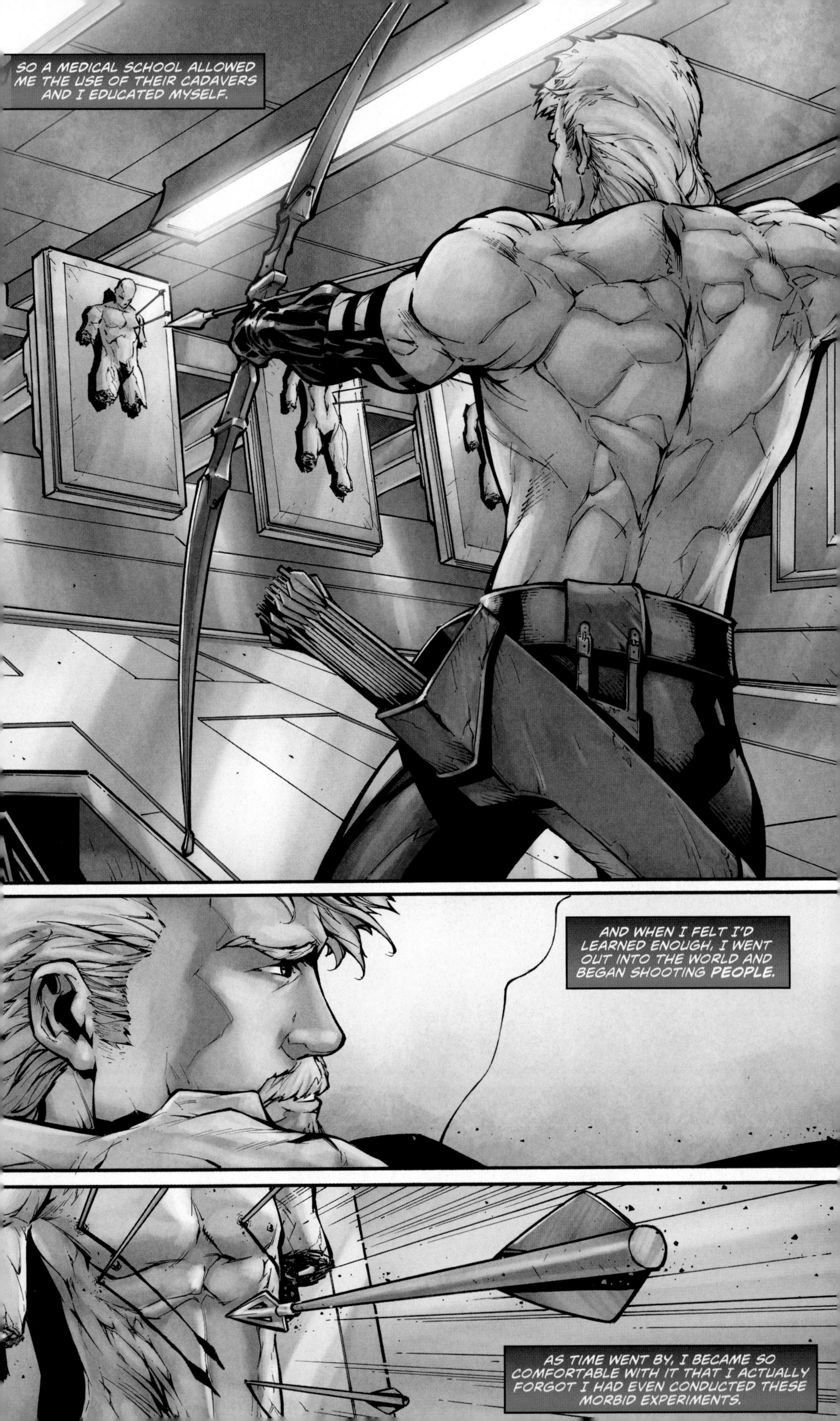
SO A MEDICAL SCHOOL ALLOWED ME THE USE OF THEIR CADAVERS AND I EDUCATED MYSELF.
AND WHEN I FELT I'D LEARNED ENOUGH, I WENT OUT INTO THE WORLD AND BEGAN SHOOTING PEOPLE.
AS TIME WENT BY, I BECAME SO COMFORTABLE WITH IT THAT I ACTUALLY FORGOT I HAD EVEN CONDUCTED THESE MORBID EXPERIMENTS.

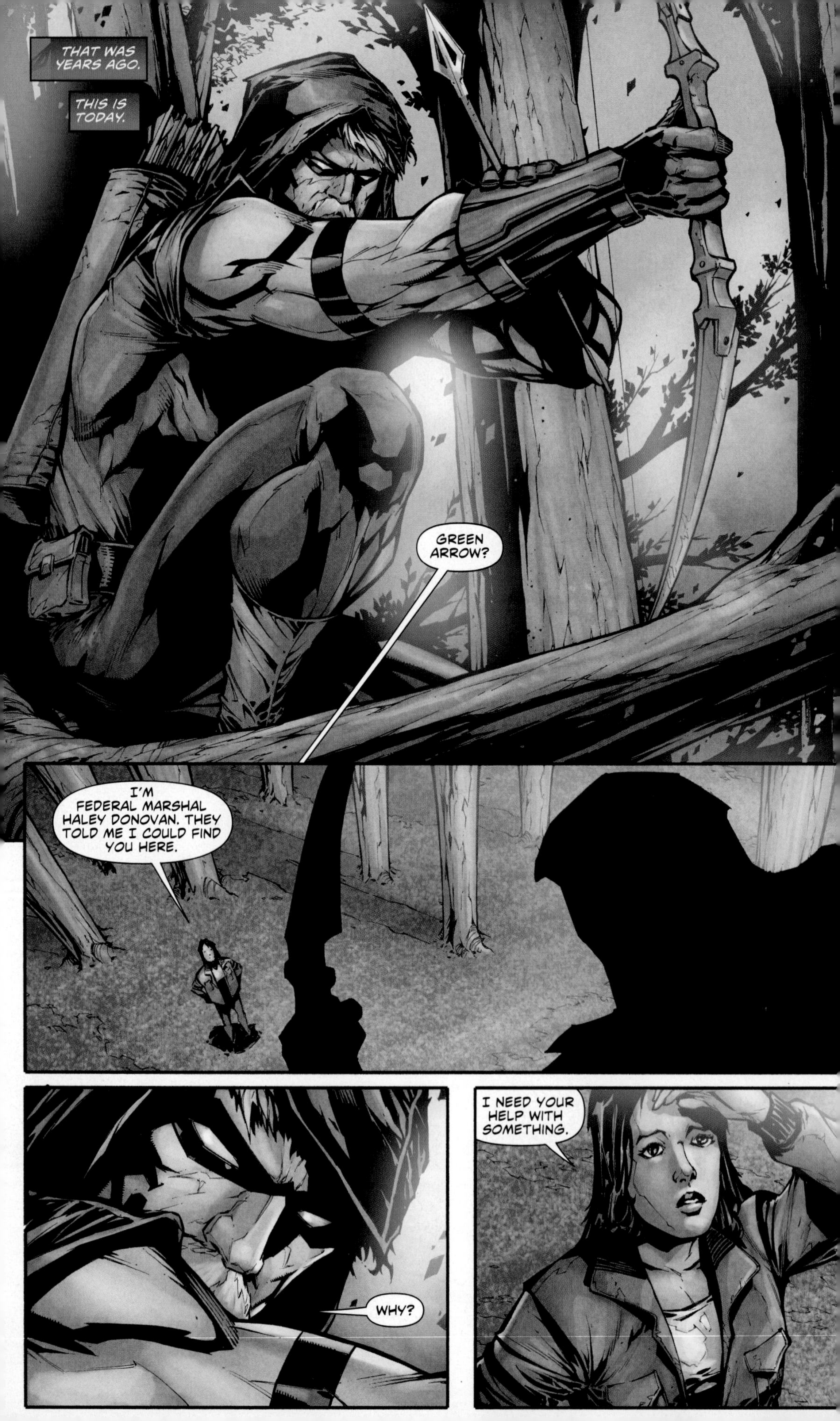
THAT WAS YEARS AGO.
THIS IS TODAY.
GREEN ARROW?
I'M FEDERAL MARSHAL HALEY DONOVAN. THEY TOLD ME I COULD FIND YOU HERE.
WHY?
I NEED YOUR HELP WITH SOMETHING.

SOMETIMES I MEET PEOPLE AND RIGHT FROM THE START I KNOW THEY'RE GOING TO BE A PROBLEM.

I KNOW RIGHT WHEN I SEE THEIR EYES THEY AREN'T JUST LOWLIFES WITH HALF-BAKED SCHEMES.

SOME MIGHT CALL THEM FUTURE ARCHENEMIES.

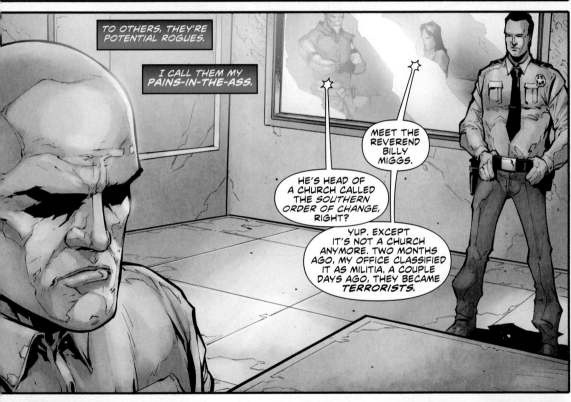

TO OTHERS, THEY'RE POTENTIAL ROGUES.

I CALL THEM MY PAINS-IN-THE-ASS.

MEET THE REVEREND BILLY MIGGS.

HE'S HEAD OF A CHURCH CALLED THE SOUTHERN ORDER OF CHANGE, RIGHT?

YUP. EXCEPT IT'S NOT A CHURCH ANYMORE. TWO MONTHS AGO, MY OFFICE CLASSIFIED IT AS MILITIA. A COUPLE DAYS AGO, THEY BECAME TERRORISTS.

"THE REVEREND" ORCHESTRATED THE SIMULTANEOUS ATTACK OF SEVERAL ORGANIZATIONS HE TARGETED AS "SINFUL." NINE PEOPLE WERE KILLED.

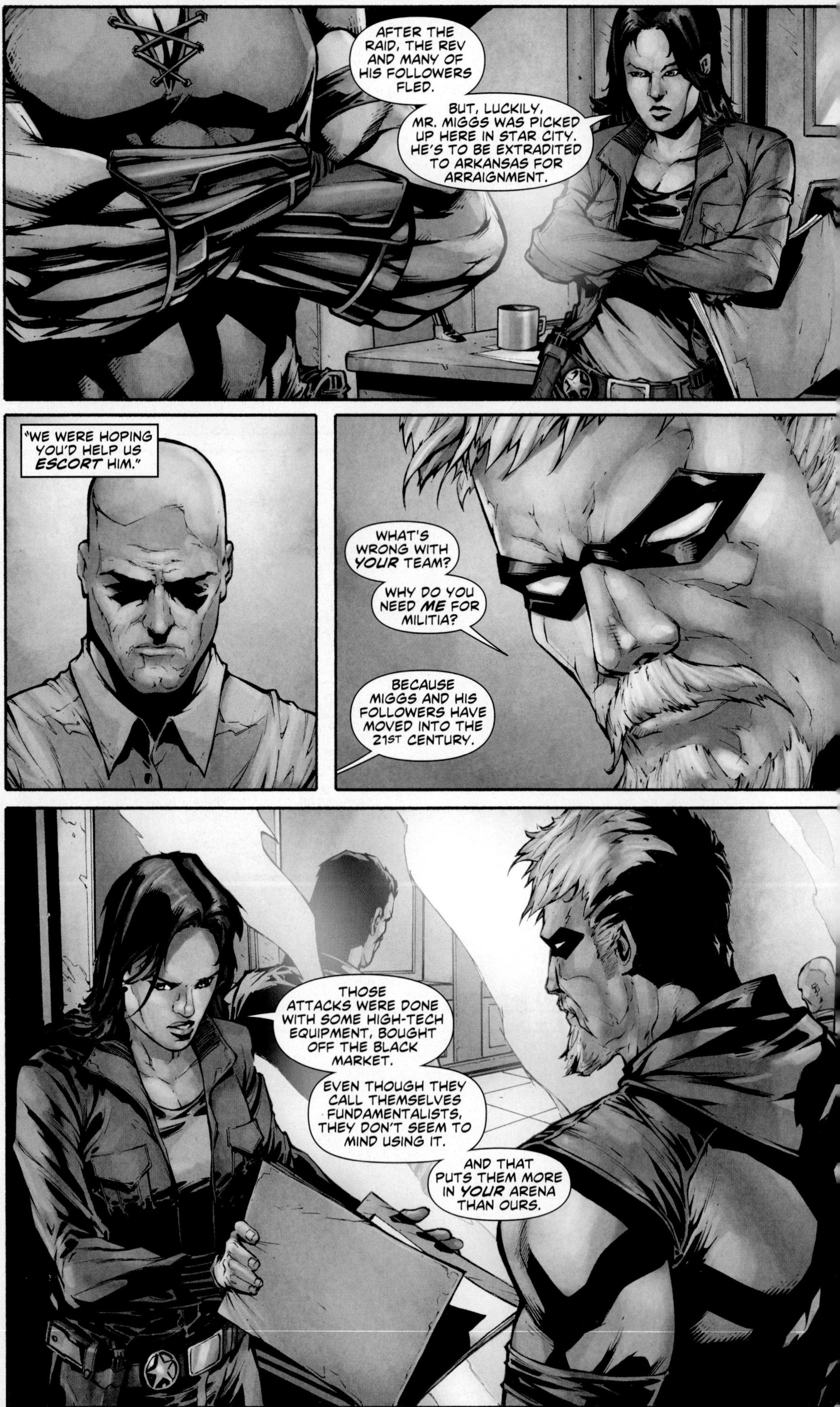
AFTER THE RAID, THE REV AND MANY OF HIS FOLLOWERS FLED.
BUT, LUCKILY, MR. MIGGS WAS PICKED UP HERE IN STAR CITY. HE'S TO BE EXTRADITED TO ARKANSAS FOR ARRAIGNMENT.
"WE WERE HOPING YOU'D HELP US *ESCORT* HIM."
WHAT'S WRONG WITH *YOUR* TEAM?
WHY DO YOU NEED *ME* FOR MILITIA?
BECAUSE MIGGS AND HIS FOLLOWERS HAVE MOVED INTO THE 21ST CENTURY.
THOSE ATTACKS WERE DONE WITH SOME HIGH-TECH EQUIPMENT, BOUGHT OFF THE BLACK MARKET.
EVEN THOUGH THEY CALL THEMSELVES FUNDAMENTALISTS, THEY DON'T SEEM TO MIND USING IT.
AND THAT PUTS THEM MORE IN *YOUR* ARENA THAN OURS.

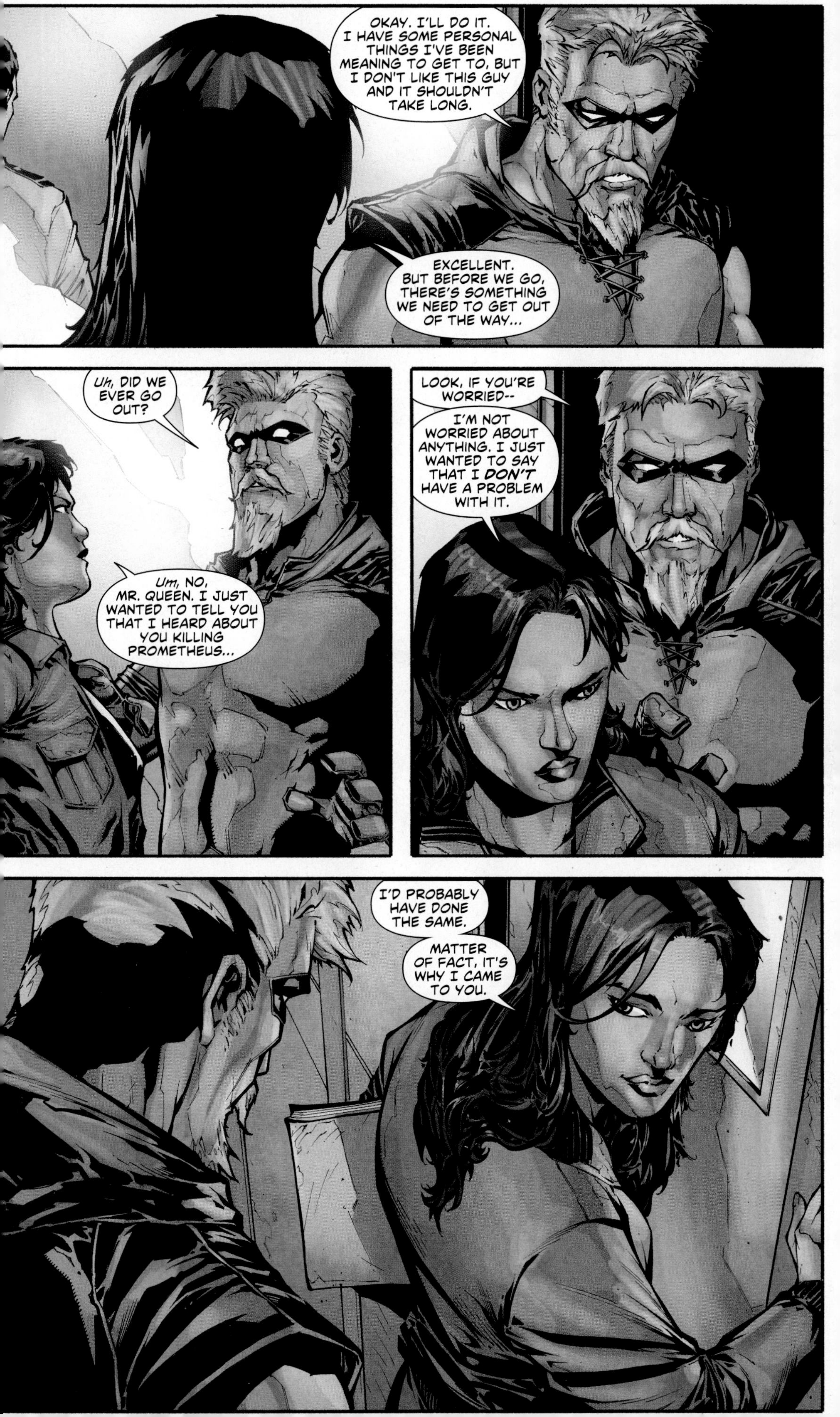
OKAY. I'LL DO IT. I HAVE SOME PERSONAL THINGS I'VE BEEN MEANING TO GET TO, BUT I DON'T LIKE THIS GUY AND IT SHOULDN'T TAKE LONG.
EXCELLENT. BUT BEFORE WE GO, THERE'S SOMETHING WE NEED TO GET OUT OF THE WAY...
Uh, DID WE EVER GO OUT?
Um, NO, MR. QUEEN. I JUST WANTED TO TELL YOU THAT I HEARD ABOUT YOU KILLING PROMETHEUS...
LOOK, IF YOU'RE WORRIED--
I'M NOT WORRIED ABOUT ANYTHING. I JUST WANTED TO SAY THAT I ***DON'T*** HAVE A PROBLEM WITH IT.
I'D PROBABLY HAVE DONE THE SAME.
MATTER OF FACT, IT'S WHY I CAME TO YOU.

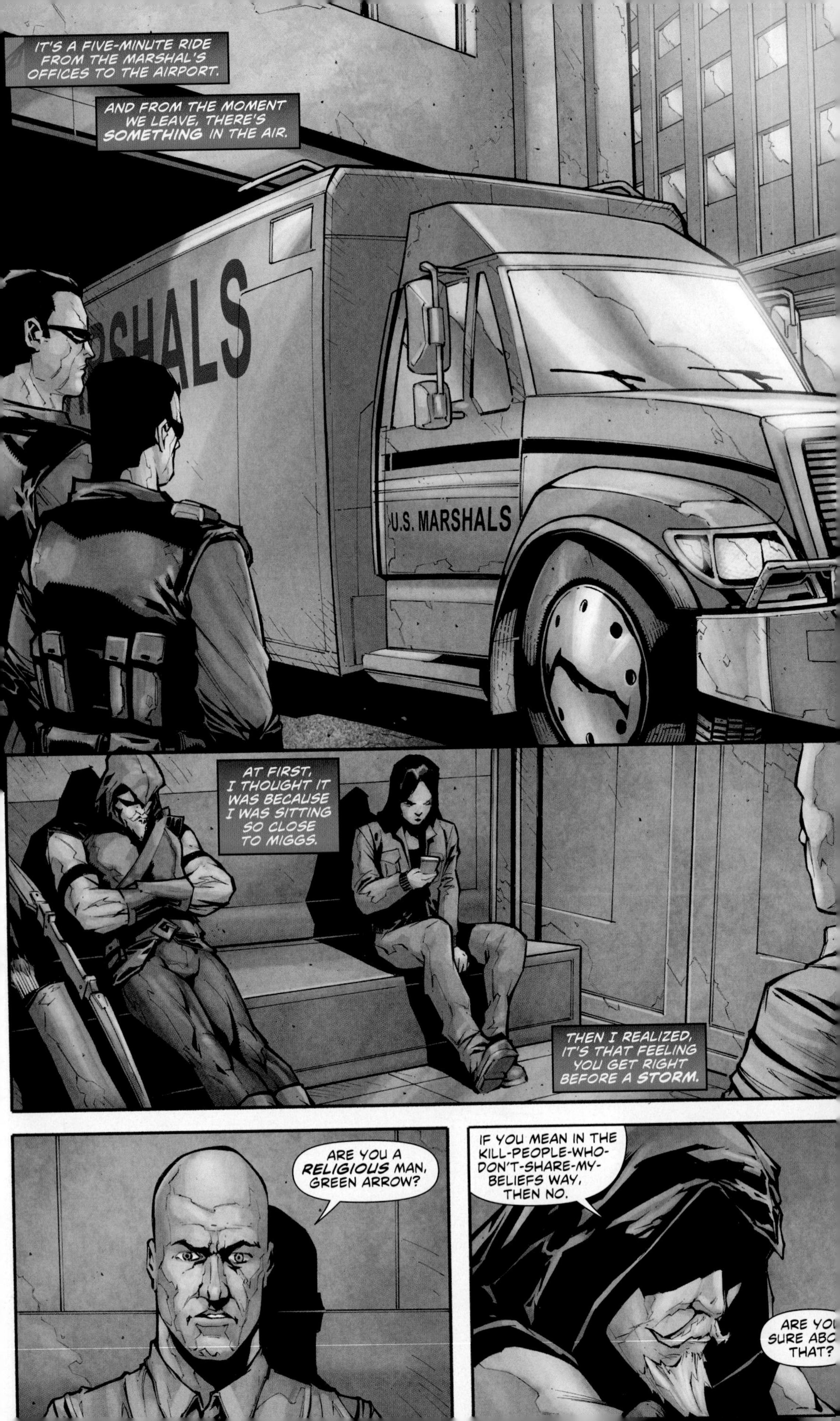

IT'S A FIVE-MINUTE RIDE FROM THE MARSHAL'S OFFICES TO THE AIRPORT.
AND FROM THE MOMENT WE LEAVE, THERE'S SOMETHING IN THE AIR.
RSHALS
U.S. MARSHALS
AT FIRST, I THOUGHT IT WAS BECAUSE I WAS SITTING SO CLOSE TO MIGGS.
THEN I REALIZED, IT'S THAT FEELING YOU GET RIGHT BEFORE A STORM.
ARE YOU A RELIGIOUS MAN, GREEN ARROW?
IF YOU MEAN IN THE KILL-PEOPLE-WHO-DON'T-SHARE-MY-BELIEFS WAY, THEN NO.

I'M NOT GOING TO DEFEND MYSELF TO YOU.

BECAUSE YOU DON'T HAVE TO. YOU AND THE MURDERERS ARE WINNING THE WAR.

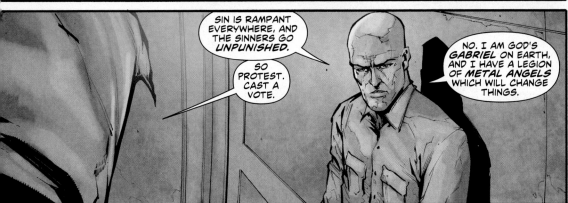

SIN IS RAMPANT EVERYWHERE, AND THE SINNERS GO *UNPUNISHED*.

SO PROTEST. CAST A VOTE.

NO. I AM GOD'S *GABRIEL* ON EARTH, AND I HAVE A LEGION OF *METAL ANGELS* WHICH WILL CHANGE THINGS.

THEY WILL SMITE OUR ENEMIES WITH FIERY WINGS, THROWING LASER-GUIDED SPEARS, AND SLINGING 7.62 MILLIMETER STONES AT 400 ROUNDS PER MINUTE.

MIGGS, IT'S TWO MORE MINUTES TO THE AIRPORT. DO YOU THINK YOU COULD SPARE US THE SERMON?

I'M DONE, MS. DONOVAN. BESIDES...

FWOOSH

...THEY'RE HERE.

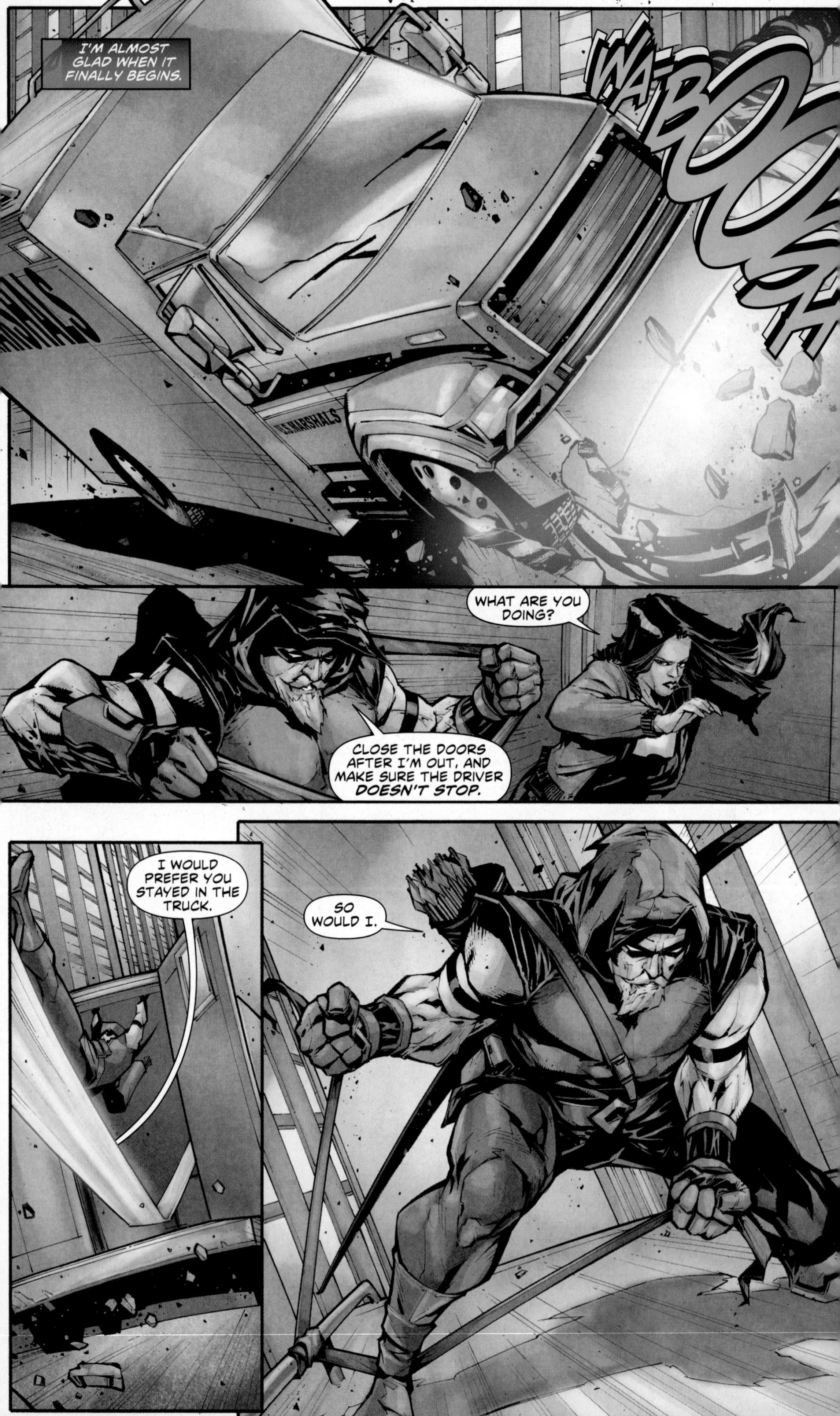
I'M ALMOST GLAD WHEN IT FINALLY BEGINS.
WA-BOOOM
U.S. MARSHALS
WHAT ARE YOU DOING?
CLOSE THE DOORS AFTER I'M OUT, AND MAKE SURE THE DRIVER DOESN'T STOP.
I WOULD PREFER YOU STAYED IN THE TRUCK.
SO WOULD I.

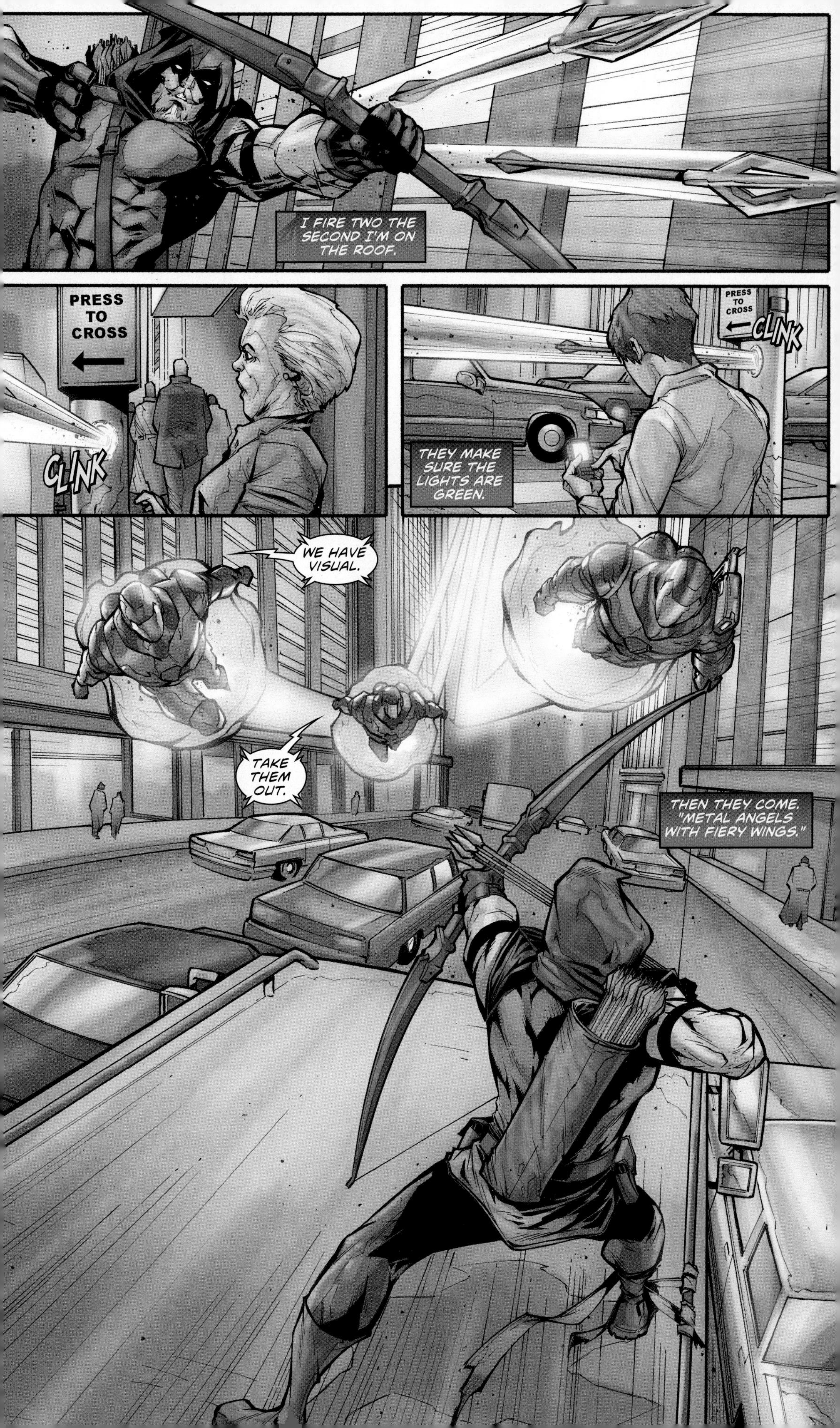
I FIRE TWO THE SECOND I'M ON THE ROOF.
PRESS TO CROSS
CLINK
PRESS TO CROSS
CLINK
THEY MAKE SURE THE LIGHTS ARE GREEN.
WE HAVE VISUAL.
TAKE THEM OUT.
THEN THEY COME. "METAL ANGELS WITH FIERY WINGS."

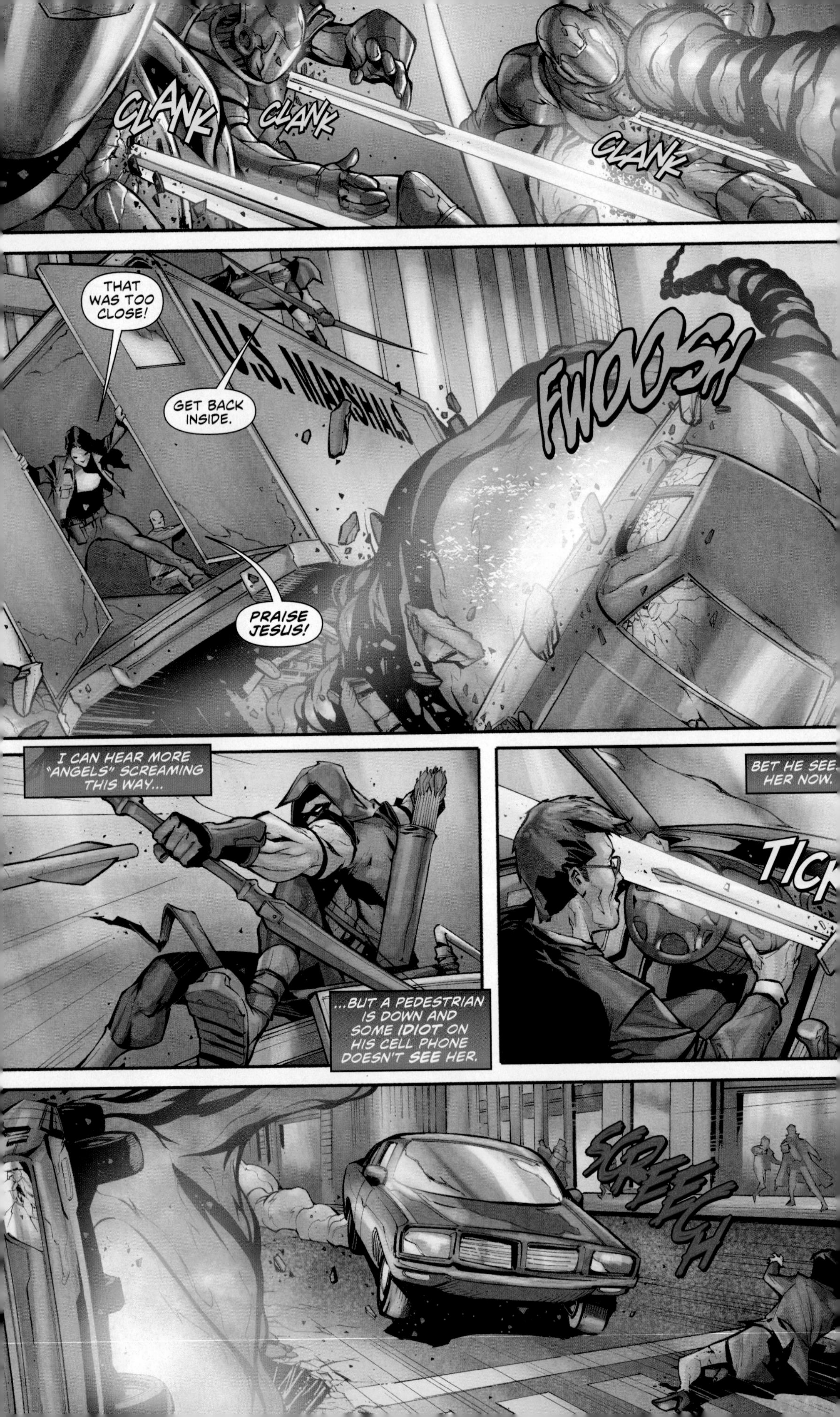
CLANK
CLANK
CLANK
THAT WAS TOO CLOSE!
GET BACK INSIDE.
U.S. MARSHALS
FWOOSH
PRAISE JESUS!
I CAN HEAR MORE "ANGELS" SCREAMING THIS WAY...
...BUT A PEDESTRIAN IS DOWN AND SOME IDIOT ON HIS CELL PHONE DOESN'T SEE HER.
BET HE SEE HER NOW.
TICK
SCREECH

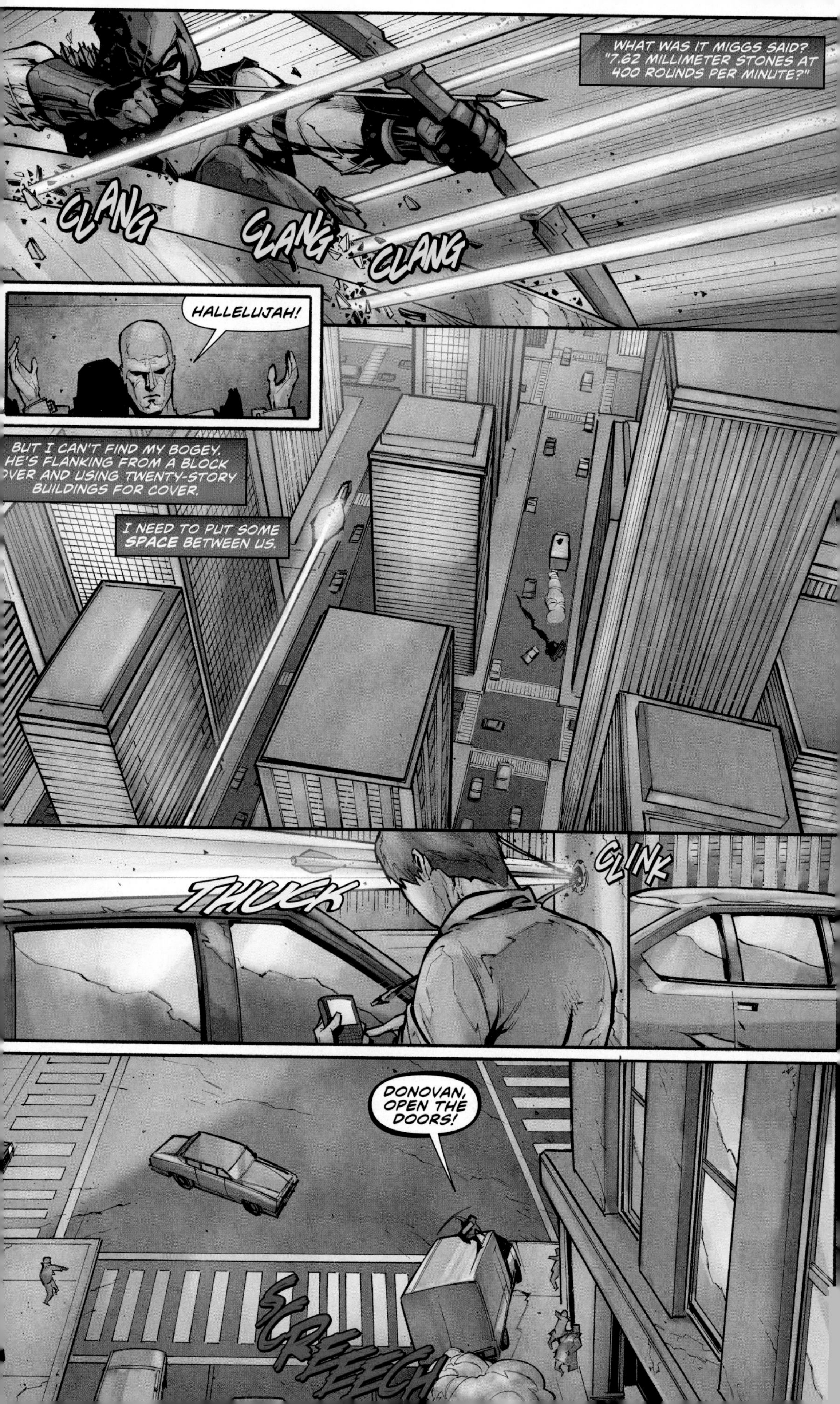
WHAT WAS IT MIGGS SAID? "7.62 MILLIMETER STONES AT 400 ROUNDS PER MINUTE?"
CLANG
CLANG
CLANG
HALLELUJAH!
BUT I CAN'T FIND MY BOGEY. HE'S FLANKING FROM A BLOCK OVER AND USING TWENTY-STORY BUILDINGS FOR COVER.
I NEED TO PUT SOME SPACE BETWEEN US.
THUCK
CLINK
DONOVAN, OPEN THE DOORS!
SCREEEECH

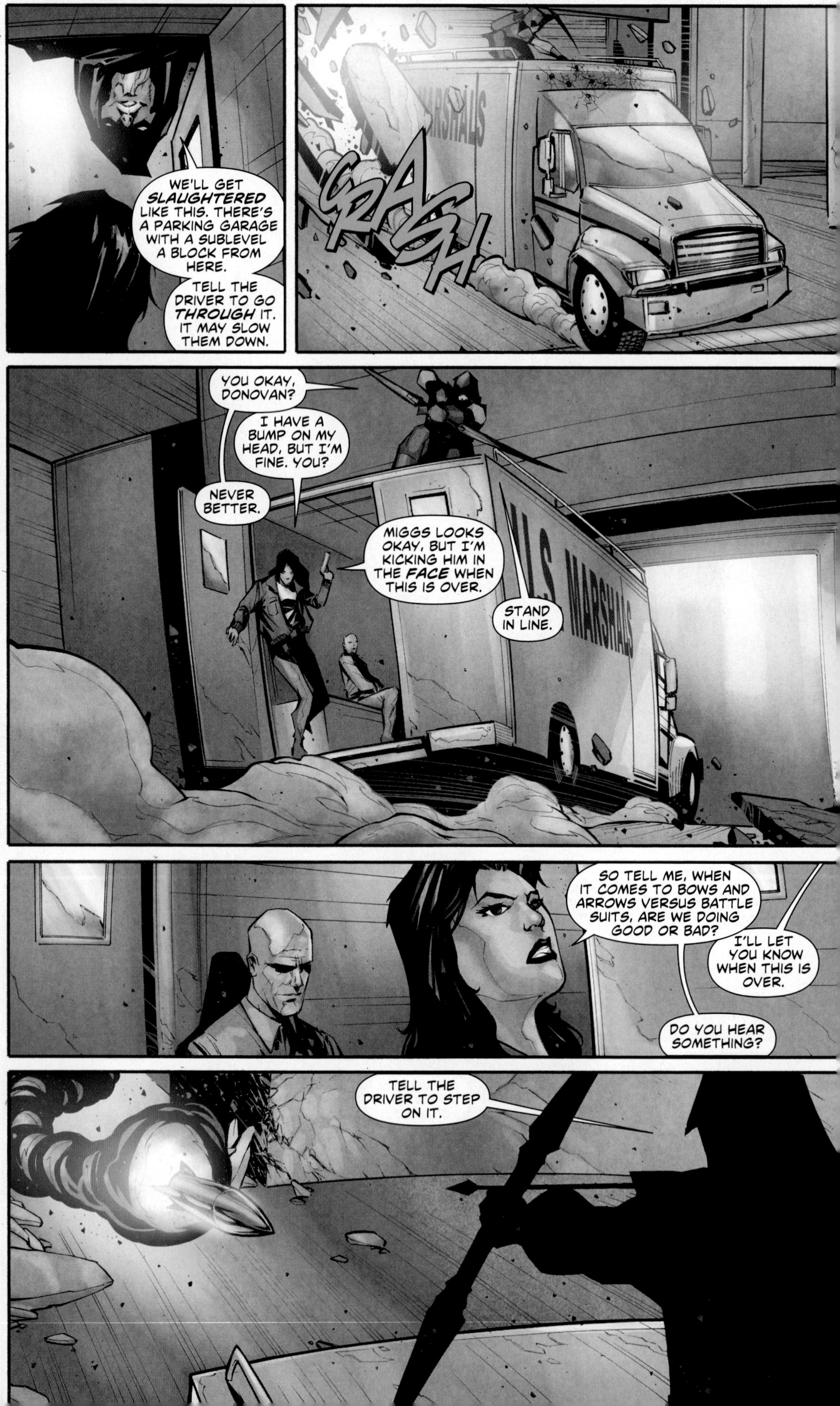
WE'LL GET SLAUGHTERED LIKE THIS. THERE'S A PARKING GARAGE WITH A SUBLEVEL A BLOCK FROM HERE.
TELL THE DRIVER TO GO THROUGH IT. IT MAY SLOW THEM DOWN.
MARSHALS
CRASH
YOU OKAY, DONOVAN?
I HAVE A BUMP ON MY HEAD, BUT I'M FINE. YOU?
NEVER BETTER.
MIGGS LOOKS OKAY, BUT I'M KICKING HIM IN THE FACE WHEN THIS IS OVER.
STAND IN LINE.
U.S. MARSHALS
SO TELL ME, WHEN IT COMES TO BOWS AND ARROWS VERSUS BATTLE SUITS, ARE WE DOING GOOD OR BAD?
I'LL LET YOU KNOW WHEN THIS IS OVER.
DO YOU HEAR SOMETHING?
TELL THE DRIVER TO STEP ON IT.

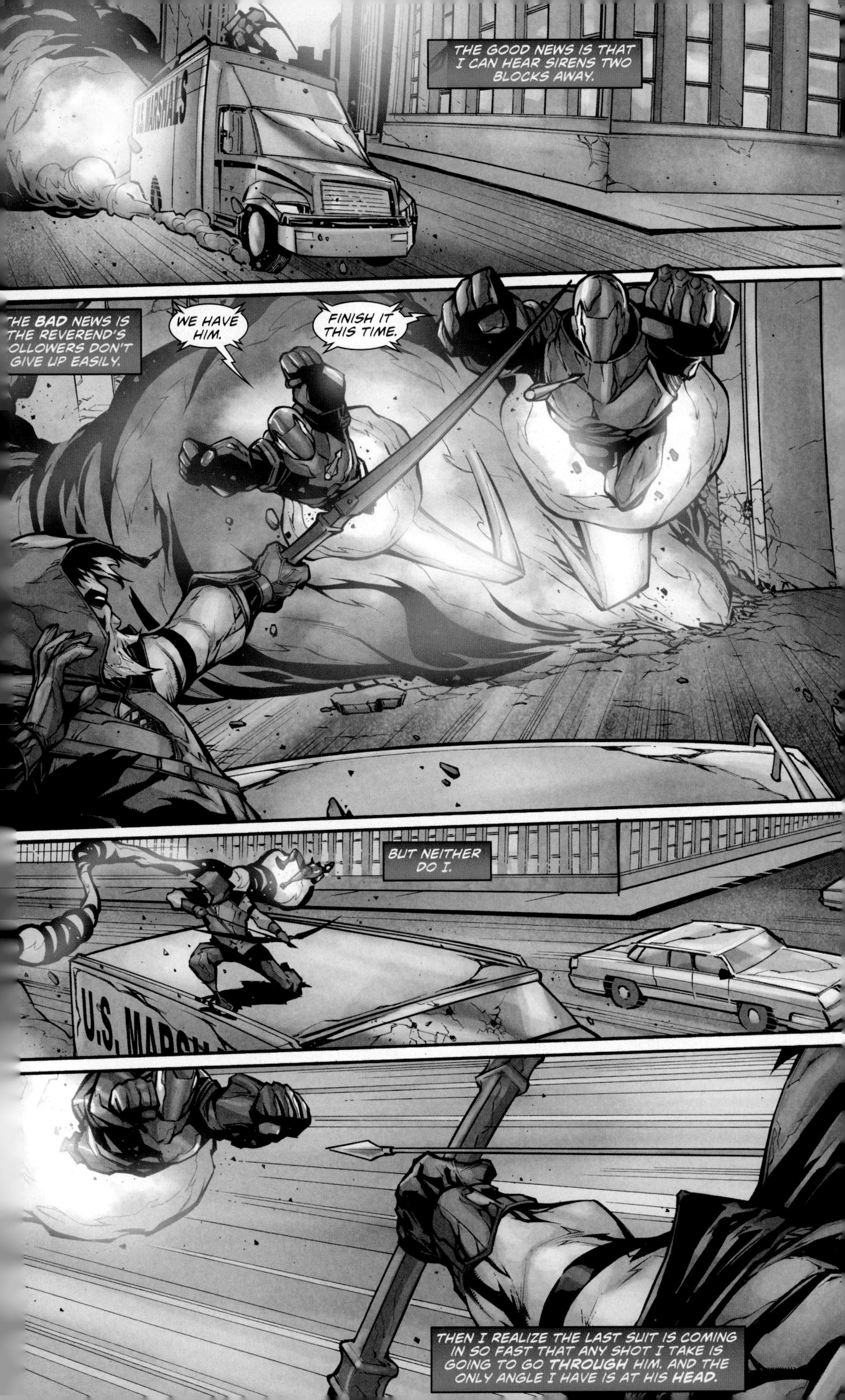
THE GOOD NEWS IS THAT I CAN HEAR SIRENS TWO BLOCKS AWAY.
U.S. MARSHALS
THE BAD NEWS IS THE REVEREND'S FOLLOWERS DON'T GIVE UP EASILY.
WE HAVE HIM.
FINISH IT THIS TIME.
BUT NEITHER DO I.
U.S. MARSH
THEN I REALIZE THE LAST SUIT IS COMING IN SO FAST THAT ANY SHOT I TAKE IS GOING TO GO THROUGH HIM. AND THE ONLY ANGLE I HAVE IS AT HIS HEAD.

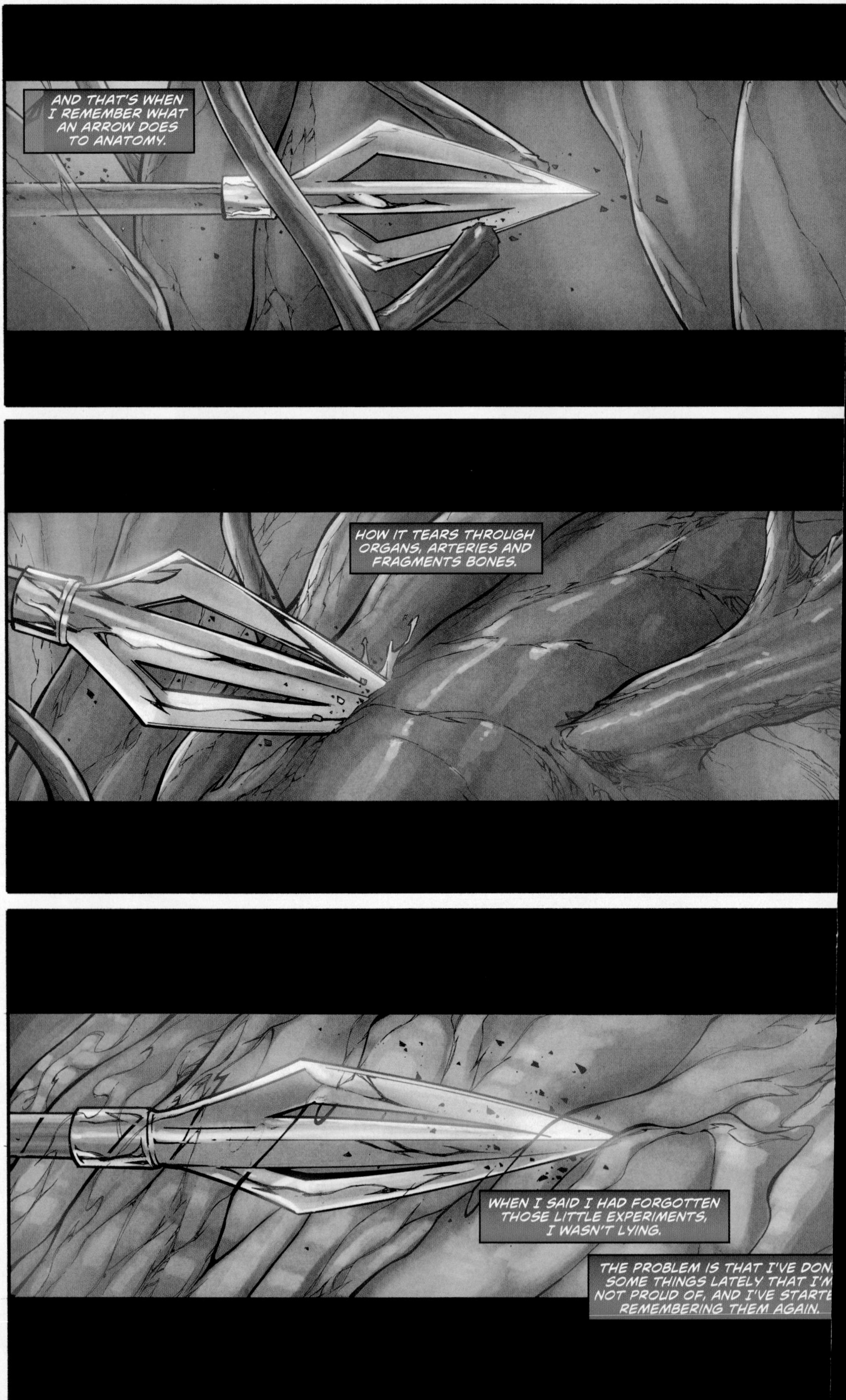
AND THAT'S WHEN I REMEMBER WHAT AN ARROW DOES TO ANATOMY.
HOW IT TEARS THROUGH ORGANS, ARTERIES AND FRAGMENTS BONES.
WHEN I SAID I HAD FORGOTTEN THOSE LITTLE EXPERIMENTS, I WASN'T LYING.
THE PROBLEM IS THAT I'VE DON SOME THINGS LATELY THAT I'M NOT PROUD OF, AND I'VE STARTE REMEMBERING THEM AGAIN.

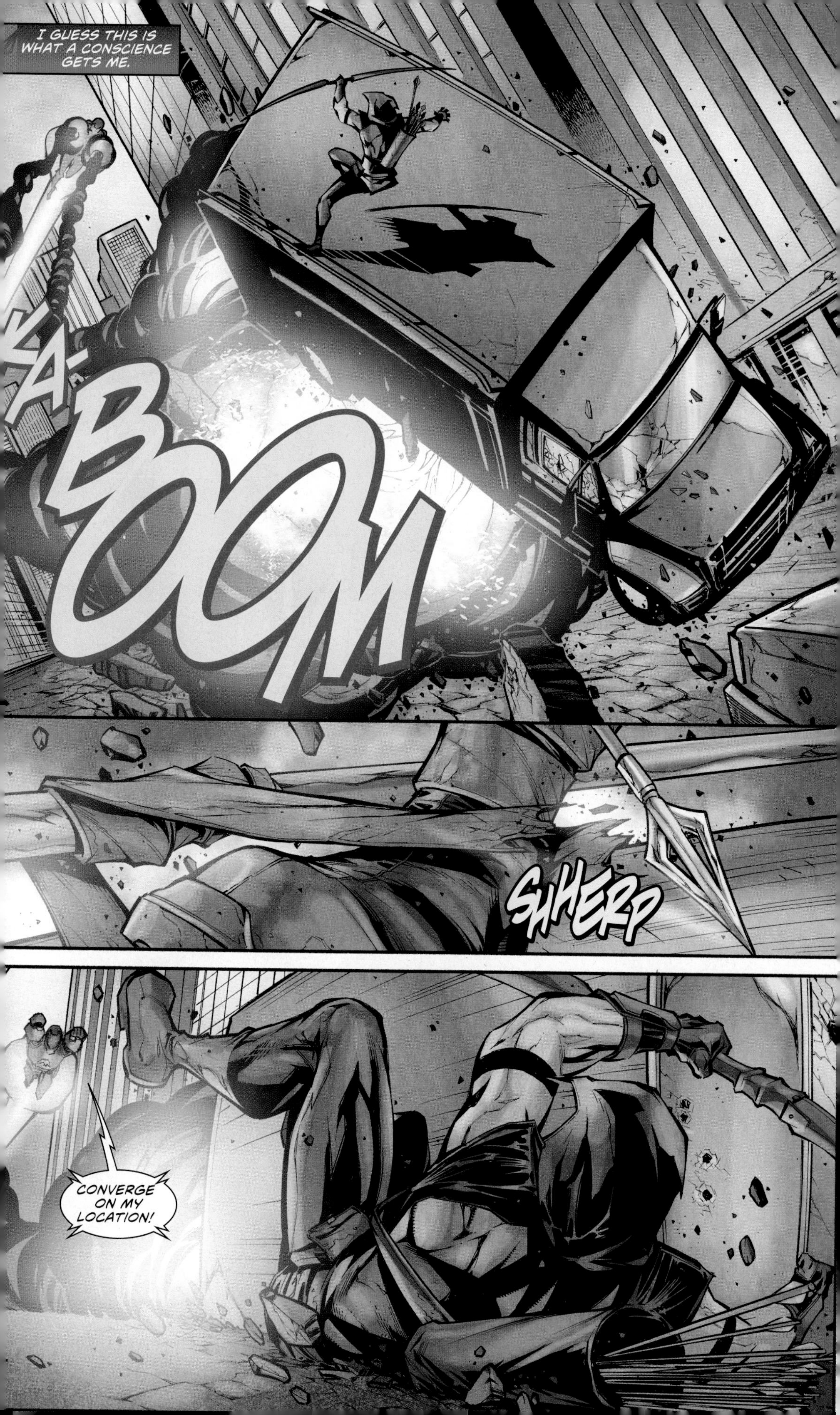
I GUESS THIS IS WHAT A CONSCIENCE GETS ME.
KA-BOOM
SHHERP
CONVERGE ON MY LOCATION!

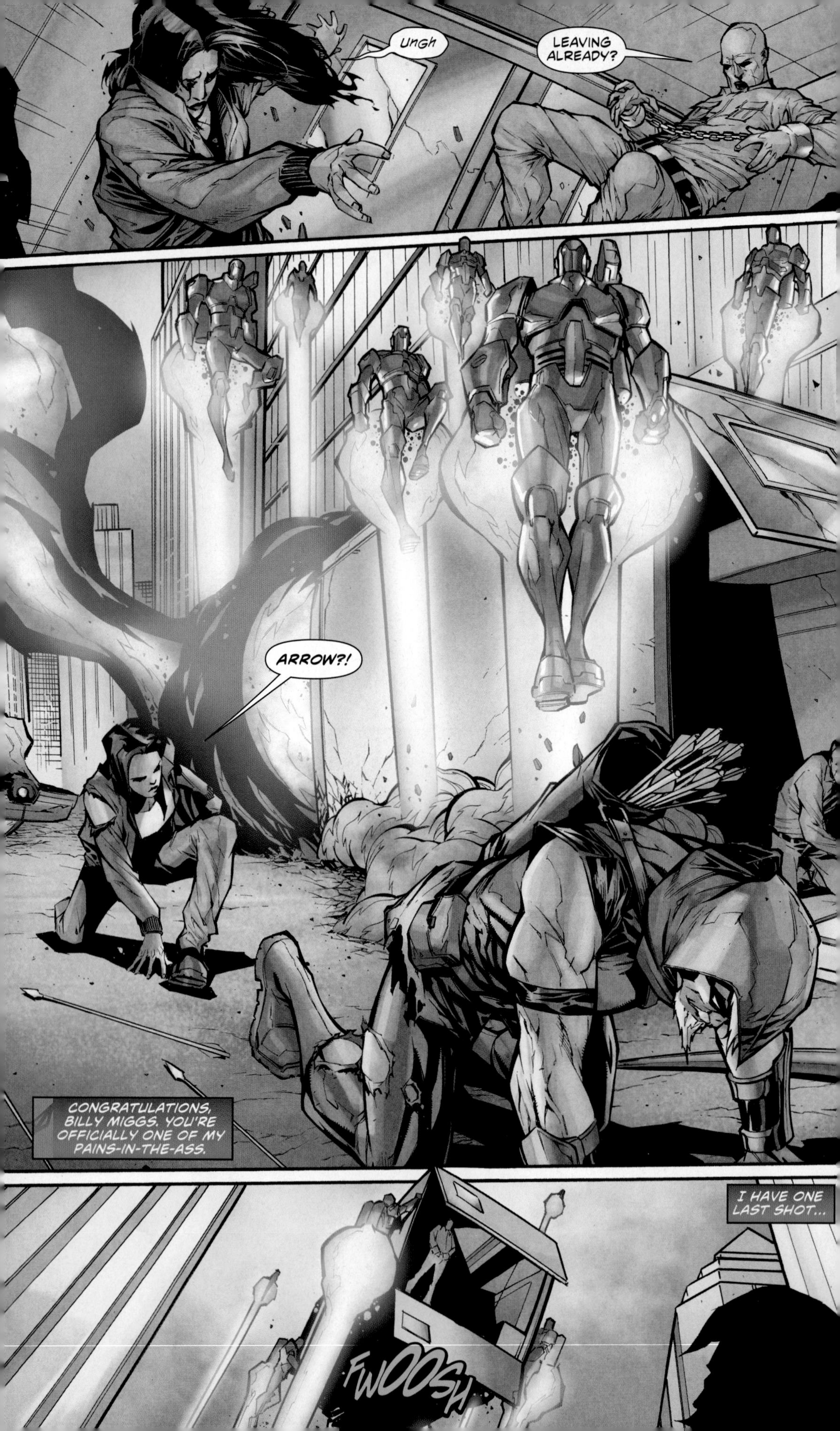

Ungh
LEAVING ALREADY?
ARROW?!
CONGRATULATIONS, BILLY MIGGS. YOU'RE OFFICIALLY ONE OF MY PAINS-IN-THE-ASS.
I HAVE ONE LAST SHOT...
FWOOSH

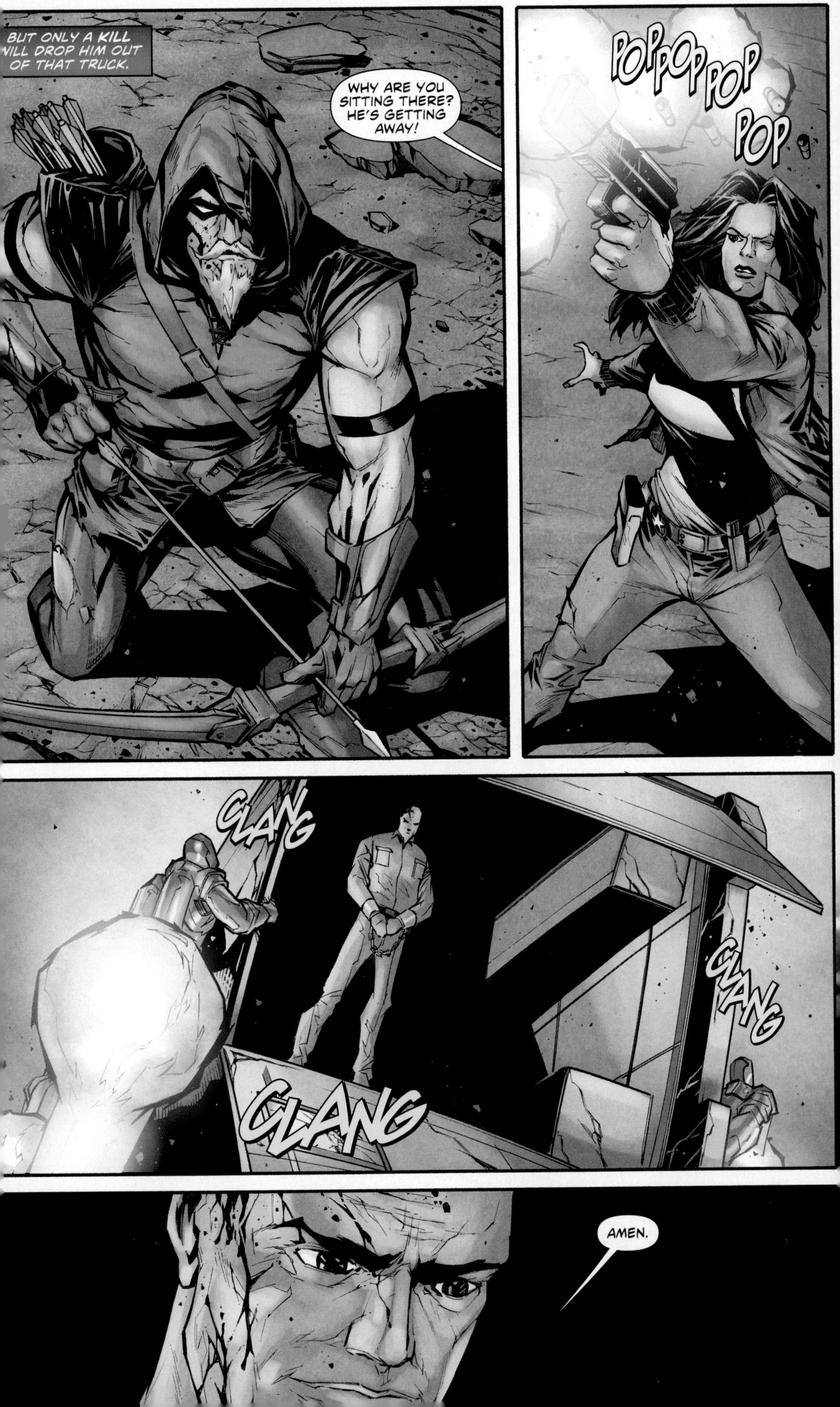
BUT ONLY A KILL WILL DROP HIM OUT OF THAT TRUCK.
WHY ARE YOU SITTING THERE? HE'S GETTING AWAY!
POP POP POP POP
POP
CLANG
CLANG
CLANG
AMEN.

I'M SORRY.

SORRY?
I CAME TO YOU BECAUSE I THOUGHT YOU'D TAKE A SHOT OTHERS *WOULDN'T.* BUT I GUESS I CHOSE THE *WRONG* MAN.

YOU *BETTER HOPE* THAT NOBODY ELSE DIES.

THERE'S NOTHING I CAN SAY.

ALL I KNOW IS... I'M GOING AFTER BILLY MIGGS.

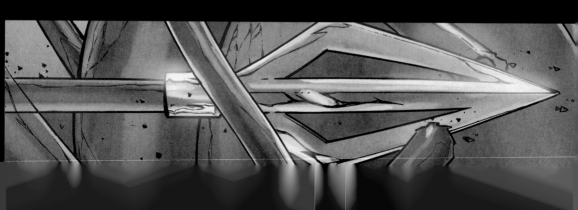

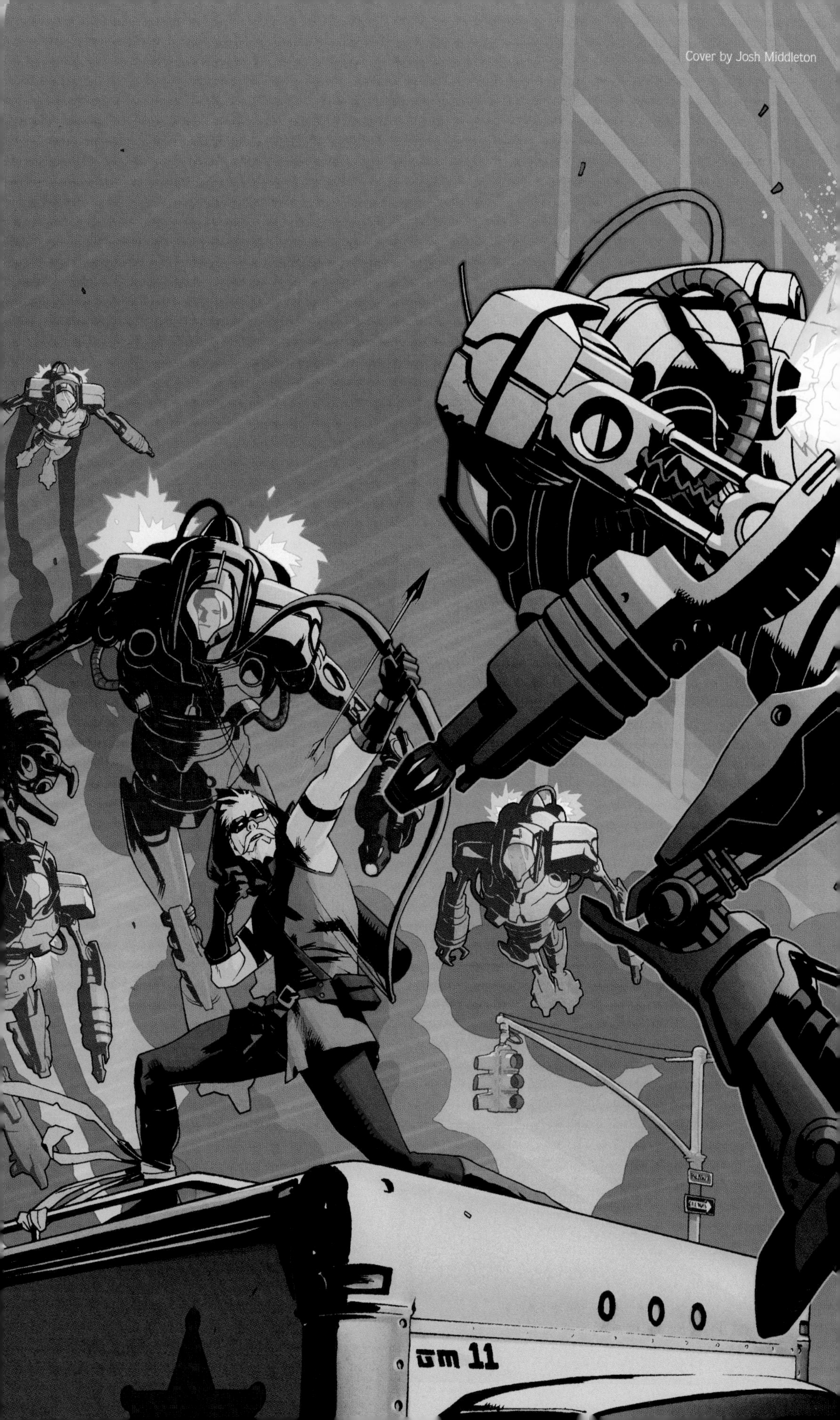
Cover by Josh Middleton

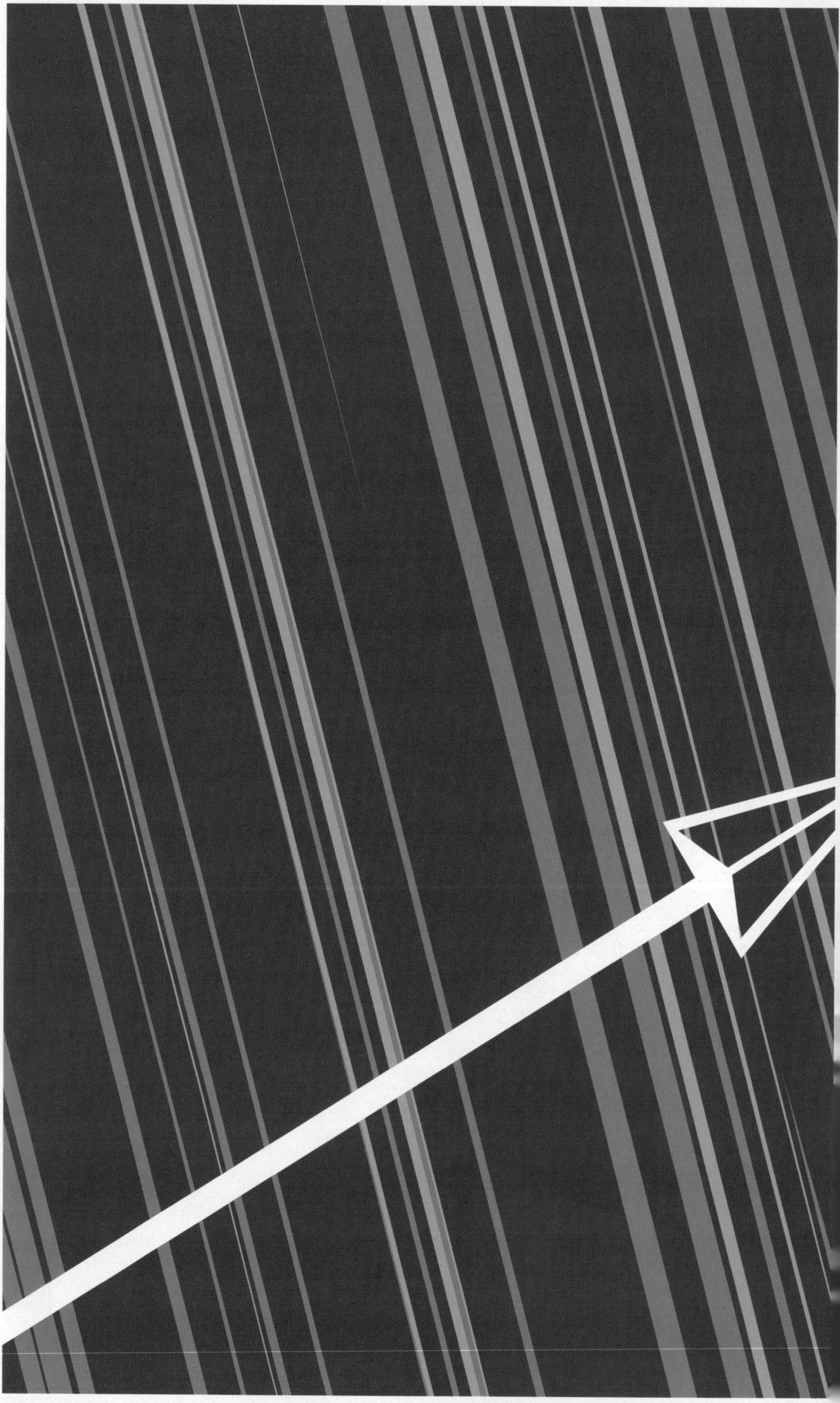

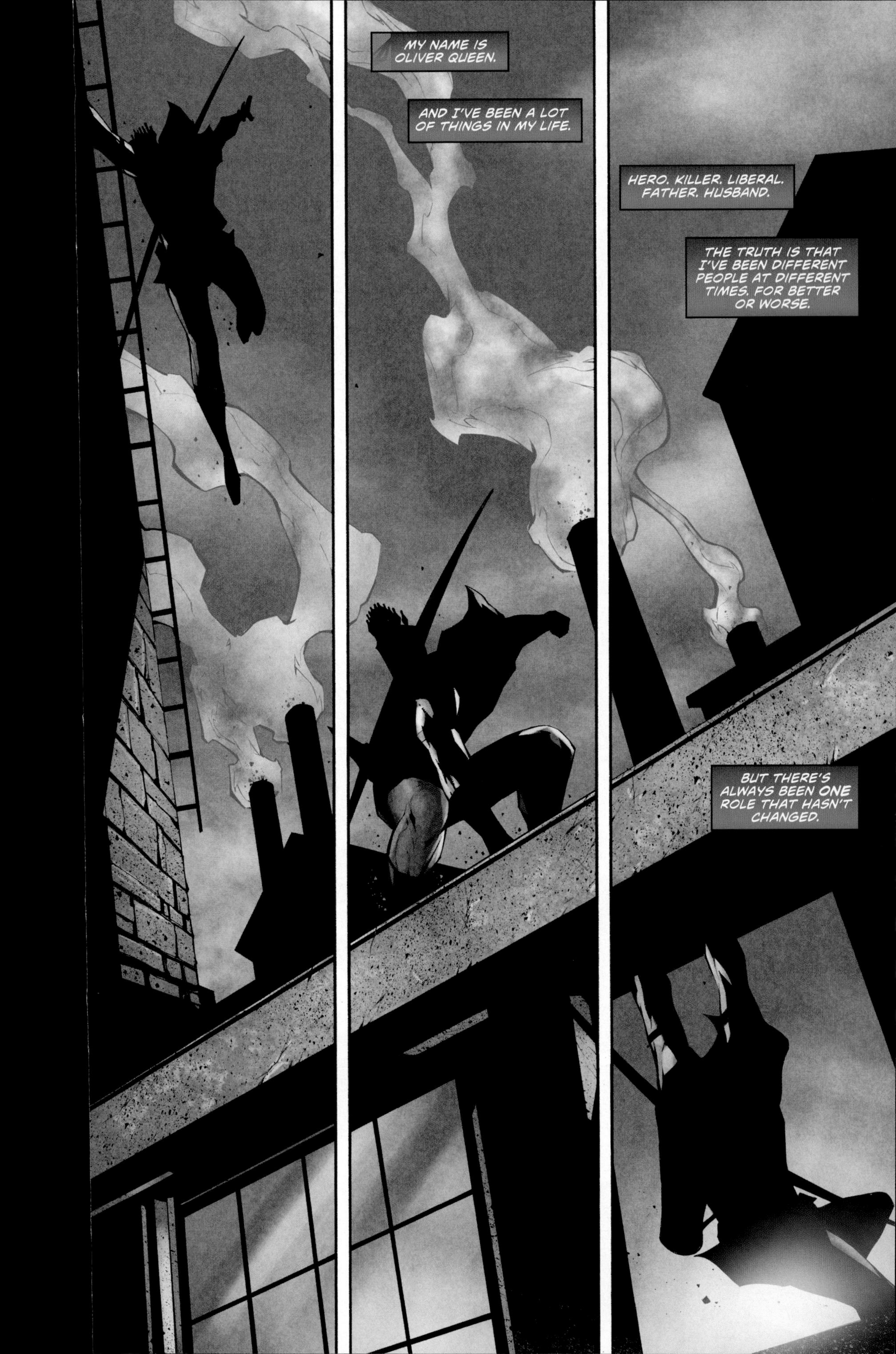
MY NAME IS OLIVER QUEEN.
AND I'VE BEEN A LOT OF THINGS IN MY LIFE.
HERO. KILLER. LIBERAL. FATHER. HUSBAND.
THE TRUTH IS THAT I'VE BEEN DIFFERENT PEOPLE AT DIFFERENT TIMES. FOR BETTER OR WORSE.
BUT THERE'S ALWAYS BEEN ONE ROLE THAT HASN'T CHANGED.

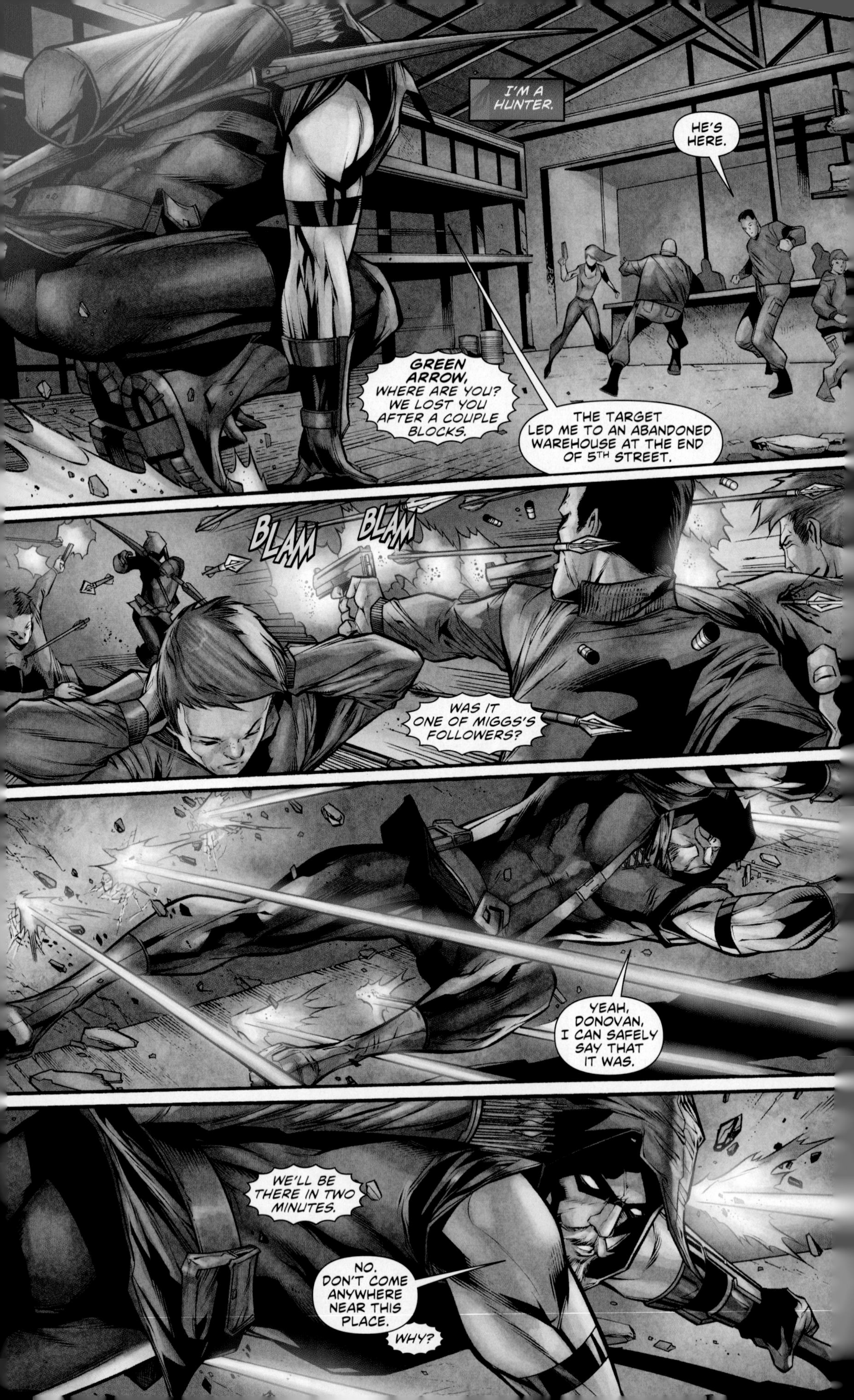
I'M A HUNTER.
HE'S HERE.
GREEN ARROW, WHERE ARE YOU? WE LOST YOU AFTER A COUPLE BLOCKS.
THE TARGET LED ME TO AN ABANDONED WAREHOUSE AT THE END OF 5TH STREET.
BLAM
BLAM
WAS IT ONE OF MIGGS'S FOLLOWERS?
YEAH, DONOVAN, I CAN SAFELY SAY THAT IT WAS.
WE'LL BE THERE IN TWO MINUTES.
NO. DON'T COME ANYWHERE NEAR THIS PLACE.
WHY?

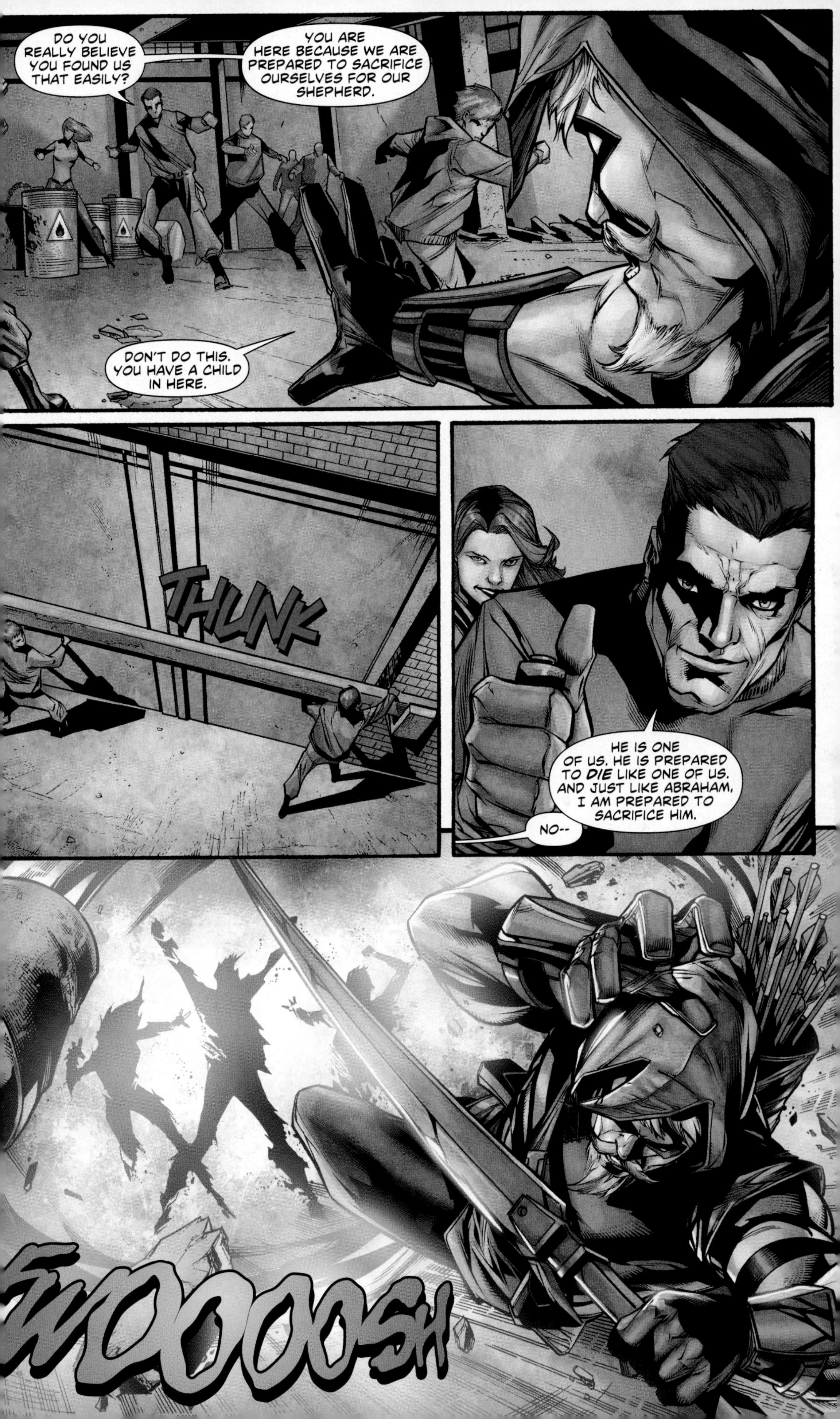
DO YOU REALLY BELIEVE YOU FOUND US THAT EASILY?
YOU ARE HERE BECAUSE WE ARE PREPARED TO SACRIFICE OURSELVES FOR OUR SHEPHERD.
DON'T DO THIS. YOU HAVE A CHILD IN HERE.
THUNK
HE IS ONE OF US. HE IS PREPARED TO *DIE* LIKE ONE OF US. AND JUST LIKE ABRAHAM, I AM PREPARED TO SACRIFICE HIM.
NO--
WOOOOSH

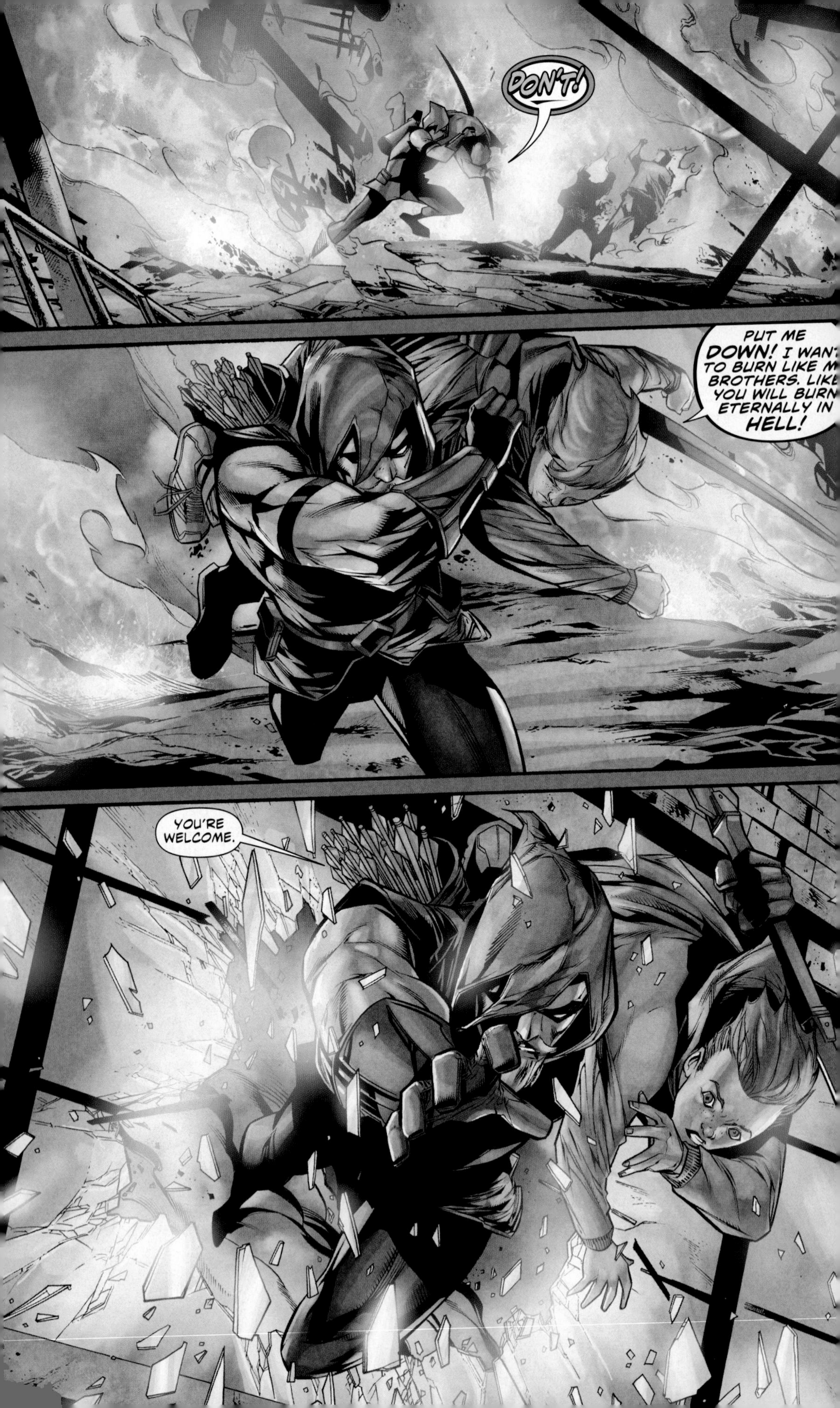
DON'T!
PUT ME DOWN! I WANT TO BURN LIKE MY BROTHERS. LIKE YOU WILL BURN ETERNALLY IN HELL!
YOU'RE WELCOME.

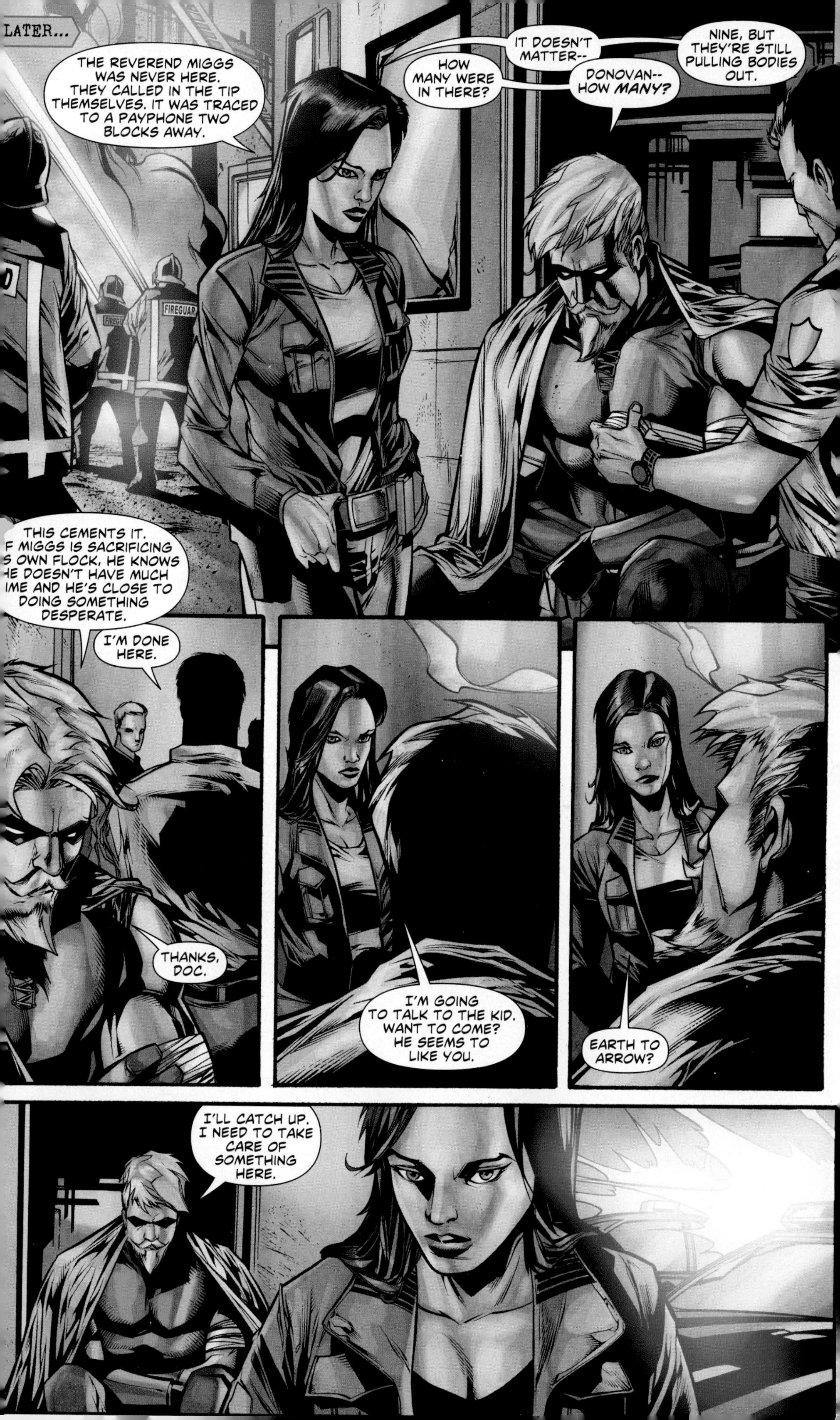
LATER...
THE REVEREND MIGGS WAS NEVER HERE. THEY CALLED IN THE TIP THEMSELVES. IT WAS TRACED TO A PAYPHONE TWO BLOCKS AWAY.
HOW MANY WERE IN THERE?
IT DOESN'T MATTER--
DONOVAN-- HOW MANY?
NINE, BUT THEY'RE STILL PULLING BODIES OUT.
FIREGUARD
THIS CEMENTS IT. F MIGGS IS SACRIFICING S OWN FLOCK, HE KNOWS HE DOESN'T HAVE MUCH IME AND HE'S CLOSE TO DOING SOMETHING DESPERATE.
I'M DONE HERE.
THANKS, DOC.
I'M GOING TO TALK TO THE KID. WANT TO COME? HE SEEMS TO LIKE YOU.
EARTH TO ARROW?
I'LL CATCH UP. I NEED TO TAKE CARE OF SOMETHING HERE.

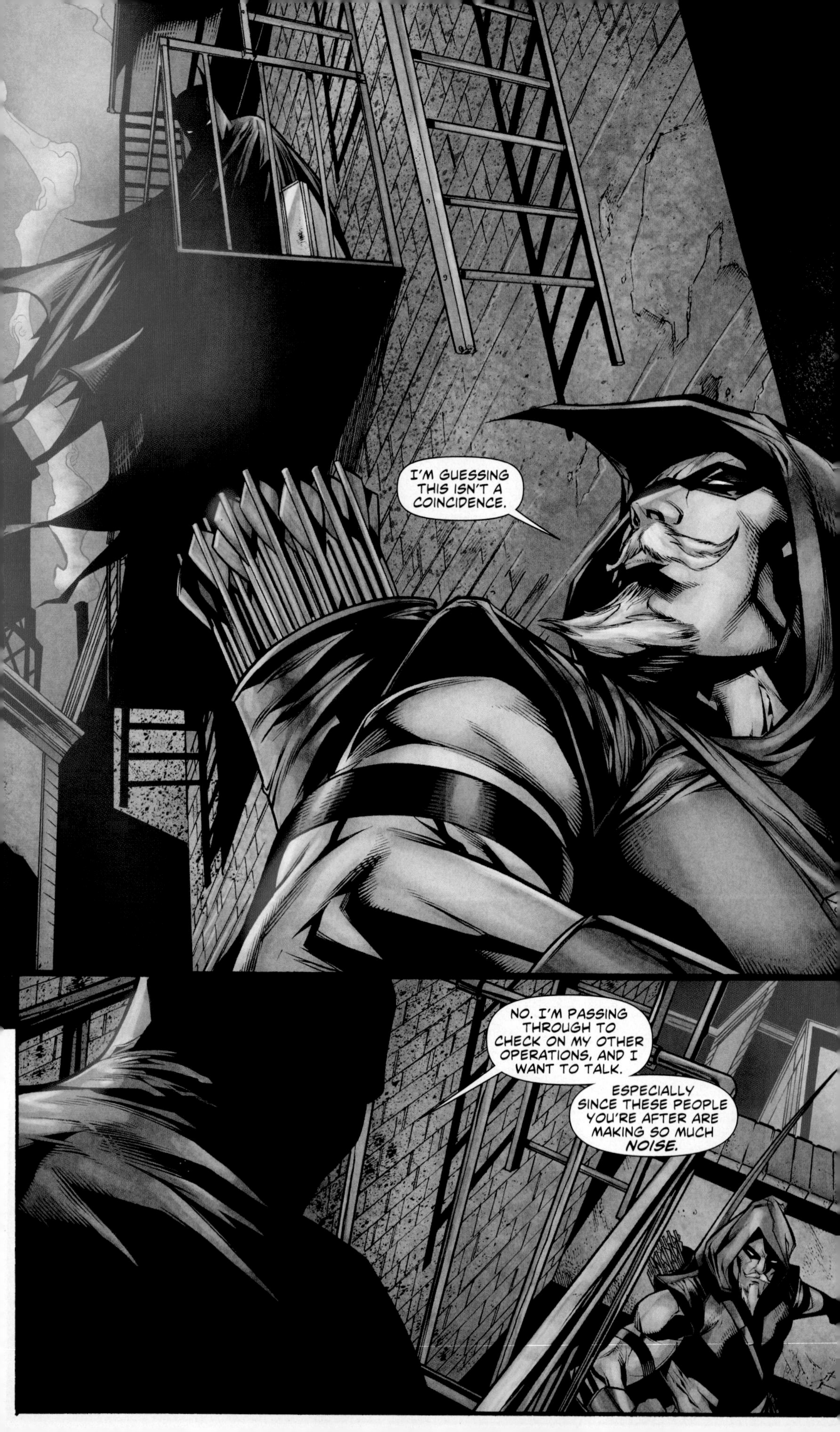
I'M GUESSING THIS ISN'T A COINCIDENCE.
NO. I'M PASSING THROUGH TO CHECK ON MY OTHER OPERATIONS, AND I WANT TO TALK.
ESPECIALLY SINCE THESE PEOPLE YOU'RE AFTER ARE MAKING SO MUCH NOISE.

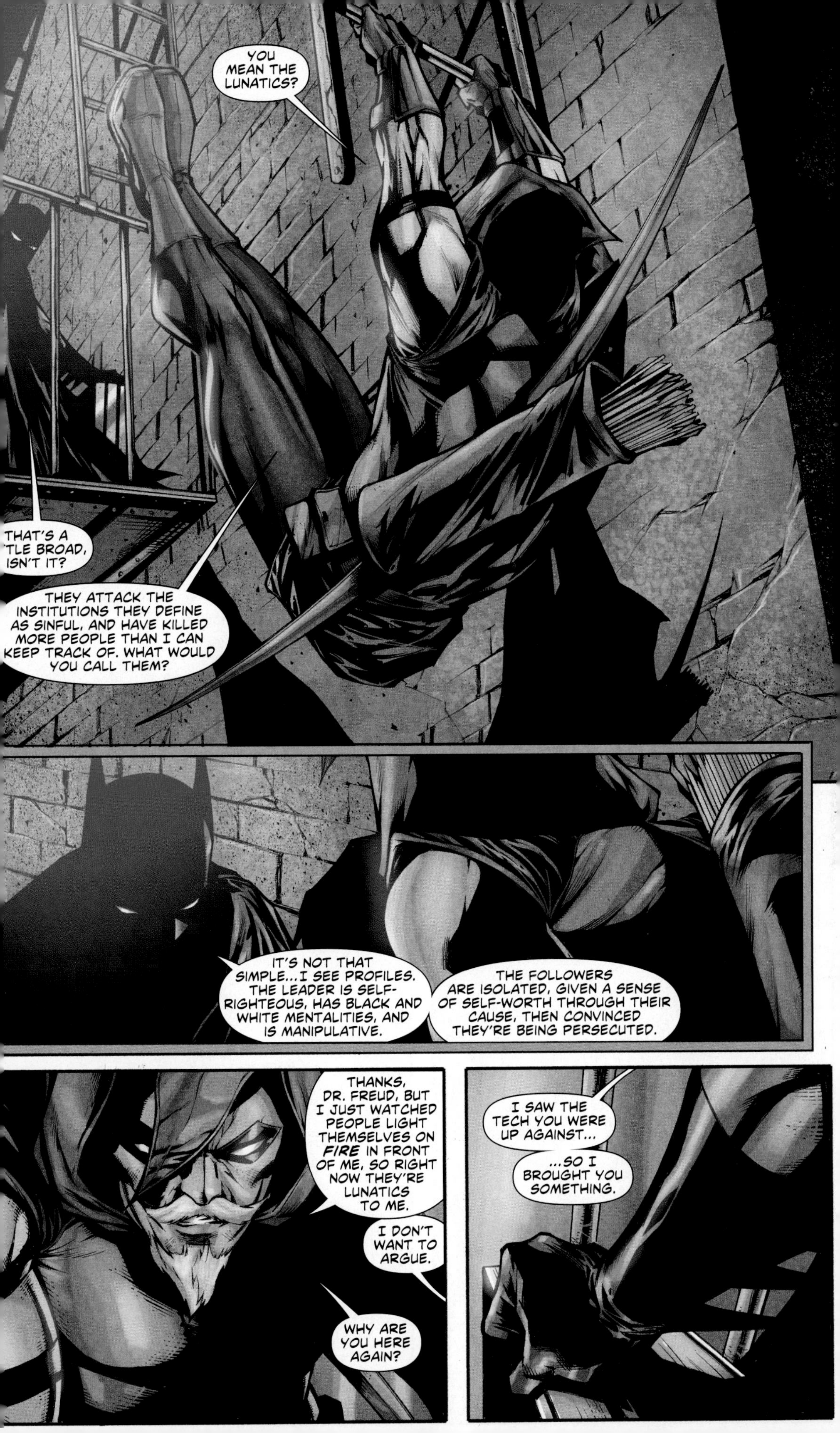
YOU MEAN THE LUNATICS?
THAT'S A 'TLE BROAD, ISN'T IT?
THEY ATTACK THE INSTITUTIONS THEY DEFINE AS SINFUL, AND HAVE KILLED MORE PEOPLE THAN I CAN KEEP TRACK OF. WHAT WOULD YOU CALL THEM?
IT'S NOT THAT SIMPLE...I SEE PROFILES. THE LEADER IS SELF-RIGHTEOUS, HAS BLACK AND WHITE MENTALITIES, AND IS MANIPULATIVE.
THE FOLLOWERS ARE ISOLATED, GIVEN A SENSE OF SELF-WORTH THROUGH THEIR CAUSE, THEN CONVINCED THEY'RE BEING PERSECUTED.
THANKS, DR. FREUD, BUT I JUST WATCHED PEOPLE LIGHT THEMSELVES ON *FIRE* IN FRONT OF ME, SO RIGHT NOW THEY'RE LUNATICS TO ME.
I DON'T WANT TO ARGUE.
WHY ARE YOU HERE AGAIN?
I SAW THE TECH YOU WERE UP AGAINST...
...SO I BROUGHT YOU SOMETHING.

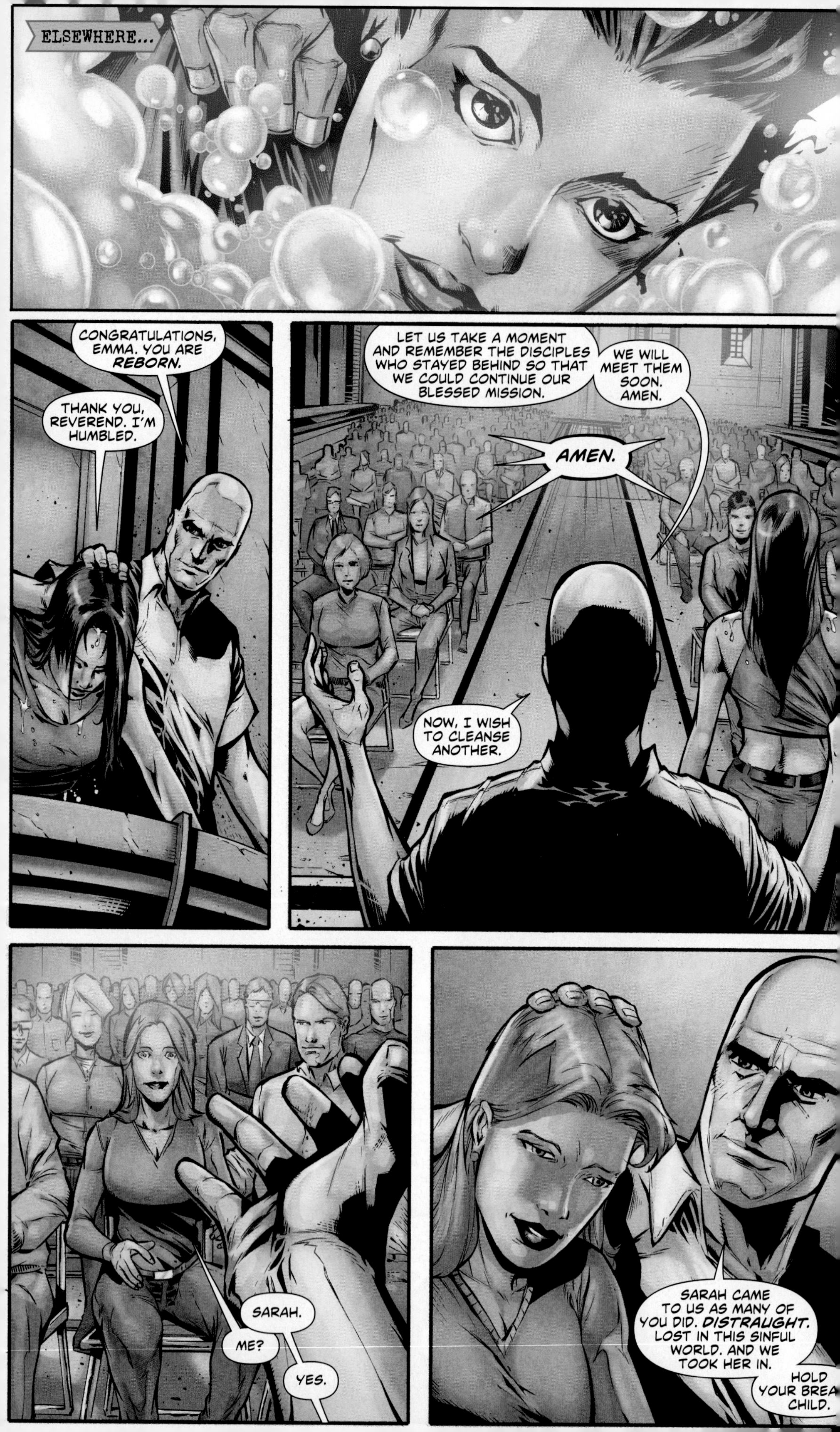
ELSEWHERE...
CONGRATULATIONS, EMMA. YOU ARE REBORN.
THANK YOU, REVEREND. I'M HUMBLED.
LET US TAKE A MOMENT AND REMEMBER THE DISCIPLES WHO STAYED BEHIND SO THAT WE COULD CONTINUE OUR BLESSED MISSION.
WE WILL MEET THEM SOON. AMEN.
AMEN.
NOW, I WISH TO CLEANSE ANOTHER.
SARAH.
ME?
YES.
SARAH CAME TO US AS MANY OF YOU DID. DISTRAUGHT. LOST IN THIS SINFUL WORLD. AND WE TOOK HER IN.
HOLD YOUR BREA
CHILD.

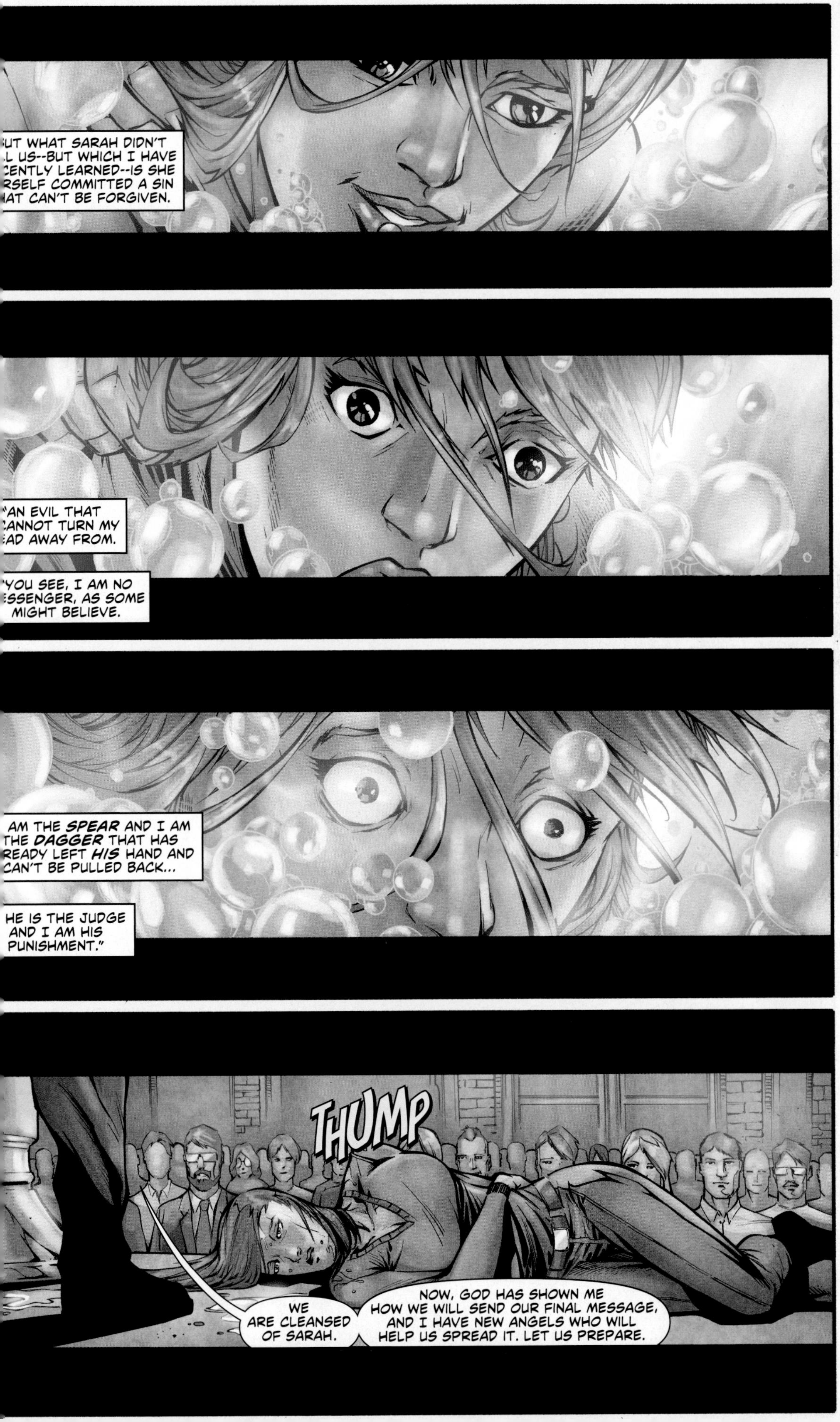

UT WHAT SARAH DIDN'T L US--BUT WHICH I HAVE CENTLY LEARNED--IS SHE RSELF COMMITTED A SIN IAT CAN'T BE FORGIVEN.
"AN EVIL THAT CANNOT TURN MY EAD AWAY FROM.
"YOU SEE, I AM NO ESSENGER, AS SOME MIGHT BELIEVE.
AM THE SPEAR AND I AM THE DAGGER THAT HAS READY LEFT HIS HAND AND CAN'T BE PULLED BACK...
HE IS THE JUDGE AND I AM HIS PUNISHMENT."
THUMP
WE ARE CLEANSED OF SARAH.
NOW, GOD HAS SHOWN ME HOW WE WILL SEND OUR FINAL MESSAGE, AND I HAVE NEW ANGELS WHO WILL HELP US SPREAD IT. LET US PREPARE.

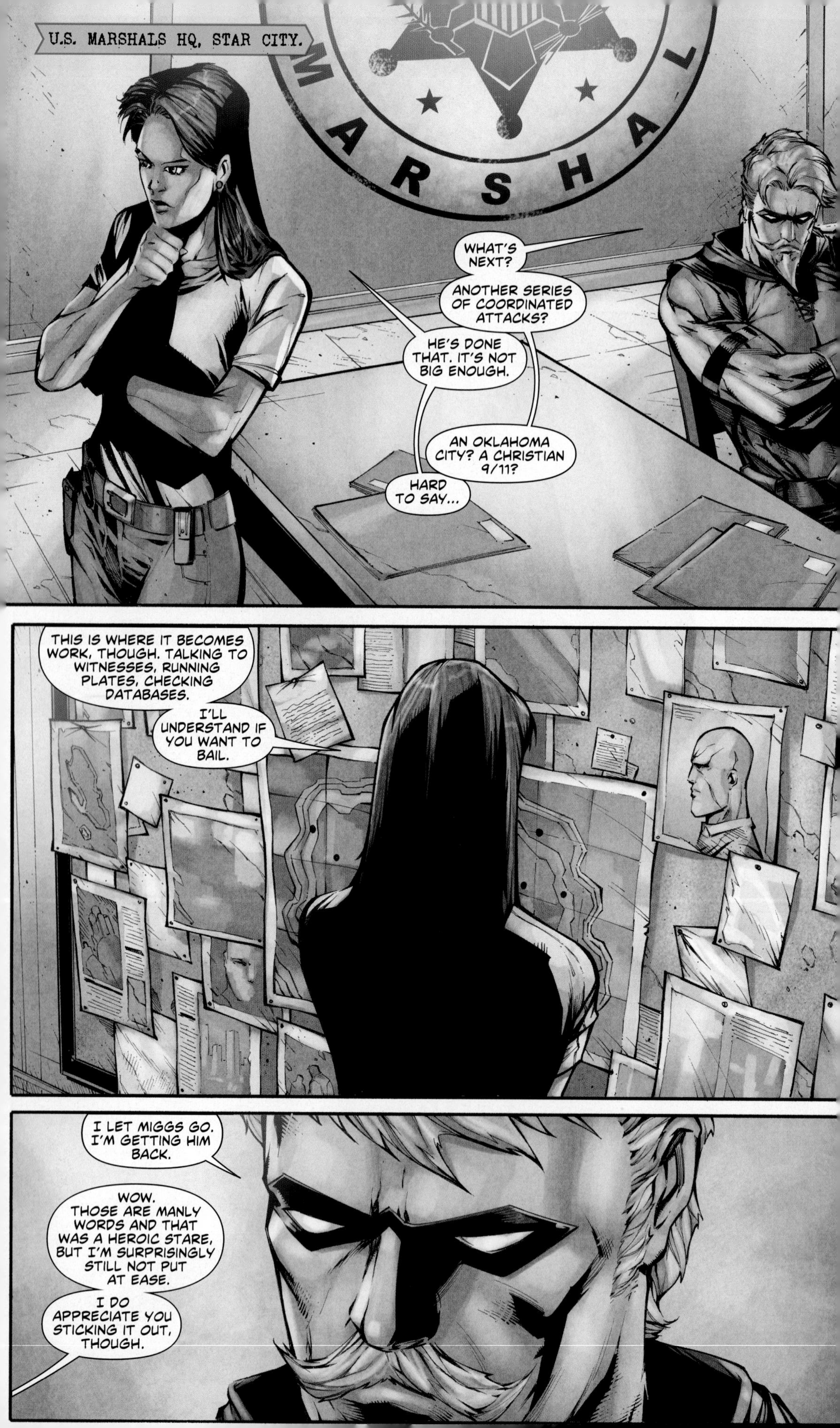
U.S. MARSHALS HQ, STAR CITY.
WHAT'S NEXT?
ANOTHER SERIES OF COORDINATED ATTACKS?
HE'S DONE THAT. IT'S NOT BIG ENOUGH.
AN OKLAHOMA CITY? A CHRISTIAN 9/11?
HARD TO SAY...
THIS IS WHERE IT BECOMES WORK, THOUGH. TALKING TO WITNESSES, RUNNING PLATES, CHECKING DATABASES.
I'LL UNDERSTAND IF YOU WANT TO BAIL.
I LET MIGGS GO. I'M GETTING HIM BACK.
WOW. THOSE ARE MANLY WORDS AND THAT WAS A HEROIC STARE, BUT I'M SURPRISINGLY STILL NOT PUT AT EASE.
I DO APPRECIATE YOU STICKING IT OUT, THOUGH.

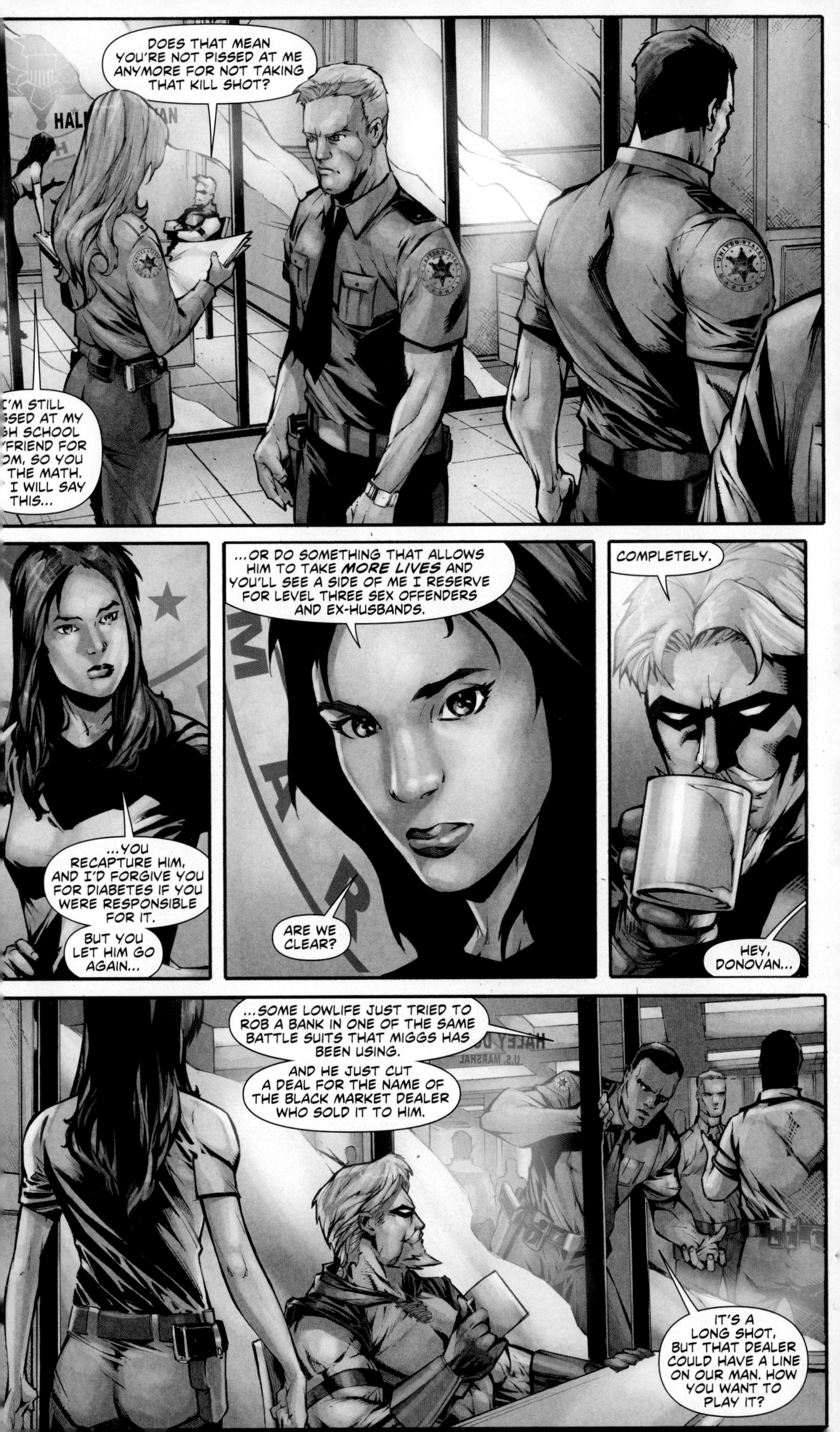

DOES THAT MEAN YOU'RE NOT PISSED AT ME ANYMORE FOR NOT TAKING THAT KILL SHOT?
I'M STILL SSED AT MY GH SCHOOL FRIEND FOR OM, SO YOU THE MATH. I WILL SAY THIS...
...YOU RECAPTURE HIM, AND I'D FORGIVE YOU FOR DIABETES IF YOU WERE RESPONSIBLE FOR IT.
BUT YOU LET HIM GO AGAIN...
...OR DO SOMETHING THAT ALLOWS HIM TO TAKE MORE LIVES AND YOU'LL SEE A SIDE OF ME I RESERVE FOR LEVEL THREE SEX OFFENDERS AND EX-HUSBANDS.
ARE WE CLEAR?
COMPLETELY.
HEY, DONOVAN...
...SOME LOWLIFE JUST TRIED TO ROB A BANK IN ONE OF THE SAME BATTLE SUITS THAT MIGGS HAS BEEN USING.
AND HE JUST CUT A DEAL FOR THE NAME OF THE BLACK MARKET DEALER WHO SOLD IT TO HIM.
IT'S A LONG SHOT, BUT THAT DEALER COULD HAVE A LINE ON OUR MAN. HOW YOU WANT TO PLAY IT?

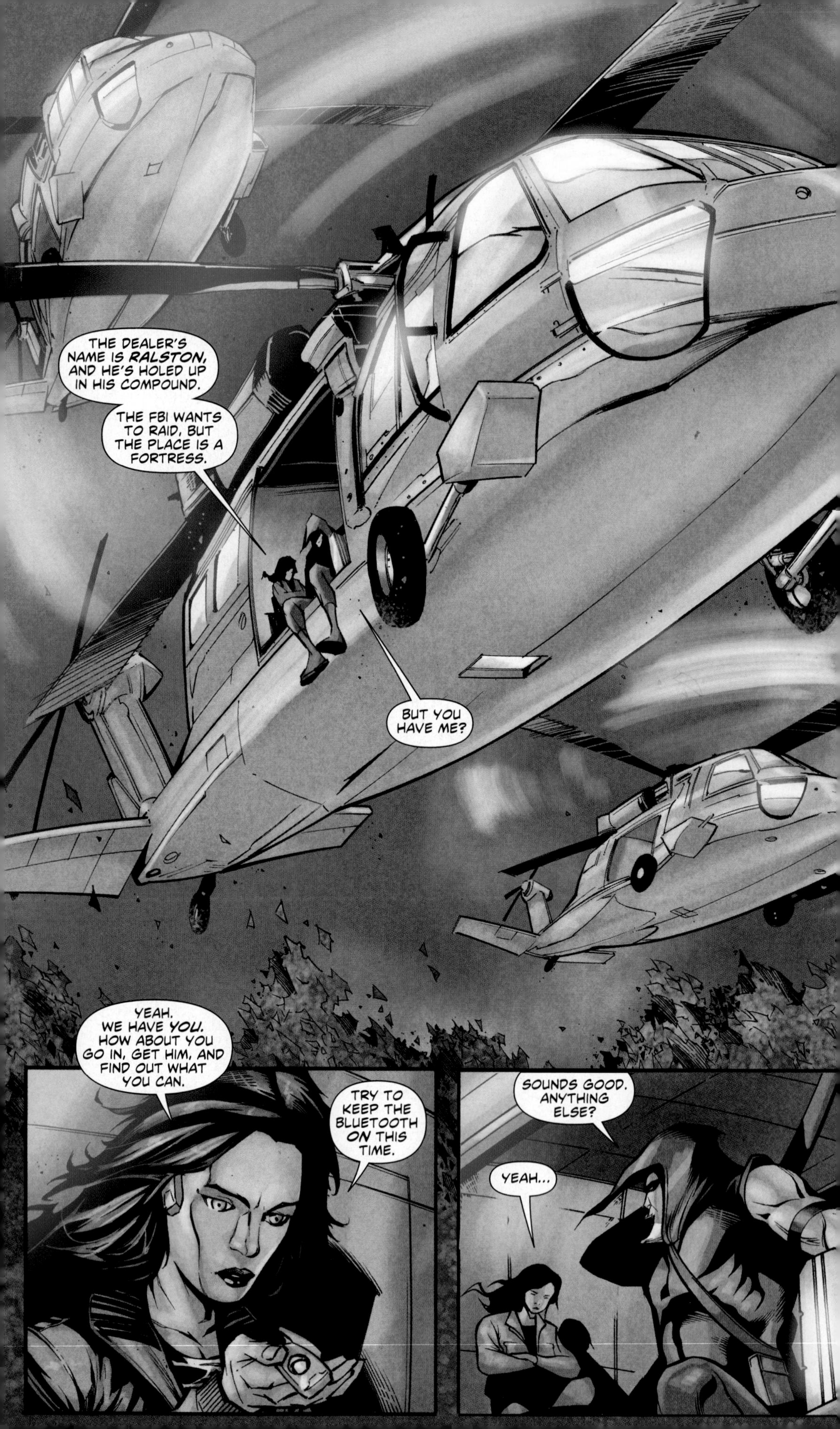
THE DEALER'S NAME IS RALSTON, AND HE'S HOLED UP IN HIS COMPOUND.
THE FBI WANTS TO RAID, BUT THE PLACE IS A FORTRESS.
BUT YOU HAVE ME?
YEAH. WE HAVE YOU. HOW ABOUT YOU GO IN, GET HIM, AND FIND OUT WHAT YOU CAN.
TRY TO KEEP THE BLUETOOTH ON THIS TIME.
SOUNDS GOOD. ANYTHING ELSE?
YEAH...

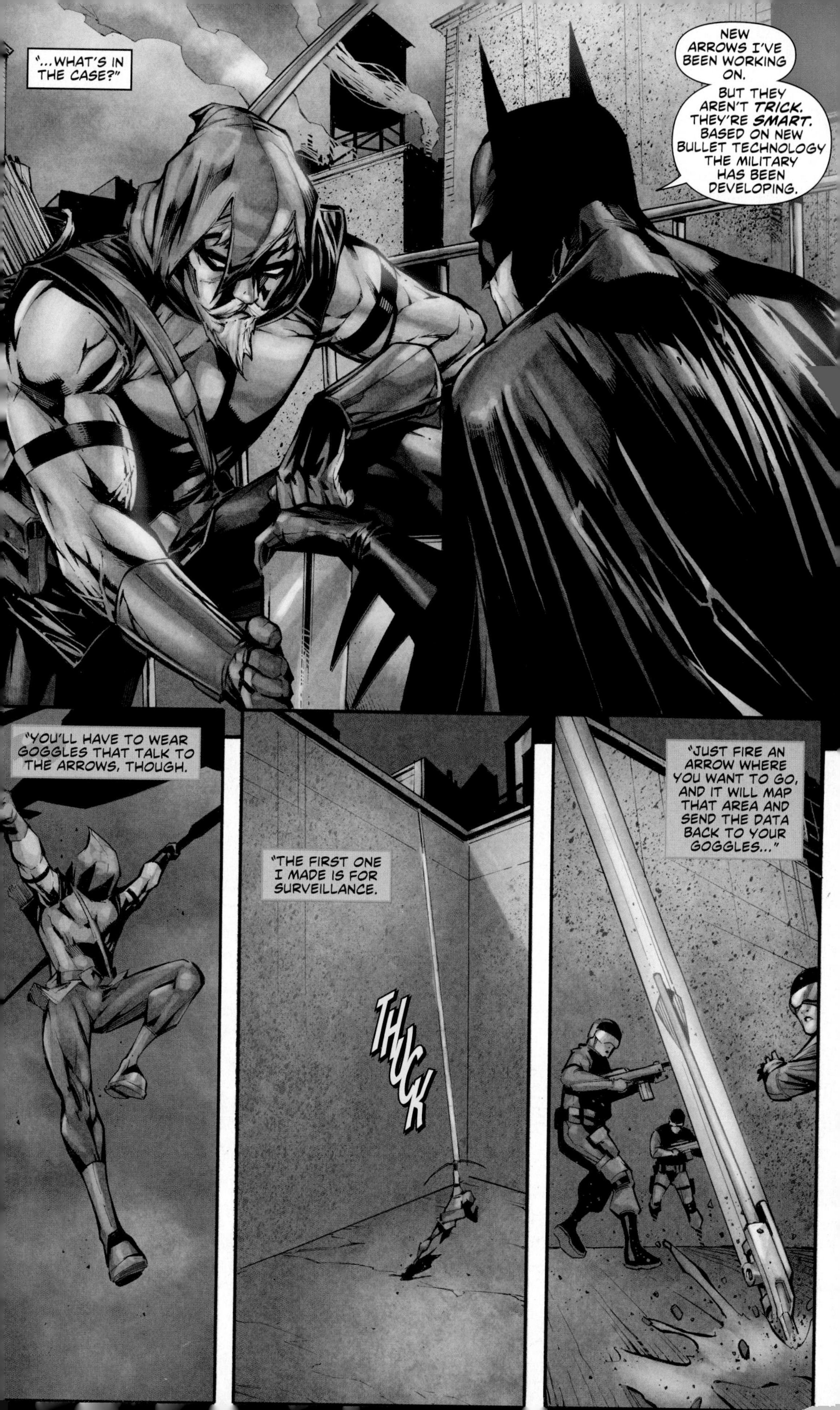
"...WHAT'S IN THE CASE?"
NEW ARROWS I'VE BEEN WORKING ON.
BUT THEY AREN'T TRICK. THEY'RE SMART. BASED ON NEW BULLET TECHNOLOGY THE MILITARY HAS BEEN DEVELOPING.
"YOU'LL HAVE TO WEAR GOGGLES THAT TALK TO THE ARROWS, THOUGH.
"THE FIRST ONE I MADE IS FOR SURVEILLANCE.
THUCK
"JUST FIRE AN ARROW WHERE YOU WANT TO GO, AND IT WILL MAP THAT AREA AND SEND THE DATA BACK TO YOUR GOGGLES..."

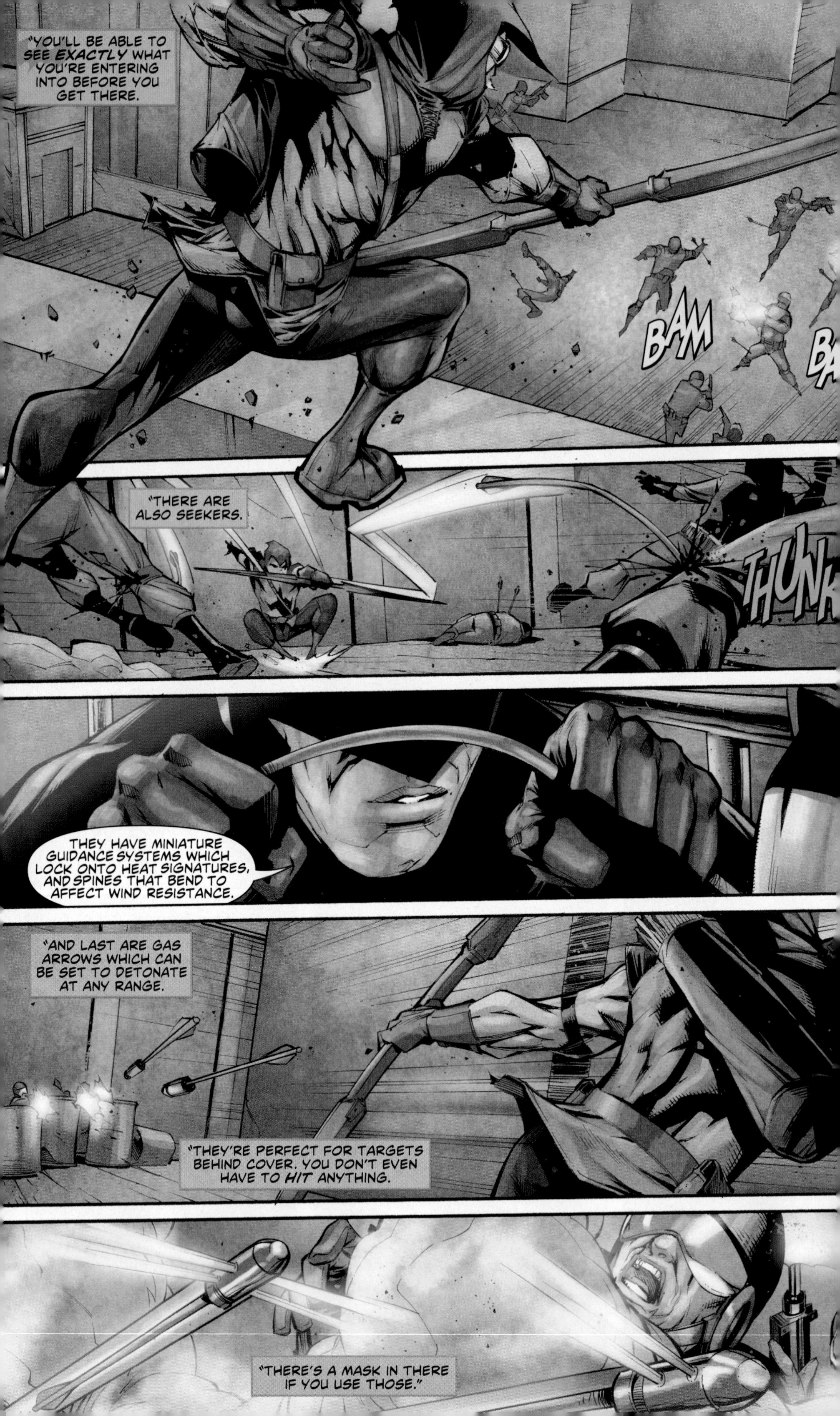
"YOU'LL BE ABLE TO SEE EXACTLY WHAT YOU'RE ENTERING INTO BEFORE YOU GET THERE.
BAM
BA
"THERE ARE ALSO SEEKERS.
THUNK
THEY HAVE MINIATURE GUIDANCE SYSTEMS WHICH LOCK ONTO HEAT SIGNATURES, AND SPINES THAT BEND TO AFFECT WIND RESISTANCE.
"AND LAST ARE GAS ARROWS WHICH CAN BE SET TO DETONATE AT ANY RANGE.
"THEY'RE PERFECT FOR TARGETS BEHIND COVER. YOU DON'T EVEN HAVE TO HIT ANYTHING.
"THERE'S A MASK IN THERE IF YOU USE THOSE."

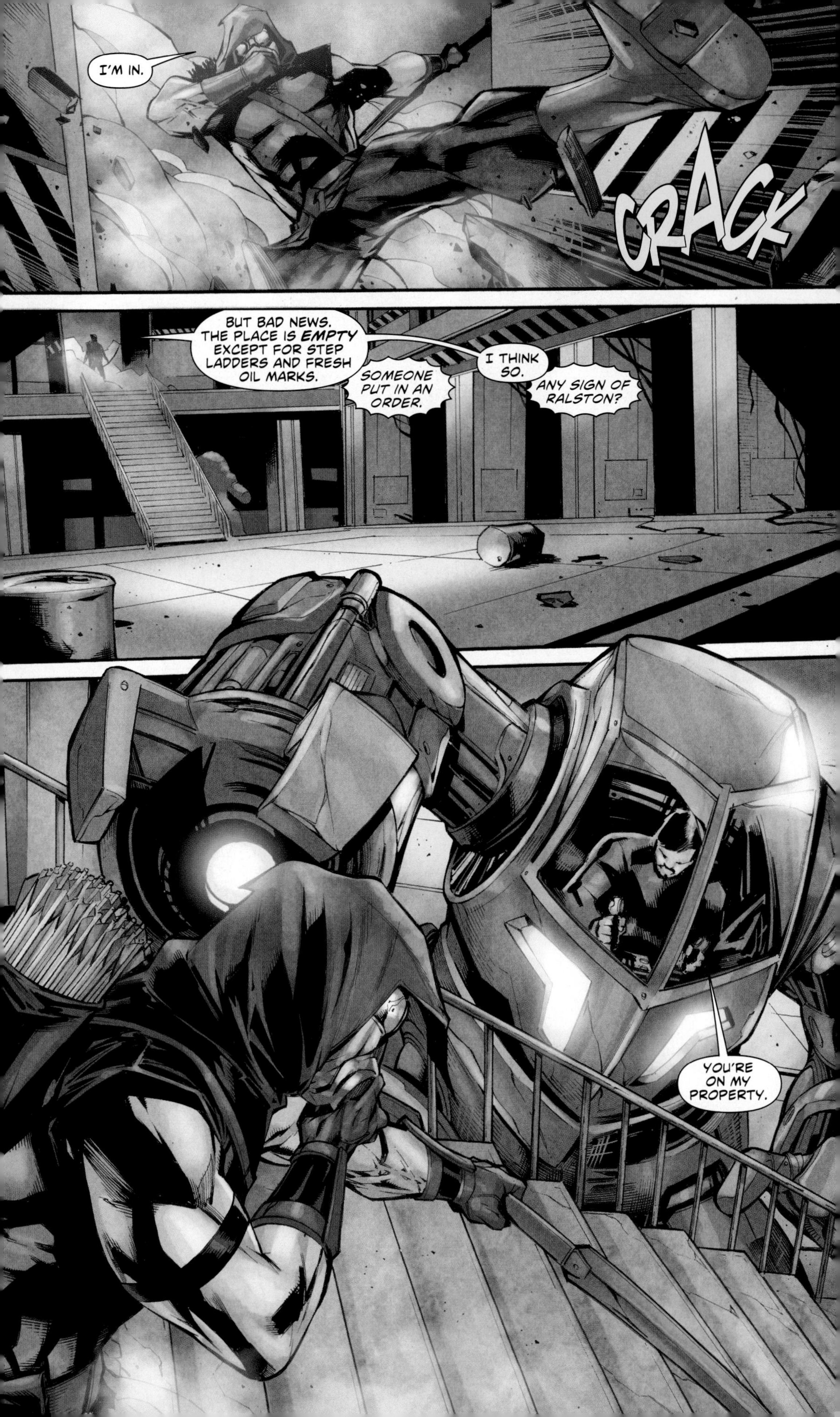
I'M IN.
CRACK
BUT BAD NEWS. THE PLACE IS EMPTY EXCEPT FOR STEP LADDERS AND FRESH OIL MARKS.
SOMEONE PUT IN AN ORDER.
I THINK SO.
ANY SIGN OF RALSTON?
YOU'RE ON MY PROPERTY.

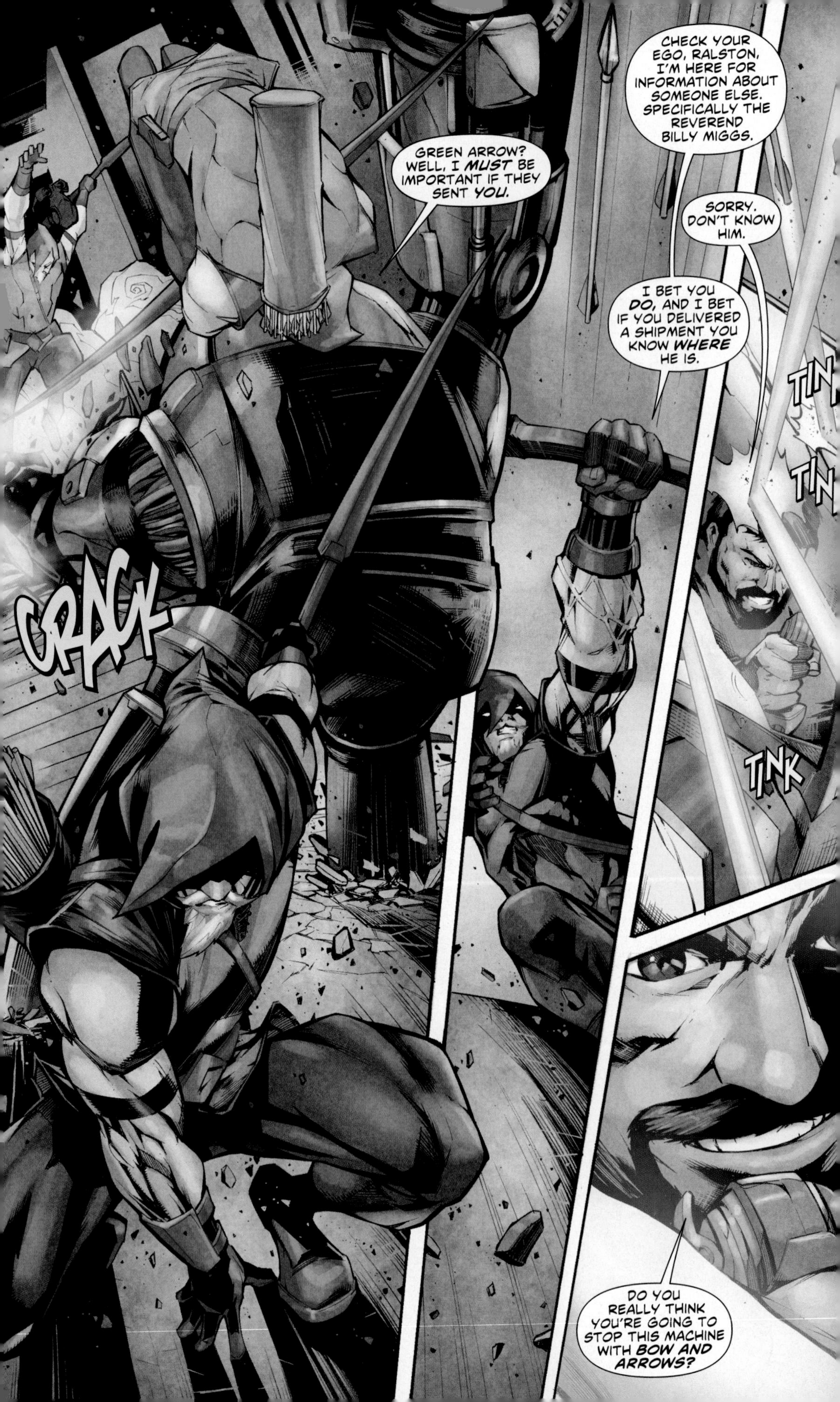
GREEN ARROW? WELL, I MUST BE IMPORTANT IF THEY SENT YOU.
CHECK YOUR EGO, RALSTON, I'M HERE FOR INFORMATION ABOUT SOMEONE ELSE. SPECIFICALLY THE REVEREND BILLY MIGGS.
SORRY. DON'T KNOW HIM.
I BET YOU DO, AND I BET IF YOU DELIVERED A SHIPMENT YOU KNOW WHERE HE IS.
CRACK
TIN
TIN
TINK
DO YOU REALLY THINK YOU'RE GOING TO STOP THIS MACHINE WITH BOW AND ARROWS?

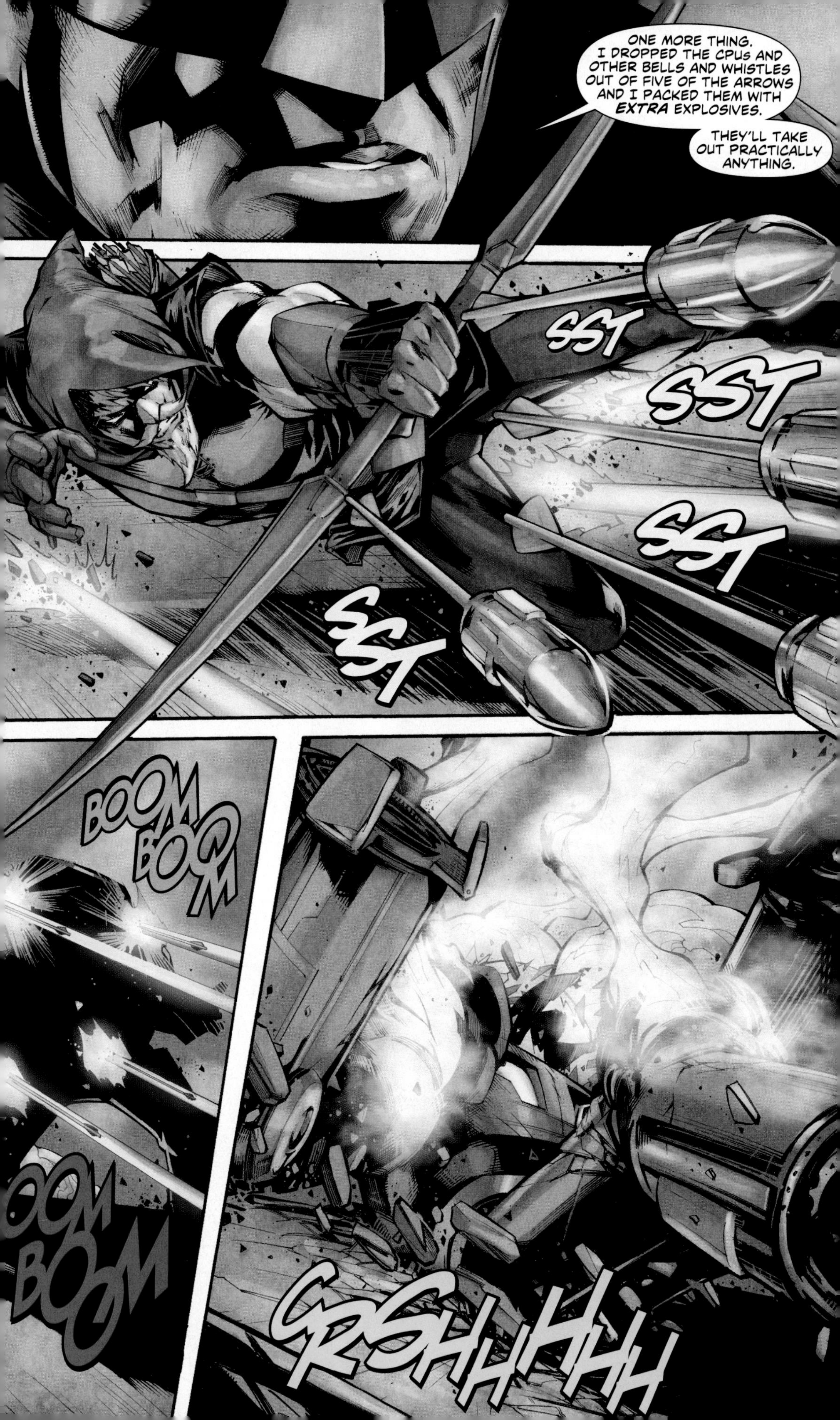
ONE MORE THING. I DROPPED THE CPUs AND OTHER BELLS AND WHISTLES OUT OF FIVE OF THE ARROWS AND I PACKED THEM WITH *EXTRA* EXPLOSIVES.
THEY'LL TAKE OUT PRACTICALLY ANYTHING.
SST
SST
SST
SST
BOOM
BOOM
BOOM
BOOM
CRSHHHHH

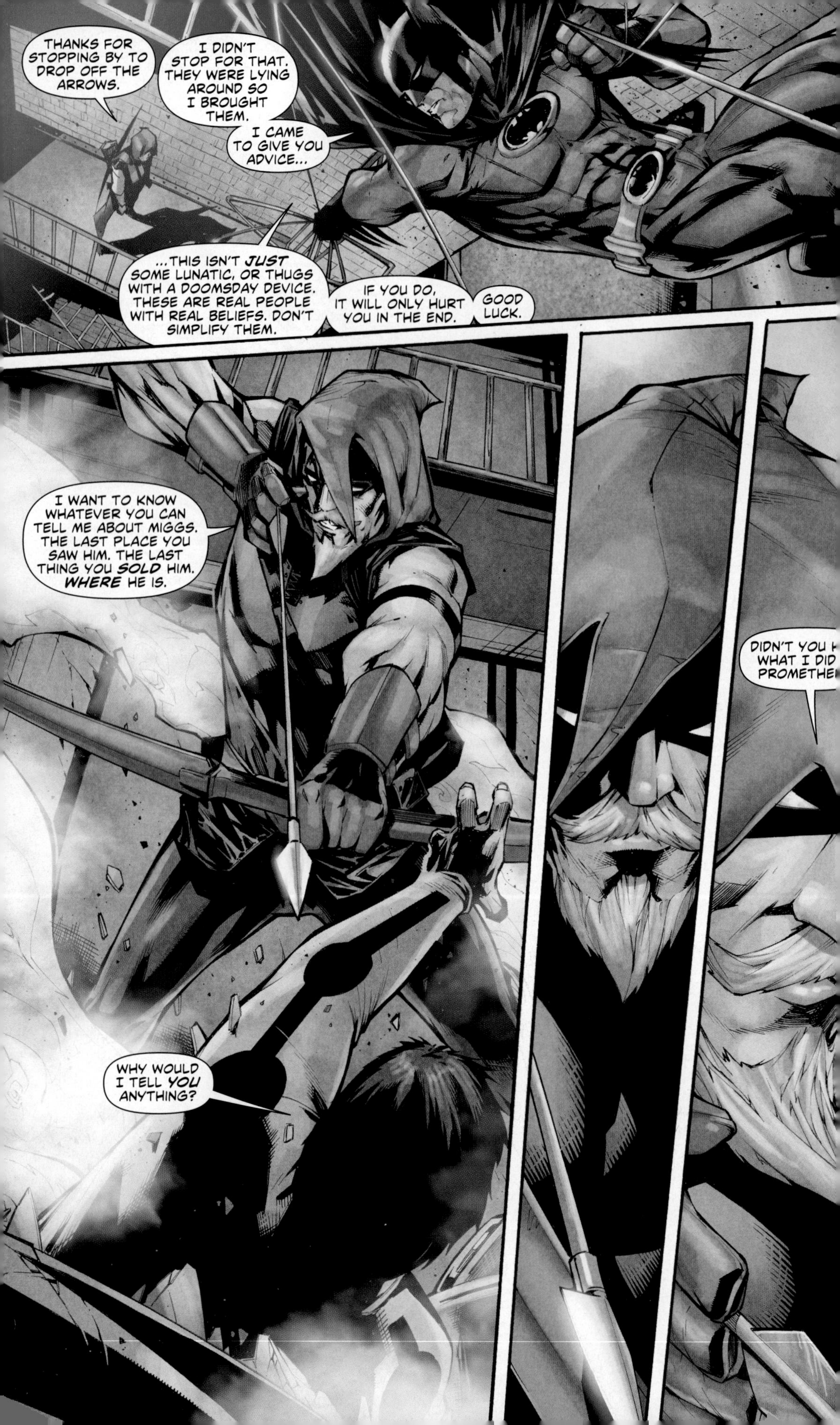
THANKS FOR STOPPING BY TO DROP OFF THE ARROWS.
I DIDN'T STOP FOR THAT. THEY WERE LYING AROUND SO I BROUGHT THEM.
I CAME TO GIVE YOU ADVICE...
...THIS ISN'T JUST SOME LUNATIC, OR THUGS WITH A DOOMSDAY DEVICE. THESE ARE REAL PEOPLE WITH REAL BELIEFS. DON'T SIMPLIFY THEM.
IF YOU DO, IT WILL ONLY HURT YOU IN THE END.
GOOD LUCK.
I WANT TO KNOW WHATEVER YOU CAN TELL ME ABOUT MIGGS. THE LAST PLACE YOU SAW HIM. THE LAST THING YOU SOLD HIM. WHERE HE IS.
WHY WOULD I TELL YOU ANYTHING?
DIDN'T YOU WHAT I DID PROMETHE

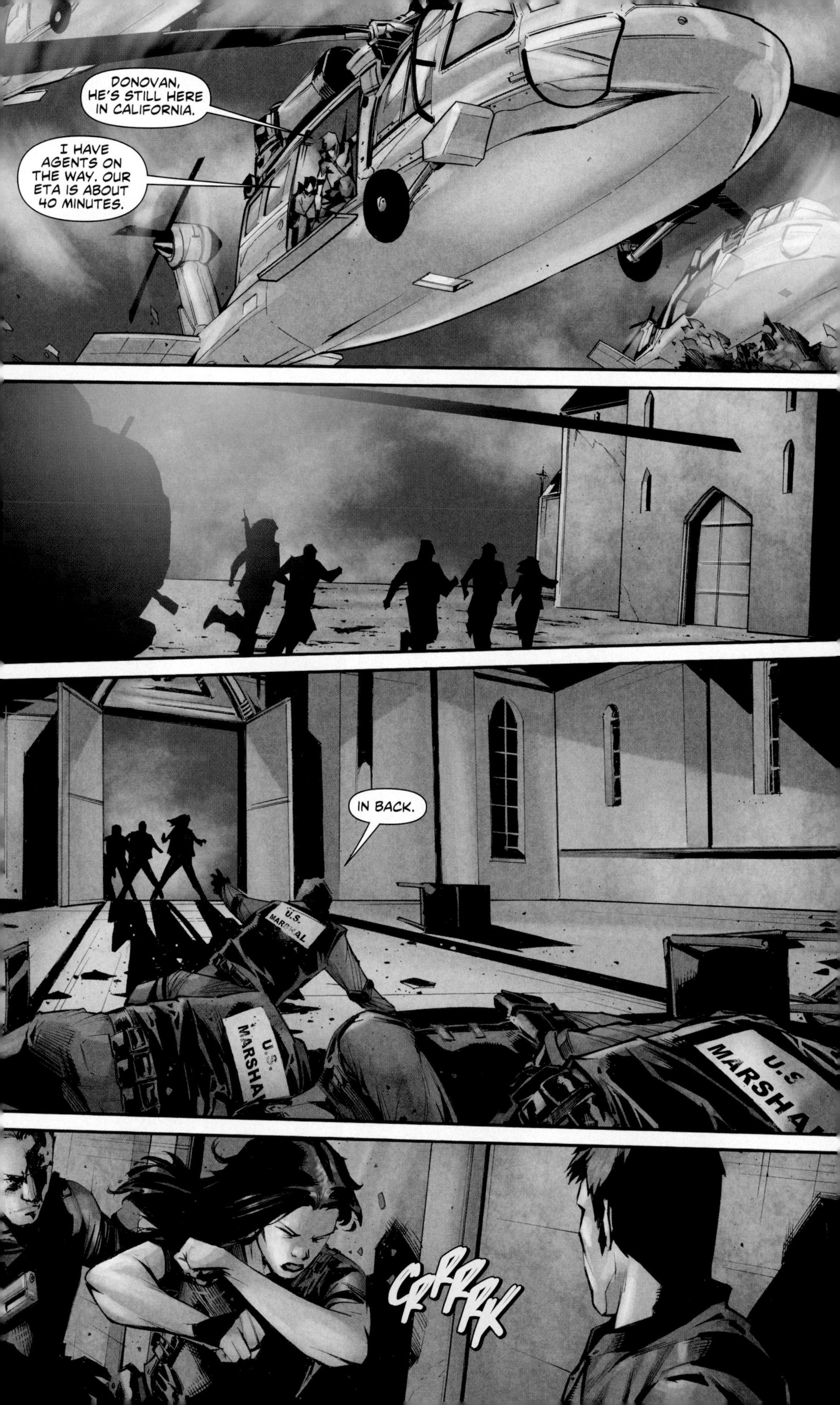

DONOVAN, HE'S STILL HERE IN CALIFORNIA.
I HAVE AGENTS ON THE WAY. OUR ETA IS ABOUT 40 MINUTES.
IN BACK.
U.S. MARSHAL
CRRRAK

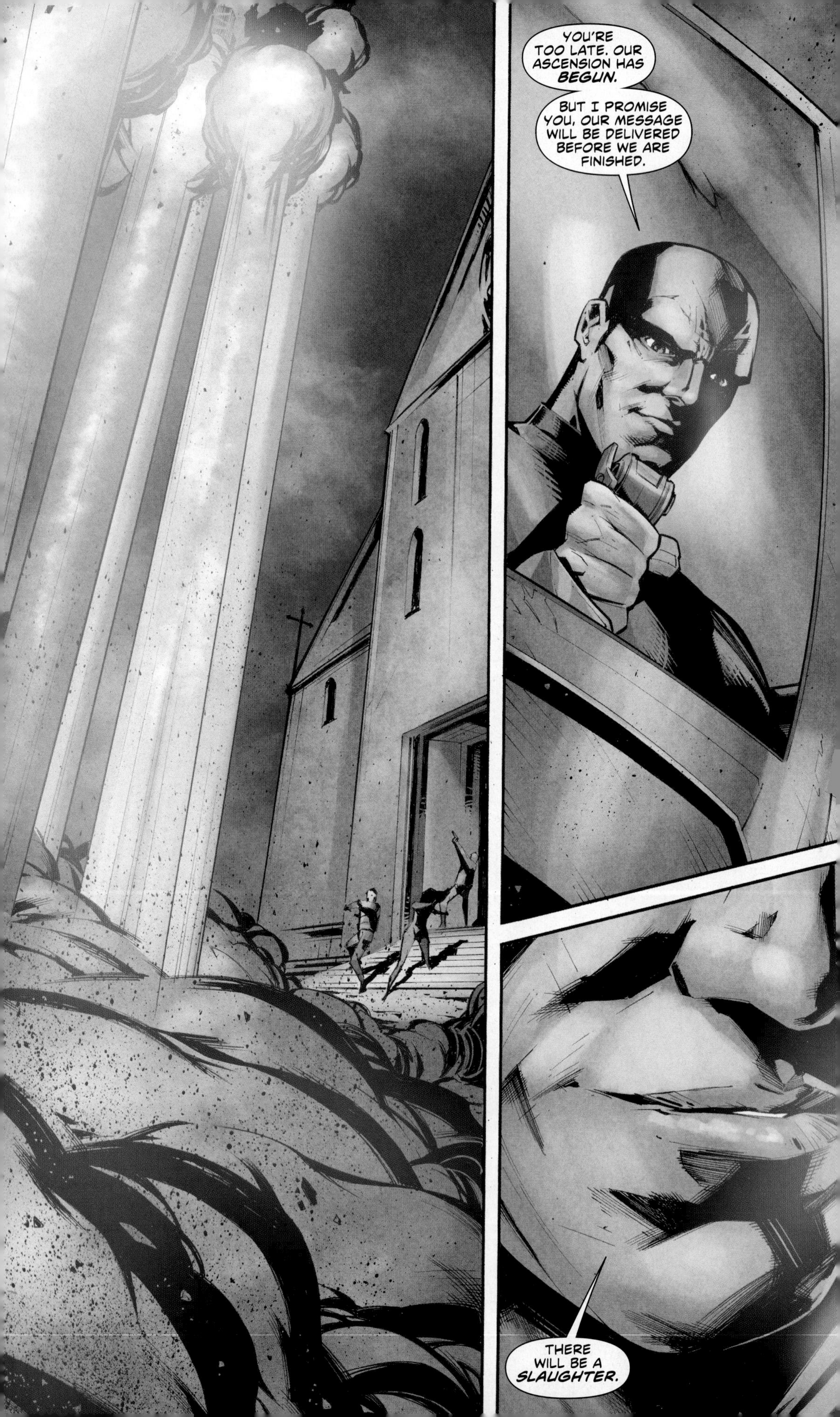
YOU'RE TOO LATE. OUR ASCENSION HAS BEGUN.
BUT I PROMISE YOU, OUR MESSAGE WILL BE DELIVERED BEFORE WE ARE FINISHED.
THERE WILL BE A SLAUGHTER.

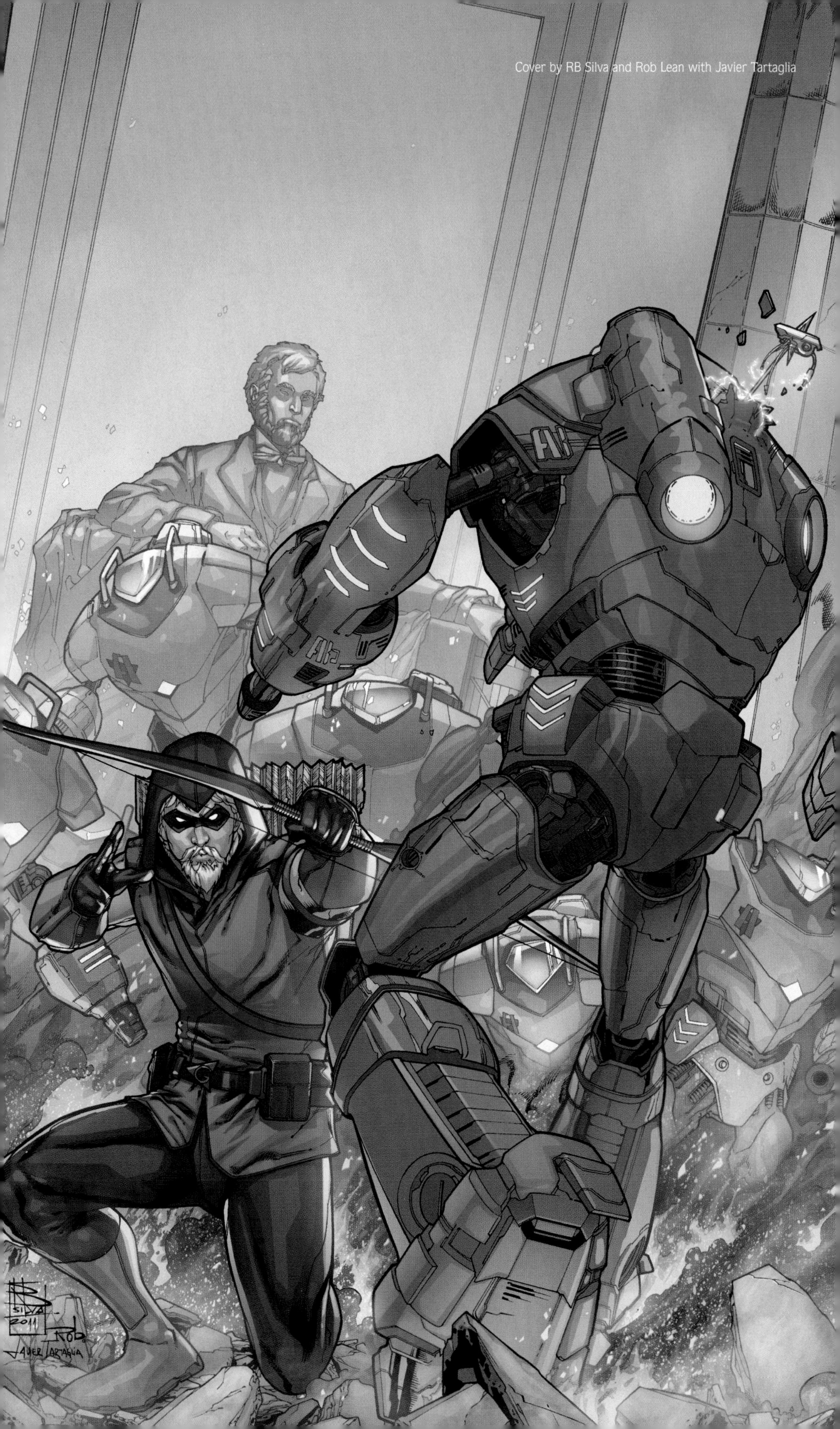

Cover by RB Silva and Rob Lean with Javier Tartaglia

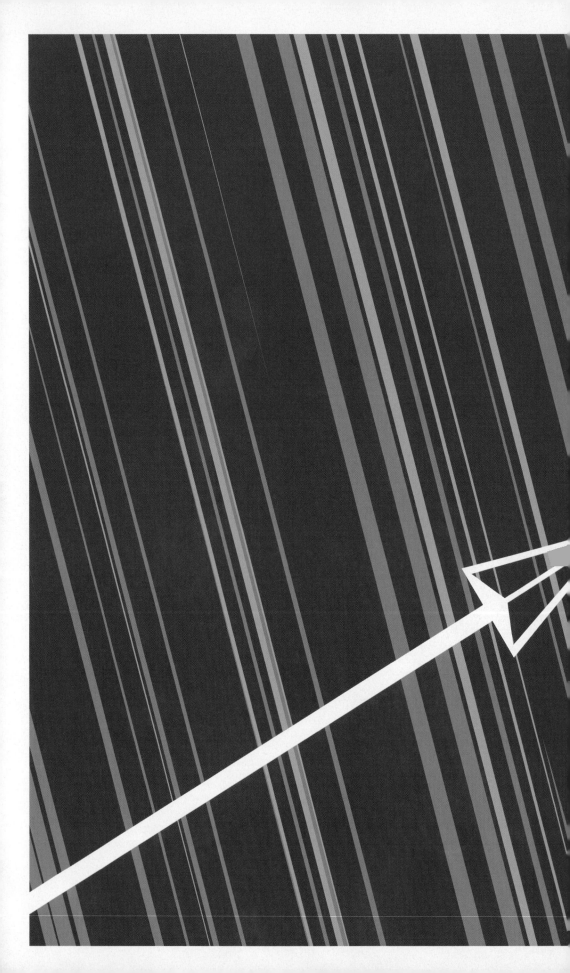

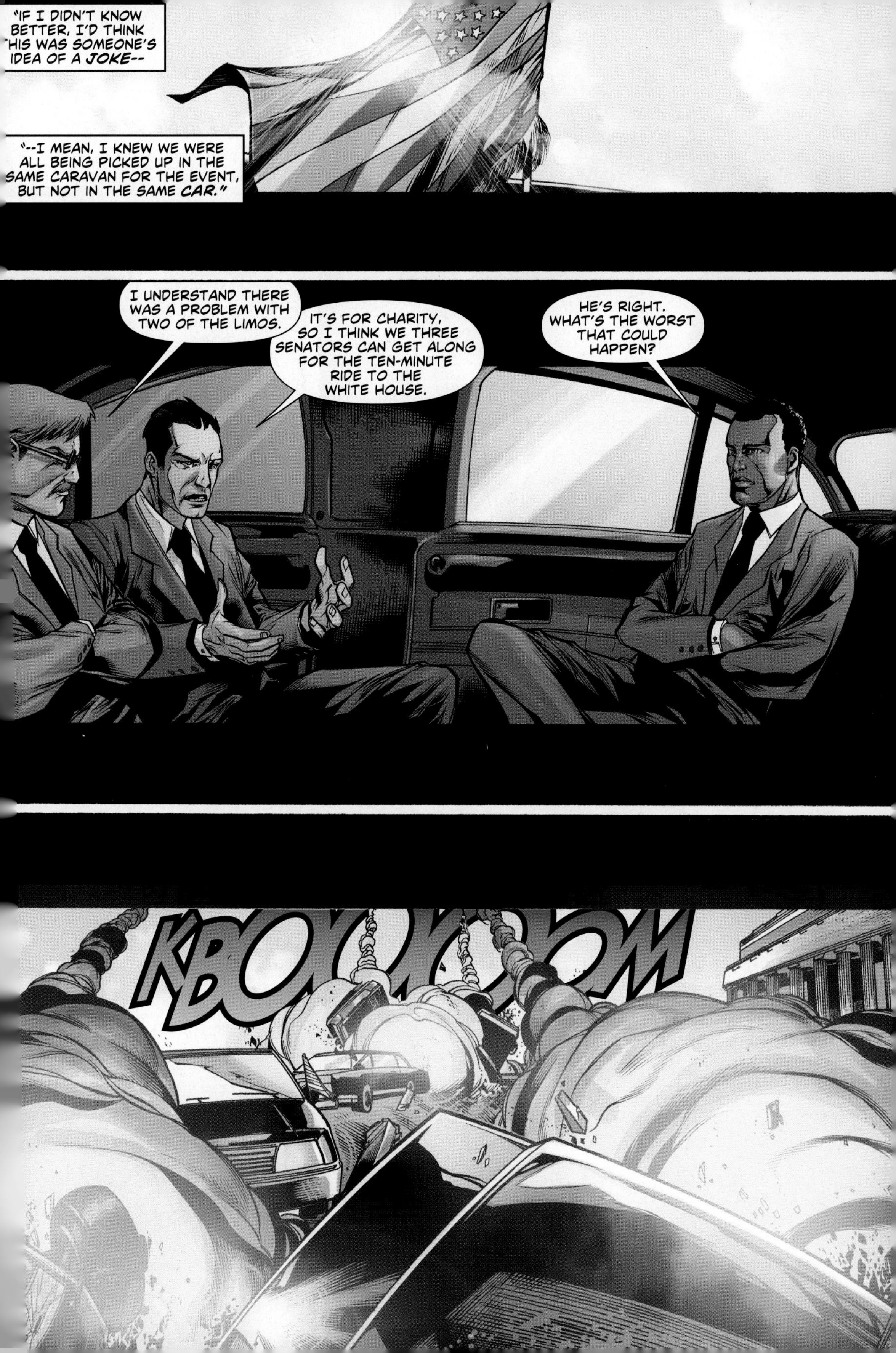
"IF I DIDN'T KNOW BETTER, I'D THINK THIS WAS SOMEONE'S IDEA OF A JOKE--
"--I MEAN, I KNEW WE WERE ALL BEING PICKED UP IN THE SAME CARAVAN FOR THE EVENT, BUT NOT IN THE SAME CAR."
I UNDERSTAND THERE WAS A PROBLEM WITH TWO OF THE LIMOS.
IT'S FOR CHARITY, SO I THINK WE THREE SENATORS CAN GET ALONG FOR THE TEN-MINUTE RIDE TO THE WHITE HOUSE.
HE'S RIGHT. WHAT'S THE WORST THAT COULD HAPPEN?

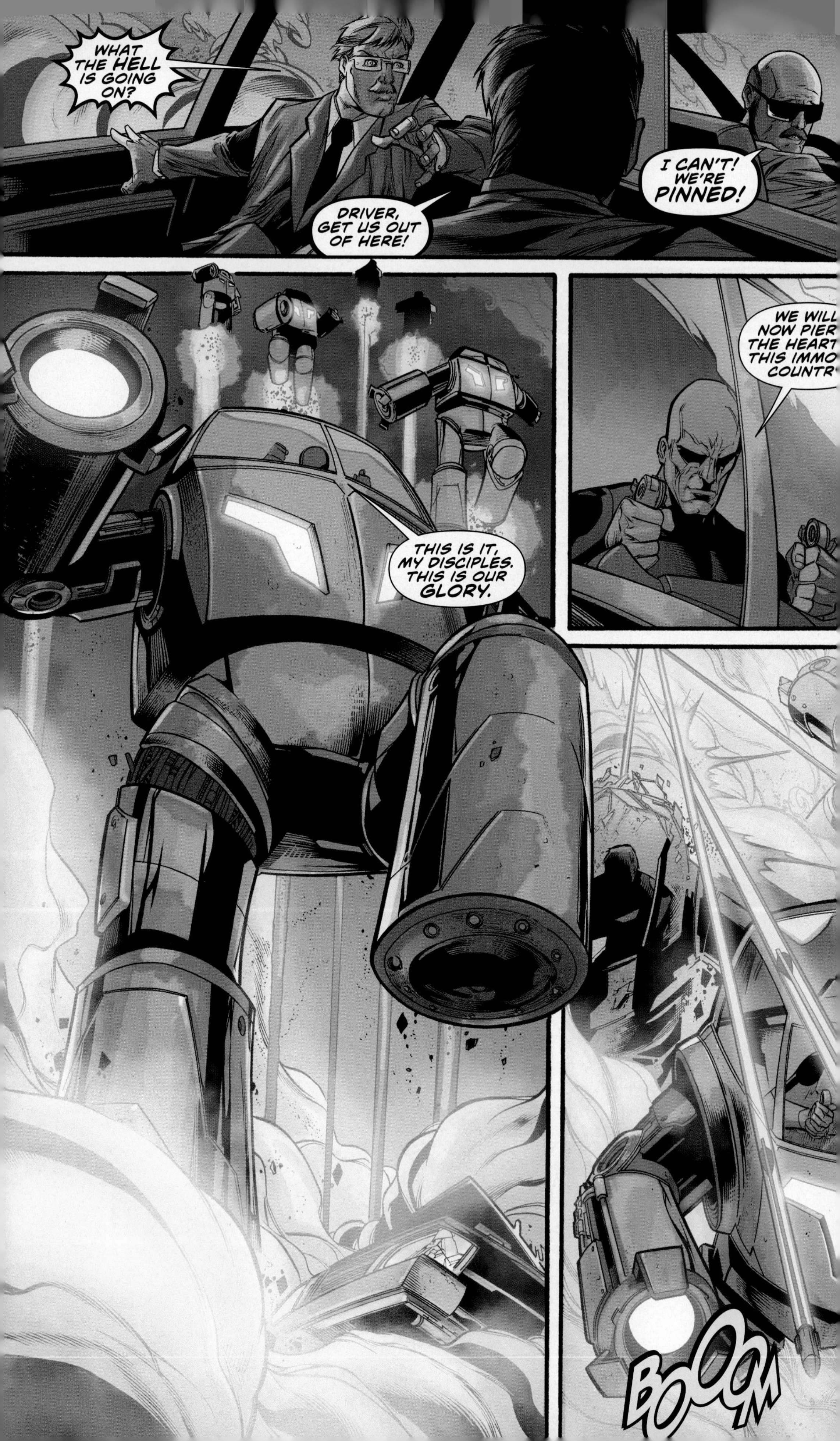
WHAT THE HELL IS GOING ON?
DRIVER, GET US OUT OF HERE!
I CAN'T! WE'RE PINNED!
THIS IS IT, MY DISCIPLES. THIS IS OUR GLORY.
WE WILL NOW PIER THE HEART THIS IMMO COUNTR
BOOOM

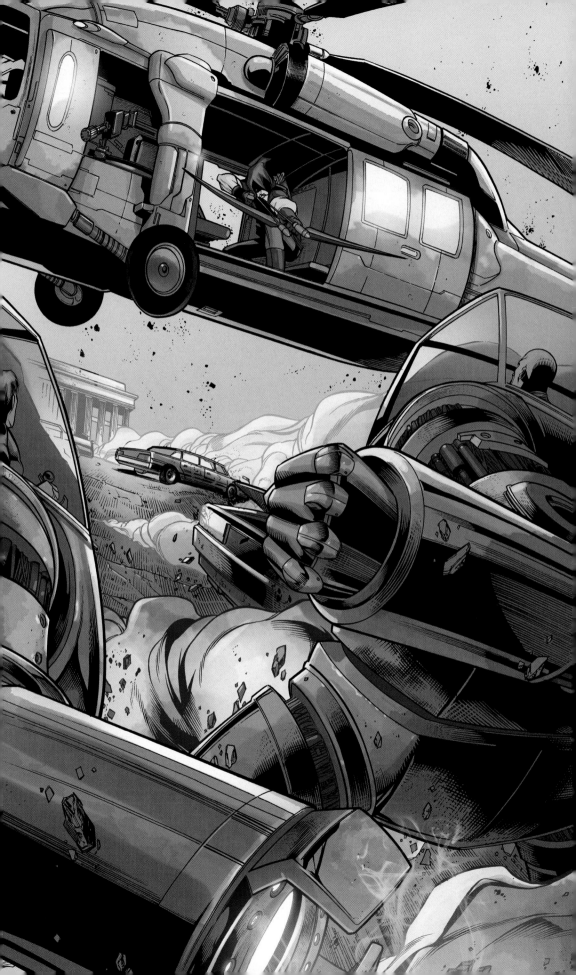

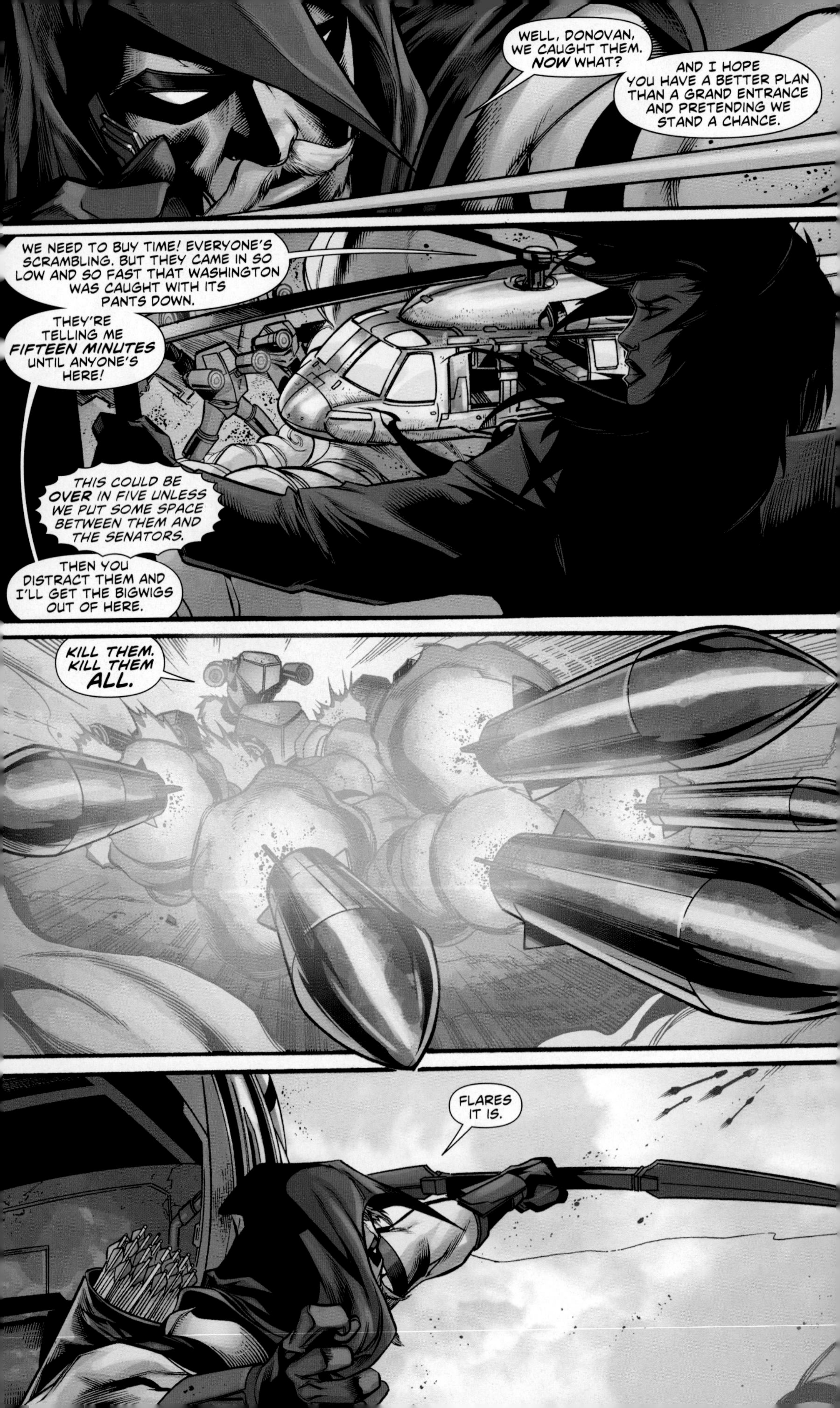

WELL, DONOVAN, WE CAUGHT THEM. *NOW* WHAT?
AND I HOPE YOU HAVE A BETTER PLAN THAN A GRAND ENTRANCE AND PRETENDING WE STAND A CHANCE.
WE NEED TO BUY TIME! EVERYONE'S SCRAMBLING. BUT THEY CAME IN SO LOW AND SO FAST THAT WASHINGTON WAS CAUGHT WITH ITS PANTS DOWN.
THEY'RE TELLING ME *FIFTEEN MINUTES* UNTIL ANYONE'S HERE!
*THIS COULD BE **OVER** IN FIVE UNLESS WE PUT SOME SPACE BETWEEN THEM AND THE SENATORS.*
THEN YOU DISTRACT THEM AND I'LL GET THE BIGWIGS OUT OF HERE.
*KILL THEM. KILL THEM **ALL.***
FLARES IT IS.

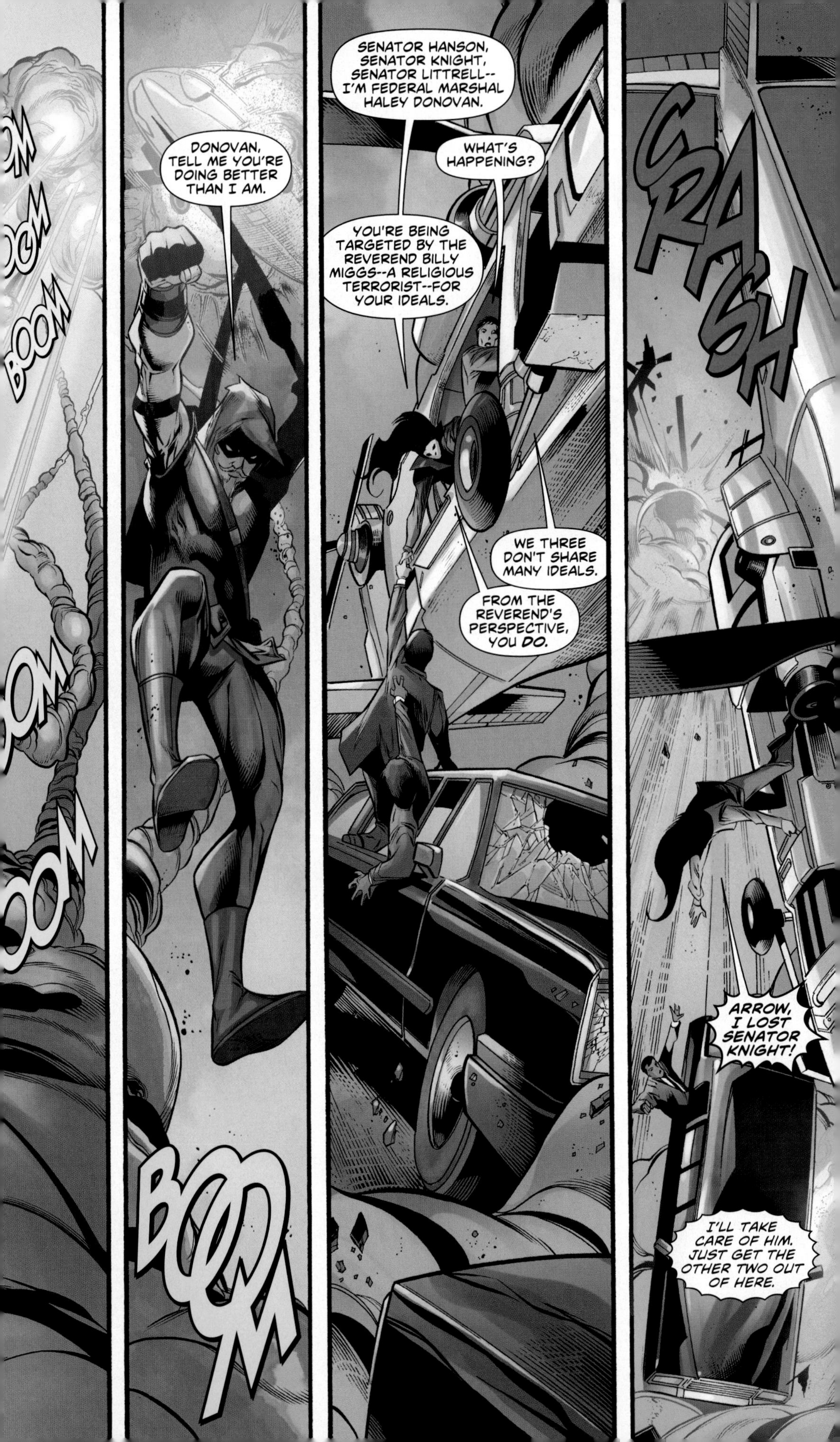

BOOM
BOOM
BOOM
BOOM
BOOM
BOOM
DONOVAN, TELL ME YOU'RE DOING BETTER THAN I AM.
BOOM
SENATOR HANSON, SENATOR KNIGHT, SENATOR LITTRELL-- I'M FEDERAL MARSHAL HALEY DONOVAN.
WHAT'S HAPPENING?
YOU'RE BEING TARGETED BY THE REVEREND BILLY MIGGS--A RELIGIOUS TERRORIST--FOR YOUR IDEALS.
WE THREE DON'T SHARE MANY IDEALS.
FROM THE REVEREND'S PERSPECTIVE, YOU *DO.*
CRASH
ARROW, I LOST SENATOR KNIGHT!
I'LL TAKE CARE OF HIM. JUST GET THE OTHER TWO OUT OF HERE.

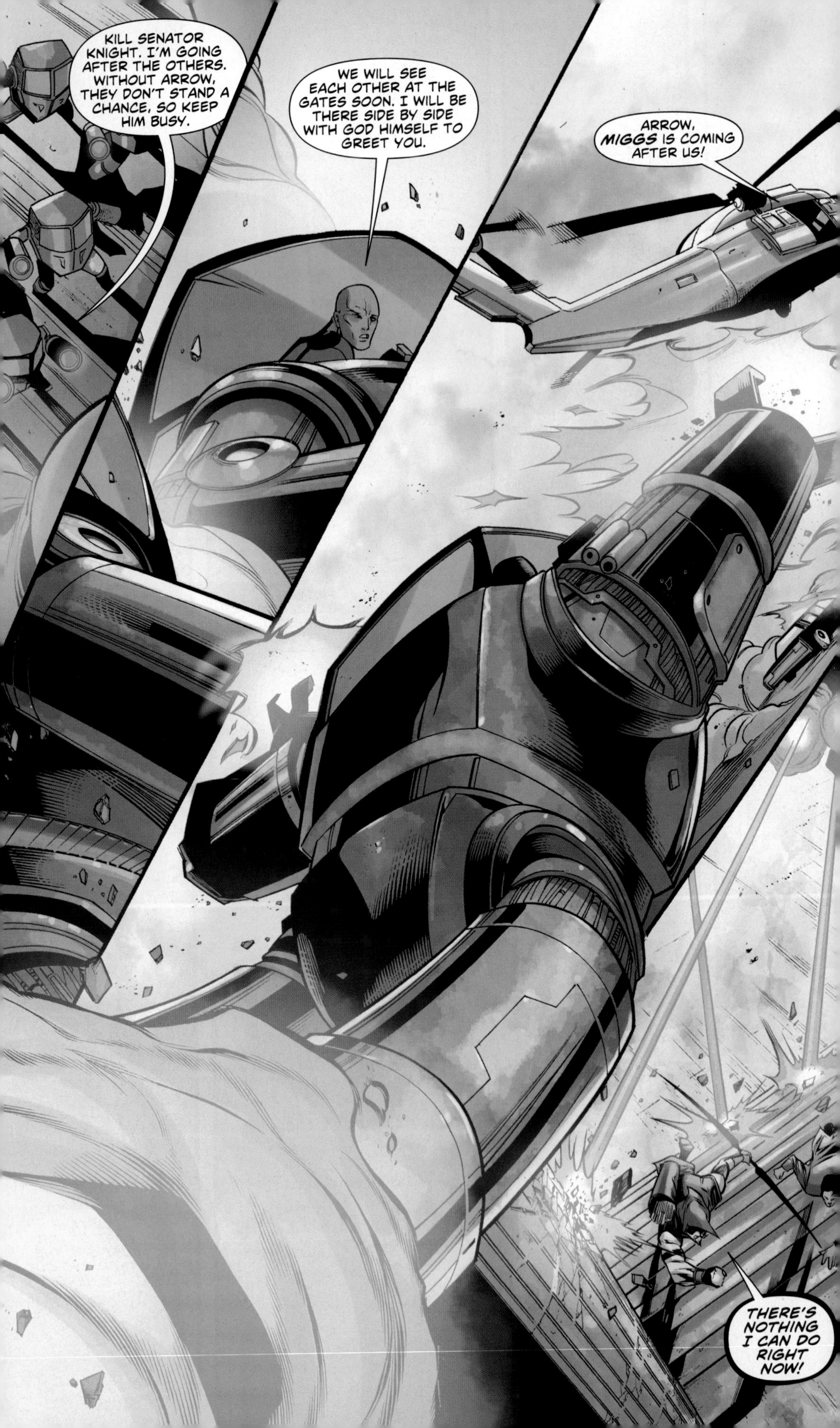
KILL SENATOR KNIGHT. I'M GOING AFTER THE OTHERS. WITHOUT ARROW, THEY DON'T STAND A CHANCE, SO KEEP HIM BUSY.
WE WILL SEE EACH OTHER AT THE GATES SOON. I WILL BE THERE SIDE BY SIDE WITH GOD HIMSELF TO GREET YOU.
ARROW, MIGGS IS COMING AFTER US!
THERE'S NOTHING I CAN DO RIGHT NOW!

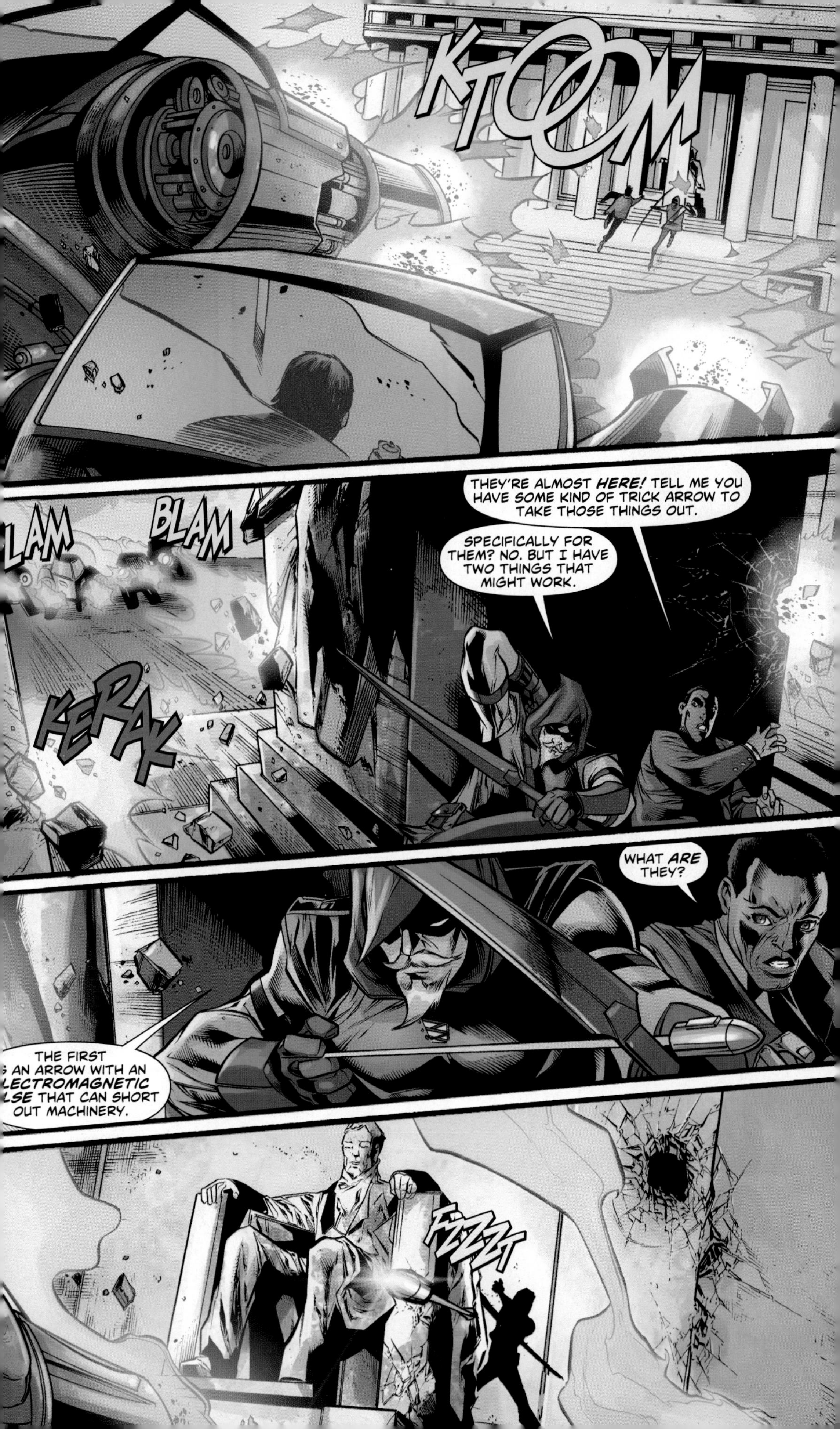
KTOOM
LAM
BLAM
KERAK
THEY'RE ALMOST HERE! TELL ME YOU HAVE SOME KIND OF TRICK ARROW TO TAKE THOSE THINGS OUT.
SPECIFICALLY FOR THEM? NO. BUT I HAVE TWO THINGS THAT MIGHT WORK.
WHAT ARE THEY?
THE FIRST S AN ARROW WITH AN LECTROMAGNETIC LSE THAT CAN SHORT OUT MACHINERY.
FZZZK

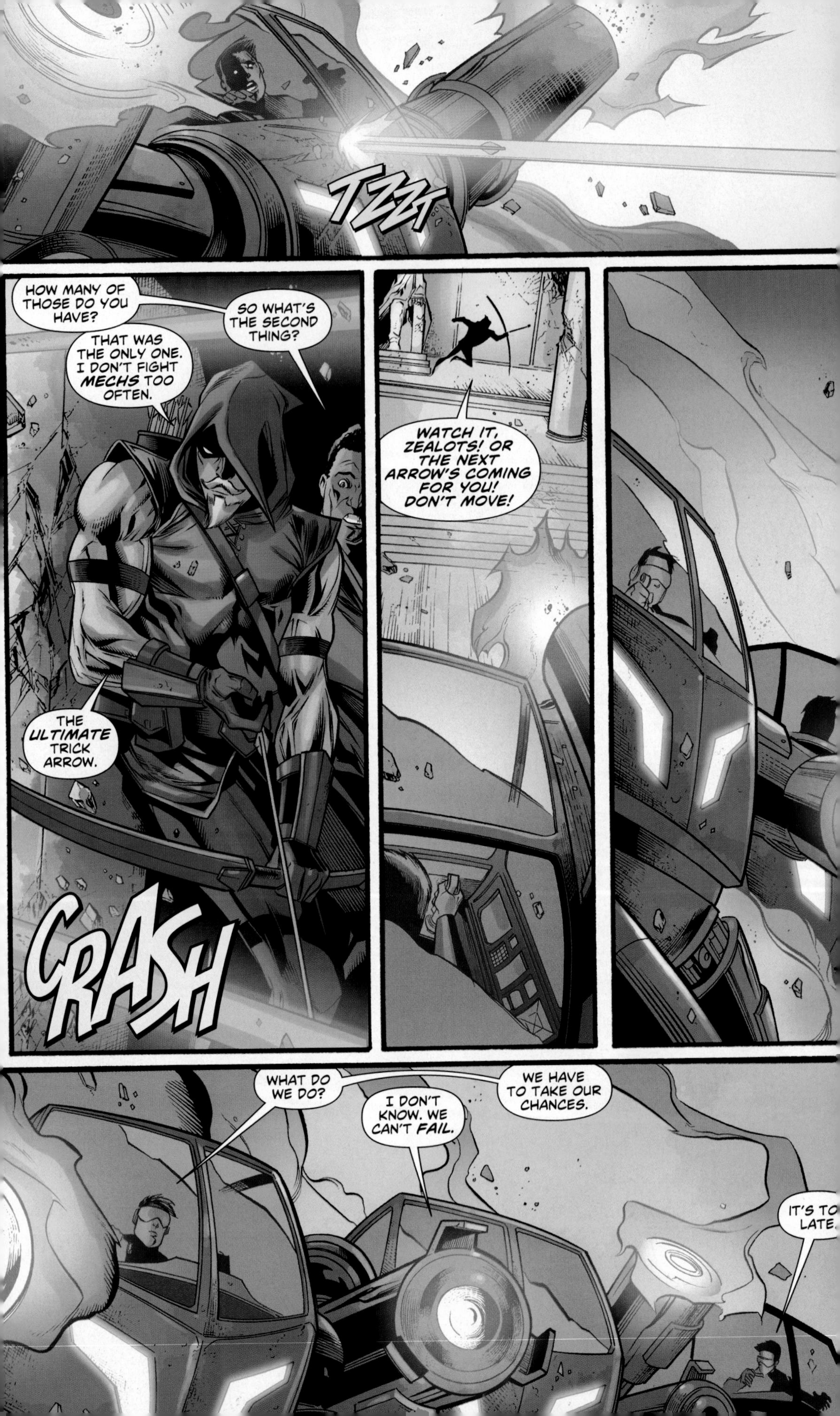
TZZT
HOW MANY OF THOSE DO YOU HAVE?
THAT WAS THE ONLY ONE. I DON'T FIGHT MECHS TOO OFTEN.
SO WHAT'S THE SECOND THING?
THE ULTIMATE TRICK ARROW.
CRASH
WATCH IT, ZEALOTS! OR THE NEXT ARROW'S COMING FOR YOU! DON'T MOVE!
WHAT DO WE DO?
I DON'T KNOW. WE CAN'T FAIL.
WE HAVE TO TAKE OUR CHANCES.
IT'S TO LATE.

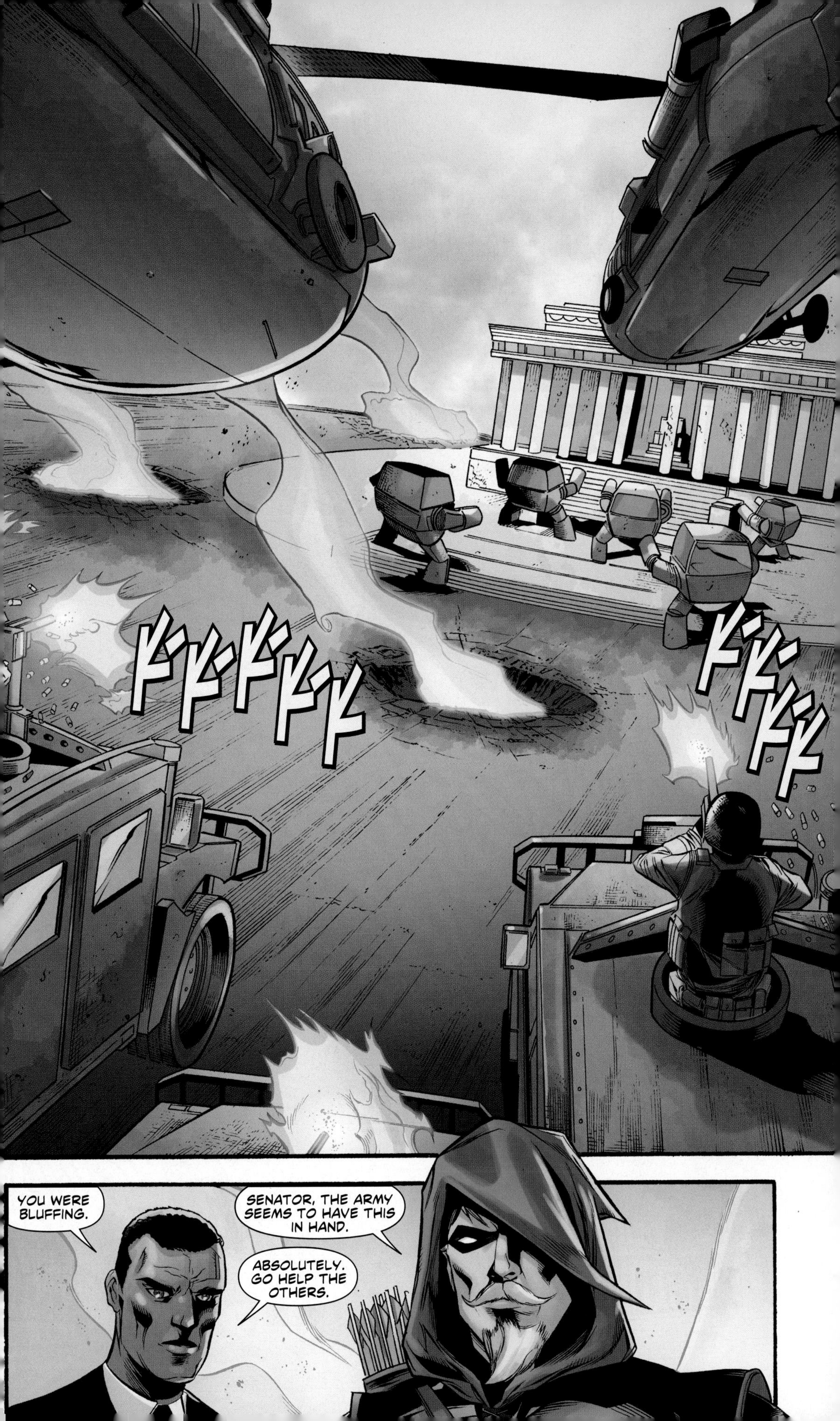
DKK-DKK-DKK-DKK
DKK-DKK-DKK
YOU WERE BLUFFING.
SENATOR, THE ARMY SEEMS TO HAVE THIS IN HAND.
ABSOLUTELY. GO HELP THE OTHERS.

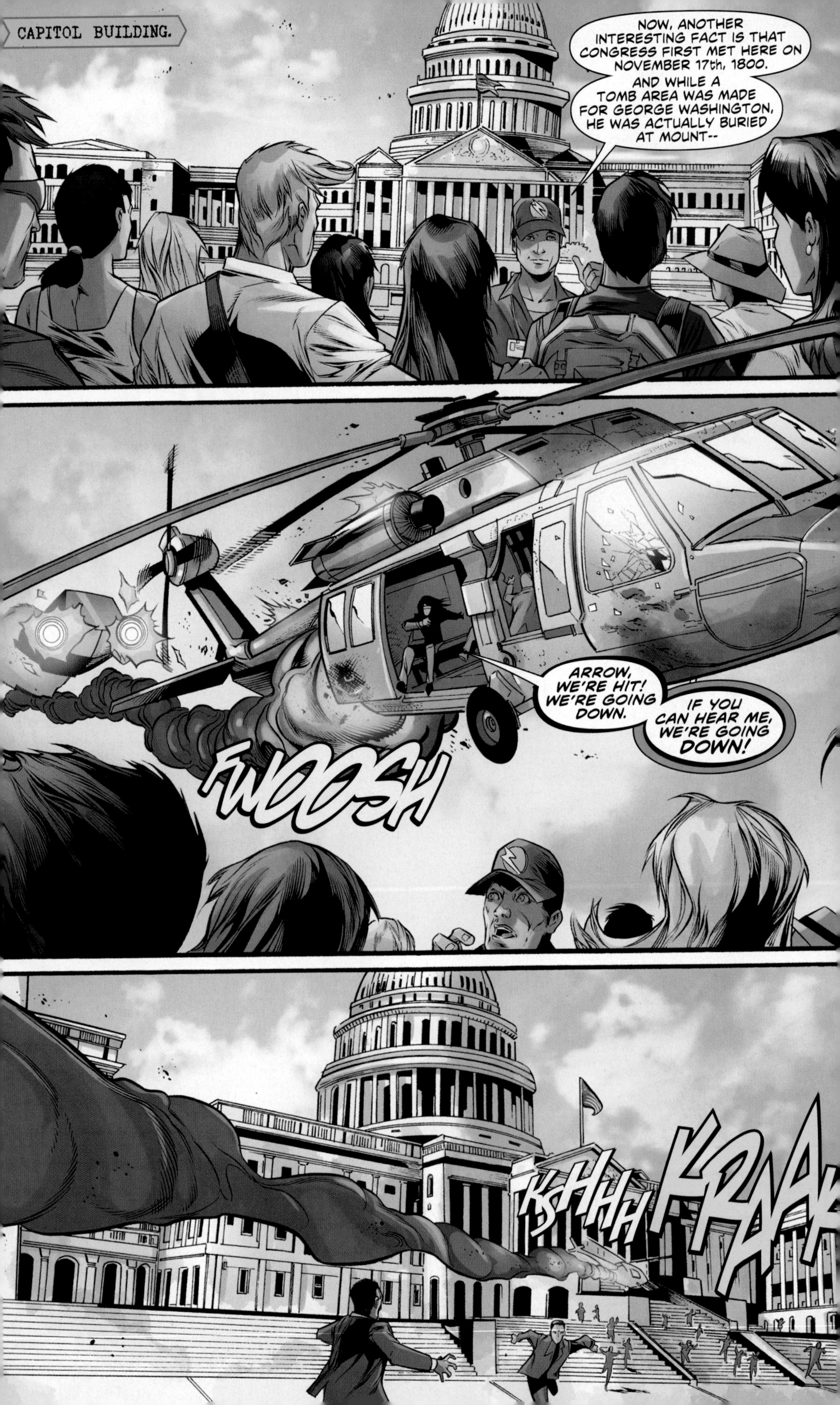
CAPITOL BUILDING.
NOW, ANOTHER INTERESTING FACT IS THAT CONGRESS FIRST MET HERE ON NOVEMBER 17th, 1800.
AND WHILE A TOMB AREA WAS MADE FOR GEORGE WASHINGTON, HE WAS ACTUALLY BURIED AT MOUNT--
ARROW, WE'RE HIT! WE'RE GOING DOWN.
IF YOU CAN HEAR ME, WE'RE GOING DOWN!
FWOOSH
KSHHHH
KRAAK

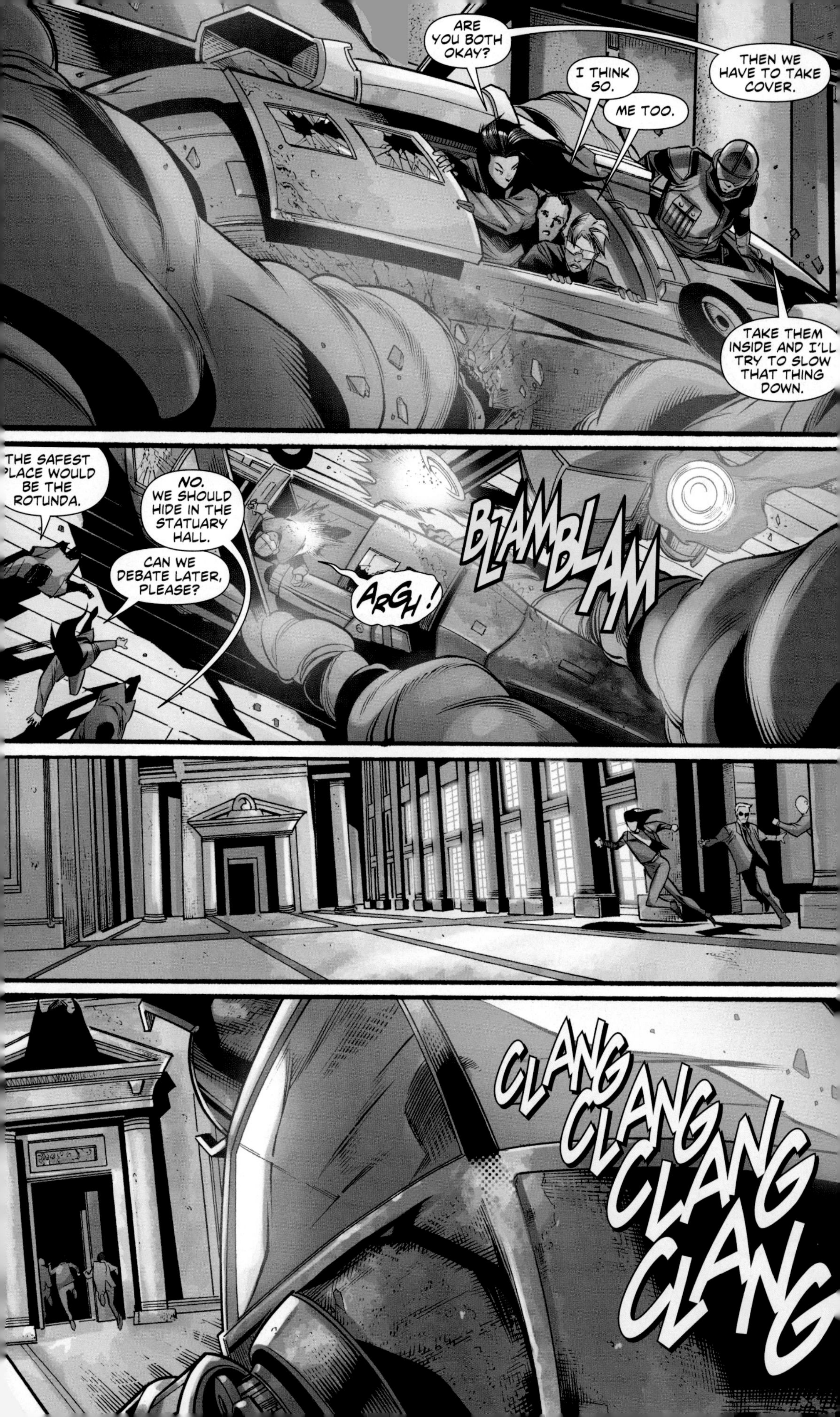
ARE YOU BOTH OKAY?
I THINK SO.
ME TOO.
THEN WE HAVE TO TAKE COVER.
TAKE THEM INSIDE AND I'LL TRY TO SLOW THAT THING DOWN.
THE SAFEST PLACE WOULD BE THE ROTUNDA.
NO. WE SHOULD HIDE IN THE STATUARY HALL.
CAN WE DEBATE LATER, PLEASE?
BLAMBLAM
ARGH!
CLANG CLANG CLANG CLANG

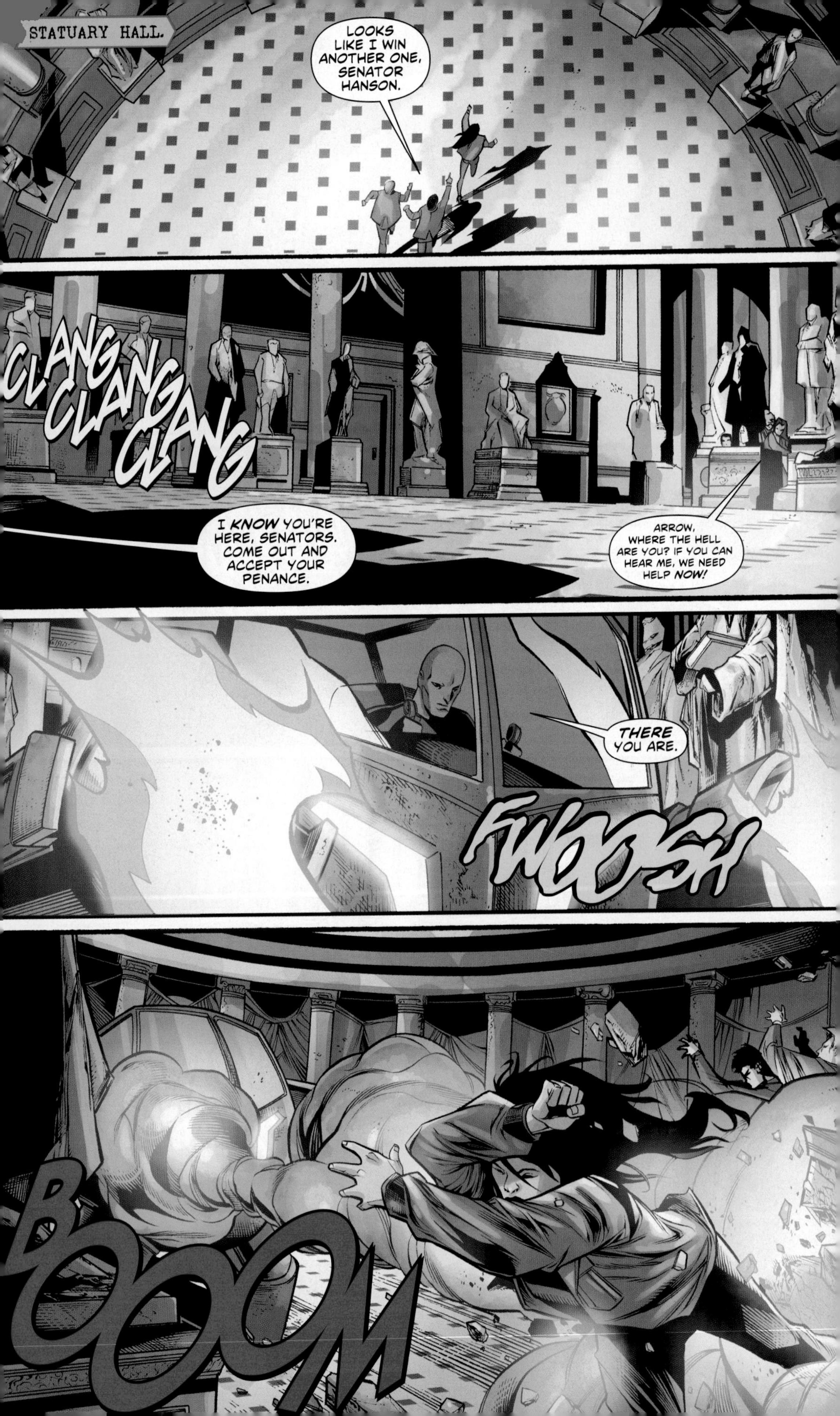
STATUARY HALL.
LOOKS LIKE I WIN ANOTHER ONE, SENATOR HANSON.
CLANG CLANG CLANG
I KNOW YOU'RE HERE, SENATORS. COME OUT AND ACCEPT YOUR PENANCE.
ARROW, WHERE THE HELL ARE YOU? IF YOU CAN HEAR ME, WE NEED HELP NOW!
THERE YOU ARE.
FWOOSH
BOOOM

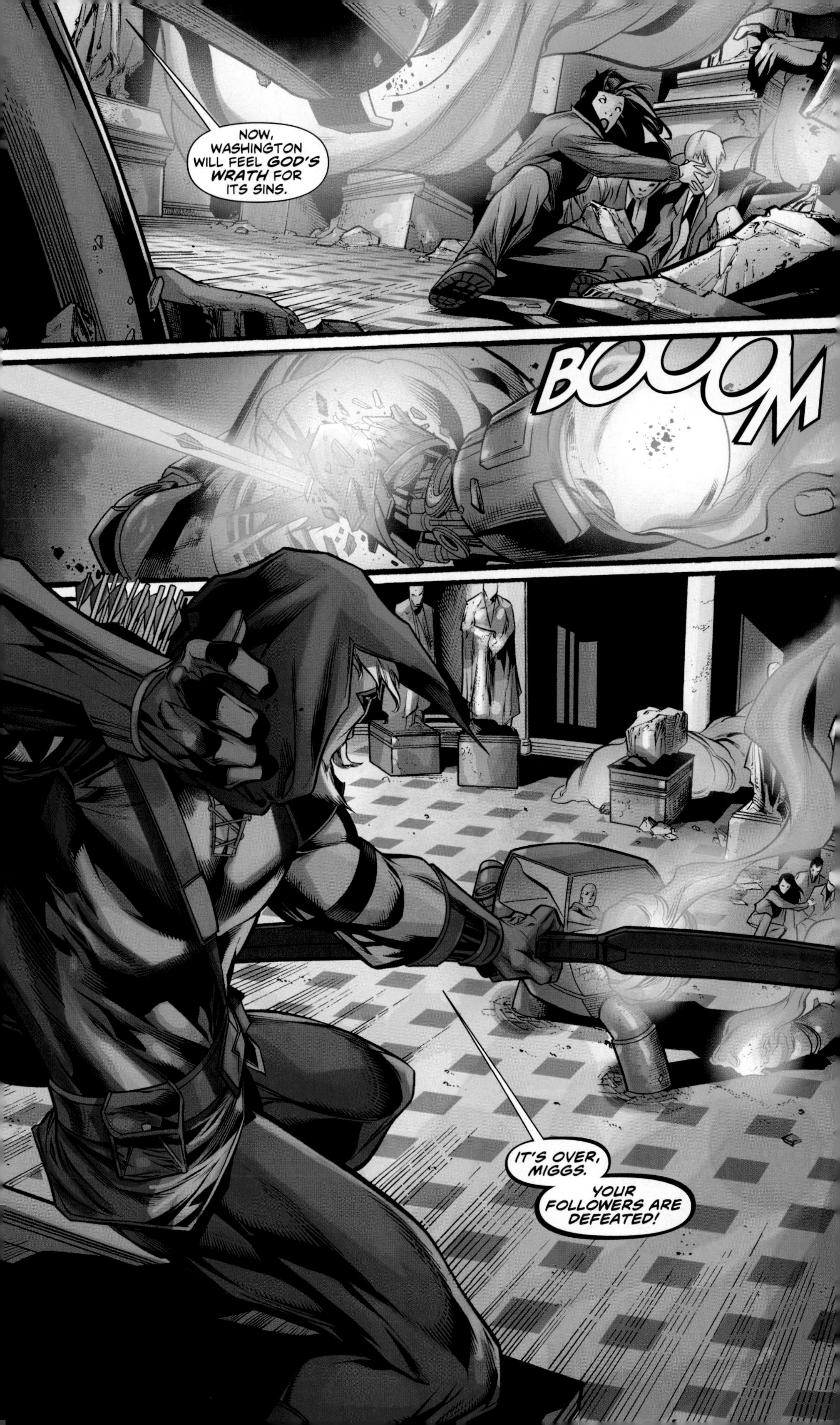

NOW, WASHINGTON WILL FEEL GOD'S WRATH FOR ITS SINS.
BOOOM
IT'S OVER, MIGGS.
YOUR FOLLOWERS ARE DEFEATED!

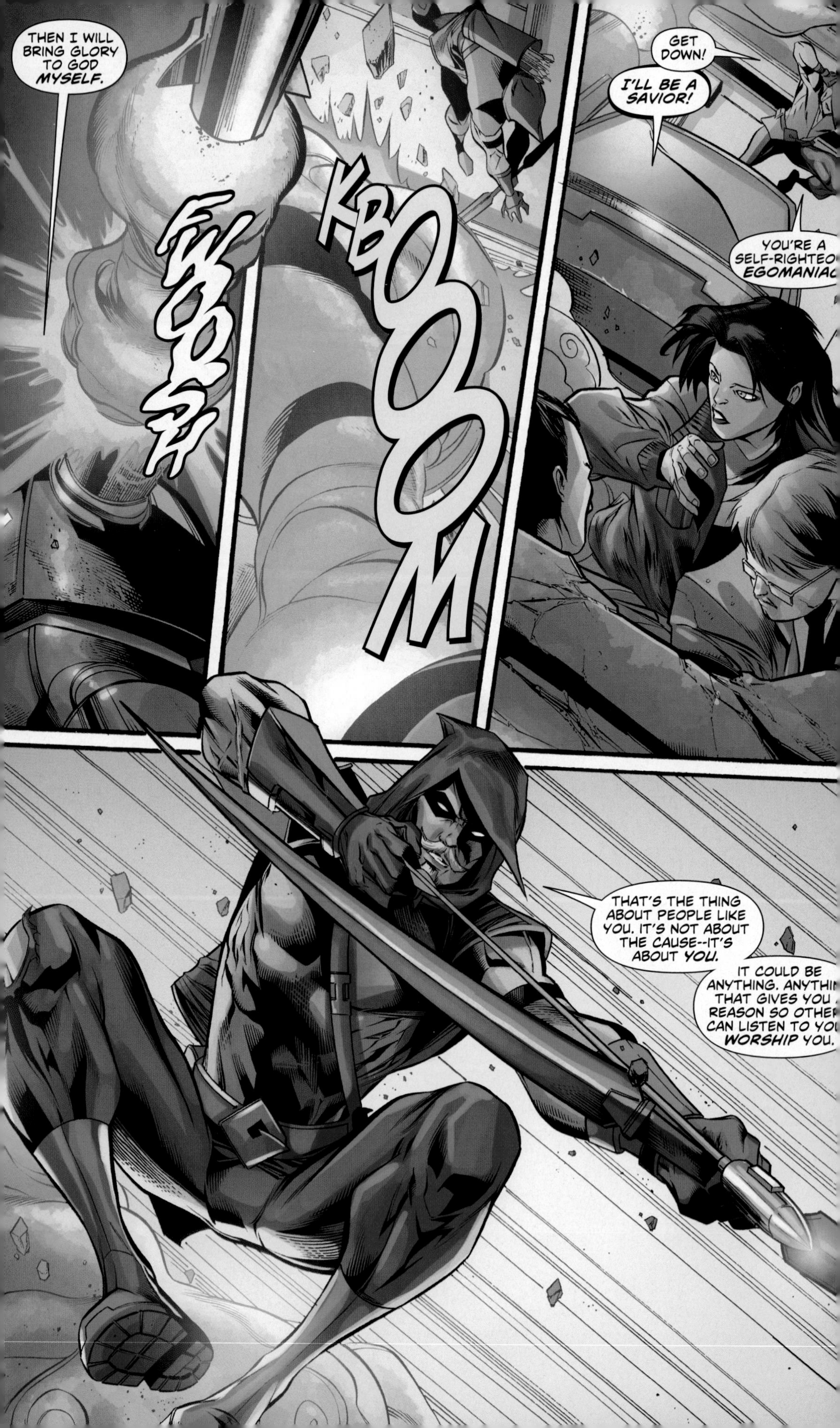
THEN I WILL BRING GLORY TO GOD MYSELF.
FWOOSH
KBOOOM
GET DOWN!
I'LL BE A SAVIOR!
YOU'RE A SELF-RIGHTEO EGOMANIAC
THAT'S THE THING ABOUT PEOPLE LIKE YOU. IT'S NOT ABOUT THE CAUSE--IT'S ABOUT YOU.
IT COULD BE ANYTHING. ANYTHI THAT GIVES YOU REASON SO OTHER CAN LISTEN TO YO WORSHIP YOU.

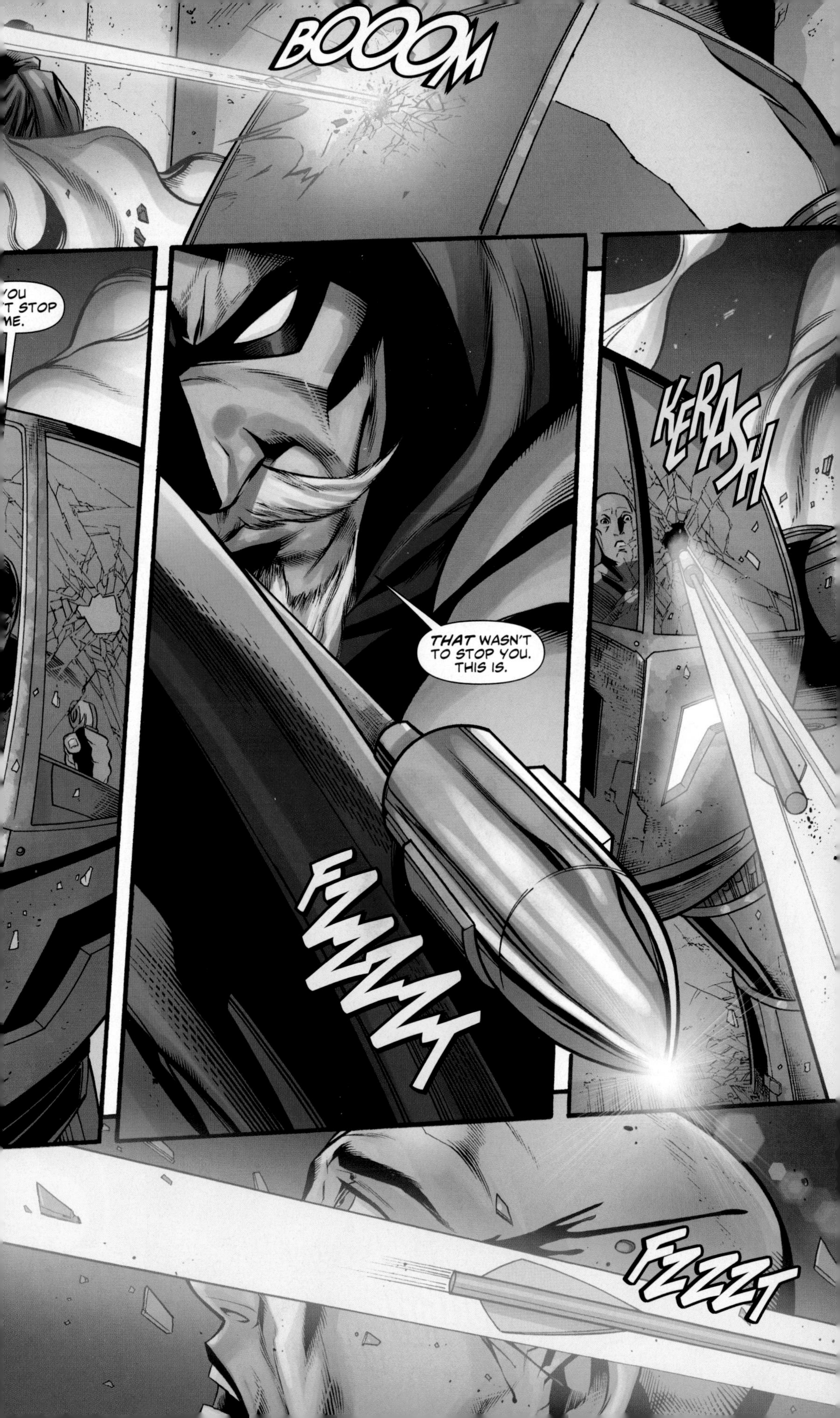
BOOOM
YOU
'T STOP
ME.
THAT WASN'T
TO STOP YOU.
THIS IS.
KERASH
FWMMM
FZZZT

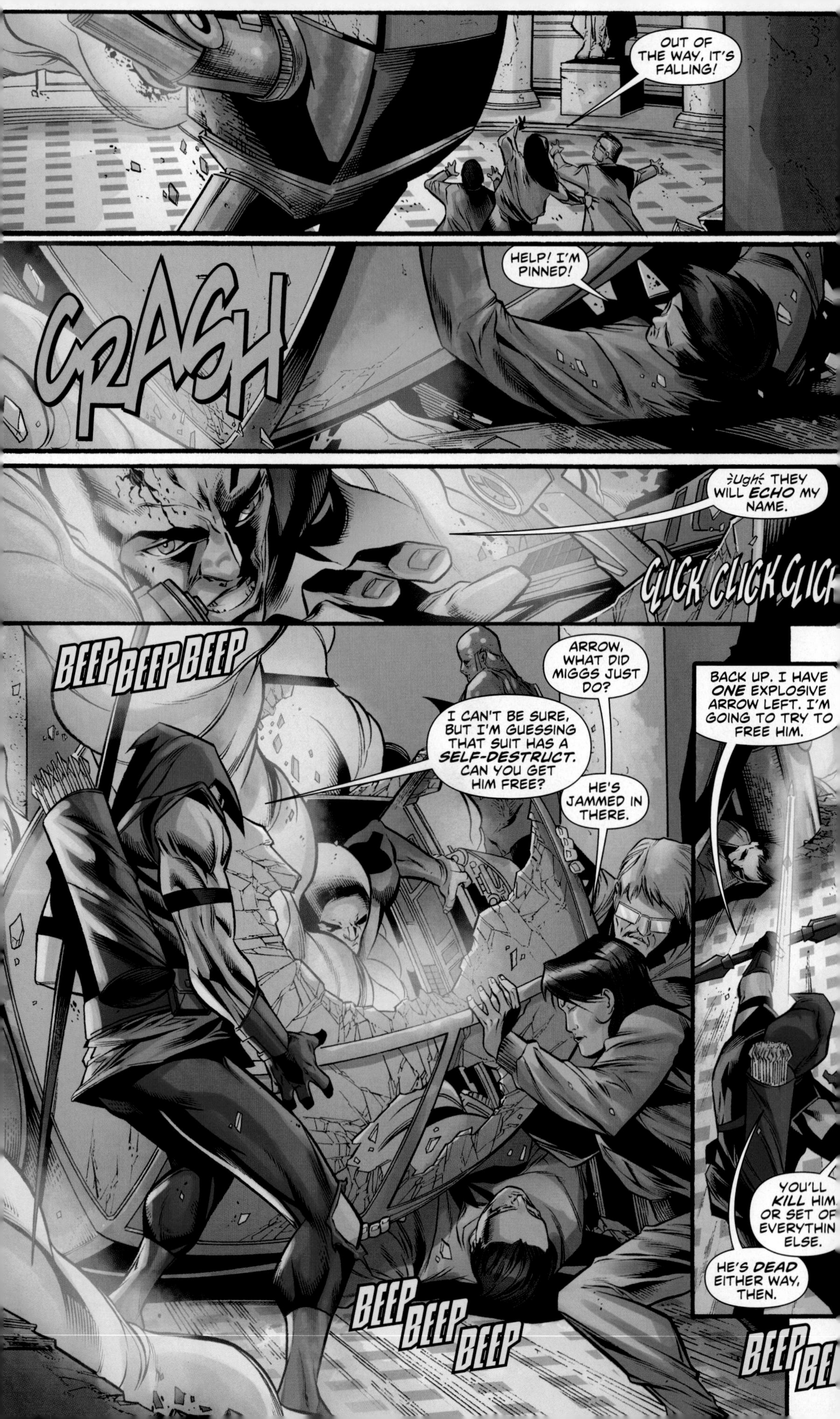
OUT OF THE WAY, IT'S FALLING!
CRASH
HELP! I'M PINNED!
ugh THEY WILL ECHO MY NAME.
CLICK CLICK CLICK
BEEP BEEP BEEP
ARROW, WHAT DID MIGGS JUST DO?
I CAN'T BE SURE, BUT I'M GUESSING THAT SUIT HAS A SELF-DESTRUCT. CAN YOU GET HIM FREE?
HE'S JAMMED IN THERE.
BEEP BEEP BEEP
BACK UP. I HAVE ONE EXPLOSIVE ARROW LEFT. I'M GOING TO TRY TO FREE HIM.
YOU'LL KILL HIM OR SET OF EVERYTHIN ELSE.
HE'S DEAD EITHER WAY, THEN.
BEEP BE

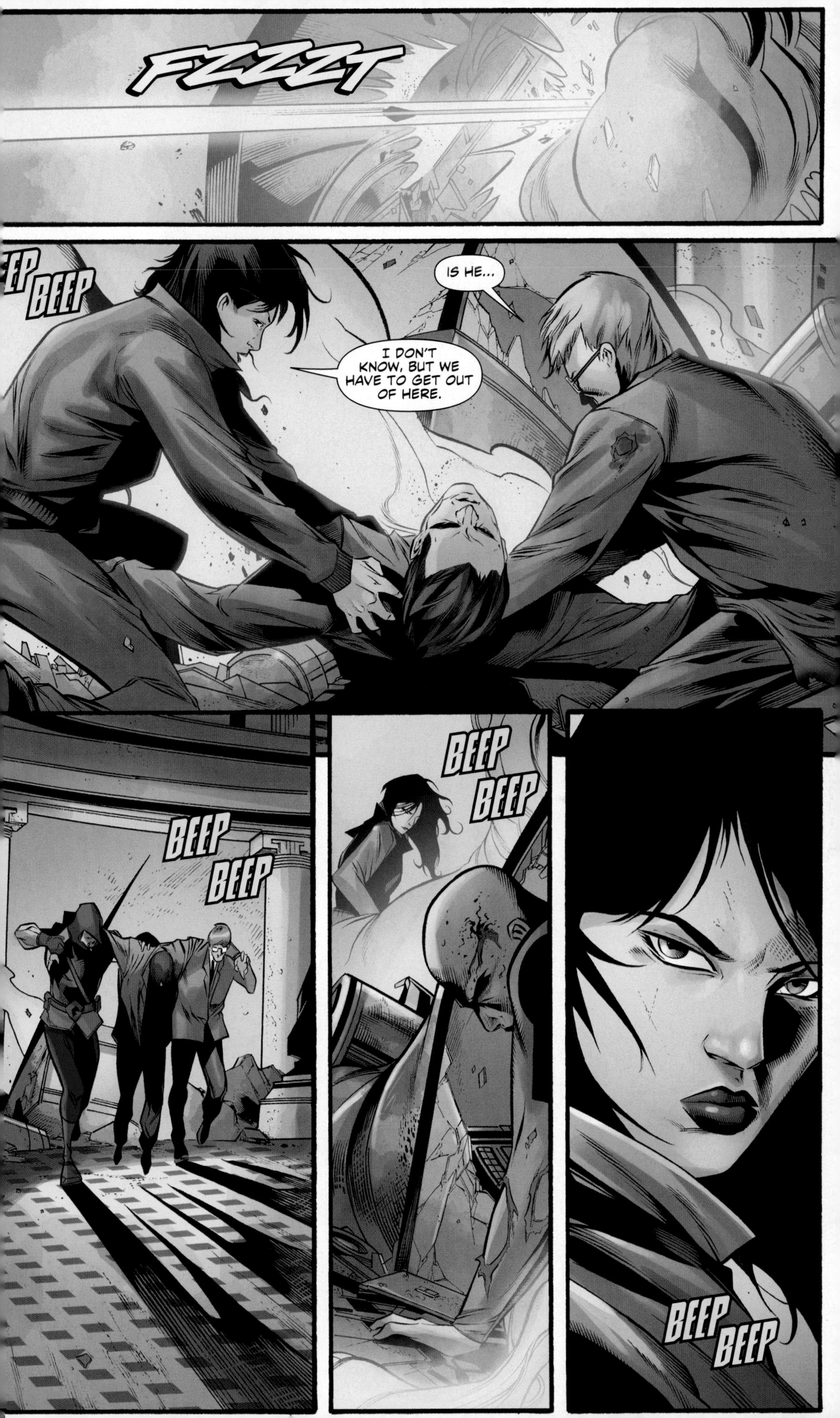
FZZZT
EP BEEP
IS HE...
I DON'T KNOW, BUT WE HAVE TO GET OUT OF HERE.
BEEP
BEEP
BEEP
BEEP
BEEP
BEEP

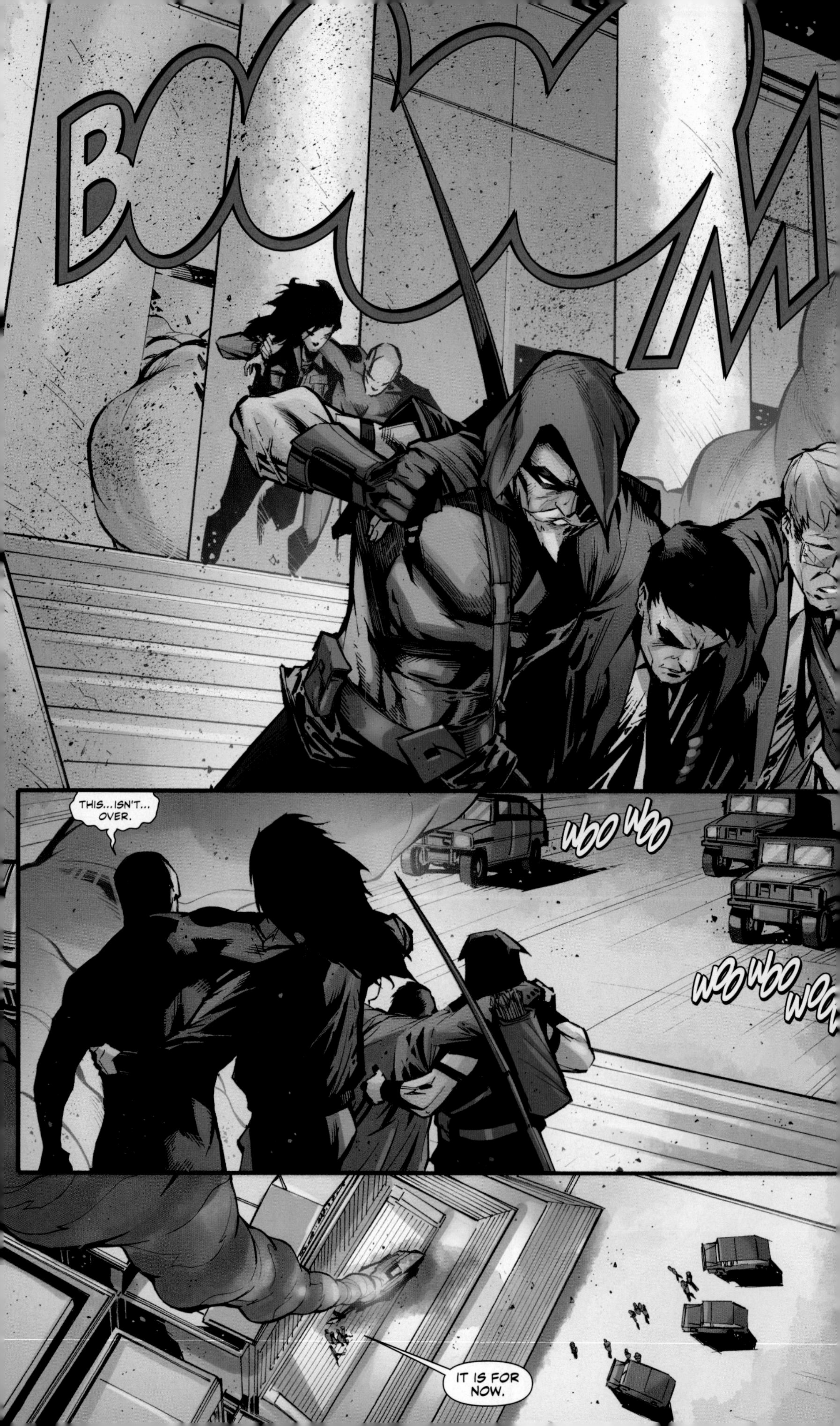
BOOM
THIS...ISN'T... OVER.
WOO WOO
WOO WOO WOO
IT IS FOR NOW.

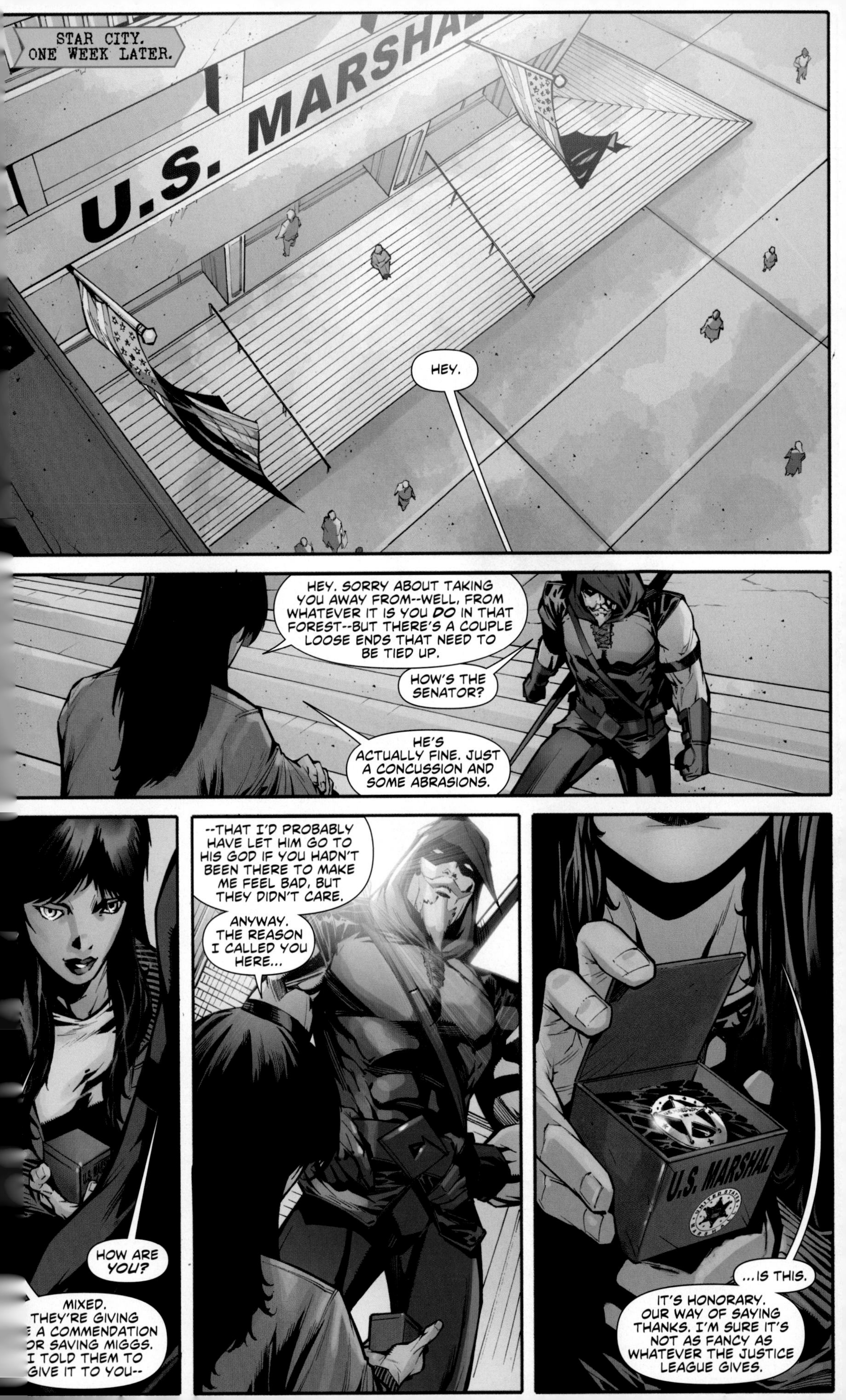
STAR CITY. ONE WEEK LATER.
U.S. MARSHAL
HEY.
HEY. SORRY ABOUT TAKING YOU AWAY FROM--WELL, FROM WHATEVER IT IS YOU *DO* IN THAT FOREST--BUT THERE'S A COUPLE LOOSE ENDS THAT NEED TO BE TIED UP.
HOW'S THE SENATOR?
HE'S ACTUALLY FINE. JUST A CONCUSSION AND SOME ABRASIONS.
HOW ARE *YOU*?
MIXED. THEY'RE GIVING E A COMMENDATION OR SAVING MIGGS. I TOLD THEM TO GIVE IT TO YOU--
--THAT I'D PROBABLY HAVE LET HIM GO TO HIS GOD IF YOU HADN'T BEEN THERE TO MAKE ME FEEL BAD, BUT THEY DIDN'T CARE.
ANYWAY. THE REASON I CALLED YOU HERE...
U.S. MARSHAL
...IS THIS.
IT'S HONORARY. OUR WAY OF SAYING THANKS. I'M SURE IT'S NOT AS FANCY AS WHATEVER THE JUSTICE LEAGUE GIVES.

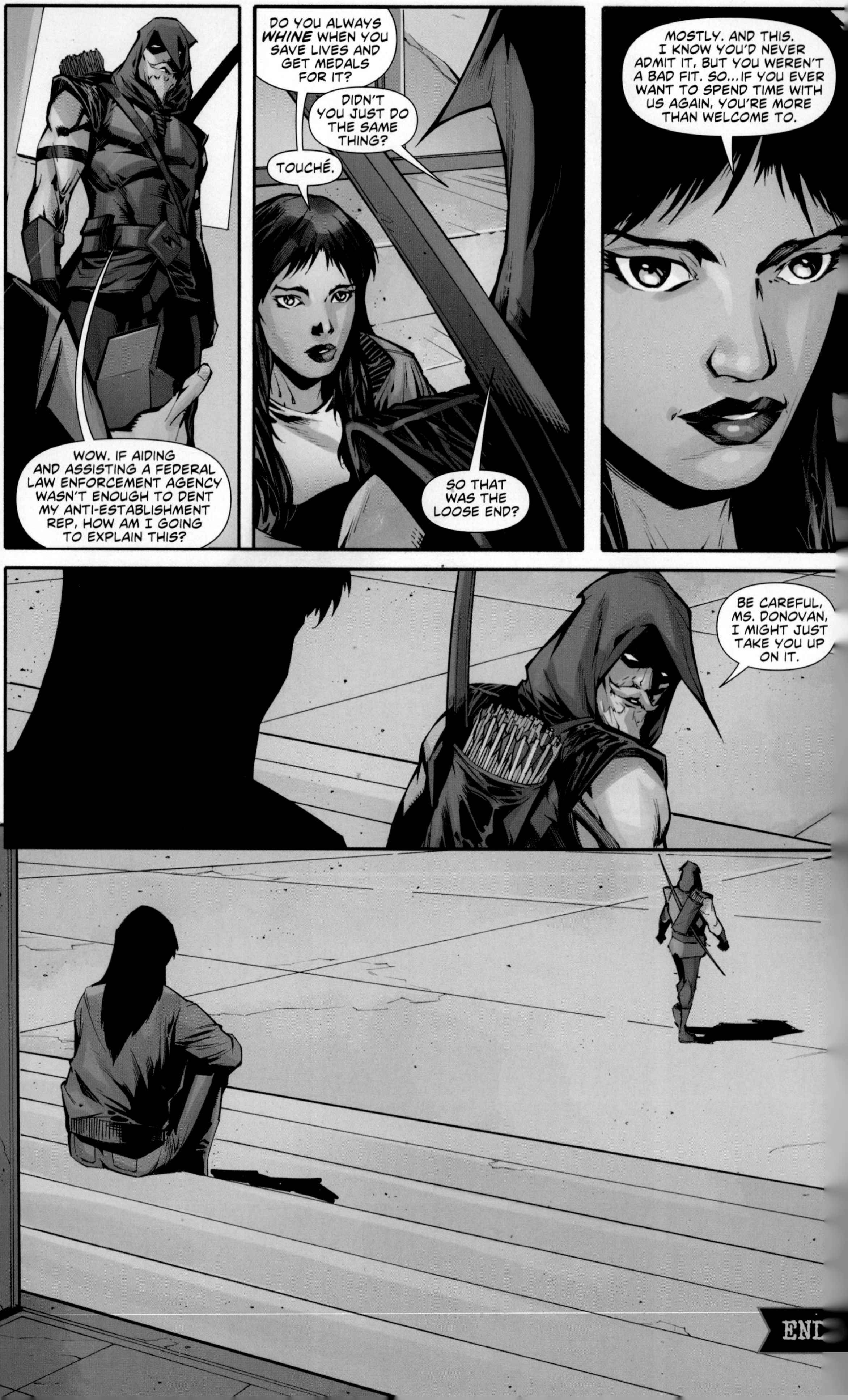
WOW. IF AIDING AND ASSISTING A FEDERAL LAW ENFORCEMENT AGENCY WASN'T ENOUGH TO DENT MY ANTI-ESTABLISHMENT REP, HOW AM I GOING TO EXPLAIN THIS?
DO YOU ALWAYS WHINE WHEN YOU SAVE LIVES AND GET MEDALS FOR IT?
DIDN'T YOU JUST DO THE SAME THING?
TOUCHÉ.
SO THAT WAS THE LOOSE END?
MOSTLY. AND THIS. I KNOW YOU'D NEVER ADMIT IT, BUT YOU WEREN'T A BAD FIT. SO...IF YOU EVER WANT TO SPEND TIME WITH US AGAIN, YOU'RE MORE THAN WELCOME TO.
BE CAREFUL, MS. DONOVAN, I MIGHT JUST TAKE YOU UP ON IT.
END

VARIANT COVER GALLERY

GREEN ARROW #8 variant by David Mack

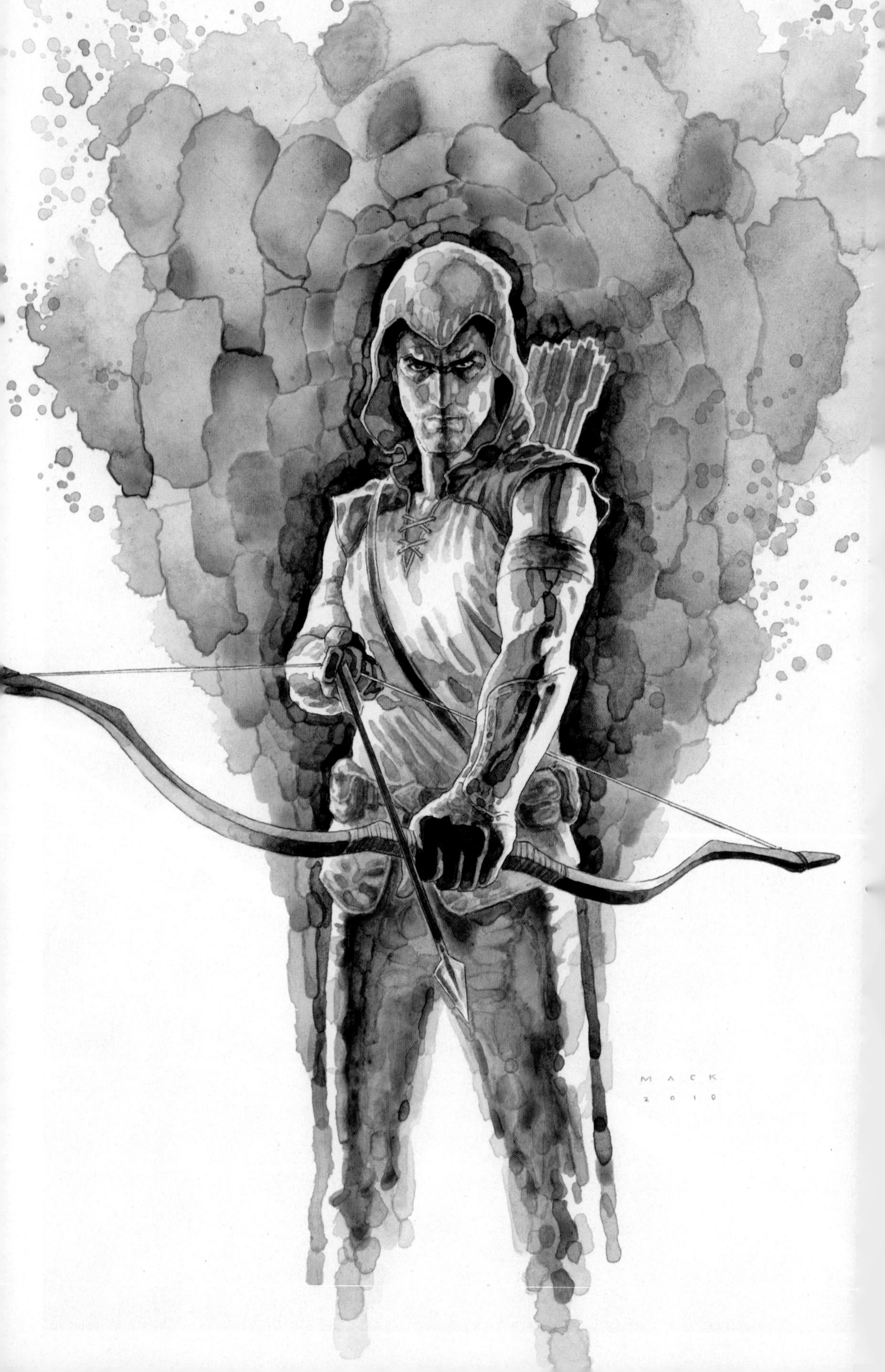
MACK
2010

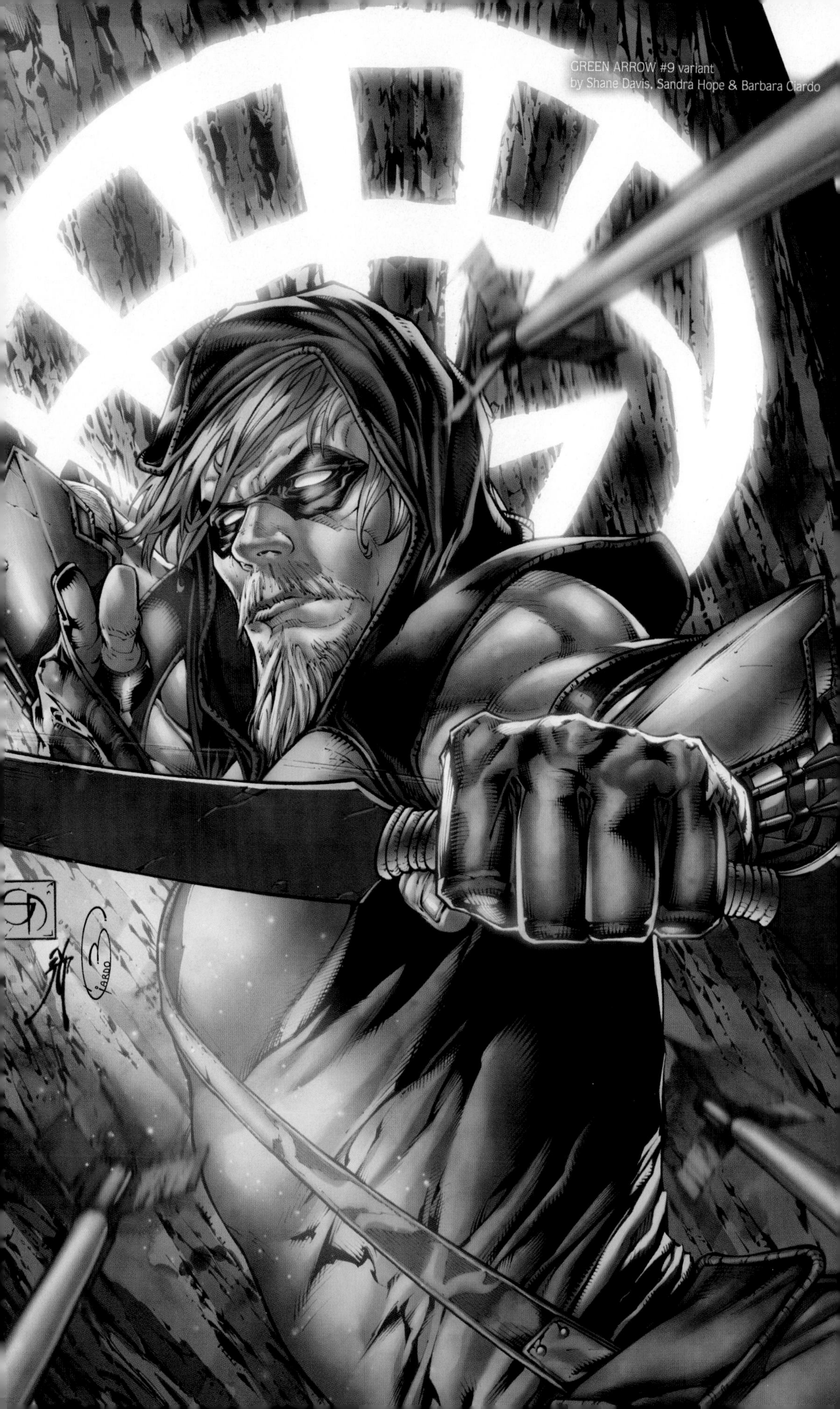

GREEN ARROW #9 variant
by Shane Davis, Sandra Hope & Barbara Ciardo

GREEN ARROW #10 variant by Tyler Kirkham, Matt Banning and Nei Ruffino

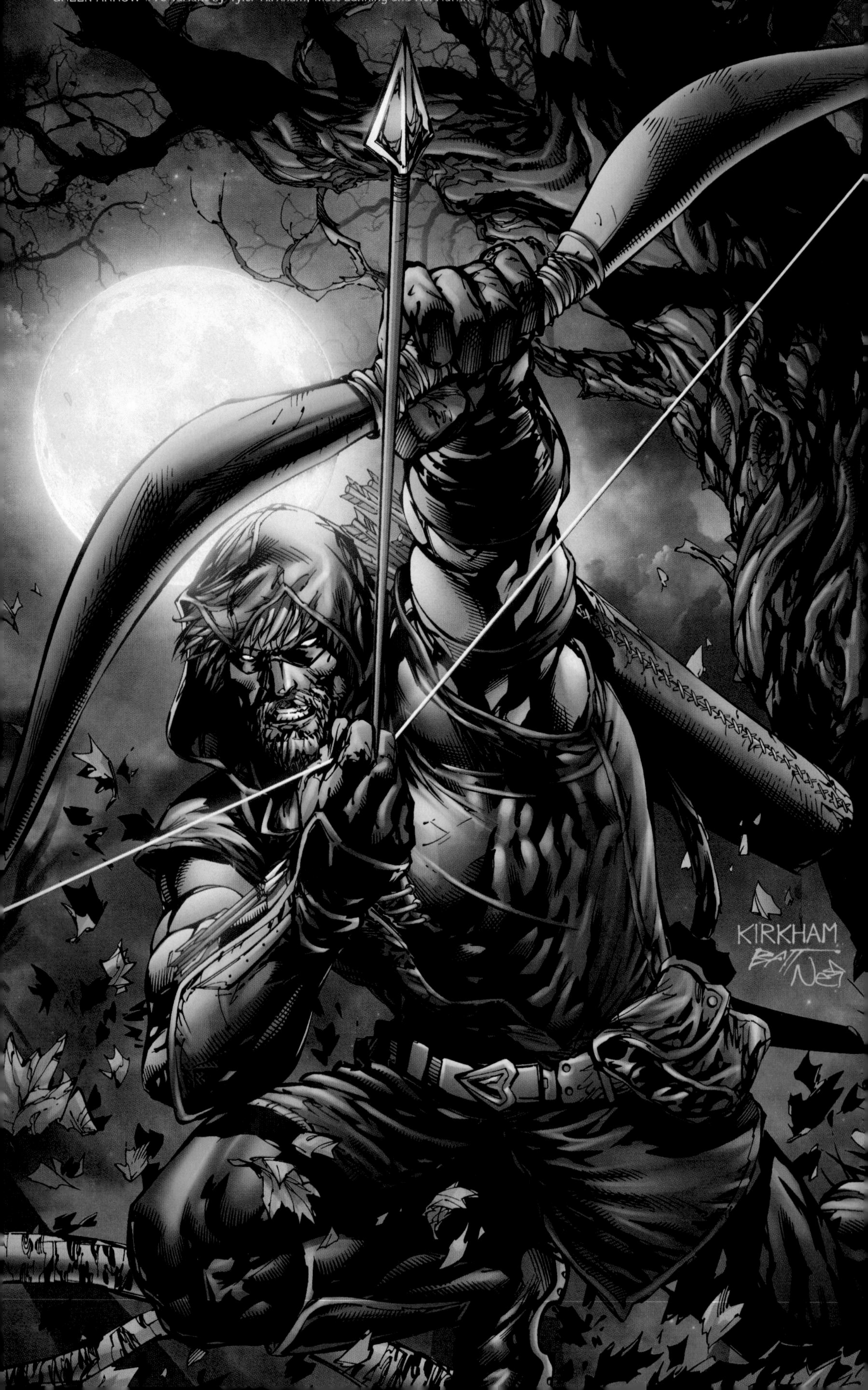
KIRKHAM